For my children:
Alexander, Pamela, Constance

CONTENTS

5   PATTERNS OF INTERACTION   **54**

6   WHAT BRITONS QUARREL ABOUT   **66**

part three   WEST GERMANY

12   THE IMPACT OF THE PAST   **142**

13   THE KEY INSTITUTIONS   **157**

14 WEST GERMAN POLITICAL ATTITUDES **170**

15 PATTERNS OF INTERACTION **183**

16   WHAT WEST GERMANS QUARREL ABOUT   **195**

part four   THE SOVIET UNION

17   THE IMPACT OF THE PAST   **210**

23   BRAZIL **313**

ANOTHER NOTE TO INSTRUCTORS

It was gratifying to learn from the publisher that there was sufficient interest in *Countries and Concepts* to warrant a second edition. A considerable number of instructors found the approach of the first edition useful in awakening students to the field of comparative politics. Instructor responses were overwhelmingly positive. One negative response, however, sticks in my mind. The professor rather liked the text but admitted, "I'm too much into teaching *political science* and not just politics!" (Emphasis in original.) I don't know if the instructor intended irony, but he certainy put his finger on one of the main dilemmas facing those who teach political science. Exactly what is it that we study, politics or political science? If we are studying political science, then we are paying a great deal of attention to methodology, statistics, time-series data, theories, and high-level abstractions. If we are studying politics, we are paying attention mostly to the conflicts that ripple through the system, including current problems.

This text has clearly opted for the politics approach; it pays little attention to theory or methodology and a good deal of attention to a country's quarrels and how they came to be. It is, admittedly, a slightly journalistic approach, but students seem to like it. I spoke with one coed from a fine institution whose instructor assigned both my book and a more "scientific" text. She confided that most of her classmates avoided reading the other book because it wasn't very interesting but that they were happy to read *Countries and Concepts*.

Let me then reaffirm the purpose of my modest attempt. It is not to create young scholars out of college sophomores. It sees, rather, comparative politics as an important, but usually neglected, grounding in citizenship that we should be making available to our young people. The author agrees with Morris Janowitz (in his 1983 *The Reconstruction of Patriotism: Education for Civic Consciousness*) that civic education has declined in the United States and that this poses dangers for democracy. Our students are often ill-prepared in the historical, political, economic, geographical, and even moral aspects of democracy and to expose such students to professional-level abstractions in political science ignores their civic education and offers them material that is largely meaningless to them. To repeat what I said in the first edition: an undergraduate is not a miniature graduate student.

Accordingly, the second edition of *Countries and Concepts* is designed to include a good deal of fundamental vocabulary and concepts, buttressed by many examples. It is readable. Many students are not doing assigned readings; with *Countries and Concepts,* they have no excuse that the reading is boring.

A couple of anonymous outside reviewers—publishers hire them in the belief that authors heed their comments—noted disapprovingly that *Countries and Concepts* contains values and criticisms. This is part of my purpose. The two go together; if you have no values you have no basis from which to criticize. Value-free instruction is probably impossible. I successful, it would produce value-free students, and that, I think, should no be the aim of the educational enterprise. If one knows something with the head but not with the heart, one really doesn't know it at all.

Is *Countries and Concepts* too critical? It treats politics as a series of ongoing quarrels for which no very good solutions can be found. It casts a skeptical eye on all political systems and all solutions proposed for political problems. As such, the book is not out to "get" any one country; it merely treats all with equal candor. *Countries and Concepts* tries to act as a corrective to analyses that depict political systems as well-oiled machines or gigantic computers that never break down or make mistakes. Put it this way: if we are critical of the workings of our own country's politics—and many, perhaps most, of us are—why should we abandon the critical spirit in looking at another land?

The second edition continues the loose theoretical approach of the first edition with the simple observation that politics, on the surface at least, is composed of a number of human conflicts or *quarrels*. These quarrels, if observed over time, usually form patterns of some durability beyond the specific issue involved. What I call *patterns of interaction,* are the relationships among politically relevant groups and inividuals, what they call in Russian *kto-kovo,* who does what to whom? There are two general types of such patterns: (1) between elites and masses, and (2) among and within elites.

Before we can appreciate these patterns, however, we must first study the *political attitudes* (both mass and elite) of a particular country, which lead us to its *political institutions* and ultimately to its *political history*. Thus we have a fivefold division in the study of each country. We could start with a country's contemporary political quarrels and work backwards, but is probably better to begin with the underlying factors as a foundation from which to understand their impact on modern social conflict. This book goes from *history* to *institutions* to *attitudes* to *patterns of interaction* to *quarrels;* however, this arrangement need not supplant other approaches. I think instructors will have no trouble utilizing this book in connection with their preferred theoretical insights.

Inclusion of the Third World in a first comparative course is problematic. Europe, especially Western Europe, hangs together fairly well; the Third World is so complex and differentiated that some observers think the concept should be discarded. The semester is only so long. But if students are going to take only one comparative course—all too often the case nowadays—they should get some exposure to three-quarters of humankind. We continue, therefore, with briefer treatment of three non-European systems: China, Brazil, and South Africa. They are not "representative" systems—what Third World countries are?—but are interesting in their three different relationships to revolution: (1) a sweeping revolution in China, (2) an aborted revolution in Brazil, and (3) a looming revolution in South Africa. Students like the stress on revolutions, and these three systems provide a refreshing counterpoise to the more settled systems of Europe.

More than ever, I believe South Africa presents students with an exciting "brain tease" in a course. South Africa is so much in the news these days that even students recognize its importance. With nearly permanent unrest and the white regime talking about concessions, we can ask: "Given what we know about politics and revolutions in other countries, what could South Africa do to avoid revolution?" If an instructor should choose not to include the section on this controversial country, the continuity would not be destroyed.

If there is to be a third edition, should I include other countries? The return cards showed scattered interest; Italy, Israel, India, and Japan were mentioned. I favored Iran—in keeping with the theme of revolutions—but concluded that things are too unsettled there and relatively little is known about Iran's internal politics. We will have to wait for what Crane Brinton called the "thermidor" before we can comprehend the Iranian revolution. I welcome your suggestions on other countries and, indeed, on any other area of the book. Some instructors responded to my invitation in the first edition for comments, corrections, and criticism. Especially valuable were the comments of Thomas P. Wolf, of Indiana University Southeast, on Britain; Waltraud Queiser Morales, of the University of Central Florida, on a summary table in the first chapter; Wayne Selcher, of Elizabethtown College, on Brazil; and, Christian Soe, of California State at Long Beach, on West Germany. Soe edits the *Comparative Politics* annual edition which serves as a useful supplement to this text. All comments are gratefuly received and can be sent to me at Lycoming College, Williamsport, PA 17701.

Williamsport, Pennsylvania   Michael Roskin

1

WHAT TO LOOK FOR

LOOKING FOR QUARRELS

One way to begin the study of a political system is to ask what its people fight about. There is no country without political quarrels. They range from calm, polite discussions over whether to include dental care in the nationalized health system to angry conflicts over minority language rights. Some controversies become murderous civil wars over who should rule the country. If you were to visit the country in question, you could get a fair idea of its quarrels by talking with its people, reading the local press, attending election rallies, and even noting the messages of posters, handbills, and graffiti.

So far, this is the approach of a good journalist. Political scientists, however, go further. They want to know the whys and wherefores of these controversies, whether they are long-standing issues or short-term problems. Our next step, then, is to observe these quarrels over time. If the basic quarrel lasts a long time—say, several years or even decades—we may conclude we're on to an important topic, that we have found a window through which to watch the country's politics.

Taking our long-term controversies as a starting point, we try to discern which groups are on which side. Who wants what and who opposes them? Here we may find political parties locked in conflict with each other, or interest groups trying to influence civil servants, or demagogues trying to sway the masses, or the army taking over power and then relinquishing it. We look, in short, for patterns.

Next we want to know why these patterns have formed. We might look first to political attitudes. Who thinks what? Are there deeply held conflicting viewpoints on how the country should be run? Are there important cleavages or splits running through the society? Equally important, we want to know something about governing institutions such as the presidency, parliament, and various political parties. These arenas are where many quarrels take place, and they are often the stakes of those quarrels as well (for example, winning the presidency or becoming the dominant party).

Ultimately, we must probe the country's history to understand how things got to be the way they are, how institutions and attitudes were formed. We may find that some patterns of interaction took shape long ago and that some of today's quarrels are the descendants of much older conflicts.

In sum, we could start studying a political system by noting a country's quarrels, observing them over time to see which are durable patterns of interaction, who is on what side in these interactions, how attitudes and institutions helped set up the interactions, and finally how the nation's past helped create the whole political structure.

To approach the problem in this order, however, might be likened to putting the cart before the horse or to reading a detective story from the conclusion backwards. While the quarrels might be the conclusion, the history is the foundation. Our approach here is to make a country's quarrels intelligible by explaining first the underlying factors.

Some Comparisons

	POPULATION millions	VOTER TURNOUT average 1945-81	PER CAPITA INCOME	GROWTH OF PER CAPITA GNP 1960-81	WORKFORCE in agric.	INFANT MORTALITY per 1,000 live births
Britain	56	77%	$7,200	2.1%	1.5%	13.3
France	55	79%	$7,200	3.8%	9%ˑ	9.ˑ
West Germany	62	87%	$11,200	3.2%	4%	13.5
Soviet Union	274	—	$3,400	—	20%	44
China	1,025	—	$566	5.0%	74%	71
Brazil	131	—	$1,500	5.1%	30%	92
South Africa	31	—	$1,300	2.3%	30%	14.9 whites 25 Indians 94 Africans
United States	235	59%	$12,800	2.3%	2%	11.2

Source: World Bank and *World Almanac*. Take all such tables with skepticism. Figures from the Third World and Communist countries are often nothing more than estimates. The Soviet Union, for example, does not publish Western-style economic figures and has kept its infant-mortality rate—a key measure of health—secret for over a decade. Changing currency parities may throw off non-U.S. economic data expressed in dollars.

THE STRUCTURE OF THIS BOOK

In this book, we take a broad look at the political systems of seven different countries in turn, considering each in a block of five sections, each focusing on a general subject area. We start with what might be termed the underlying causes of current politics. These are the "givens" or "ingredients" of a political system at a certain time. In the first three sections for each country we explore these underlying causes as we consider:

> The Impact of the Past
> The Key Institutions
> Political Attitudes

We study the *past* in order to understand the present. We are not looking for the fascinating details of history but for the major patterns that set up present institutions and attitudes. We study *institutions* to see how power is structured, for that is what institutions are: structures of power. We study *attitudes* to get a feel for the way people look at their social and political system, how deeply they support it, and how political views differ among social groups.

Moving from underlying factors to current politics brings us to the next two of each country's five sections:

> Patterns of Interaction
> What People Quarrel About

Here we get more specific and more current. The previous sections, we might say, are about the traditions, rules, and spirit of the game; the *patterns of interaction* are how the game is actually played. We look here for recurring behavior. The last section, the specific *quarrels*, represents the stuff of politics, the kind of things you might see in a newspaper in that country.

THE IMPACT OF THE PAST

Geography is not necessarily destiny, but it does help explain a country's politics. Is a country easy to invade? If so, it has to have a stronger army and probably a different governing mentality than a country that is difficult to invade. The size and regional diversity of a country may make it more difficult to unite. Natural resources are another factor, although they do not necessarily dominate. Often, poorly endowed countries achieve more prosperity and more democracy than richly endowed lands. It is human resources, not natural resources, that are basic to both economics and politics.

Was the country unified early or late? For the most part, countries are artificial, not natural, entities, created when one group or tribe conquers its neighbors and unifies them by the sword. The founding of nations is usually a pretty bloody business, and the longer ago it took place, the better. We look at Sweden and say, "What a nice, peaceful country." We look at Uganda and say, "What a ghastly bloodbath of warring tribes." We forget that if we went back far enough, Sweden might resemble Uganda. Sweden simply got most of its violence over with early.

The unification and consolidation of a country usually leaves behind regional resentments of incredible staying power. People whose ancestors were conquered centuries ago may still act out their resentments in political ways, in the voting booth or in civil violence. This is one way history has an impact on the present.

Becoming "modern" is a wrenching experience. Industrialization, urbanization, and the growth of education and communication uproot people from their traditional villages and lifestyles and send them to work in factories, usually in cities. In the process, people become "mobilized," or aware of their condition and willing to do something to change it. They become ready to participate in politics, demanding economic improvement and often that a new party take power. It's a delicate time in the life of nations. If the traditional elites do not devise some way to take account of newly awakened mass demands, the system may be heading toward revolution.

No country has industrialized in a happy manner; it is always a process marked by low wages, bad working conditions, and usually political repression. The longer ago this stage happened, the more peaceful and stable a country is likely to be. We must look for the *stage* of development a country is in. If a country is in the throes of industrialization, we can expect ample domestic tensions of the sort that were solved earlier in Europe.

Another historical point to look for is the relationship between the king and the nobles in olden days. Feudalism in Europe was a balanced relationship

The Five Crises of Nation Building

Political scientists have delineated five "crises" that nations seem to go through in sequence in their political development:

1. *Identity:* People develop a national identity over and above their tribal, regional, or local identities. Bretons come to think of themselves as French, Bavarians as Germans, and Uzbeks as Soviets. Some countries are still caught up in their identity crisis.

2. *Legitimacy:* People develop the feeling that the regime's rule is rightful, that it should be obeyed. A system without legitimacy requires massive amounts of coercion to keep it together and functioning.

3. *Penetration:* As the government's writ expands through the country, starting usually with the capital city, it encounters resistance, for many people dislike paying taxes to, and obeying the laws of, a distant authority. Local rebellions are crushed and police brought in to enforce national authority.

4. *Participation:* Once the other crises are solved, people start wanting to participate in some way in their nation's governance. There is usually a struggle to expand the electoral franchise. Parties are formed and attempt to control parliament. Mass participation in politics is usually granted only grudgingly by traditional elites, but once it's institutionalized the country is usually more stable and peaceful. Withholding participatory rights can lead to a buildup of a revolutionary anger.

5. *Distribution:* The last great crisis—probably a permanent one—is over the division of the nation's economic pie. Once the masses are participating in politics, their parties (for example, Labour in Britain, Social Democrat in Germany) demand that government use its considerable powers to distribute wealth and income in a more equitable fashion. To fund a welfare state, taxes grow. Better-off people generally fight this trend.

Fortunate is the country that has had its crises one at a time, so that its political system was able to grow and adapt with each challenge. If they all come at once—the case in much of the Third World today—they impose intolerable demands on a weak political system. Breakdowns are then frequent, usually leading to military rule.

This "sequential crises" model of political development is controversial. In some countries it seems to fit well; in others, poorly. As with all theories or models in political science, take this one with a grain of salt. See if it really applies—fully, partly, or not at all—to the country you are studying. What happens when one of more stages are bypassed or when the sequence gets jumbled? Are some countries' histories just too complicated to make the model fit at all?

in which kings and nobles needed each other. Britain preserved a rough balance between the two, and this paved the way for the limited government, civil rights, and eventually even mass political participation. In France, the king captured most of the power and created a rigid, overcentralized system incapable of handling demands for participation. The result was the French Revolution and instability ever since. Germany went the other way, falling apart into myriad petty states that unified only late, with an identity crisis and a period of explosive nationalism.

Religion is a crucial historial question. Does the country have its church-state relationship in order? If not, it's a lingering political sore. Protestant countries had an easier time of it; because their churches by definition were not linked to Rome, the state early on became stronger than church, and the church stayed out of politics. In Roman Catholic countries, where the church had power in its own right, there was a long church-state struggle called the "clerical-anticlerical split" which is still alive today in Italy. Even in France, the residues of the split still structure politics: conservatives are more religious and liberals and leftists indifferent or hostile to religion.

Instituting a democracy is a difficult historical test, one that all but two-dozen countries have so far flunked. Democracy can actually come too soon. If the people are too poor and ignorant, they are easily manipulated by political bosses. Americans often think elections are cures for all political ills, but elections in backward countries are seldom free and fair. Democracy can also come too late. If the traditional elite waits too long as the masses mobilize, the movement may turn radical and fall into the hands of revolutionary demagogues. What happened in Russia may happen again in South Africa. The slow, gradual expansion of the electoral franchise, as in Britain, is probably best.

The widening of the franchise means the rise of political parties. We ask, on what was a party first based, when was it founded, what were its initial aims, and how has it changed over the years? Was the party strongly ideological? Did it operate openly or was it driven underground? How have its early decades formed its present characteristics?

With political parties competing, we witness the introduction of the welfare issue into politics, the "distribution crisis." Left-wing parties argue that government should provide jobs, housing, medical care, and education. Other parties, on the political center or right, either reject the welfarist ideas, compromise with them, or steal them. Gradually the country becomes a welfare state. We ask what the various parties have proposed in terms of welfare and how much of it they have obtained.

Finally, history establishes political symbols that can awaken powerful emotions. Flags, monarchs, old buildings, national holidays, and national an-

Left, Right, and Center

The way delegates were seated at French assemblies during and after the Revolution gives us our terms for radical, conservative, and moderate. In a half-circle chamber, the most radical delegates were seated to the left of the speaker's rostrum, the most conservative to the right. This allowed like-minded legislators to caucus and kept apart delegates who might start fist fights.

The precise meanings of left, right, and center have varied through the ages and from country to country. In general, however, the left favors greater equality of incomes, welfare measures, and sometimes nationalization of industry. The right, now that it has shed its aristocratic origins, favors (or claims to favor) individual achievement and private industry. The center tries to synthesize the moderate elements in both viewpoints. Those just a little to one side or the other are called center-left or center-right.

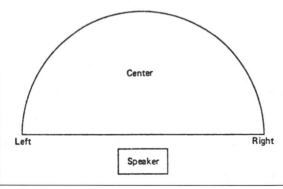

What About Names and Dates?

"Do we have to learn names and dates and details like that?" moan students of political science. This is not a history course, but obviously draws a lot from history. Historians tend to gather lots of evidence on rather narrow topics and are reluctant to generalize. Political scientists, on the other hand, utilize historical findings with an eye for patterns and generalizations rather than for details.

This does not mean we ignore names, dates, and other facts. Instead, for any given detail we ask,

"Does it matter for present-day politics?" If, for example, a current institution traces back to the actions of a certain king, it is worth remembering that king's name and century, although his exact dates may not be as important. If a current attitude traces back to early settlers, it is worth learning who they were, what they did, and why they did it. The names and dates included in this book help to explain present institutions, attitudes, and patterns. Learn them.

thems often serve as a cement to hold a country together, giving citizens the feeling that they are part of a common enterprise. To fully know a country, one must know its symbols, their historical genesis, and their current connotation.

THE KEY INSTITUTIONS

A political institution is a web of relationships lasting over time, an established structure of power. An institution may or may not be housed in an impressive building. With institutions we are looking for more or less durable sets of human relationships, not architecture.

One way to begin our search is to ask, "Who's got the power?" The nation's constitution—itself an institution—may give us some clues, but it seldom gives the whole picture. It may, for example, specify that a monarch (king or queen) is the "head of state." This sounds impressive until we learn that in most systems the head of state is a symbolic office, a sort of official greeter. In a monarchy, the head of state is a king or queen; in a republic, it's a president. This distinction, not a very important one, is called the *form of state*. Some monarchies are among the world's most democratic countries (Britain, Sweden), while some republics are terribly repressive. Of the seven countries treated in this book, only one is currently a monarchy, but all the others were monarchies earlier in their histories.

If the head of state doesn't have the power, who does? To find out, we next must discover if the system is *presidential* or *parliamentary* (see box). Both systems have parliaments, but a presidential system has a president who is elected and serves separately from the legislature; the legislature cannot vote out the president. The United States and Brazil are presidential systems. In parliamentary systems, action focuses on the prime minister, who is actually a member of parliament delegated by it to form a *government* (another word for cabinet). The prime minister and his or her cabinet can be ousted by a vote of no-confidence in parliament. Americans used to assume that presidential systems were better and more stable than parliamentary systems. The problems of the last couple of decades (Vietnam, Watergate) might make Americans aware of the advantages of a parliamentary system, which can easily oust a chief executive. Besides, parliamentary systems with the proper refinements, such as West

Parliamentary versus Presidential Systems

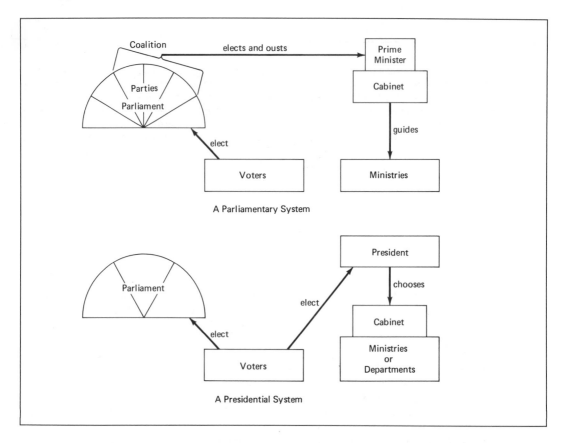

Germany's, can be quite stable. It's impossible to say which system is "better"; under various circumstances both have fallen prey to immobilism, instability, and the abuse of power.

Once we have located the center of executive power—a president or a prime minister—we ask, "How powerful is the legislature?" In most cases it is less powerful than the executive and declining. Of course, parliaments do still have the power to pass laws, but for the most part the laws originate with the civil servants and cabinet and are passed according to party wishes. In most legislatures (but not in the U.S. Congress), party discipline is so strong that a member of parliament simply votes the way party whips instruct. Further, legislators must increasingly rely on experts (often from the bureaucracy) for data and ideas in such technical areas as nuclear energy, the environment, regulation of industry, and defense affairs. But parliaments can be important in nonlegislative ways: they represent people, educate the public, structure interests, and most important, oversee and criticize executive-branch activities.

One way of classifying parliaments is by how many chambers they have:

bicameral (two) or *unicameral* (one). Two chambers are necessary in federal systems to represent the component parts, but they are often extra baggage in unitary systems. All the countries studied in this book have bicameral legislatures except China and South Africa.

Likewise, national party systems can be classified by how many parties each has. These are usually broken into three categories: one-party systems, such as the Soviet Union and China; two-party systems, such as Britain and the United States; and multiparty systems, such as France, Italy, and Sweden. (Actually, both Britain and West Germany are more accurately "two-plus" party systems, since they have relevant third parties.) In looking at party systems it is important to note how the parties compete—by sticking to the center with moderate programs or by moving to the extremes with radical positions. The two modes are called *center-seeking* and *center-fleeing*. The latter may spell dangerous polarization and system breakdown.

The number of parties is partially conditioned by a country's electoral system. Single-member districts, where a simple plurality wins elections, encourage two-party systems for the simple reason that third parties find it hard to capture that large a vote. Multimember districts, where parliamentarians are elected according to the proportion of the vote their party won, permit smaller parties to stay alive. Proportional representation, by encouraging multiparty systems, may contribute to cabinet instability as coalition members quarrel.

Political scientists now recognize that a country's permanent civil service—its bureaucracy—is one of its most powerful institutions. The bureaucracy today has eclipsed both cabinet and parliament in expertise, information, outside contacts, and sheer numbers. Some lobbyists no longer bother with the legislature; they go where the action is, to the important decision makers in the bureaucracy. Private industry is sometimes able to "capture" or "colonize" the very government offices that are supposed to be supervising them. One of our questions, then, is: How powerful and autonomous is the bureaucracy?

POLITICAL ATTITUDES

After World War II, political scientists shifted their emphasis from institutions to attitudes. The institutional approach had become suspect: for example, on paper Germany's Weimar constitution was a magnificent achievement, but it didn't work in practice because too few Germans really supported democracy. By the late 1950s, then, a new "political culture" approach to comparative politics became dominant that sought to explain systems in terms of popular attitudes. This is an important approach, but we must ask not only how attitudes determine government but how government determines attitudes. Attitudes and government are a two-way street; the two continually modify each other. Political culture can change under the impact of events. Americans became much more cynical in the wake of Vietnam and Watergate, while West Germans became more committed democrats as their country achieved economic success and political stability.

The perception of a government's legitimacy is one basic political atti-

The Civic Culture Study

In a massive 1959 study, political scientists Gabriel Almond and Sidney Verba led teams that asked approximately one thousand people in each of five countries—the United States, Britain, West Germany, Italy, and Mexico—identical questions on their political attitudes. The Civic Culture study, which was a benchmark in cross-national research, grouped its data in these categories:

Cognition: How much do people know about politics? Do they feel government has an impact on them?

Affect: Are they proud of their political institutions? Do they feel they're fairly treated by the system?

Partisanship: Why and how intensely do they support political parties? Are they tolerant of other viewpoints?

Participation: Do they feel they should participate in politics in some way?

Competence: Do they feel *able* to participate in politics? Do they feel they can influence government?

Socialization: Does the way they were raised influence their political attitudes? Do they feel most people can be trusted?

Almond and Verba discerned three types of political culture: (1) *participant,* in which people feel they should and in which they do participate in politics; (2) *subject,* in which people are aware of politics but cautious about participating; and (3) *parochial,* in which people are not even much aware of politics. They emphasized that each country is a mixture of these types, with perhaps one type dominating: participant in America, subject in West Germany and Italy, parochial in Mexico.

tude. This is not the same as its being "legal." Originally *legitimacy* meant that the rightful king was on the throne, not a usurper. Now it means a mass attitude that the government's rule is valid and that it should generally be obeyed. Governments are not automatically legitimate; they have to earn the respect of their citizens. Legitimacy can be created over a long time as a government endures and does a pretty good job of governing. Legitimacy can also erode as unstable and corrupt regimes come and go, never winning the people's respect. One quick test of legitimacy is how many police officers a country has. With high legitimacy, it doesn't need many police because people obey the law voluntarily. With low legitimacy, a country needs lots of coercive capacity, usually in the form of police.

When we look for signs of legitimacy, we ask: Do people generally obey this regime? Grudgingly or happily? Are there subgroups that regard the regime as illegitimate? Enough to make an insurrection? Does the regime have to use a lot of coercion? Is the regime taking steps to firm up its legitimacy? Is legitimacy eroding or increasing?

One way a regime can shore up its legitimacy is by using traditions and symbols. Symbols (especially time-honored ones) are the most effective and economical way of holding a system together, because one little symbol—say, the flag—can stir deep emotions. The Communists claim a revolutionary break with the past, but they cleverly use old national symbols such a the tsar's Kremlin in Moscow and the emperor's Forbidden City in Peking. The Communists in fact work hard at developing effective symbols, for they know that people are led more easily by emotion than by reason. You can learn a lot about a country by understanding its symbols.

One symbol frequently manipulated is ideology. An *ideology* is a grand plan to save or improve the country (see box). Typically, leaders at the top of a system take their ideology with a grain of salt. But for mass consumption, the Soviets and Chinese crank out reams of ideological propaganda (which, in fact, many of their people doubt).

The other political systems explored in this book are not so ideologically explicit, but all are committed to various ideologies to greater and lesser degrees: French Socialists are committed to economic modernization, British Conservatives to classic laissez-faire liberalism (also known as neoconservatism), and the South African Nationalists to a form of racism called *separate development*. Does every system have some sort of ideology? Probably. A system run on purely pragmatic grounds—if it works, use it—would be unideological, but such systems are rare. Even Americans, who pride themselves on being very pragmatic, are usually convinced of the effectiveness of the free market (Republicans) or moderate government intervention (Democrats). Thus one of our questions: How ideological or pragmatic is the system and its political parties?

What is "Ideology"?

Confusion surrounds the term *ideology.* Some use it to mean whatever politicians think, but this is too broad a definition. Political ideologies are belief systems that claim to aim at improving society. Ideologists say: "If we move in this direction, things will be much better. People will be happier, catastrophe will be avoided, society will become perfected." An ideology usually contains four elements:

1. The *perception* that things are going wrong, that society is headed down the wrong path. Fanatic ideologies often insist that total catastrophe is just around the corner.
2. An *evaluation* or analysis of why things are going wrong. This means a criticism of all or part of the existing system.
3. A *prescription* or cure for the problem. Moderate ideologies advocate reforms; extremist ideologies urge revolution and overthrow of the present system.
4. An effort to form a *movement* to carry out the cure. Without a party or movement, the above points are just talk without serious intent.

Seen in this light, Marxism-Leninism is a perfect example of ideology. First, we have Marx's perception that capitalism is doomed. Second, we have his analysis, that capitalism contains its own internal contradictions, which bring economic depressions.

Third, we have a Marxist prescription: Abolish capitalism in favor of collective ownership of the means of production, in a word, socialism. And fourth, especially with Lenin, we have the determined effort to form a strong Communist party—the "organizational weapon"—to put the cure into effect by overthrowing the capitalist system.

There are some other interesting points about ideologies. They are usually based on a serious thinker, often an important philosopher. Communism traces back to Hegel, classic liberalism to John Locke. But the philosopher's original ideas become popularized, vulgarized, and often distorted at the hands of ideologists who are trying to mass-market them. Deep thoughts are turned into cheap slogans. It often ends up that the original philosopher would reject what's being done in his name. Toward the end of his life, Marx is said to have worried about the distortions of his ideas by younger thinkers and to have commented, "One thing is for sure: I am not a Marxist."

Another point about ideologies is that they are always defective, that is, they can never deliver what they promise: perfect societies full of happy humans. Classic liberalism produced an underclass, while Marxism-Leninism produced a state bureaucracy that stepped on everyone. Still, as long as people can imagine a cure for society's ills, there will be ideologies.

Another point related to attitudes is a country's education system. Almost universally, education is the main path to political elite status. The way an education system functions—who gets educated and in what way—helps structure who gets political power and what they do with it. No country has totally

The Politics of Social Cleavages

Most societies are split along one or more lines. Often these splits, or "cleavages," become the society's fault lines along which political attitudes form. Here are some of the more politically relevant social cleavages.

Social Class

Karl Marx thought social class determined everything, that it was the only important social cleavage. Whether one was bourgeois or proletarian determined most political orientations. Marx held that middle- and upper-class people were conservative; working-class people, progressive or radical. Experience, however, makes it hard for many to swallow such a black-and-white view. Sometimes poor people are extremely conservative while middle-class intellectuals are radical.

Still, social class does matter in structuring attitudes. The working class does tend toward the left, but never 100 percent. Further, the left they tend to is apt to be the moderate left of social democracy rather than the radical left of communism. Such is the case of the West German Social Democratic party.

The student of comparative politics has to put class into perspective. By itself, social class is seldom a sufficient explanation for political orientation. Other ingredients are usually present. The question, as Joseph LaPalombara put it, is, "Class plus what?"

Geographic Region

Most countries have regional differences, and often they are politically important. Once a region gets set in its politics it can stay that way for generations. Often the attitude is a remembrance of past conquests and injustices. Scotland still resents England, and likewise the south of France resents the north. The student should learn to inquire what the regions of a nation and their politics are and how they got to be that way.

Religion

We considered how religious struggles were one of the more politically relevant items in a nation's history. In some countries they are still quite important. You can predict with fair accuracy how a French person will vote by knowing how often he or she attends Mass. You can partly predict how a German will vote by knowing if the citizen in question is Protestant or Catholic (and which region he or she lives in). It has been shown that religion accounts for the formation of more political parties than does social class.

Urban-Rural

City people are usually different politically from country people. City people tend to be more aware of politics, more participatory, and more liberal or leftist. This is especially true in the Third World, where the countryside remains extremely backward while the cities modernize. Even China, despite its revolution, has a significant urban-rural split in terms of living conditions, education, and political orientation.

There are other possible politically relevant social cleavages. In some situations sex matters, especially in Catholic countries where women tend to be more conservative than men. Occupation, as distinct from social class, can also influence political attitudes. A miner and a farmer may make the same amount of money, but chances are the miner will be leftist and the farmer conservative. Age can sometimes be an important political factor. Young people are usually more open to new ideas and more likely to embrace radical and even violent causes than older citizens. West Germany's terrorists, China's Red Guards, and South Africa's rioters were all young.

Almost any social cleavage or category can become politically relevant. The student of comparative politics can become sensitive to these categories by asking himself or herself from where they got the political views they hold. Is it your age? Did you get them from your family? And why does your family hold these views? Is it their religion? Their ethnic group? Their regional tradition?

equal educational opportunity. Even where schooling is legally open to all, social-, economic-, and (in Communist countries) even political-screening devices work against some sectors of the population. Typically, the working class is shortchanged and the middle class is overrepresented in colleges and universities. Most countries have elite universities that produce a big share of their political leadership, at times a near monopoly.

The education system leads to a country's elite system. It is usually schooling that gives a person access to elite status. Elites—the top or most influential people—are a major determinant of a country's politics. We need to answer some specific questions about them: Where and how were they educated? Did they inherit or achieve their elite status? How do elite attitudes compare to those of the masses? Is the elite system open to all of talent, or is it closed to all but a few? Are the various elites of society (business, labor, government, military, and so on) able to cooperate, or are they locked in conflict? Do elites totally control and manipulate the masses, or is there some mass input into elite deliberations?

With elites we are reminded that politics, even democratic politics, is usually the work of a few. Most people most of the time do not participate in politics, as Joseph LaPalombara has observed. But there are various kinds of elites, some more democractic and dedicated to the common good than others. Later, when considering the "Patterns of Interaction" chapters, be sure to ask yourself: How much of these interactions are an elite game with little or no mass participation?

PATTERNS OF INTERACTION

Here at last we come to what is conventionally called politics. In determining *patterns of interaction,* basically we look for who does what to whom. We look for the interactions of parties, interest groups, individuals, and bureaucracies. Do groups come together to compete or strike deals? How do political parties persuade the public to support them? In studying each country, it is the fourth section that will be the crucial one, but the other four are needed too, to fully understand this one.

We look not for one-time events but for things that occur with some regularity. Finding such patterns is the beginning of making generalizations, and generalizing is the beginning of theory. Once we have found a pattern we ask, Why? The answer will be found partly from what we have learned about each country in preceding chapters, and partly in the nature of political life where struggle and competition are normal and universal.

Some interactions are open and public; others are closed and secretive. The interactions of parties and citizenry are mostly open. Every party tries to convince the public that the party is fit to govern. This hold equally true for democratic and authoritarian systems. Do they succeed? Whom do the parties aim for and how do they win them over? By ideology? Promises? Common interests? Or by convincing people the other party is worse?

The parties interact with each other, sometimes cooperatively but more often competitively. How do they denounce and discredit each other? Under

The Politician as Balancer

One of the most common patterns in political interactions is the one politicians—if they are successful—follow in balancing parties, public opinion, interest groups, and bureaucracies. If a politician can balance these forces, usually making sure everyone gets something but not one gets everything, he or she is apt to be successful and durable.

The more we learn, for example, about so-called dictators the more we realize they can't just dictate everything but have to play off one interest against another. When the politician loses his or her balancing ability and starts forgetting about the interests of important groups, those groups can become alienated and hostile to the system. Then the system can be headed for breakdown or civil war.

what circumstances do they make deals? Is their competition murderous or moderate?

Parties interact with the government. In the Soviet Union and China they run parallel with the government. In politically more open countries, parties try to capture and retain governmental power. How do parties form coalitions? Who gets the top cabinet jobs? Once in power, is the party able to move or is it immobilized by contrary political forces? These are some questions to ask.

Politics within the parties is an important point. We ask if a party has factions. Does it have a left wing and a right wing? How do its leaders hold it together? Do they pay off factions with key jobs or merely with lip service? Do factional quarrels paralyze the party? Could it split? Do its more extreme factions frighten away voters?

Parties also interact with interest groups. Some groups enjoy "structured access" to like-minded parties. In Europe, labor unions are often linked formally to political parties. Here we need to know: Does the party co-opt the interest group or vice versa? How powerful are interest-group views in determining party policy?

As mentioned earlier, interest groups often decide it's not worth working on the electoral-legislative side and instead focus their attention on the bureaucratic. One of the key areas of politics is where bureaucracies and businesses interface. Are interest groups controlled by government or vice versa? What kind of relationships do businessmen and bureaucrats establish? Which groups are the most influential? These important interactions are generally out of the public sight. Does money change hands? Or have the two merely established identical viewpoints?

What About Democracy?

In surveying the many interactions that make up politics, we notice how few of them are "democratic," that is, allow the people as a whole to make decisions. If some of the most important interactions are out of public sight—the classic "smoke-filled back room" or the envelope full of money—what then does democracy mean? If elections depend to a considerable extent on misleading or frightening the public, what role has the citizenry in politics?

Democracy is actually rather hard to define. The countries of Eastern Europe, under Soviet tutelage, claim to be "people's democracies," better and more complete democracies than those of Western Europe. This claim leads to some crucial questions you should be asking: What is democracy? What criteria do you use to recognize it? Is democracy ultimately impossible?

WHAT PEOPLE QUARREL ABOUT

Here we move to current issues, the political struggles of the day. We start with economics, that is, the universal and permanent quarrel over who gets what. (Political scientists should have a grounding in economics; if you haven't already done it, think about taking an economics course.)

First we inquire if the economy of the country in question is growing. If so, is it expanding rapidly or slowly? Why? Are workers lazy or energetic? Are managers stupid or clever? How much of the economy gets government help and planning? Is government interference a hindrance on the economy? If the economy is declining, why? Why are some countries economic success stories and others not? How big a role does politics play in economic growth?

Other questions: Are unions reasonable or strike-happy? What political payoffs do unions seek? Are wage settlements in line with productivity, or are they inflationary? Does government try to influence wage increases? Do workers and management cooperate or battle each other? Do workers have any say in running their companies? How much imported labor is there? How much unemployment?

Once we have a realistic picture of the economic pie, we inquire who gets what slice. How equal—or unequal—is the distribution of income and wealth? Does government policy aim at making incomes more equal or at rewarding some people more than others? Does unequal distribution lead to social and political resentment?

Some governments attempt to correct a skewed distribution of income by "redistributing" it. This is what happens when taxation skims off money from better-off people and transfers it to poorer people. Redistribution is another name for a welfare system. To what extent does the system redistribute income? How high and how progressive are taxes? How many and how generous are welfare benefits? Do people want more welfare and higher taxes, or less welfare and lower taxes? Which people? In which direction is the redistribution system heading—more to the economically needy, less, or to leveling off?

There are, to be sure, noneconomic quarrels as well. Regionalism is among the nastiest. Even well-integrated Britain has a bloody regional war in

The Importance of Being Comparative

You can't be scientific if you're not comparing," political scientist James Coleman used to tell his students. Countries are not unique; they are comparable with other countries. When we say, for example, that the parliament of country X has become a rubber stamp for the executive, this is not a very meaningful statement until we note that it is also the tendency in countries Y and Z.

The "uniqueness trap" often catches commentators of the American scene off-guard. We hear statements such as: "The U.S. political system is breaking down." Compared to what? To France in 1958? To China in 1966? Or to the United States itself in 1861? Compared to these other cases, the United States today is in rather good shape. We hear statements like this one: "The trouble with this country is that the labor unions are too powerful." But what percentage of the American labor force is unionized? How does this compare to Britain and West Germany? Does U.S. labor have its own political party like some labor movements in other countries?

Our thinking on politics will be greatly clarified if we put ourselves into a comparative mood by frequently asking, "Compared to what?"

Northern Ireland. In France, Corsicans and Bretons set off bombs. In Spain, Canada, Yugoslavia, and elsewhere, long-ignored regional problems have come to the fore. Regions want different things; some want outright independence, some merely autonomy, some just a better economic deal or recognition of their language. What are a country's regions? Which of them are discontent? How much? A lot or little? Do they have a political impact? Have extremists turned to violence?

How is the central government reacting to regionalist demands? By crushing them? By setting up regional councils and home rule? Is there a move afoot to decentralize or devolve power to the regions? Or are things going the other way, with a move to centralize more power in the capital?

Some quarrels are unique to a particular country. Brazilians quarrel about whether to hold direct elections, South Africans about reforming *apartheid,* and the Chinese about introducing a market economy. The student of comparative politics keeps his or her eyes open for the quarrels that ripple through each system.

VOCABULARY BUILDING

affect	distribution	parliamentary	redistribution
anticlerical	electoral system	parochial	regionalism
authoritarian	elites	participant	social cleavages
bicameral	factions	participation	socialization
bureaucracy	form of state	partisanship	subgroup
coercion	franchise	party system	subject
cognition	generalization	pattern	symbol
comparative	identity	penetration	unicameral
competence	industrialization	political culture	unification
cynical	institution	pragmatic	urbanization
democracy	legitimacy	presidential	welfare

FURTHER REFERENCE

Almond, Gabriel, and **Sidney Verba.** *The Civic Culture: Political Attitudes and Democracy in Five Nations.* Princeton, N.J.: Princeton University Press, 1963.
————— , **eds.** *The Civic Culture Revisited.* Boston: Little, Brown, 1980.
Chilcote, Ronald H. *Theories of Comparative Politics: The Search for a Paradigm.* Boulder, Colo.: Westview Press, 1981.
Grew, Raymond, ed. *Crises of Political Development in Europe and the United States.* Princeton, N.J.: Princeton University Press, 1978.
Heidenheimer, Arnold J., Hugh Heclo, and **Carolyn Teich Adams.** *Comparative Public Policy: The Politics*

of Social Choice in Europe and America, 2nd ed. New York: St. Martin's Press, 1983.
Kramnick, Isaac, and **Frederick M. Watkins.** *The Age of Ideology—Political Thought, 1750 to the Present,* 2nd ed. Englewood Cliffs, N.J.: Prentice-Hall, 1979.
LaPalombara, Joseph. *Politics Within Nations.* Englewood Cliffs, N.J.: Prentice-Hall, 1974.
Lijphart, Arend. *Democracies: Patterns of Majoritarian and Consensus Government in Twenty-One Countries.* New Haven, Conn.: Yale University Press, 1984.
Lipset, Seymour Martin. *Political Man: The Social Bases of Politics.* expanded and updated ed. Baltimore, Md.: John Hopkins University Press, 1981.

Nordlinger, Eric A. *On the Autonomy of the Democratic State.* Cambridge, Mass.: Harvard University Press, 1981.

Ornstein, Norman J., ed. *The Role of the Legislature in Western Democracies.* Washington, D.C.: American Enterprise Institute, 1981.

Prescott, J. R. V. *Political Geography.* London: Methuen, 1972.

Putnam, Robert D. *The Comparative Study of Political Elites.* Englewood Cliffs, N.J.: Prentice-Hall, 1976.

Shively, W. Phillips. *The Craft of Political Research,* 2nd ed. Englewood Cliffs, N.J.: Prentice-Hall, 1980.

Tilly, Charles, ed. *The Formation of National States in Western Europe.* Princeton, N.J.: Princeton University Press, 1975.

part one

GREAT BRITAIN

2

THE IMPACT
OF THE PAST

"ISLAND LIKE ENGLAND"

A Polish student I once knew at UCLA had to write a paper for her English class on what she most wished for her native land. She thought for a moment and wrote: "I wish that Poland be island like England." She meant that Poland, on a plain between large hostile neighbors (Germany and Russia), has a sad history of invasion and partition. If only Poland had been an island like England, she reasoned, its history would have been much happier. In *Richard II,* Shakespeare said much the same:

> This royal throne of kings, this scept'red isle,
> This earth of majesty, this seat of Mars,
> This other Eden, demi-paradise,
> This fortress built by Nature for herself
> Against infection and the hand of war,
> This happy breed of men, this little world,
> This precious stone set in the silver sea,
> Which serves it in the office of a wall,
> Or as a moat defensive to a house,
> Against the envy of less happier lands;
> This blessed plot, this earth, this realm, this England.

The last successful invasion of England was in 1066. The barrier posed by the English Channel has kept Frenchmen, Spaniards, and Germans from conquering Britain. Politically this has meant that England could develop its own institutions without foreign interference, a luxury not enjoyed by most Continental lands. Militarily it has meant that England rarely needed or had a large army, a point of great importance in the seventeenth century when British kings were unable to tame Parliament precisely because the monarch had few soldiers. Britain's insularity also contributed to a seafaring tradition that went hand-in-hand with outward expansion and made Britain both the world's greatest empire and greatest industrial power in the nineteenth century.

Shakespeare was only partly right about the seas serving as England's moat. Centuries earlier, England had been invaded many times. For a millenium and a half, waves of Celts, Romans, Angles and Saxons, Danes, and finally Normans washed upon Britain. One tribe of Celts, the Britons, gave their name to the entire island. Britishers, like most peoples, are not of one stock but of many.

The fierce Germanic tribesmen who rowed across the North Sea during the third to fifth centuries A.D. brought over what we call Old English or *Anglisch,* the language of the Angles, akin to the Frisian of Holland. "England" was simply the land of the Angles. The Angles and Saxons slowly moved across England, destroying towns and massacring inhabitants. The Celts were pushed back to present-day Wales and Scotland, which became a "Celtic fringe" to England. Some fleeing Celts crossed over to France and gave their name to Brittany. Preserving their distinct identity and languages (Cymric in Wales, Gaelic in Scotland), Britain's Celts never quite forgot what the newer arrivals did to them.

Other invaders followed. In the ninth century Danish Vikings held much of eastern England (the Danelaw), but they were eventually absorbed. Another group of Vikings had meanwhile settled in France; these Norsemen (Normans) gave their name to Normandy. In 1066, with the English throne in dispute, William of Normandy put forward his own dubious claim to it and invaded with a force gathered from all over France. He defeated the English King Harold at the famous battle of Hastings, and England changed dramatically.

The United Kingdom

The full and official name of Britain is the United Kingdom of Great Britain and Northern Ireland. "Great Britain" refers to the whole island that includes Wales and Scotland as well as England.

The British flag, the "Union Jack," stands for three saints representing different parts of the United Kingdom. The larger red cross is the Cross of St. George of England, the white is the Cross of St. Andrew of Scotland, and the thinner, diagonal red cross is that of St. Patrick of Ireland. (Note that this cross is off center.) The Union Jack is a potent symbol, calculated to evoke both regional pride and national unity.

William the Conqueror replaced the entire Saxon ruling class with Norman nobles, who earned their fiefdoms by military service. Since at first the Norman conquerors spoke only French, vast numbers of French words soon enriched the English language. Backed by brutal military power, administration was better and tighter. William ordered a complete inventory of all lands and population in his new domain; the resulting Domesday Book provided a detailed tool for governance. The Exchequer—the name derived from the French word for a checkered counting table—became the king's powerful treasury minister, a title and office that exist today. Further, since William and his descendants ruled both England and parts of France, England was tied for centuries to the affairs of the Continent.

Britain's French Legacy

Dating from the Norman Conquest, many English expressions, especially those related to royalty and the courts, are still in ancient Norman French. An English court is called to order with Oyez! Oyez! (hear ye). The motto of the elite Order of the Garter, which was founded in 1348 for the best jousters, is *Honi soit qui mal y pense* (evil to him who thinks evil).

Although the king or queen no longer has any real political power, the royal assent is still needed to turn into law an act of Parliament—itself a French word, meaning a place where people *parley* (talk). When His Majesty approves a nonfinancial bill, the monarch still writes, *Le Roy le veult* (the king wishes it). For a financial bill, which originally meant that Parliament granted money to the monarch, the formula is appropriately grateful: *Le Roy remercie ses bons sujets, accepte leur benevolence et ainsi le veult* (the king thanks his good subjects, accepts their benevolence, and thus wishes it). The royal veto—used for the last time by Queen Anne in 1707—is a cautious *Le Roy s'avisera* (the king will consider it).

MAGNA CARTA

The Normans brought to England a political pattern that had emerged on the Continent, feudalism. The feudal system was a contractual agreement between lords and vassals in which the lords would grant the vassals land (or the use of it) and protection while the latter would support the former with military service. Feudalism tends to appear naturally when central authority has broken down and a money economy disappears, for then land and fighting ability take on tremendous importance. In Europe, the collapse of the Roman Empire meant that kings could survive and thrive only if they had enough knights to fight for them. The knights in turn got land. Power here was a two-way street: the king needed the knights and vice versa.

The mixed monarchy of the Middle Ages was a balance between king and nobles. Its feeling can be summed up in the oath the nobles of Aragon (in the northeast of Spain) swore to a new ruler: "We who are as good as you swear to you, who are no better than we, to accept you as our king and sovereign lord provided you observe all our statutes and laws; and if not, no."

This oath, curiously, fitted England better than Aragon, for centuries of English history were dominated by the struggle to make sure the king did not exceed his feudal bounds and become an absolute monarch (which is what happened in most of Europe). This English struggle laid the foundation for limited, representative government, democracy, and civil rights, even though the participants at the time had no such intent.

The Great Charter that the barons forced upon King John at Runnymede in 1215 is nothing so far-reaching or idealistic; it never mentions liberty or democracy. What the barons and top churchmen wanted from John was to stop his encroachment on feudal customs, rights, and laws by which they held sway in their localities. In this sense the Magna Carta, one of the great documents of democracy, was feudal and reactionary. Far more important than its actual content, however, was the principle of limiting the monarch's powers and making sure he stayed within the law.

The Magna Carta meant that the king was in a kind of balance with the nobles and that as long as they balanced, there would be neither despotism nor anarchy, the twin ills of the Continent. In Europe, countries either went to absolutism, a kind of royal dictatorship, as in France, or broke up into small princi-

The Common Law

One of England's contributions to civilization is the Common Law, the legal system now practiced also in the United States, Canada, Australia, and other countries once administered by Britain (but not South Africa). Common Law grew out of the customary usage of the Germanic tribal laws of the Angles and Saxons, which stressed the rights of free men. It developed on the basis of precedent set by earlier decisions and thus has been called "judge-made law."

When the Normans conquered England, they decided that the purely local nature of this law was un-suitable to governing the country as a whole, so they set up central courts to systematize the local laws and produce a "common" law for all parts of England—hence the name.

Common Law differs from the Roman Law that is practiced throughout Continental Europe (and in Scotland). Common Law emphasizes precedent while Roman Law stresses formal legal codes. This gives the Common Law flexibility to adapt and change over time.

palities, as in Germany. British, and by extension, American, democracy owes a lot to the strength and stubbornness of English barons who stood up for their traditional rights.

THE RISE OF PARLIAMENT

During the same century as the Magna Carta, English kings started seeing the utility of calling to London, by now the capital, two to four knights from each shire (roughly a county) and a similar number of burghers from the towns to consult with the king on matters of the realm. Kings did this not out of the goodness of their hearts but because they needed to firm up the support of those who had local power and to raise taxes. The fact that English kings also had French holdings meant that England fought wars in France. These were expensive, and the only way to raise revenue to pay for them was by inviting local notables to participate, at least symbolically, in the affairs of state. Little did the kings know that they were founding an institution in the thirteenth century that would overshadow the monarchy by the seventeenth century.

Parliament began as an extension of the king's court but over the centuries took on a life of its own. Knights and burghers formed what we call a *lower house*, the House of Commons. Those of noble rank, along with the top churchmen, formed what we call an *upper house*, the House of Lords. In time, a leading member of the Commons became its representative to the king; he was called the Speaker. In order that business could be conducted unhampered, parliamentary privileges developed to prevent the arrest of members.

The Commons at this stage was not a "representative" institution, at least not in our sense. It represented only people who were locally wealthy or powerful, not a cross-section of the English people. That came much later, in the nineteenth century. But Parliament, especially the Commons, played a role even more important than accurate representation of the nation. It continued the blocking mechanism of the Magna Carta: it diffused power and prevented the king from getting too much. Parliament thus laid one of the foundation stones of democracy without knowing it.

HENRY VIII

Parliament got a major boost during the reign of Henry VIII (1509–47), when Henry declared a partnership with Parliament in his struggle against Rome. On top of underlying tensions between the Vatican and London–the universal Church on the one hand and growing nationalism on the other–Henry wanted the pope to grant him a divorce. His marriage to Catherine of Aragon had failed to produce the male heir that Henry felt he needed to insure stability after him. (Ironically, it was his daughter Elizabeth who went down in history as one of the greatest English monarchs.)

The pope refused—Catherine's Spanish relatives at that time controlled Rome—so Henry summoned a parliament in 1529 and kept it busy for seven years, passing law after law to get England out of the Catholic church and the

Catholic church out of England. The new Anglican church, called Episcopalian in America, was at first identical to the Roman Catholic church (it turned Protestant later), but at its head was an Englishman, not the pontiff of Rome. The new church granted Henry his divorce in 1533. He married a total of six wives—and had two of them beheaded. But Henry was not simply eager for young brides; he was desperate for a male heir for dynastic reasons.

Whatever his motives, the impact of Henry's break with Rome was major. England was cut free from papal guidance and direction. Countries that stayed Catholic, such as France, Spain, and Italy, experienced wrenching splits for centuries between pro-church and anticlerical forces. England (and Sweden) avoided this nasty division because the state early on was stronger than the church and controlled it. This meant that in England it was far easier to secularize society and politics than in Roman Catholic countries, where the church was still an independent power.

Parliament became more important than ever; Henry needed its support for his momentous break with Rome. In 1543 Henry praised Parliament as an indispensible part of his government: "We be informed by our judges that we at no time stand so highly in our estate royal as in the time of parliament, wherein we as head and you as members are conjoined and knit together into one body politic." A century later Parliament chopped the royal head off one of his successors.

PARLIAMENT VERSUS KING

In the late fifteenth century several European monarchs were able to expand their powers and undermine the old feudal mixed monarchy. The weakened power of Rome in the sixteenth century gave kings more independence and introduced the notion that kings ruled by divine right, that is, that they got their authority directly from God without the pope as intermediary. Political theorists searched for the seat of *sovereignty,* the highest legal authority in the land, and concluded that it must lie in one person, the monarch. This movement was called *absolutism.* By 1660 absolute monarchs governed most lands of Europe— but not England.

The seventeenth century was one of almost uninterrupted turmoil for England: religious splits, civil war, a royal beheading, and a military dictatorship wracked the country. The net winner, when the dust had settled, was Parliament.

Trouble started when James I came down from Scotland to take over the English throne after the death of Elizabeth in 1603. James united the crowns of Scotland and England, but they remained separate countries until the 1707 Act of Union. James I was intelligent and well educated but imbued with absolutist notions then common throughout Europe. He didn't like to share power and thought existing institutions should simply support the king. This brought him into conflict with Puritanism, an extreme Protestant movement that aimed to reform the "popish" elements out of the Anglican church. James preferred the Anglican church to stay just the way it was, for it was one of the pillars of his regime. James's harassment of Puritans caused some of them to run away to Massachusetts.

Premature Democrats

Among the antiroyalists were a group of out-and-out republicans called Levellers, who wanted to make men politically more equal. Sergeants and enlisted men in the New Model Army argued that people like themselves—tradesmen, artisans, and farmers—should be allowed to vote. They were influenced in their thinking by Puritanism, which among other things taught that all men were equal before God and needed no spiritual or temporal superiors to guide them. (This Puritan influence also had a powerful impact on American democracy.)

One group of Levellers, meeting in Putney in 1647, even went so far as to advocate one man, one vote. This idea was a good two centuries ahead of its time, and the more conservative forces of England, including Cromwell himself, would stand for no such change. Still, the Putney meeting had introduced the idea of the universal franchise—that is, giving everybody the right to vote.

By now Parliament had grown to feel coequal with the king and, in the area of raising revenues, his superior. Hard up for cash, James tried to impose taxes without the consent of Parliament, which grew angry over the move. James's son, Charles I, who took over in 1625, fared even worse. He took England into separate wars with Spain and France; both were unsuccessful and increased the king's desperation for money. Charles tried to play the role of a Continental absolute monarch, but the English people and Parliament wouldn't let him.

When the Royalists fought the Parliamentarians in the English Civil War, 1642–48, the latter proved stronger, for the Parliamentarian cause was aided by Puritans and the growing merchant class. The Parliamentarians created a "New Model Army," which trounced the Royalists. (The king, as was mentioned, had no standing army at his disposal.) Charles was captured, tried by Parliament, and beheaded in 1649.

CROMWELL'S COMMONWEALTH

From 1649 to 1660 England had no king. Who then was to rule? The only organized force left was the army, and it was under Oliver Cromwell. Briefly England became a *republic*—a term that simply means a country not headed by a monarch. It was called the Commonwealth, and Cromwell was the leading figure. Problems, however, did not die down; in fact, discord grew worse. To restore order, Cromwell in 1653 was designated Lord Protector, a sort of uncrowned king, and soon imposed a military dictatorship on England. When Cromwell died in 1658, most Englishmen had had enough of turbulent republic-

Acton's Dictum

The nineteenth-century British historian and philosopher Lord Acton distilled the lessons of centuries of English political development in his famous remark: "Power tends to corrupt; absolute power corrupts absolutely." Acton feared the tyrannical tendencies of the modern state. Lord Acton's dictum is as close as political science can get to a law.

anism and longed for stability and order. In 1660, Parliament invited Charles II, son of the beheaded king, to return from Dutch exile and take the throne. The English monarchy was restored, but it was a different kind of monarchy, one in which Parliament was much stronger and had to be treated with respect.

THE "GLORIOUS REVOLUTION"

Charles II knew he could not be an absolute monarch; instead, he tried to manipulate Parliament discreetly. A showdown came over religion. Charles was pro-Catholic and secretly ready to return his allegiance to Rome. In 1673 he issued the Declaration of Indulgence, lifting laws against Catholics and non-Anglican Protestants. What we might see as an act of tolerance toward minority religions Parliament saw as an illegal return to Catholicism, and it blocked the royal move. Anti-Catholic hysteria swept England with fabricated stories of popish plots to take over the country.

When Charles II died in 1685, his openly and proudly Catholic brother, James, took the throne as James II. Again a Declaration of Indulgence was issued, and again Parliament took it as a return to both Catholicism and absolutism. Parliament dumped James II (but let him escape) and invited his Protestant daughter, Mary, and her Dutch husband, William, to be England's queen and king. This was the "Glorious Revolution": a major shift of regime took place with scarcely a shot fired. In 1689 a "Bill of Rights"—unlike its U.S. namesake—spelled out Parliament's relationship to the Crown: no laws or taxes without the former's assent.

The vast majority of Englishmen thoroughly approved, through their Parliament. If it wasn't clear before then, it was now: Parliament was supreme and had the ability to invite and dismiss monarchs. In 1714, for example, Parliament invited George I from Hanover in Germany to become king; the present royal family is descended from him. Since that time, the English monarch has been increasingly a figurehead, one who reigns but does not rule.

THE RISE OF THE PRIME MINISTER

One of the consequences of bringing over George I in 1714 was that he couldn't really govern even if he wanted to. He spoke no English and preferred Hanover to London. So he turned to an administrative device that had been slowly developing and allowed it to assume top executive power—the *cabinet*, composed of ministers and presided over by a first, or prime, minister. Under Sir Robert Walpole, from 1721 to 1742, the cabinet developed into approximately its present form but lacked two important present-day features: the prime minister could not pick his ministers (that was reserved for the king), and the cabinet was not responsible—meaning, in its original sense, "answerable"—to Parliament.

Royal power had one last gasp. George III managed to pack the Commons with his supporters and to govern with the obedient Lord North. One unforeseen result of this temporary absolutist resurgence was the language of the U.S. Declaration of Independence, which sought to regain the traditional rights of Englishmen against a too-powerful king. Following the British defeat, William Pitt the younger restored the cabinet and prime ministership to power and made them responsible only to the Commons, not to the King. This began the tradition—it still has no statutory backing—that the "government" consists of the leader of the largest party in the House of Commons plus other people that he or she picks. As party chief, top person in Parliament, and head of government combined, the prime minister became the focus of political power in Britain.

THE DEMOCRATIZATION OF PARLIAMENT

Parliament may have been supreme by the late eighteenth century, but it was hardly democratic or even representative. In the country, the right to vote was limited to those who owned land that yielded an income of at least forty shillings a year. In towns, there were often not more than a dozen or two men eligible to vote, although in the cities the franchise was much wider.

In the eighteenth century, parties began to form. At first they were simply parliamentary caucuses, meetings of people from the same area. Only in the next century did they begin to strike roots in the electorate outside of Parliament. The labels "Whig" and "Tory" first appeared under Charles II, connoting his opposition and his supporters respectively. Both were derisive names: the original Whigs were Scotish bandits, and the original Tories were Irish bandits.

During the nineteenth century a two-party system emerged. The Whigs grew into the Liberal party and the Tories into the Conservative party. British Conservatives to this day are nicknamed Tories. Whatever their party label, parliamentarians were not ordinary people. The House of Lords, of course, was limited to hereditary peers. The House of Commons, despite its name, was the home of gentry, landowners, and better-off people. Elections were often won by bribing the small number of voters.

By the time of the American and French revolutions in the late eighteenth century, however, Parliament noticed that the winds were stirring in favor of expanding the electorate. People began talking about political democracy and the right to vote. Under the impact of the industrial revolution and economic growth, two powerful new social classes arose, the middle class and the working class. Whigs and Tories, both heavily aristocratic in their makeup, at first viewed demands for the mass vote with disdain and even horror; it reminded them of how democracy ran amok during the French Revolution.

Gradually, though, it dawned on the Whigs that the way to head off revolution was to incorporate some of the new social elements into politics and give them a stake in the system. Furthermore, that party which supported broadening the franchise would most likely win the votes of those who were newly enfranchised. After much resistance by Tories in the Commons and by the entire House of Lords, Parliament succeeded in passing the famous Reform Act of 1832.

At the time, the Reform Act hardly looked like a momentous breakthrough. It let more of the middle class vote but still only expanded the electorate by about half: only about 7 percent of adults could then vote. The Reform Act established the principle, though, that the Commons ought to be representative of, and responsive to, the broad mass of citizens, not just the notables. In 1867, it was the Conservatives' turn. Under Prime Minister Disraeli the Second Reform Act doubled the size of electorate, giving about 16 percent of the adult Britons the vote. In 1884, the Third Reform Act added farm workers to the electorate and thus achieved nearly complete male suffrage. Women finally got the vote in 1918.

The interesting point about the growth of the British electorate is that the process was slow. New elements were added to the voting rolls only gradually, giving Parliament time to assimilate the forces of mass politics without going through an upheaval. The gradual tempo also meant that citizens got the vote when they were ready for it. In some countries where the universal franchise—one person, one vote—was instituted early, the result was not democracy but tyranny as crafty officials rigged the voting of people who didn't understand electoral politics. Spain, for example, got universal suffrage in the 1870s, but election results were set in advance. By the time the British working class got the vote, they were ready to use it intelligently.

With the expansion of the voting franchise, political parties turned from parliamentary clubs into modern parties. They had to win elections involving

Conservative Geniuses: Burke and Disraeli

As befits a country that favors tradition, Britain's greatest political thinkers have been conservatives who stressed continuity with the past and respect for traditional symbols.

Edmund Burke was a Whig member of Parliament during the American and French revolutions. He urged Britain to leave the thirteen colonies alone (they were only trying to recover the traditional rights of Englishmen), but he recoiled in horror at the French Revolution, warning well in advance that it would end up a military dictatorship (it did). The French revolutionists had broken the historical continuity and smashed the symbols that make a system work, argued Burke. People need traditions to restrain and guide them, he wrote. Scrap traditional authority—as the French did—and society breaks down only to end under a tyranny. Burke's views on representation in Parliament are also interesting. Burke told his constituents in Bristol that he was not their messenger boy in the Commons; he respected their opinions but voted the way he thought best. The Burkean view of a legislator is a far cry from the extreme constituency orientation of the modern American congressional representative.

Benjamin Disraeli, a Christianized Jew who became prime minister in the 1870s, understood that, to survive, the Tories must offer the workingman the vote and thereby win his support. He led the Conservatives to expand the electorate to encompass most workers. This gave many workingmen a stake in the system. Rather than turning revolutionary like workers in much of Europe, most British workers stayed pragmatic and moderate. Many British working people support the Conservative party to this day. Disraeli's expansion of the electorate was a gamble that paid off: it increased democracy but didn't hurt the Conservatives.

Both Burke and Disraeli understood that to be conservative does not mean to stand pat, never to budge in the face of change. True conservatism, they saw, means constant, but never radical, change. Wrote Burke: "A state without the means of some change is without the means of its conservation." Progress comes not from chucking out the old but from gradually modifying the parts that need changing while preserving the overall structure, keeping the form but reforming the contents.

thousands of voters. This meant organization, programs, promises, and continuity. The growth of the electorate forced parties to become vehicles for democracy.

THE RISE OF THE WELFARE STATE

By the turn of the century, with workingmen having the right to vote, British parties had to pay attention to demands for welfare measures—public education, housing, jobs, and medical care—that the upper-crust gentlemen of the Liberal and Conservative parties had earlier been able to minimize. Expansion of the electoral franchise led to the growth of the welfare state.

One force goading Liberals and Conservatives into supporting welfare measures was the new Labour party, founded in 1900. At first, most working-class voters went with the Liberals, but by the end of World War I, the Labour party had won them over and pushed the Liberals into the weak third-party status they have languished in to this day. Unlike many Continental socialists, the British Labourites were never Marxist. Instead, they combined militant trade unionism with intellectual social democracy to produce a pragmatic, gradualist ideology that sought to level class differences in Britain. As one observer put it, the British Labour party "owed more to Methodism than to Marx."

The British labor movement of the late nineteenth century was tough, a quality it retains today. Resentful of being treated like dirt, many workingmen went into politics with a militant snarl that still characterizes many of their heirs in the 1980s. In the 1926 General Strike, the trade unions attempted to bring the entire British economy to a halt to gain their wage demands. They failed.

Briefly and weakly in power under Ramsay MacDonald in the 1920s, La-

---

Comparing: The Genesis of Two Welfare States

Both Britain and Sweden are welfare states, Sweden more so than Britain. How did this come to be? In comparing their histories, we get some clues.

• Swedish King Gustav Vasa broke with Rome in the 1520s, a few years earlier than Henry VIII. In setting up churches that were dependent on their respective states—Lutheran in Sweden, Anglican in England—the two countries eliminated religion as a source of opposition to government.

• Because of this, politics in both lands did not get stuck in a clerical–anticlerical dispute over the role of the church, as was the case in France, Italy, and Spain. In Britain and Sweden, the main political split was along class lines, working class versus middle class.

• Britain and Sweden both developed efficient and uncorrupt civil services, an absolute essential for the effective functioning of welfare programs.

• Both countries formed strong—but not Marxist—labor movements, the TUC in Britain and LO in Sweden.

• These two labor movements gave rise to moderate worker-oriented parties, Labour in Britain and the Social Democrats in Sweden, which demanded, and over time got, numerous welfare measures passed. One big difference is that the Social Democrats have been in power in Sweden for all but six years since 1932 and have implemented a more thorough—and more expensive—welfare state.

bour won resoundingly in 1945 and implemented an ambitious program of welfare measures. Since at least then, the chief quarrel in British politics has been between people who like the welfare state and people who don't.

VOCABULARY BUILDING

absolutism	divine right	Magna Carta	Tory
Anglican Church	electorate	mixed monarchy	United Kingdom
Bill of Rights	English Channel	notables	vassal
caucus	Exchequer	Reform Acts	welfare state
Commons	feudalism	secularization	Whig
conservatism	Levellers	shilling	
Continent	Lords	sovereignty	
Cymric			

FURTHER REFERENCE

Beer, Samuel H. *Modern British Politics: Parties and Pressure Groups in the Collectivist Age.* New York: W. W. Norton, 1982.

Chrimes, S. B. *English Constitutional History.* London: Oxford University Press. 1967.

Dangerfield, George. *The Strange Death of Liberal England.* New York: Capricorn Books, 1935.

Greenleaf, W. H. *The British Political Tradition,* 2 vols. London: Methuen, 1983.

Halevy, Elie. *The Triumph of Reform, 1830—1841.* London: Ernest Benn, 1961.

Lloyd, T. O. *Empire to Welfare State: English History 1906—1976,* 2nd ed. New York: Oxford University Press, 1979.

Robbins, Keith. *The Eclipse of a Great Power: Modern Britain 1870—1975.* New York: Longman, 1982.

de Schweinitz, Karl. *England's Road to Social Security.* Philadelphia: University of Pennsylvania Press, 1943.

Trevelyan, G. M. *History of England: III. From Utrecht to Modern Times: the Industrial Revolution and the Transition to Democracy.* London: Longmans, Green and Co., 1926.

3

THE KEY INSTITUTIONS

AN UNWRITTEN CONSTITUTION

It is commonly said that Great Britain has no written constitution. This is not completely true, for parts of the British constitution are written. It is more correct to say that the British constitution does not consist of a single document but is rather a centuries-old collection of Common Law, historic charters, acts passed by Parliament, and, most important, just plain custom.

This eclectic quality gives the British constitution flexibility. With no single, written document to refer to, nothing can be declared "unconstitutional." Parliament—specifically the House of Commons—can pass any law it likes. The British political system can therefore grow and change over time without suffering a systemic crisis. Franklin D. Roosevelt's problems with the Supreme Court, which ruled some of his measures unconstitutional, could not have come up in Britain.

The negative side of this, however, is that there is no absolute standard by which to judge acts of Parliament or of the bureaucracy. The British press, for example, is not as free as the American. The Pentagon Papers, a secret history of U.S. decisions on Vietnam, which was leaked to the press and published in 1971, would have sent both leaker and publisher to jail in Britain. The U.S. Constitution sets a clear standard for civil rights.

In the hands of unscrupulous people, the flexibility of the British constitution could be seriously abused. But in British politics, with its tradition and sense of fair play, such abuse is rare.

The British often speak of "the Crown" but have a devil of a time defining it; often they don't even try. The Crown is an all-encompassing term meaning the powers of government in general. Originally the Crown meant the king, but over the centuries it has broadened to mean everyone helping the king or queen, and this includes Parliament, the cabinet, and civil servants. Let us consider some of these.

THE MONARCH

In Britain there is a clear distinction between "head of state" and "head of government." In America this distinction is sometimes ignored because the two are merged into one in the presidency. In most of the rest of the world, however, there is a top figure without much power who symbolizes the nation, receives foreign ambassadors, and gives speeches on patriotic occasions. This person— often a figurehead—can be either a hereditary monarch or an elected president, although not a U.S.-style president. Britain, Sweden, Norway, Denmark, the Netherlands, Belgium, and Spain are monarchies. This doesn't mean they aren't democratic; it just means that the head of state is a carry-over from the old days.

A hereditary head of state can be quite useful. Above politics, a monarch can serve as psychological cement to hold a country together even without taking an important role in government. Because theoretically the top position in the land—what royalist philosophers used to call the sovereign—is already occupied, there are no political battles over it. The nastiest struggles in the world are precisely over who is to be sovereign; in Britain the issue has long been settled.

Prince Charles, Britain's future king and head of state, with his wife, Princess Diana, and their first child, Prince William, also a future king. (British Information Services)

The great commentator on the British constitution, Sir Walter Bagehot, divided it into "dignified" and "efficient" parts. The monarch as head of state is a dignified office with lots of symbolic but not real political power. He or she "reigns but does not rule." The king or queen nominally appoints a cabinet of His or Her Majesty's servants (see box), but otherwise a monarch is more like an official greeter.

The "efficient" office in Britain is that of the head of government, the prime minister, a working politician who fights elections, leads his or her party, and makes political deals. Despite the very significant prestige attached to being prime minister, it does not carry nearly the degree of "dignity" that being the monarch does. Is there an advantage in the way Britain and other countries split the two positions? There is. If the head of government does something foolish or

Comparing: The Last Political Monarch

Unlike other European monarchs, King Juan Carlos of Spain retains some crucial political functions. Juan Carlos took over as head of state after Franco's death in 1975 and initiated and backstopped a process that turned Spain from dictatorship to democracy. He named a prime minister who dismantled the Franco structure, carried out Spain's first free elections in forty-one years, and drafted a new constitution—all with the open approval of the king.

Juan Carlos's real test as a defender of democracy came in 1981 when some disgruntled officers tried to carry out a coup; they actually held the entire *Cortes* (Spain's parliament) at gunpoint. In full military uniform, the king addressed the nation on television and ordered the troops back to their barracks. They complied, and democratic Spaniards of all parties thanked God for the king. Democracy and monarchy are not antithetical; one can support the other. ¡ *Viva el rey!*

illegal, he or she will catch the public's ire, but the blame will fall on the individual prime minister, and respect will not diminish for the head of state, the "dignified" office. The system retains its legitimacy. Where the two offices are combined, as in the United States, and the president is involved in something like Watergate, the public gets disgusted at both the working politician and the nation's symbolic leader.

The Queen Chooses a New Prime Minister

In 1979 an old ritual was repeated. Ostensibly Queen Elizabeth II chose a new prime minister and cabinet, but of course she really had no choice at all. Events unrolled according to the fiction that the prime minister is still chief advisor to the monarch.

Britain's Conservatives, a minority in the Commons, saw the parliamentary support of Prime Minister James Callaghan's Labour government dwindle, chiefly due to the defection of the small Scottish National party. Sensing their chance, the Tories introduced a simple motion, "That this House has no confidence in Her Majesty's government." They won by a single vote.

Callaghan faithfully followed the traditional script. The next day he called on Queen Elizabeth to offer his resignation as prime minister and "suggest" that Parliament be dissolved (simply declared over), with elections held in three weeks. She agreed, as she had to. The May elections were an overwhelming endorsement for the Conservatives and their leader, Margaret Thatcher. The day after the elections the queen called Thatcher to Buckingham Palace and "asked" her to form a new government. Thatcher ritually kissed the Queen's hands and humbly acceded to her request.

THE CABINET

The British cabinet is also quite different from the U.S. cabinet. The former consists of members of Parliament (most in the Commons, a few in Lords) who are high up in their parties and important political figures. Most have lots of experience, first as ordinary "MPs" (members of Parliament), then as junior ministers, and finally as cabinet ministers. The American cabinet often consists of presumed experts from universities, law offices, and businesses, mostly politically unknown and without experience in winning elections or serving in Congress. A British cabinet member is a political being with real clout, someone the prime minister must listen to. The American counterpart can be more safely ignored by the president.

Originally the British cabinet consisted of ministers to the king. Starting in the seventeenth century, however, the cabinet became more and more responsible to Parliament and less and less to the king. A British minister does not necessarily know much about his or her "portfolio" (ministerial job) but is carefully picked by the prime minister for political qualifications. Both major British parties contain several viewpoints and power centers, and prime ministers usually take care to see they are represented in the cabinet. When Prime Minister Thatcher ignored this principle and picked as ministers only Tories loyal to her and her philosophy, she was criticized as dictatorial and courted a "backbenchers' revolt." Balancing party factions in the cabinet helps keep the party together in Parliament and in power.

Notice that the British cabinet bridges a gap between "executive" and "legislative." British ministers are both; the elaborate American separation of powers (adopted by the Founding Fathers from an earlier misperception of British government by Montesquieu) doesn't hold in Britain. The United Kingdom has more nearly a *fusion,* or combining of powers.

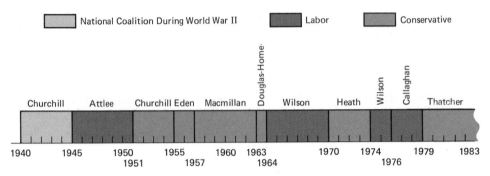

British Cabinets and Prime Ministers

The British cabinet practices "collective responsibility," meaning that they all stick together and support the final consensus. Ministers often argue heatedly in the secret, twice-weekly cabinet meetings, but once a policy is agreed upon, they all publicly support it. Occasionally, over a major controversy, a minister resigns in protest at the cabinet's decision.

In recent years, the cabinet has consisted of more than twenty ministers, although this number and portfolio titles change. The Commons routinely approves the prime minister's requests to add, drop, or combine ministries. Below cabinet rank are more than thirty noncabinet "departmental ministers" and a similar number of "junior ministers" assigned to help cabinet and departmental ministers. All totaled, at any given time about a hundred MPs are also serving in the executive branch. The hope of being named to one of these positions insures the loyalty and obedience of most younger MPs.

For all intents and purposes, in Britain (and in most parliamentary systems) cabinet equals government; the two terms are used interchangeably. When the "government falls" it simply means that the cabinet has resigned. Britain is often referred to as "cabinet government," although some call it "prime ministerial government."

The Hierarchy of Britain's Ruling Party

In the cabinet	One prime minister 20 or more cabinet ministers
In the executive but not the cabinet	30 or more departmental ministers 30 or more parliamentary undersecretaries ("junior ministers")
In Parliament only	30–40 parliamentary private secretaries over 200 other MPs, "backbenchers"

THE PRIME MINISTER

The prime minister, PM for short (don't get it confused with MP, which he or she also is), is the linchpin of the British system. In theory, the PM's powers could be nearly dictatorial. Because the prime minister picks and controls the cabinet and heads the largest party in Parliament, theoretically he or she should be able to get nearly any measure passed. British parliamentarians are well disciplined; party "whips" make sure their MPs turn out for "divisions" (votes) and vote the straight party line. Yet even with the reins of power so tightly held by one person, prime ministers still do not turn into dictators.

The chief reason is that general elections are never more than five years away. Prime ministers are usually cautious about introducing measures that might provoke public ire. When Margaret Thatcher embarked on a painful economic policy in 1979, she knew it had to show positive results by 1984 when she would have to "go to the country" with new elections. More typically, prime ministers introduce only piecemeal measures to avoid offending key blocks of voters. The fear of losing the next election keeps most prime ministers cautious.

Further, a prime minister has to be careful of the major currents of opinion within party ranks. As in the United States, the two large British parties contain left, right, and center wings, as well as regional and idiosyncratic viewpoints. As was mentioned earlier, a prime minister usually constructs the cabinet with top MPs representing several views within the majority party. In cabinet meetings the PM tries to fashion a consensus from the several stands. Then the cabinet has to sell the policy to their MPs back in the Commons. Party discipline is good but rarely total. The prime minister, through the chief whip, has a hold on the MPs. One who does not "take the whip" (follow the party line on a vote) risks losing his or her nomination for reelection—or, in effect, getting fired from Parliament. But this is a two-way street. If a party policy really bothers an MP, the member can threaten to quit and make a stink. In 1979 one Labour MP was so upset by what he saw as left-wing domination of his party that he quite Labour and ran (successfully) as a Conservative, the ultimate slap at party leadership. If a PM fails badly, he or she can even be dumped by MPs, as Harold Macmillan was in 1963. Several times in the past two decades both Labour and Conservative cabinets have had to withdraw or water down legislative proposals for fear of a backbenchers' revolt within the ranks of their own party.

The PM does have a potent political weapon: the power to call new elections whenever he or she wishes. By law, Commons can go up to five years without a general election. By-elections to fill vacancies when an MP dies or retires can come any time; they are closely watched as political barometers. A crafty prime minister calls for new general elections when he or she thinks the party will do best. A good economy and sunny weather tend to produce a happy electorate, one that will increase the seats of the incumbent party. In 1974 Britain even had two general elections because Prime Minister Harold Wilson thought he could boost Labour's strength in Commons. (He did.) In 1983 Margaret Thatcher called elections a year early to take advantage of Britain's victory over Argentina in the Falklands in 1982; she won handily. Public-opinion polls and by-elections help the prime minister decide when to ask the king or queen to dissolve Parliament and hold new elections.

The Deceptive No. 10 Downing Street

Since 1735 British prime ministers have resided in an ordinary brick row house, No. 10 Downing Street. Except for a couple of London bobbies on guard outside, a passer-by might take it for a typical private home. But this is deceptive, for behind the walls, Downing Street is actually the nerve center of Whitehall, the British executive branch.

Upstairs at No. 10, the prime minister has his or her apartment. On the ground floor, in the back, the cabinet meets in a long white room. No. 10 connects to No. 12 Downing Street, the residence of the chief whip, the prime minister's parliamentary enforcer. They can visit without being seen from the street. Also connecting out of sight is No. 11 Downing Street, residence of the important Chancellor of the Exchequer, head of the powerful treasury ministry. Next door is the Foreign Office. At the corner of Downing Street, also with a connecting door to No. 10, is the cabinet secretariat, responsible for communication and coordination among the departments. What looks from the street like an ordinary row house is actually the focal point of British government.

COMMONS

One can look at the cabinet as a committee of the House of Commons sent from Westminster (the Parliament building) to nearby Whitehall (the main government offices) to keep administration under parliamentary control. Another way is to view the Commons as an electoral college that stays in operation even after it has chosen the executive (the cabinet).

The two main parties in the Commons—Conservatives and Labour—face each other. The largest party is automatically His or Her Majesty's Government and the other His or Her Majesty's Opposition.

The physical structure of the House of Commons explains a lot. It is very small, measuring only 45 by 68 feet (14 by 21 meters) and was originally designed for only about 400 members. How then can it possibly hold the current membership of 650? It doesn't, at least not comfortably. Members have no individual desks, unlike most modern legislators. When there's an important vote, MPs pack in like sardines and sit in the aisles.

By keeping the House of Commons small, the British insure that members can face each other in debate a few yards apart. The parallel benches go well with the two-party system; the half-circle floor plan of most Continental legislatures facilitates pielike division into multiparty systems. But the main reason for the chamber's small size is that it was always small, ever since 1547 when Henry VIII first gave the Commons the use of the St. Stephen's royal chapel. During World War II when the Commons was damaged by German bombs, Prime Minister Winston Churchill ordered it rebuilt exactly the way it had been.

On each side of the oblong chamber there are five rows of benches. The front row on either side is reserved for the leading team of each major party, the cabinet of the government party and the "shadow cabinet" of the opposition. Behind them sit the "backbenchers," the MP rank and file. A neutral Speaker, elected for life from the MPs, sits in a thronelike chair at one end. The Speaker, who never votes or takes sides, manages the floor debate and preserves order. A table in the center, between the party benches, is where legislation is placed (the

An Iron Lady for Prime Minister

In May 1979, Margaret Thatcher, 53, became Britain's—and Europe's—first woman head of government. Yet although the innovation was revolutionary, everything else about Thatcher was conservative. Born in the Lincolnshire town of Grantham above her father's grocery shop, Thatcher was instilled with the old-fashioned virtues of hard work and high achievement. A grimly determined student, at age nine she won a school prize. Her headmistress told her she was lucky. "I wasn't lucky," replied little Margaret. "I deserved it." Later, to get into Oxford she needed Latin, not offered in her school. In three months, with a tutor, she learned Latin. To gain an upper-class accent, she took elocution lessons.

(British Information Services)

A chemistry major at Oxford, Thatcher became president of the Oxford University Conservative Association; politics had been in her blood since childhood. Following graduation, she worked as a chemist but was active in the Conservative party. The Tories let her try her wings in the 1950 election in a safe Labour seat in Kent. The 24-year old Thatcher didn't have a chance, but Tory leaders marked how her energy and ability to remember everyone's name pushed the Conservative vote there from 36 percent in 1950 to 40 percent on her second try in 1951.

With time out for marriage and twin babies— typical Thatcher efficiency, remark her friends— Thatcher, by now a tax attorney, was adopted to run in Finchley, a safe Tory seat near London. This time, in 1959 at age 33, she won, becoming one of Parliament's few women members. In the Commons, diligence and competence rather than brilliance pushed her to the front bench. When the Conservatives won the 1970 elections, Thatcher was named education minister. On education policy, she stressed individual achievement rather than strict equality.

In 1975, the cold, distant Edward Heath was dumped by the Conservative party. At that fall's party conference, Thatcher rounded up enough support to become the Conservative leader herself, the first woman party chief in British history. Hammering away at Labour's shortcomings and stressing her own hard-work and free-market approach, the "Iron Lady," as she was now called, counted heads in Commons and at the right time—when the eleven Scottish Nationalist MPs had deserted the Labour government—forced a vote of no-confidence that toppled the Callaghan cabinet and led to the 1979 Thatcher cabinet.

origin of the verb "to table" a proposal). The Speaker calls the house to order at 2:30 in the afternoon, and sessions can go on until late in the evening. Unless "the whip is on"—meaning an MP had better be there because an important vote is expected—many MPs are busy elsewhere.

HOW COMMONS WORKS

Each session of Parliament opens with a Speech from the Throne by the queen, another tradition. The MPs are ritually summoned by Black Rod, the queen's messenger, from the Commons and file into the nearby House of Lords. (Neither monarchs nor lords are allowed to enter the House of Commons.) From a gold-paneled dais in Lords, Her Majesty reads a statement outlining what policies "my government" will pursue. The amusing aspect is that the speech has been written by the prime minister with the queen serving merely as an announcer. A conservative king, George VI, had to read a Labour speech in 1945 promising extensive nationalization of industry. This he did without batting an eye.

   Just as the queen takes her cues from the cabinet, so does the Commons. Practically all legislation is introduced by the "government" (that is, the cabinet), and it stands a high chance of passing nearly intact because of the party discipline discussed above. What the cabinet wants, the cabinet usually gets. When a

View from the Speaker's Chair of the British House of Commons

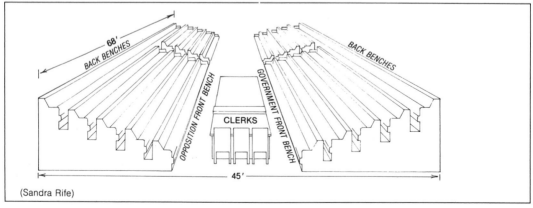

(Sandra Rife)

Conservative cabinet introduces bills into the Commons, Conservative MPs—unlike their American counterparts in Congress—rarely question them. Their job is to support the party, and individual conscience seldom gets in the way.

The task of challenging proposals falls to the opposition, seated on the Speaker's left. From the opposition benches come questions, denunciations, warnings of dire consequences, anything that might make the government look bad. Government MPs, particularly the cabinet and subcabinet ministers on the front bench, are duty bound to defend the bills. In situations like these, the famous rhetorical ability of MPs produces debates in the House of Commons unmatched in any other legislature.

While the rhetoric is brilliant and witty, the homework is weak. Because they are expected simply to obey their party, few MPs bother specializing.

What to Do with Lords?

The British Parliament is nominally bicameral. But the House of Lords over the centuries has seen its power erode. Early on, Commons established supremacy in the key area of money, raising revenues and spending them. (The U.S. Constitution provides that money bills originate in the lower chamber, the House of Representatives, an echo of the English tradition.) In Britain, the Civil War and Glorious Revolution of the seventeenth century centered around the power of Commons, and Commons emerged as the winner; Lords gradually took a back seat. By 1867 Bagehot considered Lords a "dignified" part of the constitution.

Since Britain's unwritten constitution does not specify or make permanent the powers of the two chambers, it was legally possible for Commons to push Lords into retirement. Its powers now are severely limited. The 1911 Parliament Act allows Lords to delay legislation not more than thirty days on financial bills and three years (since 1949, one year) on other bills. The Lords can amend legislation and send it back to the Commons, which in turn can (and usually does) delete the changes by a simple majority. Every few years, however, Lords jolts the system with an independence of mind lacking in the House of Commons. In 1984, for example, it embarrassed the Thatcher government and its Commons majority by rejecting a plan to abolish elections to the London regional government. Even many Tory lords thought Thatcher was going too far, and she backed down.

Lords, then, does play a somewhat larger role than a debating club. It is the only British institution in a position to check the potentially dictatorial powers of a prime minister who has a large and disciplined majority of Commons. It can thus be seen as a weak analog to the U.S. Supreme Court, a sort of "conscience of the nation." Because the status of the members of Lords as "peers" is untouchable—they can't be voted out—they can consider measures calmly and in depth. In some cases they have been able to point out weaknesses in bills coming from the more-pressured atmosphere of the Commons. They are also able to debate questions that are too hot for elected officials to handle, for example, laws concerning abortion and homosexuality.

There are some twelve hundred Lords and Ladies of the Realm; most of the titles are hereditary, but since 1958, an increasing number have been named just for their lifetime (the title does not pass on to children) for distinguished contributions in science, literature, politics, business, and the arts. Usually less than three hundred turn up in the House of Lords; a quorum is three. A few Lords are named to the cabinet or to other high political or diplomatic positions.

Can anything else be done with Lords? There have been numerous suggestions to revitalize that august body, to give it a greater political role to play. One is to increase the number of "life peers" until Lords is composed mostly of people who have earned distinction rather than inherited it. Another scheme suggested by both parties' leaders in 1968 would create a two-tier chamber with only life peers having the right to vote but hereditary peers having the right to participate in debates. (A backbenchers' revolt shelved the idea.) A radical proposal would turn Lords into a democratically elected body based on proportional representation, unlike the Commons's single-member districts. In 1983 the Labour party came out in favor of abolishing the House of Lords altogether.

Traditionally, British parliamentary committees too were unspecialized; they went over the precise wording of bills but called no witnesses and gathered no data. The structure of the committees of legislatures is an important key to their power, and gradually some MPs have seen the need for a more American type of committee system. Since the late 1960s, specialized committees have been set up to scrutinize Whitehall, but compared to their U.S. counterparts the British committees are weak. They have little staff and cannot force ministers to testify.

Neither Tory nor Labour governments have been enthusiastic about specialized committees that can monitor and criticize executive functions. That may be part of the U.S. system of separation of powers, some Britishers have argued, but it has no place in the U.K. system of fusion of powers. In general, the British cabinet would like to use Commons to rubber-stamp its decisions. Fortunately, such rubber-stamping is not always the case, as we shall explore later.

THE PARTIES

The House of Commons works as it does because of the British party system. This is a fairly recent development; only since the time of the French Revolution (1789) has it been possible to speak of coherent parties in Britain. Parties are now the cornerstone of British government. The party that gets the most MPs elected controls Commons; and the party that controls Commons forms the government.

Britain is usually described as a two-party system. This is not completely accurate, for there are small parties that sometimes can make or break a government. In 1979, for example, the withdrawal of support by the eleven Scottish Nationalists in the Commons brought down the Callaghan government in a rare vote of no-confidence. Here we can see how sometimes one of the large parties, in this case Labour, depends on the support in Parliament of a small party. We could more accurately label Britain a "two-plus" party system.

The British electoral system tends to keep two parties big, however, by penalizing smaller parties. Britain, like the United States, Canada, and Australia, uses "single-member districts" as the basis for elections. This means that each electoral district or constituency sends one person to the legislature, the candidate that gets the most votes even if less than a majority. Single-member districts with plurality victors tend to produce two large political parties. The reason: there is a big premium in such districts to combine small parties into big ones in order to edge out competitors. If one of the two large parties splits, which sometimes happens, the election is thrown to the other party, the one that hangs together. In proportional representation, for instance, in some Continental countries, there is not such a great premium on forming two large parties, and that contributes to party splintering.

British parties are more cohesive and centralized than American parties. It's fair to say there are more differences within the two big American parties than between them; in Britain it would probably be the other way around. The taxes. The Conservatives, nicknamed Tories, urge less government involvement in society and the economy and lower taxes. Internal party differences arise from the *degree* to which party members support these general points of view.

British Labourites, who are sometimes called Socialists—a term they don't object to—favor more nationalization of industry, more welfare measures, and higher

Two-Party Systems: Variations on a British Theme

The countries that inherited the British electoral system of single-member constituencies with simple plurality winners all tend toward two large parties at the national level. At the state or province level there may be more parties, as for example, Canada's socialist New Democrats or the separatist *Parti Québeçois*. But in the main, this electoral system results in two parties, one to the left, the other to the right:

United States	*Democratic*	*Republican*
Australia	*Labour*	*Country and Liberal*
New Zealand	*Labour*	*National*
Canada	*Liberal*	*Progressive Conservative*

In 1981, the more moderate wing of the Labour party split off to form a centrist Social Democratic party. They argued that Labour had fallen under the control of radicals and had turned sharply leftward. The Social Democrats faced the problem that had long beset Britain's third party, the middle-of-the-road Liberals, namely, that single-member plurality districts severely penalize smaller parties.

The Liberal party illustrates how smaller parties suffer under the British system of electing MPs. In the last century the Liberals were one of the two big parties, but by the 1920s they had been pushed into a weak third place by Labour. Now, although the Liberals are often able to win nearly one vote out of five, they rarely get more than a dozen seats in the Commons. The reason: the Liberal vote is territorially dispersed so that in few constituencies does it top Tories or Labourites.

In 1983, the Liberals and the Social Democrats ran as the Liberal-Social Democratic Alliance to improve their chances. They polled a strong third but, because they were spread rather evenly, won fewer than two dozen seats in Commons. Alliance leaders voiced strong support for a proportional representation system that would give them seats in proportion to votes, but there is no way the Conservative or Labour parties will give up the built-in advantage that the system of single-member districts with plurality wins confers on the two largest parties.

Scottish and Welsh nationalist parties have shown spurts of growth and decline. Although they are now weakened, their territorial concentration enables them to obtain a few seats in Parliament. We will explore patterns of interaction among the parties and the voters in chapter 5.

VOCABULARY BUILDING

backbencher	constitution	head of state	single-member
by-election	*Cortes*	junior minister	district
cabinet	Crown	minister	Westminster
collective respon-	eclectic	opposition	whip
sibility	head of govern-	portfolio	Whitehall
Common Law	ment	prime minister	

FURTHER REFERENCE

Beloff, Max, and Gillian Peele. *The Government of the United Kingdom: Political Authority in a Changing Society.* New York: W. W. Norton, 1980.

Birch, Anthony H. *The British System of Government,* 6th ed. Winchester, Mass.: Allen & Unwin, 1982.

Borthwick, R. L., and J. E. Spence, eds. *British Politics in Perspective.* New York: St. Martin's Press, 1984.

Bromhead, Peter. *Britain's Developing Constitution.* New York: St. Martin's Press, 1974.

Hansom, A. H., and Malcolm Walles. *Governing Britain: A Guide-Book to Political Institutions.* London: Fontana/Collins, 1970.

Mackintosh, John P. "Reform of the House of Commons: The Case for Specialization," in *Modern Parliaments: Change or Decline?,* ed. by Gerhard Loewenberg. Chicago: Aldine, 1971.

Norton, Philip. *The British Polity.* New York: Longman, 1984.

———. *The Constitution in Flux.* Totowa, N.J.: Martin Robertson, 1983.

Punnett, R. N. *British Government and Politics,* 4th ed. London: Heinemann, 1980.

Verney, Douglas V. *British Government and Politics: Life Without a Declaration of Independence,* 3d ed. New York: Harper & Row, 1976.

Wilson, Harold. *The Governance of Britain.* New York: Harper & Row, 1977.

4

BRITISH POLITICAL ATTITUDES

A TOUCH OF CLASS

"England is a snob country," one long-time American resident in London told me. She added: "And I'm a snob, so I like it here." Her candor touched one of the facets of British political life, one that explains a great deal about modern England: the large and often invidious distinctions made between and by social classes.

Social class can be analyzed two ways, objectively and subjectively. The objective approach uses data such as income to put people into categories. The subjective approach asks people to put themselves into categories. There are often discrepancies between the two, as when a self-made businessman, thinking of his humble origins, describes himself as working class, or when a poorly paid schoolteacher, thinking of her university degrees, describes herself as middle class. In Britain and most industrialized democracies the main politically relevant distinction is between working class and middle class.

Objectively, class differences in Britain are not so great; they are basically no different from the rest of Western Europe. The time has long passed when a Disraeli could write that Britain was not one nation but two, the rich and the poor. Since that time, the British working class has grown richer, the middle class bigger, and the small upper class poorer.

But subjectively or psychologically, class differences remain. Working-class people live, dress, speak, and enjoy themselves in markedly different ways from the middle class. They seem to like these differences and try to preserve them.

According to Ralf Dahrendorf, a German sociologist who heads the London School of Economics, the key word in Britain is not class but *solidarity*. While there has been a leveling of objective class differences, Dahrendorf holds, the idea of individual competition and improvement has not caught on in Britain as in other industrial countries. Rather than struggling upward individually, many Britons relish the feeling of solidarity they get by sticking with their old jobs, neighborhoods, and pubs. "Britain is a society in which the values of solidarity are held in higher esteem than those of individual success at the expense of others," Dahrendorf wrote.

Whether one calls it class or solidarity, these divisions influence British politics in many ways. They contribute to the way Britons vote. They color the attitudes of labor unions and of the Labour party. And—very important—they give birth to Britain's elites through the education system.

"PUBLIC" SCHOOLS

One pillar of the British class system is the "public" school. Actually, these are private boarding schools—costing an average of $3,500 a year, a sum well beyond the reach of working-class families—that got their name from their avowed purpose of training boys for public life in the military, civil service, or politics (Conservative). Eton, Harrow, Rugby, St. Paul's, Winchester, and other famous

Comparing: Class in Britain and America

Over two-thirds of Britons identify themselves as *working*-class. A similar percentage of Americans call themselves *middle*-class. Why the big difference? Part of the problem is the way the question is asked: many U.S. surveys do not include the category "working-class," just upper, middle, and lower.

The responses reflect two different cultures: one where class distinctions are played up and one where they are played down. Britons are taught about class differences; Americans are taught to act as if all are equal.

Are the Americans kidding themselves? *Middle-class* used to connote people with their own property and some financial independence, such as shopkeepers and small-business people. In post-World War II America it came to mean earning a middle level of income regardless of source. But, steel or auto workers (who make more than most college professors!) are not really middle class. Their comfortable situation can vanish with layoffs, factory closings, and foreign imports. The economic upheavals of the 1980s—in which American workers had to take substantial pay cuts—reminded many that they were still working class. In Britain, the working class knows it is working class and doesn't pretend to be middle class.

academies have for generations molded the sons of the upper and upper-middle classes into a ruling elite. At present about 6 percent of English children receive a private education.

What they learn from ages 13 to 18 is more than their demanding curriculum. At least as important is the style they pick up: self-confident to the point of arrogance, self-disciplined, bred to rule. Spy novelist John Le Carré recalled with loathing his years in a public school during World War II: "We doubled up with mirth at the sound of lower-class accents." His schoolmates called such people "oiks" and felt nothing but contempt for them. In 1945 Attlee was simply "A Leftie who had seduced the oiks into getting rid of Churchill." In terms of class relations, added Le Carré, "nothing, but absolutely nothing, has changed" since the 1940s.

The English private-school system generates an "old boy" network that assists graduates later in life. The years of floggings, vile food, and bullying upper-classmen forge bonds among old schoolmates, and they often arrange for each other to get positions in industry and government. A large portion of Britain's elite have gone to private boarding schools, including some three-fourths of Conservative MPs (but few Labour MPs).

While the upper and upper-middle classes send their sons to "public" schools, the middle class send theirs to "grammar" schools, where pupils wear uniforms but do not live in. Until 1944, there was no free high-school system in Britain, but since the advent of the first Labour government nearly two hundred grammar schools receive state subsidies to enable them to take in working-class youths; these are called direct-grant schools. Some 80 percent of English schoolchildren, however, especially those of the working class, go to "comprehensive" and technical schools that lead most of them to the workplace. In spite of all the efforts of the Labour party since World War II, British education is still strongly divided along class lines.

What to Do with "Public" Schools?

The British Labour party has long sought to do away with the country's private boarding schools. Labourites regard them as a pillar of the class system where boys of better-off families learn nothing but privilege. As mentioned, most Conservative politicians have attended "public" schools, but few Labour politicians have. Conservatives want to maintain the schools, arguing that they train the best people and imbue them with a sense of public service.

In the past, Labour governments essentially let the private boarding schools alone while they tried to upgrade the quality of publicly supported "comprehensive" schools. If anything, the private schools grew stronger as more parents decided they were the only way to insure their children would get into a good university.

"OXBRIDGE"

The real path to position and power in Britain is through the elite universities of Oxford or Cambridge, collectively dubbed "Oxbridge." Typically half of Conservative MPs are Oxford or Cambridge graduates (usually after attending a public school such as Eton), while a quarter of Labour MPs are Oxbridge products. In the cabinet, these percentages are much higher, for the leaders of the two big parties are heavily Oxbridge. And prime ministers are almost always graduates of either Oxford or Cambridge. The only exception in recent years was Labour Prime Minister James Callaghan (1976–79), who regretted that he had never gone to college. Perhaps in no other industrialized country are the political elite drawn so heavily from just two universities.

As with secondary (high-school) education, British university education is also elitist. A far greater proportion of Americans go to a university than do Britishers. British university admission is slanted in favor of better-off families, especially those who send their children to "public" schools. Since World War II, with higher education open to the working and lower-middle classes by direct-grant secondary schools and scholarships for deserving youths, Oxford and Cambridge have become less class-biased in their admissions.

Only a small percentage of Oxbridge students go into politics, but those who do receive a major boost. In the first place, an Oxford or Cambridge

The Establishment

So homogeneous are Britain's ruling elites—in terms of education, dress, speech, mentality, and so on—that critical writers in the 1950s began referring to them as the Establishment, as if they were a sort of exclusive club that only the right kind of people could get into. While obviously an exaggeration, there is some truth to the charge that an "establishment" runs Britain. Whether the government is Conservative or Labour, the same types of people always seem to be in charge.

A typical member of the Establishment went to a private (often boarding) school, then to Oxford or Cambridge, then used connections to get a good position in the civil service or a seat in Parliament. Of the twenty-two ministers in Thatcher's first cabinet, for example, twenty had attended "public" schools and seventeen were Oxbridge graduates.

degree—which takes three years to earn—commands respect. Further, the Oxbridge experience hones political skills. One popular major for aspiring politicians is "PPE"—philosophy, politics, and economics—in effect, how to run a country. Debating in the Oxford or Cambridge Union trains students to think on their feet and confound their opponents with rhetorical cleverness, a style that carries over into the House of Commons. Perhaps the main advantage an Oxbridge education confers, however, is the "sense of effortless superiority" that the graduate carries all his or her life.

CLASS AND VOTING

Britain used to be offered as a good example of "class voting"—a situation where most of the working class votes for the left party (in this case, Labour) while most of the middle class votes for the right (in this case, the Conservatives). Actually, class voting in Sweden is higher than in Britain, but nowhere is it 100 percent. Two shifts dilute class voting in Britain and elsewhere: (1) some working-class people vote Conservative, and (2) some middle-class people vote Labour. Class differences may be part of Britain's political culture, but they do not translate into class voting on a one-to-one basis.

What happens to dilute class voting? Some working-class people are simply convinced that Conservatives do a better job governing than Labourites. Some workers have a sentimental attachment to the country's oldest party. Some issues have little to do with class. The Tories won over a large part of the working class in 1983 on the issues of personality and the Falklands War.

Going the other way, many middle-class educated people are intellectually convinced that socialism is the answer to what they see as an establishment-ruled, snobbish class system. Such intellectuals sometimes provide important leadership in the Labour party. In the 1980s, the leader of the Labour left was an aristocrat, Anthony Wedgewood Benn, or, as he liked to be known, Tony Benn. Further, some middle-class people grew up in working-class families and have sentimental ties to the way their parents voted.

Class voting changes over time. The British generation that came to political maturity during and after World War II, especially the working class, has been quite loyal to the Labour party, which it swept to power in 1945. Since then, class voting has fallen off in Britain and in many other West European countries. Class is not what it used to be in British voting patterns.

Class, nonetheless, is still a factor. Typically, political scientists find that voting behavior is influenced by social class plus one or more other factors such as region, ethnic group, religion, and urban-rural differences. The 1983 British general election seems to bear this out (see box). Tories were strongest in England, especially the south of England, and in small towns and rural areas. They were weaker in Scotland and Wales and in the big industrial cities, places with a long-term Labour identification and concern over unemployment. Class by itself explains only a part of British voting patterns. Class plus region explains a good deal more.

THE DEFERENTIAL BRITISH?

One image of the British that has been widely promulgated is that they are "deferential," that is, the average Briton defers to the political judgment of elites. According to the deferential model, working- and middle-class Britons recognize the superior leadership qualities of the Oxbridge-educated Establishment and let it take the lead.

The deferential model of British political attitudes has been oversold, for many Britons defer only grudgingly or not at all. Perhaps in the last century, when class differences were enormous, the working class deferred to its social betters. But while they were tipping their hats, it seems likely they were also building a store of resentment. As noted in chapter 2, the labor movement came into British politics in the last century with a snarl. In some sectors of the British working class, resentment is as strong as ever and comes out in the militant socialism on the left wing of the Labour party, indifferent work attitudes, and one of the highest rates of strikes in the world. The deferential model cannot explain such behavior.

The 1983 Elections: Class Plus Region

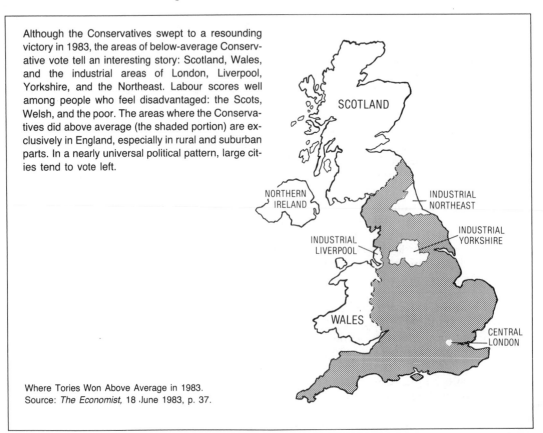

Although the Conservatives swept to a resounding victory in 1983, the areas of below-average Conservative vote tell an interesting story: Scotland, Wales, and the industrial areas of London, Liverpool, Yorkshire, and the Northeast. Labour scores well among people who feel disadvantaged: the Scots, Welsh, and the poor. The areas where the Conservatives did above average (the shaded portion) are exclusively in England, especially in rural and suburban parts. In a nearly universal political pattern, large cities tend to vote left.

SCOTLAND

NORTHERN
IRELAND

INDUSTRIAL
NORTHEAST

INDUSTRIAL
YORKSHIRE

INDUSTRIAL
LIVERPOOL

WALES

CENTRAL
LONDON

Where Tories Won Above Average in 1983.
Source: *The Economist,* 18 June 1983, p. 37.

The "working-class Tory" has been explained as a working-class person who defers to the Conservatives and votes for them. But the working-class Tory voter can be explained without the notion of deference. Many such voters think the Conservatives have the right policies, that the Labour party has swung too far left, and that there are too many nonwhite immigrants. No more deference is probably to be found in Britain today than anywhere else in Western Europe.

BRITISH CIVILITY

Civility here means keeping reasonably good manners in politics and avoiding getting abusive. In Britain, civility is based on a sense of limits: don't let anything go too far, don't let the system come unstruck. Thus while Labourites and Conservatives have serious arguments, neither party, when in power, moves in for the kill. The game is not one of total annihilation, as it has sometimes been in France, Germany, and Russia. Accordingly, British politicians are fairly decent toward each other.

But civility, like deference, has its limits in Britain. In Parliament a cabinet minister presenting a difficult case sometimes faces cries of "Shame!" or "Treason!" from the opposition benches. Margaret Thatcher faced Labourites chanting "Ditch the bitch." It should be pointed out that insults and heckling are a normal part of British debates and are not viewed as out of bounds; some see them as tests of a debater's cool.

Civility is usually the case out in public too—but not always. Amateur orators at the famous Speakers' Corner of Hyde Park in London can have their say on any subject they like, although they too must face heckling. But British politics turned very uncivil on the question of race, which we'll discuss later, and there have been riots and demonstrations that have resulted in deaths. Murder, rather than civility, became the norm for Northern Ireland. British civility has been overstated; Swedes are far more civil.

PRAGMATISM

The term *pragmatic* has the same root as practical and means using what works without paying much attention to theory or ideology. British attitudes, like American or Swedish ones, are generally pragmatic. The Conservatives pride themselves on being the most pragmatic of all British parties. They have been willing to adopt the policies of another party if they are vote catchers. In the last century, Disraeli crowed that he had "dished the Whigs" by stealing their drive to expand the voting franchise. In the 1950s, the returning Conservative government did not throw out Labour's welfare state; instead they boasted that Tories ran it more efficiently. The most ideological move the Conservatives had undertaken in decades was the laissez-faire economic program of Prime Minister Thatcher. The pain her program entailed contributed to ideological debates within and between the two large and usually pragmatic parties.

The British Labour party has historically been mostly uninterested in Marxism or any other theory. With the Callaghan government in the 1970s, ide-

The British Art of Queuing

On my first visit to Britain long ago I hitched a ride to a seaport to catch a ship for Germany. Upon hearing where I was going, my host told me Germans were terrible people. "They don't know how to queue," he exclaimed, as if the ability to form a neat, orderly line was the great test of civilization.

The queue (pronounced *kew*) is practically a British art form. Probably no other nationality so obedi-ently and spontaneously forms a line at bus stops, ticket windows, bars, and so on. But in this area too, Britain is slipping. In recent years observers have noticed people cutting into line, pushing to the head, or not queuing at all. Some suggest the decline of queuing mirrors the general decline of British civility and obedience to rules.

ological controversy engulfed Labour. Callaghan was a very moderate, pragmatic Labourite, hard to distinguish from many Conservatives. Many Labour personalities, including the heads of some trade unions, resented Callaghan's centrism and rammed through a clearly socialist party platform. The moderate wing of the Labour party in 1981 split off to form a centrist party, the Social Democrats. We will explore ideology within the two main parties more fully in the next chapter.

The long-term tendency for both major British parties is probably to stick close to the pragmatic center. In the first place, most British voters want results, not theories. When Prime Minister Thatcher's economic policies failed to achieve their desired effect and angered voters, Tory backbenchers urged her to soften the policies. When fairly extreme socialists took over the Labour party at about this same time, Labour chiefs saw many voters desert them for the moderate Social Democrats. They tempered their rhetoric accordingly.

There is and always has been a certain amount of ideology in British politics, but it has always been balanced with a shrewd practical appreciation that ideology neither wins elections nor effectively governs a country. The ideological flare-up of the 1980s in Britain will probably not endure as long as will the underlying tendency to middle-of-the-road pragmatism.

One aspect of British pragmatism is their "muddling through" style of problem solving. The British tend not to thoroughly analyze a problem and come up with detailed options or "game plans" in the American manner. Instead, they try to "muddle through somehow," improvising as they go. This often works with small problems, but with a big problem, such as Northern Ireland, it amounts to a nonsolution.

TRADITIONS AND SYMBOLS

As noted earlier, British politics has a good deal of tradition. Things are often done in the old ways, even by left-wing socialists, who, whether they recognize it or not, subscribe to Burke's idea of keeping the forms but changing the contents. As Burke saw, traditions and symbols contribute to society's stability and continuity; people feel disoriented without them.

The British man or woman in the street usually likes traditions and symbols. Fewer than one Briton in five, for example, would abolish the monarchy in favor of a republic with a president. Parades with golden coaches and horsemen in red tunics are not just for tourists—although they certainly help Britain's economy—they also serve to deepen British feelings about the rightness of the system.

Traditions can also tame political radicals. Once they win seats in the Commons, radicals find themselves having to play according to time-hallowed parliamentary usages. "Well, it simply isn't done, old boy," is the standard lesson taught to newcomers in Parliament. In a few years, the would-be radicals are usually more moderate. In terms of parliamentary behavior, it's hard to distinguish Labour from Tory MPs.

LEGITIMACY AND AUTHORITY

One definition of *legitimacy* is a feeling of rightness about the political system. As was pointed out in chapter 1, originally the word meant that the right king was on the throne, not a usurper. As used by political scientists, it refers to public attitudes that the government's rule in general is rightful. Legitimacy is a feeling among the people; it does not mean "legal."

When a political system enjoys high legitimacy, people generally obey it. They will even do things they don't want to, such as paying their income taxes. When a political system has little legitimacy, it is much harder to govern; instead of voluntary obedience it must rely on coercion. Simply put, societies with high legitimacy need few policemen; those with low legitimacy need many.

Legitimacy is closely related to the idea of authority, obeying duly constituted officials. British legitimacy and authority were long cited as models, but they were exaggerated and oversold. British policemen used to be famous for not carrying guns and for their good relations with people on their beat. Political scientists used to cite such points to illustrate Britain's nonviolent qualities. During the 1970s, however, Britain turned more violent. The Irish Republican Army spread their murderous tactics from Ulster, planting bombs that killed dozens. In 1984, one bomb blew up near Thatcher. Criminals started using handguns. In Britain's inner cities, relations between police and youths, especially black youths, grew hateful and contributed to urban riots (which nonetheless cost very few lives). Some British policemen now carry guns and riot gear, a symbol of the erosion of legitimacy and authority in Britain.

THE ULSTER ULCER

While we can say that Britons on the whole still have attitudes of civility, pragmatism, legitimacy, respect for authority, and nonviolence, we must also note that Northern Ireland stands as a massive exception. The case of the six counties of Ireland known as Ulster illustrates that a system that works when there is widespread consensus at the grass-roots level fails when underlying consensus is lacking. Unlike the rest of Britain, Ulster is a split society, more like those of Latin Europe—France, Spain, Italy—where part of the population does not see the government as legitimate.

The Ulster problem has its roots in history. For eight centuries England ruled Ireland, at times treating the Irish as subhuman, seizing their land, deporting them, even outlawing the Catholic faith. A low point came with the 1846–54 Potato Famine in which a million Irish starved to death while the English, with plentiful food stocks, watched. (An example of what happens when you make too many babies, admonished English Malthusians.) At that time about a million and a half Irish emigrated, mostly to the United States. The Irish problem was the great issue of nineteenth-century British politics, "the damnable question" of whether to keep it firmly under British control to grant it "home rule."

At Eastertime in 1916, while the English were hard-pressed in World War I, the Irish Republican Army (IRA), in what is known as the Easter Rising, rose up with guerrilla-warfare tactics. By 1922, after brutally crushing the rising, the British had had enough; Ireland became a "free state" of the British Commonwealth. In 1949, the bulk of Ireland ended this status and became a totally independent republic, Eire.

The IRA: Ballots and Bullets

The Irish Republican Army is illegal in both Eire and Ulster, but its political arm, Sinn Fein (pronounced *shin fain*) is not. In 1983 close to half of Northern Ireland's Catholics voted for Sinn Fein and elected extremist Gerry Adams to Parliament from West Belfast. Adams, who never intended taking his seat in Westminster, denies belonging to the IRA but does not condemn its violence: "I honestly see no other way by which the British can be forced to withdraw from this country, except by a mixture of struggle which involves properly controlled, interactive armed struggle." Some people, he says, should be shot.

Electing IRA people is not new for Ulster's Catholics. In 1981 they elected Bobby Sands, an imprisoned IRA gunman, who starved himself to death in a hunger strike. The fact that so many men and women of Ulster are willing to vote for an extremist party indicates the depth of hatred and difficulty of compromise.

But this did not solve the Ulster problem; 60 percent of its 1.5 million people in these six northern counties are Protestant (descended from seventeenth-century Scottish immigrants), and they are determined to remain part of Britain. Fiercely Protestant, for years these "Orangemen" (after the Protestant King William of Orange) treated Ulster Catholics as a different race and feared "popish" plots to bring Ulster into the Catholic-dominated Irish Republic to the south. The Protestant majority systematically shortchanged the Catholic minority in jobs, housing, and political power. For many years, most Catholics didn't even have the right to vote for the local legislature.

In 1968 Catholic protests started, modeled on U.S. civil-rights marches. But peaceful demonstrations turned violent. A "provisional" wing of the IRA (itself illegal even in the Republic of Ireland) emerged to enroll Catholic fanatics in a program of murder. A Protestant counterpart, the Ulster Defense Association, reciprocated in kind. Assassination became nearly random. Over twenty-four hundred people have been killed—most of them civilians, many of them innocent bystanders. Still patrolled by the British army, Northern Ireland continues in a state of low-level civil war. No major political party has a solution to the problem that for a time made the United Kingdom Europe's most violent nation.

A CHANGING POLITICAL CULTURE

We are trying to put British political attitudes into some kind of perspective. Britons are neither angels nor devils. Political scientists used to present Britain as a model of stability, moderation, calm, justice, and just plain niceness. In contrast, France was often presented as a model of instability and immoderate political attitudes. The contrast was overdrawn; neither the British nor the French are as good or as bad as sometimes portrayed.

Observations of a country's political culture can err in two ways. First, if you are favorably disposed toward a country—and Americans are great anglophiles—you may tend to overlook some of the nasty things lurking under the surface or dismiss them as aberrations. For years American textbooks on British politics managed to ignore or play down the violence in Northern Ireland. Such "incivility" seemed so un-British that no one wanted to mention it. The 1981 riots caught many observers by surprise.

Second, we may forget that studies of political culture are carried out at certain times, and that things change. The data for one famous book, Almond and Verba's *Civic Culture,* were collected a generation ago. The authors' composite portrait of Britain as a "deferential civic culture" is no longer valid. Since the late 1950s, Britain has undergone some trying times, especially in the area of economics. Difficult times did not erase British attitudes wholesale; they simply made manifest what had been latent. Political attitudes change; they can get nastier.

VOCABULARY BUILDING

anglophile	Easter Rising	muddling through	pragmatism
civility	equalitarian	Oxbridge	public schools
class voting	Establishment	Potato Famine	social class
deferential	legitimacy	PPE	working-class Tory

FURTHER REFERENCE

Alford, Robert R. *Party and Society: The Anglo-American Democracies.* Chicago: Rand McNally, 1963.

Almond, Gabriel A., and Sidney Verba. *The Civic Culture: Political Attitudes and Democracy in Five Nations.* Princeton, N.J.: Princeton University Press, 1963.

Arthur, Paul. *Government and Politics of Northern Ireland,* 2d ed. New York: Longman, 1983.

Dahrendorf, Ralf. *On Britain.* Chicago: University of Chicago Press, 1982.

Guttsman, W. L. *The British Political Elite.* New York: Basic Books, 1963.

Kavanagh, Dennis. "Political Culture in Great Britain: The Decline of the Civic Culture," in *The Civic Culture Revisited,* ed. Gabriel A. Almond and Sidney Verba. Boston: Little, Brown, 1980.

Madgwick, Peter, and Richard Rose, eds. *The Territorial Dimension in United Kingdom Politics.* Atlantic Highlands, N.J.: Humanities Press, 1982.

Nordlinger, Eric A. *The Working-Class Tories: Authority, Deference and Stable Democracy.* Berkeley: University of California Press, 1967.

Robertson, David. *Class and the British Electorate.* New York: Basil Blackwell, 1984.

Rose, Richard, ed. *Studies in British Politics: A Reader in Political Sociology,* 3d ed. New York: St. Martin's Press, 1976.

_____ . *Governing Without Consensus: An Irish Perspective.* Boston: Beacon Press, 1972.

_____ . *Politics in England: An Interpretation,* 3d ed. Boston: Little, Brown, 1980.

Stewart, Angus, ed. *Contemporary Britain.* Boston: Routledge & Kegan Paul, 1983.

Wald, Kenneth D. *Crosses on the Ballot: Patterns of British Voter Alignment since 1885.* Princeton, N.J.: Princeton University Press, 1983.

5

PATTERNS OF INTERACTION

PEOPLE AND PARTIES

In Britain, as in most democratic countries, the relationship between people and political parties is complex, a two-way street in which both influence the other. The parties project something called "party image," what people think of the party's policies, leaders, and ideology. Most voters, on the other hand, carry in their heads a "party identification," a long-term tendency to think of themselves as "Tory" or "Democrat" or whatever. The strategy of intelligent party leadership is to project a party image that will win the loyalty of large numbers of voters and get them to identify permanently with that party. If they can do this, the party becomes powerful and enjoys many electoral successes.

Both party image and party identification are reasonably clear in Britain: most Britons recognize what the three main parties stand for in general terms, and a large portion of British voters identify with a party. The situation is never static, however, for the parties constantly change the images they project, while some voters lose their party identification and shift their votes.

In every country, parents contribute heavily—but never totally—to the party identification of their children. In Britain, political scientists David Butler and Donald Stokes found that if both parents are of the same party, some 90 percent of the children first identify with that party, although this figure later erodes as young people develop their own perspectives. By the same token, party images are rather clear, and most Britons are able to see differences between their two largest parties, Labour aiming at helping working people through welfare measures and sometimes nationalization of industry, and Conservatives aiming at economic growth through hard work without social experiments.

For deeply confirmed Labour or Conservative voters—those whose party identification closely matches the image of their preferred party—there is little doubt about whom to vote for. Until recently, most British voters were reliably Labour or Conservative. The element that changes from one election to another—because either their party identification is not strong or their perceptions of the parties' images shifts, or both—is called the "swing" vote. A swing of a few percentage points can determine who will form the next government, for if each constituency shifts a little one way, say, toward Labour, the Labour candidate will be the winner in many constituencies. Single-member districts often exaggerate percentage trends and turn them into large majorities of seats. A "swing" of only one percentage point nationwide usually translates into a dozen or more parliamentary seats changing hands, sometimes changing the majority in Commons (see box).

The game of British electoral politics consists of the parties trying to mobilize all of their party identifiers—that is, making sure their people bother to vote—plus winning over the uncommitted swing vote. Mobilization is the key. In 1970 the Labour government of Harold Wilson suffered a surprise defeat by the Conservatives under Edward Heath. It wasn't that Labour identifiers suddenly switched sides—they didn't—but rather that some were unhappy with Wilson's policies and simply stayed away from the voting booth.

1983: Tories Win Again

In the elections of June 1983, a "swing" from Labour to Conservative of 6 percent translated into an additional 58 Tory seats, increasing their majority in Commons. The curious thing is that the Tory vote actually went *down* 0.4 percent from 1979. The Conservatives won more seats because in 1983 their opposition was divided between Labour and the new Liberal-Social Democrat Alliance. In Britain, few elections give the winning party a *majority* of votes cast; rather, they usually win a *plurality,* and in single-member districts this gives them an overrepresentation. Grossly underrepresented in 1983 was the Alliance.

The election was not a total endorsement of the Tories. The Thatcher economic program had brought inflation down to 5 percent, but unemployment was a staggering 13 percent. Thatcher did project strength and determination, something aging Labour chief Michael Foot did not. The growth of the Liberal-Social Democrat Alliance was mostly at the expense of the Labour party, which projected a too-strong leftist image. Much of the working class abandoned the Labour party—some for the Conservatives, others for the Alliance. Even union members—long Labour's backbone—voted only 39 percent for the Labour party. Unless it turned back toward the moderate center, many analysts feared the Labour party might be doomed.

	% VOTES MAY 1979	% VOTES JUNE 1983	SEATS 1979	SEATS 1983
Conservative	43.9	43.5	339 (54%)	397 (61%)
Labour	36.9	28.3	268 (42%)	209 (32%)
Alliance	13.8 (Liberal)	26.1	11 (1.7%)	23 (3.5%)

NATIONAL AND LOCAL PARTY

Political scientists used to describe the British national party—Conservative or Labour—as nearly all-powerful, able to dictate to local party organizations whom to nominate for Parliament. As usual, though, when you look more closely you find that things are more complicated.

The name of the game for parliamentary candidates is the "safe seat" and getting adopted by the local constituency organization to run for it. A safe seat is one in a district with a known, dependable majority for your party. Party leaders are normally assigned very safe seats, for it is highly embarrassing if one of them loses his or her seat in the Commons. About 400 (of 650) seats are usually considered safe. There is a bargaining relationship between the parties' London headquarters—the Conservatives' Central Office or Labour's Transport House—and the local constituency party. The local party often requests lists of possible candidates from headquarters, settles on one, and then gets it approved by the central headquarters. Unlike the U.S. system, there is both national and local input into British candidate selection with a veto on both sides.

Some constituency organizations insist that a candidate actually live in the district. Americans expect all candidates to reside in the district they represent; those who don't are called "carpetbaggers" and have an uphill battle. Most countries, however, including Britain, impose no such requirements, although being a local person can help. Some British constituencies like their people to establish a residence there once they've won. But many constituencies couldn't care less if their MP actually lives there; after all, the MP's job is mainly in

London, and periodic visits are sufficient for him or her to hear complaints and maintain ties with electors. Besides, in Britain, party is more important than personality. In any given House of Commons, few MPs are natives of the constituency they represent.

What about the unsafe seats, those where the other party usually wins? These are the testing grounds for energetic newcomers to politics. Central Office or Transport House may send a promising beginner to a constituency organization that knows it doesn't have much hope of winning. Again, the local unit must approve the candidate. Even if the candidate loses, his or her energy and ability are carefully watched—by measuring how much better the candidate did than the previous one—and promising comers are marked. For the next election, the London headquarters may offer the candidate a safer constituency, one where he or she stands a better chance. Finally, the candidate either wins an election in a contested constituency, is adopted by a "safe" constituency, or bows out of politics. Many of Britain's top politicians, including several prime ministers, lost their first races and were transferred to other constituencies. There's no stigma attached; it's normal, part of the training and testing of a British politician.

POLITICS WITHIN THE PARTIES

British political parties, like British cabinets, are balancing acts. A party leader must neither pay too much attention to his or her party's factions nor totally ignore them. In constructing their policies, leaders usually try to give various factions a say but keep the whole thing under moderate control with an eye to winning the next election.

Party leaders must balance a pretty fine line between sometimes extremist party militants and a generally moderate voting public. If a party takes too firm an ideological stand—too left in the case of Labour or too right in the Conservative case—it can cost the party votes. Thus party leaders tend to hedge and moderate their positions, trying to please both the true believers within their party and the general electorate. If they slip in this balancing act, they can lose either party members or voters, or both. When Labour veered left in the 1980s and the Conservatives followed their hard-right Thatcher course, the Alliance sprung into life in the center, a warning to both major parties.

Although long described as ideologically moderate, both the British Labour and Conservative parties have important ideological viewpoints within their ranks. The Labour party is divided into "left" and "right" wings. The Labour left, springing from a tradition of militant trade unionism and intellectual radicalism, wants more nationalization of industry, the dismantling of "public" schools, higher taxes on the rich, to quit the Common Market, and no nuclear weapons, British or U.S. Some Marxists and Trotskyists have won Labour offices. The Labour right, on the other hand, is moderate and gradualist. It favors the welfarist approach of some Continental social-democratic parties such as the German SPD and shies away from government take-overs of industry. It has no illusions about the Soviets and is pro-NATO, pro-Common Market, and pro-American in foreign policy. The rightists in Labour argue that the left-wing's ideas are extremist and cost the party votes. In 1981, several Labour rightists walked out to form a new centrist party (see box).

As an amorphous party proud of its pragmatism, Conservatives were long thought immune to ideological controversy or factional viewpoints. This is not completely true, for the Tories comprise two broad streams of thought, which we might label as "classic" and "neoconservative" tendencies. The classic Tory is not a U.S.-style conservative, advocating a totally free economy with no

Can Kinnock Save Labour?

From its 1983 electoral disaster, the Labour party struggled to recover. Part of its problem was a too-left party image. Another part was its doddering and ineffective leader, Michael Foot. At its annual conference that fall in Brighton, the Labour party tried to repair both areas by overwhelmingly choosing as its new leader Neil Kinnock, a silver-tongued Welshman as charming as Margaret Thatcher is aloof. At 41, Kinnock, son of a coal miner, was the youngest Labour leader ever. Although of Labour's left, Kinnock's leftist leaning is the "soft" rather than the "hard" variety that repelled so many voters. In a balancing act,

the conference also elected rightist Roy Hattersley as deputy leader, a recognition that the two strands will have to cooperate to resurrect the party.

Kinnock, a gifted orator, reflected this balancing act as he used a radical *tone* to keep control over his party's left while offering unthreatening generalities ("lifting the yoke of Thatcherism") that appeal to many moderate voters. Within a few months, Labour's strength grew close to the Tories' in public-opinion polls. Kinnock, although he has never had any experience as a minister, had made himself a plausible candidate for prime minister.

(British Information Services)

government intervention. Instead, the old-fashioned Tory wants a party that takes everybody's interests into account, plus traditional ways of doing things, under the guidance of people born and bred to lead.

The neoconservative wing (which intellectually traces back to nineteenth-century *liberalism*) is much more like American conservatives: they want to roll back government and free the economy. After World War II this view crept into the Conservative party and, with the 1975 election of Margaret Thatcher as party chief, became predominant. Businessman Sir Keith Joseph, education minister in the Thatcher cabinet, is regarded as chief theoretician. Under Thatcher, the classic Tories were dubbed "wets," the militant Thatcherites "dries."

The trouble here is that some old-style British Conservatives find total capitalism almost as threatening as socialism. Many British farmers, industrialists, and fishermen survive—or think they can survive—only with protective tariffs and subsidies. When the Thatcherites forced them to compete in a free market, they howled in pain and fear. Prime Minister Thatcher faced a revolt of Tory "wets" against her excessively "dry" policies and fired "wet" Foreign Secretary Francis Pym from her cabinet. British industrialists, hit by the highest bankruptcy rate in their history, pleaded for a little "wetter" policy.

A New Center Party?

If the Labour party sinks any lower than it did in 1983, its place as main opposition force could be taken by the Liberal-Social Democratic Alliance. In almost half of Britain (313 constituencies out of 650), it was the Alliance that came in second after the Tories, not Labour. But the Alliance has some problems that may stunt it:

- It isn't a party. The Liberals and SDP have not merged. In 1983 they ran merely as an electoral alignment, with Social Democrats supporting Liberals in some constituencies and Liberals supporting Social Democratic candidates in others. There are no "Alliance" members of Parliament, just seventeen Liberals and six Social Democrats.

- Liberals and Social Democrats do not see eye to eye. The SDP is more welfare-oriented, for example, whereas the Liberals are more critical of the U.S. leadership of NATO.

- Liberals think the new, untried SDP got too good a deal in the Alliance. They argue that the Alliance's main electoral support and organizational strength was Liberal.

- The Alliance contains two powerful, ambitious personalities, Liberal chief David Steel and SDP leader Dr. David Owen, neither of whom would gladly accept the second spot in a merged party.

- If the new Labour party leadership succeeds (see box), it will win back the moderate Labour voters who fled in 1983 from the party's leftism to the new Alliance.

PARTIES AND INTEREST GROUPS

What politicians say and what they deliver are two different things. Politicians speak to different audiences. To party rank and file they affirm party gospel (championing either the welfare state or free enterprise, as the case may be). To the electorate as a whole they tone down their ideological statements and offer vague slogans, such as "You've never had it so good," or "Time for a change." But quietly, usually behind the scenes, politicians are also striking important deals with influential organizations representing industry, commerce, professions, and labor. These are known as interest groups, and about half of the British electorate belong to at least one of them.

Although British interest groups are sometimes rather intimately involved with their favored parties, politicians usually disavow that any interest groups dominate party policy. The Labour party has a particularly difficult time of this, for labor unions are constituent members of the Labour party, controlling a majority of votes at Labour's annual conference, contributing some 80 percent of the party's budgets and campaign funds, and providing grass-roots manpower and organization. Especially important are the views of the head of the ten-million-member labor federation known as the Trades Union Congress (TUC), which is similar to the American AFL-CIO but proportionately bigger and stronger. No Labour party leader can ignore the wishes of Britain's union leaders.

This has opened Labour to charges that it is run by and for the unions, which have earned a reputation as too far left, too powerful, and strike-happy. To counteract this, both Labour party and union leaders deny union dominance. Indeed, one Labour party campaign tactic is to claim that only the Labour party can control the unions, rather than the other way around. The close association of labor federation to social-democratic party is the norm for the industrialized countries of Northern Europe, as we shall see when we study West Germany.

Dozens of union members sit as Labour MPs in Parliament; dozens more MPs are beholden to local unions for their election. This union bloc inside the Labour party can force a Labour government to moderate or withdraw measures that might harm unions. To say that the unions run the Labour party, however, is an exaggeration, for repeatedly Labour party chiefs have made union leaders back down, explaining to them that if the unions get too much the Labour party will lose the next elections. To reiterate, to be a party leader means performing a balancing act among several forces.

MPs known to directly represent special interests—an "interested member"—are not limited to the Labour side. Numerous Tory MPs are interested members for various industries and do not try to hide it.

The conservative mirror image of the TUC is the powerful Confederation of British Industry (CBI), formed by an amalgamation of three smaller groups in 1965. The CBI speaks for most British employers but has no formal links to the Conservative party, even though their views are often parallel. The CBI was delighted at the antinationalization stance of the Conservative party, although British industrialists gulped when they found this meant withdrawal of subsidies to *their* industries. Under Thatcher, the CBI sometimes joined with Tory "wets" to complain about the damage her policies were inflicting on the economy. Thatcher could not totally ignore them, for CBI members and money find their way into Tory circles, and dozens of CBI-affiliated company directors occupy Conservative seats in Commons. The first director-general of CBI, John Davies, became minister for trade and industry in the 1970 Tory cabinet.

THE PARTIES FACE EACH OTHER

There are two ways of looking at British elections. The first is to see them as three-week campaigns coming once every few years, each a model of brevity and efficiency. Another, however, is to see them as nearly permanent campaigns that begin the day a new Parliament reconvenes after the latest balloting. The formal campaign may be only three weeks, but long before then the opposition party is thinking of little but ousting the current government.

The chief arena for this is the House of Commons. Unlike the U.S. Congress, British parliamentarians are seldom animated by a spirit of bipartisanship. The duty of the opposition is to oppose, and this they do by accusing the government of everything from incompetence and corruption to sexual scandal. The great weapon here is embarrassment, making a cabinet minister look like a fool. The time is the Question Hour, held Monday through Thursday from 2:30 P.M. (when Commons opens) to 3:30. By tradition, this hour is reserved for MPs to aim written questions at the various cabinet ministers who are in attendance on the front bench. Each written question can be followed up by supplementary oral questions. The opposition tries to push a minister into an awkward position where he or she has to tell a lie, fluff an answer, or break into anger. Then the opposition smirks, "You see, they're not fit to govern."

The Profumo Scandal

In the time-honored game of embarrassment played in the House of Commons, the classic play came with the 1963 Profumo affair. The Labour opposition got wind that Tory War Minister (at the departmental, not the cabinet, level) John Profumo was dating a party girl who at the same time was also seeing the Soviet naval attaché, a known spy. Questioned by Labour in the Commons, Profumo swore there had been no impropriety in his relationship with Christine Keeler and threatened to sue anyone who said otherwise. Being a gentleman of impeccable credentials—Harrow, Oxford, army brigadier—Profumo was believed by the Macmillan government. But the scandal refused to die down; it began to appear that security had been breached and that Profumo was being set up for blackmail.

Labour took full advantage of sensational news stories to charge the Conservative government with laxity on national security, covering up for one of its "old boys," and debauchery at the highest levels of the Establishment. There was some truth to the charges, and Profumo resigned in shame. It was not, however, the shame of a married man, 48, caught with a 21-year-old call girl. That was forgivable. What was unforgivable was that a gentleman had lied to Parliament. The Tory government mishandled the incident; Conservative MPs lost confidence in Prime Minister Macmillan, and voters lost confidence in the Conservative party, which was voted out the following year.

THE CABINET AND THE CIVIL SERVANTS

As we discussed earlier, British cabinet ministers are generalists, not specialists, and are chosen more for political reasons than for any special ability to run their departments. Who then does run them? The nominal head of each British department is the minister; he or she represents that ministry in cabinet discussions and defends it in the Commons. But the minister doesn't run the department; civil servants do.

Ministers come and go every few years; the highest civil servants, known as "permanent secretaries" are there much longer. The permanent secretary often has an edge on his or her minister in social and economic terms as well. Most permanent secretaries are knighted while few ministers are. Although knighthood is now purely honorific in Britain, it still conveys a certain social superiority. Permanent secretaries earn more than ministers, in some cases nearly twice as much. A minister finds it nearly impossible to fire or transfer a permanent secretary. Further, permanent secretaries have a say in determining who will replace them when they retire or leave for lush positions in private industry; they tend to be a self-selecting elite. Permanent secretaries always play the role of humble, obedient servants, but some ministers come to wonder just who's boss around their departments.

The permanent secretary is assisted by several deputy secretaries who in turn are supported by undersecretaries and assistant secretaries. These names look like those of an American department, but there's a major catch: In most U.S. departments all or most of these people are political appointees, serving at the pleasure of the president and resigning when a new president takes office. In Britain, only the ministers assisted by some junior ministers—about a hundred persons in all—change with the political winds. What in America are temporary political appointees, in Britain are permanent officials.

The Utility of Dignity

Another seemingly quaint British holdover from the past is the queen's bestowal of honors such as knighthood. But more than just a quaint practice, it's a clever payoff system that serves a number of purposes. The granting of titles is a reward and an encouragement to retire, solving the problem of senility and dead wood at the top. A person looking forward to a knighthood (Sir) or a peerage (Lord) is more likely to go quietly. Getting one of these honors also has a civilizing effect on the recipients; even the most militant union leaders and rapacious businessmen start talking philosophically about the common good once they have a title in front of their name.

Although the queen awards these and other distinctions, she does so only on the advice of the prime minister. A small staff keeps track of meritorious civil servants, business people, unionists, soldiers, politicians, scholars, artists, and writers and recommends who should get what. In addition to becoming knights and peers, distinguished Britons may be named to the Order of the British Empire, Order of the Garter, Order of Merit, Order of the Bath, the Royal Victorian Order, and many others. The granting of honors is a part of British politics, a way of bolstering loyalty to, and cooperation with, the system.

This gives them a lot of power. They are not amateurs but know their department: its personnel, problems, interests, and desires. Knowledge is power, and over time top civil servants come to quietly exercise a lot of it. While a permanent secretary or his or her assistants never—but never—go public with their viewpoints, they make them felt through the kinds of ideas, programs, bills, and budgets they submit to the minister, their nominal boss. The minister theoretically can command them, but in practice he or she simply doesn't know enough about the workings of the ministry. Instead, the minister relies on them. Accordingly, while most bills and budget proposals *pass through* the cabinet, they do not *originate* there. The permanent civil servants do the jobs that are the stuff of governance.

Treasury: The Real Power

Among the many British ministries, one holds all the others in awe: the Treasury. Sometimes called the "department of departments," Treasury has the last word on who gets what among the ministries and, since a lot of the British economy is government linked, a major say in the island's economic life. Anyone with a bright idea in British government—a new minister or an innovative civil servant—soon comes up against the stone wall of Treasury, the ministry that says "no."

Britain's treasury minister goes by the old name of Chancellor of the Exchequer—originally the king's checker of taxes—and is now the second most powerful figure in any cabinet, just after the prime minister. Many Chancellors of the Exchequer later become prime ministers, so the person in that office is watched closely.

Under the Chancellor are the usual secretaries and civil servants, but they are a breed unto themselves, smarter and more powerful than other bureaucrats. Operating on a team-spirit basis, Treasury chaps trust only other Treasury chaps, for only Treasury can see the whole picture of the British government and economy and how the many parts interrelate. The other departments see only their corner, hence they should not be heeded. This attitude gives Treasury and its people an image of cold, callous remoteness, "government by mandarins," but no one has been able to replace them.

This brings us to a fine irony. In centuries of British political evolution we have seen how Britons marched toward democracy by first limiting the power of the monarch and then expanding participation. If we look closely, though, we notice that much important decision making is only partly democratically controlled. Civil servants make a great deal of policy without democratic input. Many political scientists stress the importance of interest groups in determining policies, but we must add that one of the most powerful interest groups is the civil-service bureaucrats.

Does this mean there is no real democracy in Britain? No, it means we must understand that no country exercises perfect control over its bureaucracy and that parties and elections are only *attempts* to do so.

THE CIVIL SERVICE AND INTEREST GROUPS

We mentioned the relationship of interest groups and political parties earlier. But this is only one way interest groups make their voices heard; it is often not the most important way. Much of the impact of interest groups is in their quiet, behind-the-scenes contact with the bureaucracy. Indeed, with Parliament's role curtailed as a result of powerful prime ministers and cabinets, and the cabinet ministers themselves dependent on the permanent civil servants, many interest groups ask themselves, "Why bother with Parliament? Why not go straight to where the action is, the bureaucracy?"

This approach is especially true of business and industry; the major effort of the unions is still focused on the Labour party. The reason for this is partly in the nature of what trade unions want as opposed to what business groups want. Unions want *general* policies on employment, wages, welfare, and so on, that apply to tens of millions of people. Industry usually wants *specific,* narrow rulings on taxes, subsidies, regulations, and the like that apply to a few firms. Thus unions tend to battle in the more open environment of party policy while business groups often prefer to quietly take a government official to lunch.

In working closely with a branch of Britain's economic life, a given department comes to see itself not as an impartial administrator but as a concerned and attentive helper. After all, if that industry falters, it reflects on the government agency assigned to supervise it. In this manner civil servants come to see leaders of economic interest groups as their "clients" and to reflect their clients' views. When this happens—and it happens in every country—the industry can be said to have "captured" or "colonized" the executive department.

Reinforcing this pattern is the interchange between civil service and private industry. A permanent secretary can make much more money in a corporation than in Whitehall; every now and then one of them leaves government service for greener pastures. (We will also see this pattern in France.) By the same token, business executives are sometimes brought into high administrative positions on the theory that if they can run a company well, they can do the same for government. The point is that fairly cozy relationships develop between civil servants and private business.

WHAT ABOUT DEMOCRACY?

Most of the interactions we have talked about are not under any form of popular control. Ideological infighting, the influence of interest groups on parties and the bureaucracy, the relationship of top civil servants with ministers, the granting of knighthood—these and other interactions are removed from democratic control. The people do not even choose whom they get to vote for; that is a matter for party influentials. All the people get to do is vote every few years, and the choice is limited.

Again, does this mean there is no democracy in Britain? No, not at all. Some people have an exaggerated vision of democracy as a system in which everyone gets to decide on everything. Such a system never existed at the national level, nor could it. The most we can ask of a democracy is that the leading team—in Britain, the prime minister and cabinet—are held accountable periodically in elections. This keeps them on their toes and anxious to pay attention to the public good, hold down special favors and corruption, and make sure the bureaucracy functions. It is in the *anticipation* of electoral punishment that Britain, or any other country, qualifies as a democracy. What has been called the "rule of anticipated reactions" keeps the governors attentive. We will learn not to expect much more of political systems.

VOCABULARY BUILDING

Central Office	ideology	party identification	subsidy
classic conservatism	interested member	party image	swing
classic liberalism	knighthood	peerage	Trades Union
Confederation of	laissez faire	permanent secretary	Congress
British Industry	mobilization	Question Hour	Transport House
constituency	neoconservative	safe seat	Treasury

FURTHER REFERENCE

Bentley, Michael, and John Stevenson, eds. *High and Low Politics in Modern Britain.* New York: Oxford University Press, 1983.

Butler, David, ed. *Coalitions in British Politics.* New York: St. Martin's Press, 1978.

——— , and **Donald Stokes.** *Political Change in Britain.* New York: St. Martin's Press, 1976.

——— , **and Dennis Kavanagh.** *The British General Election of 1983.* New York: St. Martin's Press, 1984.

Campbell, Colin. *Governments Under Stress: Political Executives and Key Bureaucrats in Washington, London, and Ottawa.* Toronto: University of Toronto Press, 1983.

Cyr, Arthur. "Cleavages in British Politics," in *Faction Politics: Political Parties and Factionalism in Comparative Perspective,* ed. Frank Belloni and Dennis Beller. Santa Barbara, Calif.: ABC-Clio, 1978.

Economist. *Political Britain Today.* New York: Cambridge University Press, 1984.

Headey, Bruce. *British Cabinet Ministers: The Roles of Politicians in Executive Office.* London: George Allen Unwin, 1974.

Leys, Colin. *Politics in Britain: An Introduction.* Toronto: University of Toronto Press, 1983.

Ranney, Austin, ed. *Britain at the Polls, 1983.* Durham, N.C.: Duke University Press, 1984.

Rodgers, William. *The Politics of Change.* London: Secker & Warburg, 1982.

Särlvik, Bo, and **Ivor Crewe.** *Decade of Dealignment: The Conservative Victory of 1979 and Electoral Trends in the 1970s.* New York: Cambridge University Press, 1983.

Warde, Alan. *Consensus and Beyond: The Development of Labour Party Strategy since the Second World War.* Manchester: Manchester University Press, 1983.

Whiteley, Paul. *The Labour Party in Crisis.* New York: Methuen, 1983.

6

WHAT BRITONS
QUARREL ABOUT

THE "BRITISH DISEASE"

Britain has been in economic decline for decades. At first it was only relative decline as the economies of Western Europe and Japan grew more rapidly than the British. By the 1970s, however, Britain was suffering absolute decline that left people with lower living standards as inflation outstripped their wage increases. On a world scale, the first industrial nation saw its share of world trade in manufactured goods sink to a paltry 7.5 percent in 1981. In Britain, deindustrialization seemed to be taking place; in some years the British GNP shrank.

Why did Britain decline? There are two basic approaches to such a complex problem. One begins with what happens in people's attitudes—a psycho-cultural approach. The other begins with what happens in the physical world—the politico-economic approach. The two are not mutually exclusive but have a chicken-egg relationship to each other: one feeds into the other.

Some writers put their emphasis on British nonwork attitudes as the root of the problem. The old feudal aristocracy, which disdained hard work as tawdry moneymaking, was never thoroughly displaced in Britain. Rather, the rising entrepreneurs tried to ape the old elite and become gentlemen of leisure and culture. In public schools and Oxbridge, young Britons learn to despise commercial and technical skills in favor of the humanities. The emphasis is on having wealth rather than creating it. Accordingly, Britain lacks daring and innovative capitalists.

The British class system makes matters worse. British managers—mostly middle class—are snobbish toward workers; they do not mix with them or roll up their sleeves and get their hands dirty. British workers react by showing solidarity with their "mates" and more loyalty to their union than to their company. If the psycho-cultural approach is correct, the only way to save Britain is to change British attitudes. But deep-seated attitudes change slowly.

The other approach, the politico-economic, argues that the bad attitudes

"Pluralistic Stagnation"

Harvard political scientist Samuel Beer advances a provocative thesis on the cause of Britain's decline: too many interest groups making too many demands on parties who are too willing to promise everyone everything. The result is "pluralistic stagnation" as British groups scramble for welfare benefits, pay hikes, and subsidies for industry. The two main parties bid against each other with promises of more benefits to more groups. In the late 1960s, a strong "counterculture" emerged in Britain, which wrecked traditional attitudes of civility and deference and made groups' demands more strident. With every group demanding and getting more, no one saw any reason for self-restraint that would leave them behind. It was as if everyone was looking jealously over his shoulder to see what the other fellow was getting from the system. Government benefits fed union wage demands, which fed inflation, which fed government benefits . . .

The interesting point about the Beer thesis is that it blames precisely what political scientists have long celebrated: pluralism, the autonomous interaction of society's many groups on themselves and on government. In U.S. political science especially, this is supposed to be a good thing, the foundation of freedom and democracy. Beer demonstrates, though, that it can run amok; groups block each other and government, leading to what Beer calls the "paralysis of public choice." Any comparison with your system?

are a reflection of faulty governmental policy. Change the policy so as to provide a new context, and attitudes will change. The Thatcherites are among the chief proponents of this view. The problem, they argue, is the growth of government, especially since Labour won with its socialistic program in 1945. The welfare state lets many consume without producing and subsidizes inefficient industries. Unions, given free rein by Labour governments, raise wages and lower productivity. The growing costs of the welfare state drain away funds that should be used for investment. Insufficient investment means insufficient production, which means stagnating living standards. Cut both welfare benefits and industry subsidies and you will force—with some pain—a change in attitudes.

The Flip Side of the Welfare State

The other side of the welfare state is how expensive it is. In 1980, taxes took these percentages of GNP:

Sweden	51.5
Holland	45.8
France	42.9
Britain	37.4
West Germany	37.2
Canada	32.9
United States	30.7
Switzerland	30.5
Japan	26.1

Source: Lloyds Bank.

THE THATCHER CURE

The Thatcherites' analysis of Britain's problems parallels that of Beer (see box). The permissive policies of both Labour and previous Conservative governments had expanded welfare programs beyond the country's ability to pay for them. Unions won wage increases that were entirely out of line with productivity. Nationalized and subsidized industries were money-losers. The result: hefty inflation and falling production that were making Britain the sick man of Europe. The cure: the "monetarist" theory of American economist (and Nobel Prize winner) Milton Friedman, who sees too-rapid growth of the money supply as the cause of inflation. Thatcher cut government bureaucracy, the growth of welfare, and subsidies to industry in an effort to control Britain's money supply and restore health to its economy.

Some Britons wondered if the cure wasn't worse than the disease. Unemployment surged to 14 percent of the work force, thousands of firms went bankrupt, and Britain's GNP growth was still anemic. Even moderate Conservatives pleaded for her to relent, but Thatcher wasn't called the Iron Lady for nothing. "The lady's not for turning," she intoned. She saw the economic difficulties as a purge Britain had to experience to get well. One of her econo-

Comparing: Dutch and Belgians Also Cut Welfare

Virtually all the lands of Northern Europe have constructed similar welfare states, and all face the same economic problems. Many are trying cures similar to Thatcher's. In the Netherlands in 1982 a Christian Democrat-Liberal (both pretty conservative) coalition took power under Ruud Lubbers and carried out cuts much deeper than Thatcher's. "The majority of the voters accept the idea that we need to scale down," said a Dutch journalist. Belgium, with a Christian Democrat-Liberal coalition, made similar cuts into welfare spending. In both countries—as in Britain—resistance came from unions, especially public-service unions, and people on social security.

mists said: "I don't shed tears when I see inefficient factories shut down. I rejoice." Thatcher and her supporters repeated endlessly, "You can't consume until you produce."

Gradually the argument began to take hold. Many Britons had to admit that they had been consuming more than they were producing, that subsidized facories and mines were a drain on the economy, and that bitter medicine was necessary to correct matters. It was almost as if Britons had become guilty at their free rides and knew they now had to pay up. In 1983, slightly more working-class Britons voted Tory than voted Labour. Even many people who had been thrown out of work by Thatcher's "dry" economics voted for her.

Thatcher had changed the terms of Britain's political debate. In 1945, Labour had shifted the debate to the welfare state, and Tories had to compete with them on their own terms, never seriously challenging the underlying premise that welfare is good. With the 1979 and 1983 elections, Thatcher made the debate one about productivity—no production, no goodies—and now Labour had to compete on *her* terms. It was a historic shift, and one that influenced the political debate in other lands, including the United States.

But did Thatchernomics work? After six years the picture was mixed, but with some positive signs. Inflation was down. Growth was not bad, but unemployment set records. And the pound sterling slid toward parity with the dollar. State-owned British Steel, British Leyland (motor vehicles), and other industries that had been nationalized since the war to prevent unemployment, trimmed their bloated, inefficient work forces and raised productivity. Some plants were sold off, a process called "privatization." Many unions eased their wage and other demands, and total union membership dropped by about a million. Many weak firms went under, but thousands of new small and middle-sized firms sprang up. Capital and labor were channeled away from losing industries and into winners, exactly what a good economic system should do. A California-like computer industry produced a "silicon glen" in Scotland and a "software valley" around Cambridge University.

Some workers were genuinely frightened about their jobs, though. When the government's National Coal Board decided to close hundreds of unprofitable pits and eliminate twenty thousand jobs, miners staged a long and violent strike in 1984, which was supported by some other unionists. Thatcher would not back down; after a year, the miners did. The number of British fami-

Comparing: Thatchernomics and Reaganomics

On two sides of the Atlantic, conservative chief executives implemented similar economic programs at about the same time. The main difference was that U.S. problems were not nearly as acute as Britain's, so President Reagan's policies didn't have to be as drastic and painful as Prime Minister Thatcher's. Nonetheless, the parallels are remarkable:

• Both cut the number of civilian government bureaucrats to save money and "deregulate" the economy.

• Both followed, to varying degrees, Friedman's monetarist approach and tried to restrain growth of the money supply. The United States was more successful in this, under the stern eye of Federal Reserve Chairman Paul Volcker. In both countries, however, the policy shot up interest rates.

• Both said they would cut welfare expenditures, but neither succeeded; welfare programs are too firmly entrenched in both lands. Both did succeed in halting the growth of such programs.

• During their first couple of years in office, both witnessed recession, heightened unemployment, and continued inflation; their policies seemed to have failed. But by 1983, both economies were showing improvement, with inflation down and productivity up. U.S. unemployment improved, but Britain's stayed high.

• Both created massive budgetary deficits, inadvertently subscribing to the Keynesian economic theory of deficit government spending to induce prosperity. This was ironic, for both claimed to despise Keynesianism.

• Both met strong union resistance—Reagan faced air traffic controllers and postal workers, Thatcher coal miners—and both refused to back down. Their respective showdowns helped persuade unions to lower their demands, and this contributed to curbing inflation. Both were accused of "union busting," and union membership declined.

• Both said they would cut taxes. Reagan did, and this stimulated economic recovery. Thatcher merely shifted taxes—from income to value-added, a sort of national sales tax—which wasn't as stimulative but did contribute to increased investment.

• Both changed the terms of political debate in their respective countries, putting welfare-minded Democrats and Labourites on the defensive and making people think about production instead of consumption. This was their greatest impact.

lies below the poverty line increased under Thatcher. High youth unemployment led to urban riots.

Furthermore, on closer examination, Thatcher did not really apply stringent monetarist prescriptions. As unemployment soared, so did automatic unemployment compensation. Welfare expenditures did not shrink, and Britain's money supply still grew too fast. Some industries were still subsidized. Thatcher's words were tougher than her deeds.

The Tories won the 1983 election because (1) many people thought Thatcher was right; (2) the Labour party was too far left and lacked a dynamic leader; (3) the opposition was divided between Labour and the Alliance; and (4) the Falklands War with Argentina rallied Britons to their leader. In the next election, which must be called by 1988, some or all of these factors will have disappeared. Thatcher, therefore, has a very definite time limit to show that her brand of economics really works.

The Trouble with National Health

The centerpiece of Britain's extensive welfare state is the National Health Service, which went into operation in 1948 as part of Labour's longstanding commitment to improving the lot of working Britons. Before the war, British medical care was spotty. When millions were examined for military service during the war, many were scrawny and unhealthy. Conservatives and the British Medical Association fought the NHS, but the tide was against them.

Did the NHS work? The answer is both yes and no. The British population is much healthier than it used to be. Infant mortality, one key measure of overall health standards, dropped from 53 out of 1,000 live births in 1938 to 13.3 in 1984 (still almost double the rates of Sweden and Japan). The British working class has especially benefited.

But NHS has some negative aspects. Costs skyrocketed. The British population has become more elderly, and old people consume several times as much medical care as younger people. Technical advances in medicine work wonders, but they are terribly expensive. The system requires many bureaucrats. The NHS became the largest employer in Western Europe, but personnel and facilities have not kept pace with demand. If surgery isn't for an emergency, patients may wait two years. Some three-quarters of a million Britons are on waiting lists for medical treatment.

The upshot is that private medical care has quietly returned to Britain. A growing number of Britons are willing to pay for speedy, personal, private treatment. Some British employers offer private medical insurance to their employees as a fringe benefit, just like in the United States. Britain actually has a dual health system, one national, funded by taxes, and another private, funded by direct payment or private insurance. Labour's great effort to provide medical treatment for all has succeeded, but its efforts to eliminate class differences in medical treatment has failed.

SCOTTISH AND WELSH NATIONALISM

The United Kingdom has problems with its unity. In addition to the low-level civil war in Northern Ireland, Scotland and Wales present problems of regionalism. Wales has been a part of England since the Middle Ages; the thrones of England and Scotland were united in 1603, and in 1707 both countries agreed to a single Parliament in London. But old resentments never quite died. Wales and Scotland were always poorer than England, provoking the feeling among Welsh and Scots that they were economically exploited.

In the twentieth century the political beneficiary of these feelings has been the Labour party, which holds sway in Wales and Scotland. But in the 1960s the small Plaid Cymru (pronounced *plyde kum-REE*, meaning "Party of Wales") and the Scottish Nationalist party began to grow, and in the 1974 election the Welsh Nationalists won three Commons seats and the Scottish Nationalists eleven.

Local nationalism grew in many countries during the 1970s: Corsican and Breton in France, Quebecer in Canada, Basque and Catalan in Spain. It was hard to pinpoint the cause for this upsurge in local separatism. Economics plays a role; local nationalists usually claim their regions are shortchanged by their central governments. Nationalists often emphasize their regions' distinct languages and cultures and demand that they be taught in schools. Some of the impulse behind local nationalism is the bigness and remoteness of the modern state, the feeling that important decisions are out of local control, made by far-away bureaucrats. And often smoldering under the surface are historical resentments of a region that once was conquered, occupied, and deprived of its own identity. Whatever the mixture, local nationalism sometimes turns its adherents into fanatics willing to wreck the entire country to get their way. Happily, this did not happen in Britain. The Scots and Welsh never became as extreme as Basques in Spain or Quebecers in Canada.

In Scotland, the economic factor played a large part. When oil was discovered in the North Sea off Scotland in the 1960s, some Scots didn't want to share the petroleum revenues with the United Kingdom as a whole. "It's Scotland's oil!" cried the Scottish Nationalists whose electoral fortunes rose with the offshore discoveries. Oil offered Scotland the possibility of economic independence and self-government, of becoming something more than a poor, northerly part of Britain.

Wales had no oil (just coal), but it also felt economically exploited. Most important for Welsh nationalists, however, was language, the ancient Celtic tongue of Cymric (pronounced *kim-rick*). About one Welsh person in ten still speaks Cymric, and many are elderly. In recent years, however, there has been an upsurge of people learning Welsh, and the language is now officially coequal with English within Wales. There is even a Welsh TV channel.

The strategy of the Labour government of the 1970s was to offer home rule or autonomy to Scotland and Wales. This was called "devolution," the granting of certain governing powers by the center to the periphery. In 1977 Commons passed the Scotland and Wales Bills, which would have set up Scottish and Welsh assemblies and executives. These were to have powers over local affairs in much the same way that American states have, although it would be an exaggeration to equate devolution with American-style federalism.

The catch was that the devolution plans has to be approved in a referendum by 40 percent of all eligible Scottish and Welsh voters, a harder task than getting a simple majority. The Welsh plan was rejected by four Welsh voters out of five, and only 33 percent of Scots voted for their plan, short of the required 40 percent. Many Scottish and Welsh voters thought local nationalism was a nice romantic idea but impractical. Some feared it would just add another layer of bureaucracy. In the parliamentary elections of 1979 and 1983, each nationalist party retained only two seats as Scotland and Wales swung overwhelmingly to Labour. Voting Labour in Scotland and Wales, in fact, has become a form of local nationalism, a way of repudiating rule by England, which goes almost totally Conservative. Devolution as a political plan was dead, but Scottish and Welsh resentments were as high as ever.

BRITISH RACISM

British intellectuals, especially those on the left, used to criticize the United States for racism. Then the British left took to denouncing South Africa. That sort of thing, Britishers used to say, could never happen in tolerant, civilized Britain. At least since the 1958 Notting Hill race riot in London, the English have had to face the fact that they, too, have a race problem and that there are no easy solutions to it.

What to do with Ulster?

Northern Ireland is a major problem for Britain—Ulster's heavily subsidized economy and security costs Britain some $2 billion a year—but not yet a major quarrel, for no one offers a plausible solution. Fewer than one Briton in three wants to keep Ulster, but none know how to get rid of the problem gracefully. A 1973 act of Parliament guarantees that Northern Ireland will never "cease to be part of the United Kingdom without the consent of the majority." This guarantee is one of the stumbling blocks to any solution, for a majority of Ulster voters—especially Protestants—will not consent to a sweeping change.

Prime Minister Thatcher often assures Ulster's Protestants that she will not "sell them out." Flying in the face of her free-market philosophy, Thatcher has not dared cut Ulster's massive subsidies. Labour is at least willing to entertain—but not endorse—more radical solutions. When Labour was in power in the 1970s, it briefly considered British withdrawal as one option but discarded it for fear of increased sectarian bloodshed. Labour leftist Tony Benn still sometimes talks about pullout.

Five options for Ulster have been suggested:

- REUNIFICATION with Eire, possibly under a federal setup that would leave Ulster with local autonomy. Unification is exactly what Irish nationalists have been demanding for decades, but Orangemen won't hear of it, and they have veto power.

- INDEPENDENCE for Ulster, making it a separate country. Protestant extremists have suggested this as a last-ditch option to prevent unification, but Catholics would balk, and full-scale civil war might break out.

- DEVOLUTION, or home rule, as was proposed for Scotland and Wales. Let them manage their own affairs, says this option. But Ulster already had home rule, and it made things worse. From 1921 to 1972 Ulster had its own parliament at Stormont, but its Protestant majority disenfranchised and ignored Catholics. In 1972 the Stormont parliament was suspended and London began "direct rule."

- INTEGRATION with Britain. Ulster has an anomalous "provincial" status within the United Kingdom. Why not make it the same as Yorkshire? But Ulster Catholics don't like the idea as it would give Protestants power, and Protestants don't like it because they would lose their local autonomy.

- JOINT AUTHORITY, or two flags over Belfast, one British and one Irish. This 1984 suggestion of a study group called New Ireland Forum was welcomed by most British and Irish political leaders as a starting point for negotiations. Ulster men and women could pick one nationality or have both. But how could London and Dublin share responsibility equally? Again, Protestants would have none of it. It looks like Britain will be stuck with its Ulster problem for a long time.

The race problem in Britain is a legacy of empire. Britain in 1948 legally made the natives of its many colonies British "subjects," entitled to live and work in the U.K. Although the colonies were granted independence in the 1950s and 1960s as members of the British Commonwealth—a loosely structured organization of countries which call the queen their nominal sovereign—their people were still entitled to immigrate to Britain. In the 1950s, West Indians arrived from the Caribbean, then Indians and Pakistanis. Immigrants were willing to take the lowliest jobs that many Englishmen didn't want. Then they would send for their wives, children, fiancées, and cousins. Britain's "colored" population is now about 2.2 million, 4 percent of Britain's total.

White resentment soon grew, especially among the working class, who believed the recent immigrants wanted their housing, jobs, wallets, and daughters. Britons began to discover they were racists. In 1967 an openly racist National Front party formed, advocating the expulsion of all "coloreds" back to their native lands. Some National Front leaders had earlier been members of Britain's tiny Fascist party. Young toughs supporting the Front went in for "Paki bashing." In the 1970s, votes for National Front candidates grew, although the Front never won a seat in Parliament. Meanwhile, the minute Trotskyist Socialist Workers party attacked Front rallies, and hundreds of police had to hold the two sides apart.

The British race question is not confined to the fringes of politics. Many ordinary Britons view the nonwhites as a social problem and would like them to return to their native lands, although by now many have been born in Britain. Some of the swing to the Conservatives in 1979 can be attributed to Margaret Thatcher's call for a "clear end to immigration" before it "swamped" British culture.

In point of fact, immigration to Britain has been successively tightened by both parties since 1962 and has now become quite restrictive (see box). Demographers say there is no chance the immigrants will swamp anything. But the question poses serious ethical dilemmas. The British gloried in their empire for more than a century; now they have responsibility for what they created. Particularly poignant was the situation of "Asians" (Indians and Pakistans) in East Africa. Brought to Kenya and Uganda by the British decades ago as laborers, Asians soon became small business people and monopolized commercial life. Native Africans bitterly resented the Asians and applauded government policies to "Africanize" commerce—meaning kicking out the Indians and Pakistanis. The Asians pleaded to be let into Britain. With most of Hong Kong due to revert to Communist China in 1997, many residents of that British crown colony likewise pleaded to be let into Britain.

Third-Class Citizens

In 1983 a new law took effect in Britain that created three classes of citizenship. For the Tory government, which introduced the Nationality Act, it was the fulfillment of one of Thatcher's campaign promises to stem nonwhite immigration. For critics, it was a racist attempt to clean up Britain's "debris of empire." The act ended the seven-centuries-old *ius soli* (right of the soil) tradition—still used by the United States—of granting citizenship to any child born on British soil. The three classes of British citizenship created by the act:

• All present citizens of Britain, plus the Falkland Islands and Gibraltar, have the right to live and work in Britain and to pass this right on to their children.

• Citizens of British Dependent Territories, covering some three million people in Hong Kong, Bermuda, Belize, and some other island territories, are nominal British subjects but have no automatic right of residence in Britain.

• British Overseas Citizens, about 1.5 million minority overseas Chinese and Indians who opted for British nationality when East Africa and Malaysia gained independence, have no residency right and cannot pass their citizenship on to their children.

BRITAIN AND EUROPE

The British have never thought of themselves as Europeans. Indeed, most English people look down upon anyone from across the English Channel—even if their income is higher and their products better. Rather than working toward a united Europe after World War II, as the main Continental countries did, Britain emphasized its Commonwealth ties and its "special relationship" to the United States. London faced westward, across the Atlantic, rather than eastward, across the Channel.

Rather than signing the 1957 Treaty of Rome, which set up the European Community (EC), Britain in 1960 built a much looser grouping known as the European Free Trade Association (EFTA). While the EC Six (France, West Germany, Italy, Belgium, Netherlands, Luxembourg) surged ahead economically, the EFTA Outer Seven (Britain, Austria, Denmark, Finland, Iceland, Norway, Portugal, Sweden, and Switzerland) found themselves slowly cut off from the main European market. In 1963, Britain applied to get in to the Common Market. French President Charles de Gaulle vetoed British entry, charging that Britain was still too tied to the Commonwealth and the United States to be a good European. He was right.

By the time de Gaulle resigned in 1969, Britain was again ready to join the EC, but there were domestic political complications. Not all Britons liked the idea. For old Conservatives it meant giving up a little bit of British sovereignty to the EC headquarters in Brussels and even treating Europeans as equals. For everyone it meant higher food prices. For manufacturers it meant British products would have to compete with possibly better and cheaper Continental imports that would come in tariff-free. For fisherman it meant British fishing areas would be open to all Common Market fishermen. For workers it meant possible unemployment. In short, a lot of Britons were frightened of change and competition.

The arguments in favor of joining stressed that Britain needed change and competition, the very forces that had invigorated European industries. Further, geographically, strategically, economically, even spiritually, Britain really was a part of Europe and should start acting like it. Britain was no longer a great empire and could not stand on its own; the "special relationship" with the United States was unreliable and made Britain into a U.S. dependency.

The Common Market debate cut across party lines, sometimes producing a strange coalition of right-wing Tories and left-wing Labourites, each opposing EC entry for their own reasons. In general, however, Conservatives were pro-Market; Labour, anti-Market. In 1971, under a Tory government, the Commons voted 356 to 244 to join; 69 Labour MPs defied their party whip to vote in favor while 39 Conservatives, freed from party discipline, voted "no" along with Labour. The vote graphically demonstrated that British party discipline is not perfect. On January 1, 1973, Britain, along with Denmark and Ireland, made the Common Market Six, the Nine.

When Labour returned to power, Prime Minister Harold Wilson offered the British public a first—a referendum. Referendums—mass votes on issues rather than on candidates—are quite common in France, but Britain, with its tradition of parliamentary supremacy, had never held one before. The 1975 British referendum on the Common Market found that most Britons wanted to stay in Europe, but one-third voted no.

There is still grumbling that Britain made a mistake and should pull out. In 1983 the Labour party, dominated by its left wing, vowed that as soon as they are back in power they will initiate negotiations with the EC to withdraw. The Conservatives support EC membership in general but are highly critical of current financial arrangements that penalize Britain. Prime Minister Thatcher demanded a cut in Britain's contribution to the Common Market, which devotes two-thirds of its budget to agricultural subsidies, chiefly to French farmers. If Thatcher didn't like subsidizing British producers, she certainly didn't like subsidizing French ones. Thatcher's stubbornness, until she got some of what she wanted, almost caused the collapse of the Common Market in 1984. If Britons do not feel that they are benefiting from EC membership, their eventual withdrawal is possible.

No Nukes, British Style

The British left, including the Campaign for Nuclear Disarmament and the current Labour leadership, wants a nuclear-free Britain, with neither U.S. nor British nuclear weapons. The Conservatives support both the small British nuclear program as well as the presence of U.S. nuclear forces on British soil. The Social Democrats walked out of Labour partly because they thought unilateral nuclear disarmament was foolish pacifism, but they would like dual U.S.-British control over American missiles in Britain. The Liberals would abandon the expensive independent British nuclear deterrent—based on U.S.-made Trident missiles—but are split on U.S. missile bases in Britain.

Matters came to a head in 1983 when the United States began installing ninety-six cruise missiles at a Royal Air Force base at Greenham Common. Women CND protesters set up a camp by the base lasting for years (legal) and tried to block entrance to the base with their bodies (illegal). One leading Labourite, using a nationalistic theme, charged Thatcher was turning Britain into "an American aircraft carrier." Another said, "When they talk about limited nuclear war in the States, they mean it would be limited to us." The Tories stood firm, arguing the cruise missiles were part of a NATO effort to offset Soviet rockets aimed at Western Europe. In 1983, the British electorate sided with the Tories, but this verdict did not silence the substantial antinuclear minority in Britain.

GREAT BRITAIN OR LITTLE ENGLAND?

This sums up the dilemma of modern Britain: the problem of scaling down its vision of itself. Britain in the course of a century has clearly declined, both internationally and domestically. When Britain was a mighty empire and the most industrialized country in the world it had power, wealth, and a sense of mission. This in turn fostered order, discipline, and deference among the British people. Losing its empire and slipping down to become one of the weaker economies of West Europe, decay, violence, and resentment appeared.

Britain offers a refutation to the idea that progress is unilinear—onward ever, backward never. On the contrary, in the case of Britain we see that what goes up can eventually come down. But this process is never static. Once Britain adjusts to its new reality—as one European country among many—regeneration can begin. It may have already begun. To see how another country has turned around, how a society and economy can change from static to dynamic, let us now consider France.

VOCABULARY BUILDING

absolute decline	EC	National Health	productivity
British disease	EFTA	Service	referendum
devolution	monetarism	periphery	relative decline
		privatization	unilinear

FURTHER REFERENCE

Beer, Samuel H. *Britain Against Itself: The Political Contradictions of Collectivism.* New York: W.W. Norton, 1982.

Benyon, J., ed. *Scarman & After: Essays Reflecting on Lord Scarman's Report, the Riots and Their Aftermath.* New York: Pergamon Press, 1983.

Drucker, Henry, et al. *Developments in British Politics.* New York: St. Martin's, 1983.

Gamble, Andrew. *Britain in Decline: Economic Policy, Political Strategy and the British State.* Boston: Beacon Press, 1982.

Griffith, John, ed. *Socialism in a Cold Climate.* Winchester, Mass.: Allen & Unwin, 1983.

Jenkins, Simon. "The Trouble with Ulster," *The Economist,* 2 June 1984.

Riddell, Peter. *The Thatcher Government.* New York: Basil Blackwell, 1984.

Sampson, Anthony. *The Changing Anatomy of Britain.* New York: Random House, 1983.

Thompson, Grahame. *Mrs. Thatcher's Economic Policy: The First Five Years.* Dover, N.H.: Longwood Publishing Groups, 1985.

Wiener, Martin. *English Culture and the Decline of the Industrial Spirit, 1850–1980.* New York: Cambridge University Press, 1981.

part two

FRANCE

7

THE IMPACT
OF THE PAST

THE SPLIT HEXAGON

"France has everything," the French like to boast. They are nearly right. Roughly the shape of a hexagon, with three sides on seas and three on land, France is simultaneously an Atlantic country, a Mediterranean country, and an Alpine country. It has lush farmland, navigable rivers, many minerals, and a moderate climate. It does not, however, have the safety of England's moat. France is vulnerable to land attack from the north and east. While England historically did well without standing armies, France needed large armies, a point that helps explain the rise of French absolutism. French kings had their troops to rely on.

Internally, France is divided into a North and a South. Culturally and temperamentally the two regions are rather different and until the late Middle Ages even spoke different languages. The Germanic northerners spoke *langue d'oïl*, "the tongue of oïl," their word for yes, which grew into the modern French *oui*. The Mediterranean southerners spoke *langue d'oc*, after their word for yes, *oc*. It declined after the Paris kings conquered the South in the thirteenth century. To this day, southerners may speak with a different accent and resent the region's subjugation to Paris.

THE ROMAN INFLUENCE

Like most peoples, the French are a mixture of ethnic stocks. In the centuries before Christ, tribes of Celts pushed into France and merged with the native Ligurians. The Romans conquered the area and called it Gallia (Gaul). The Roman influence in France was longer and deeper than in England. The Anglo-Saxons obliterated England's Roman influence, but the Germanic tribes that moved into Gaul became Romanized themselves. Thus English is a Germanic language and French a Romance language.

By the time the Roman Empire collapsed, one Germanic tribe had managed to take over most of present-day France; these were the Franks. Their chief, Clovis—from whom came the name Louis—was baptized in 496, and France has been mostly Catholic ever since, the "eldest daughter of the Church." The Franks under Charles Martel turned back the invading Moors in 732, possibly saving Christianity in Europe. Charles Martel's grandson, Charlemagne, carved out a gigantic kingdom—the Holy Roman Empire—that encompassed what someday would amount to most of the six original Common Market countries. Although the empire soon disintegrated, Charlemagne had planted the idea of European unity.

THE RISE OF FRENCH ABSOLUTISM

In the confusion that followed Charlemagne, France was reduced to several petty kingdoms and dukedoms, as was Germany. While Germany stayed divided until the nineteenth century, French kings pursued unification and centralization of their power with single-minded determination. Pushing outward from the Paris area, the *Ile de France* (Island of France), the Capetian kings added territory while retaining control in Paris.

Great French Expressions: "Paris is Worth a Mass"

During the Reformation, French Protestants, called Huguenots, were controlled, massacred, and driven into exile. In 1589, however, the royal line of succession fell to a Huguenot, Henry of Navarre. The French Roman Catholic church, horrified at the thought of a non-Catholic king, offered the throne to Henry only if he would convert to Catholicism. In what has become a model of opportunism, Henry shrugged and said, "Paris is worth a Mass." The new convert became Henry IV, an excellent king and founder of the Bourbon dynasty (which still reigns in Spain).

Feudalism in France began to give way to absolutism with Louis (pronounced *Lwie*) XI, who ruled from 1461 to 1483. The crafty Louis XI doubled the size of France until it was nearly its present shape, weakened the power of the feudal nobles, ignored the Estates-General (the parliament), and developed a royal bureaucracy to increase taxation. It was a pattern that was to be strengthened for at least three centuries, leaving the France of today still highly centralized. Louis XI also cultivated relations with Rome. There was never an English-style break with the Vatican; instead the Catholic church became a pillar of the French monarchy.

Under Louis XIII, Cardinal Richelieu became chief minister and virtual ruler from 1624 to 1642. Obsessed with French power and glory, Richelieu further weakened the nobles, recruited only middle-class bureaucrats, and sent out *intendants* to control the provinces for Paris. Richelieu was an organizational genius who put his bureaucratic stamp on France for all time.

The French nobles did try to fight back, but they lost. In 1648 and again in 1650 some French aristocrats staged an uncoordinated revolt called the *Fronde*. Recall that at this time English nobles and their commoner allies beheaded a king who tried to act like an absolute monarch. In France, the nobles were quickly broken and lost the autonomy enjoyed by English lords.

LOUIS XIV: THE HIGH POINT OF ABSOLUTISM

By the time Louis XIV became king in 1661, French absolutism was already well developed; he brought it to a high point. Louis's emblem was the sun, around which all things revolved. The "Sun King" further increased centralization and bureaucratization, all aimed at augmenting his own and France's power. Louis used his large army in almost continual warfare. He acted as his own prime minister and handled much administration personally. He never bothered convening the Estates-General. He constructed the gigantic Versailles palace and made thousands of nobles live there, diverting them from power seeking to game playing—games of intrigue, love, and flattery. While English lords ruled as small kings on their estates, French nobles were reduced to courtiers.

Great French Expressions: "L'état, c'est moi."

"The state—that's me," Louis XIV is often quoted as saying. While there is no record that he actually uttered the words, there is evidence that he lived them.

Louis's policies of "war and magnificence" were terrible financial drains. To harness the French economy to serve the state, Louis's minister, Colbert, practiced "mercantilism," the theory that a nation was as wealthy as the amount of gold it possessed and that the way to amass gold was for the government to supervise the economy with plans, subsidies, monopolies, and tariffs. This helped set a pattern found in most European countries and in Japan: instead of purely free-market economics, the government is expected to play a helping role.

Louis XIV was an able monarch who impressed all of Europe. Other kings tried to imitate him, and French cuisine, architecture, dress, and language dominated the Continent. From the outside, the France of Louis XIV looked more impressive than England. Without "checks and balances" to get in the way, the centralized monarchy of France was able to accomplish great things. But the English, by slowly developing political participation, had actually devised a more stable system.

WHY THE FRENCH REVOLUTION?

For all its external splendor, France in the eighteenth century was in difficulties. Its treasury was often near bankruptcy. Especially costly was French support for the American colonists against Britain; the French did it more for revenge than for love of liberty. The bureaucracy was corrupt and inefficient. Recognizing too late that mercantilism was bad economics, the regime tried to move to a free market, but by then French industry and agriculture had become used to state protection and objected. Also important was the spread of new ideas on "liberty," "consent of the governed," and "the general will." Ideas can be dynamite, and great thinkers expounded ideas that undermined the *ancien régime* (old regime).

As Alexis de Tocqueville pointed out, revolutions seldom start when things are bad but, rather, when they are getting better. The French people enjoyed improving economic conditions for most of the eighteenth century, but that increased expectations and awakened jealousies toward people who were getting richer faster. As we saw in Iran under the shah, economic growth can be highly destabilizing. Further, Louis XVI had decided to reform the political system and provide for some kind of representation. But as we shall see in Russia and South Africa, the reforming of an unjust and unpopular system is extraordinarily difficult, a bit like taking the lid off a pressure cooker under full steam.

In the spring of 1789, Louis XVI convened the Estates-General for the first time since 1614. Its three estates—the clergy, nobility, and commoners—

were elected by nearly universal suffrage. The Third Estate, commoners, demanded that all three houses meet together, meaning that the more numerous Third Estate could override the conservative First and Second Estates. The Third Estate argued that it represented the popular will, but Louis resisted. By the time he gave in, many parliamentarians were angry and radicalized and voted themselves into a National Assembly, which is the name for the present legislature.

Great French Expressions: "Let Them Eat Cake."

One reason the French monarchy of Louis XVI was unpopular was the frivolous and extravagant queen, Marie Antoinette. She was said to have once inquired why there had been riots and was told it was because the people had no bread. "No bread?" she was said to have tittered. "Then let them eat cake." Marie Antoinette may have never said these words—they were written earlier by Rousseau—but the masses hated her for such attitudes. She was guillotined in 1793 a few months after her husband, Louis XVI's, execution.

Shortly afterward, the common people of Paris, who hated the haughty queen and were furious over rising bread prices, stormed the Bastille, an old fort, on July 14, 1789. Bastille Day became the French national day. Upon hearing of the Bastille the king exclaimed, *"C'est une révolte,"* meaning something that could be put down. A duke corrected him: *"Non, Sire, c'est une révolution."* It was the first modern usage of the word revolution.

Three French Geniuses: Voltaire, Montesquieu, Rousseau

Each in his own way, these three eighteenth-century thinkers helped persuade a good portion of Frenchmen—especially middle-class intellectuals—that the *ancien régime* was rotten and that it was possible to construct a better system. Their common weapon was reason—abstract, Cartesian, logical—in contrast to English thinkers, who relied more on empirical reality. The French dislike reality for failing to live up to their logical constructs, an approach that lends itself to radicalism.

Voltaire (1694–1778) was the epitome of the Enlightenment, doubting and ridiculing everything stupid he saw around him, of which there was plenty. His number one target: the Catholic church, which he saw as intolerant, irrational, and hypocritical. Voltaire's phrase, *"Ecrasez l'infâme"* ("crush the infamous thing"—meaning the Catholic church), became a rallying cry for anticlericalists—people opposed to Roman Catholic influence in society and politics—and spread through most of the Catholic countries of Europe.

The Baron de Montesquieu (1689–1755) traveled all over Europe to gather material for one of the first books of comparative politics, *The Spirit of the Laws.* Montesquieu, like Voltaire, was especially impressed with English liberties, which he thought resulted from the "checks and balances" of the different parts of their government. Montesquieu was actually describing an idealized model of an English system that had already passed into history, but the American Founding Fathers read him literally. Montesquieu's book suggested that countries could more or less rationally choose their governmental institutions. The French have been choosing and discarding them ever since.

Jean Jacques Rousseau (1712–1778), who was born in Geneva but lived mostly in France, was the most complex and some say the most dangerous of these thinkers. Rousseau hypothesized man in his original "state of nature" as free, happy, and morally good. What ruined him? Society was the culprit, corrupting man with private property, which leads to inequality and jealousy. Rousseau, in a famous phrase at the beginning of his book *The Social Contract,* said: "Man is born free but everywhere he is in chains." How can man be saved? Rousseau further hypothesized that beneath all the individual, petty viewpoints in society there is a "general will" for the common good. This general will could be discovered and implemented even though some people might object; they would be "forced to be free." Critics of Rousseau charge that he laid the intellectual basis for both nazism and communism in his theory of the general will because it provided dictators with the rationale that they "really know" what the people want and need.

The French political thinkers tended to call for major, sweeping change; English thinkers, for slow, cautious change. The French thinkers fundamentally hated their government; the English didn't.

FROM FREEDOM TO TYRANNY

In 1791 the National Assembly constructed a constitutional monarchy, and if things had stopped there, the French Revolution might have resembled the English Revolution of a century earlier. But the French constitutional monarchy was undermined from two sides, from the king and some aristocrats who wanted to restore absolute power and from a militant faction known as the Jacobins, who wanted a thorough revolution. The king was found to be conspiring with foreign monarchs to invade France and restore him to full power. And the attempted invasion of 1792 helped the Jacobins take over. With a makeshift but enthusiastic citizen army—"the nation in arms"—they repelled the invaders at Valmy.

Power fell into the hands of the misnamed Committee of Public Safety under Maximilien Robespierre, a provincial lawyer and fanatic follower of Rousseau who was determined to "force men to be free." Instituting the Reign of Terror, Robespierre and his followers guillotined more than twenty thousand people, starting with the king, queen, and nobles but soon spreading to anyone who doubted Robespierre. Finally, in 1794, Robespierre's comrades, afraid they might be next, guillotined *him*, and the Terror came to an end.

During all this turmoil, the army became more important, and especially one young artillery officer, the Corsican Napoleon Bonaparte, who had won fame leading French armies in Italy and Egypt. In 1799 a coup d'état overthrew the weak civilian Directory and set up a Consulate with Bonaparte as First Consul. Brilliant in both battle and civil reform, Napoleon crowned himself emperor in 1804.

A Tale of Two Flags

The Bourbon flag had been blue and white with fleur-de-lis (iris):

The post-Napoleon restoration brought back the old flag, for the tricolor symbolized everything the Bourbons hated. In 1830, the Orleanist monarchy, to mollify revolutionary sentiment, brought back the tricolor, France's flag ever since.

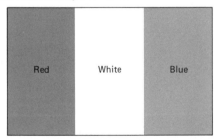

The Revolution introduced the tricolor of red, white, and blue.

The Original Chauvinist

> The original chauvinist was Nicolas Chauvin (pronounced *show-VAN*), a possibly fictitious Napoleonic soldier, who was so rabidly nationalistic his name be-
>
> came synonymous with blind patriotic fervor. The French Revolution and Napoleonic wars unleashed the concept of nationalism all over Europe.

Above all, Napoleon loved war. As Henry Kissinger has pointed out, a revolutionary power like France in the midst of hostile conservative monarchies can feel secure only by conquering all its neighbors. Napoleon made France master of all Europe, using dashing tactics and an enthusiastic army to crush one foe after another until at last they went too far. Facing a British-led coalition, harassed by guerrilla warfare in Spain, and frozen in the Russian winter, Napoleon was defeated and exiled to the Mediterranean island of Elba in 1814. The next year he tried a comeback and thousands of his old soldiers rallied around him to fight at Waterloo.

Napoleon left an ambiguous legacy. While he claimed to be consolidating the Revolution, he actually set up a tyrannical police state. Trying to embody Rousseau's elusive general will, Napoleon held several plebiscites, which he always won. Napoleon was not just a historic accident, though, for we shall see similar figures emerging in French politics. When a society is badly split, as France was over the Revolution, power tends to gravitate into the hands of a savior, and democracy doesn't have a chance.

A Theory of Revolution

The late Harvard historian Crane Brinton in 1938 published *The Anatomy of Revolution,* which argued that all revolutions pass through similar stages. He compared several revolutions, but his main model was the French. Brinton's stages:

- The old regime loses its governing effectiveness and legitimacy. It becomes inept and indecisive. Intellectuals especially become alienated from it. An improving economy provokes discontent and jealousy.

- The first stage of revolution comes with the growth of anti-regime groups. Triggering the revolution is a political problem—such as whether the three estates should meet separately or together—that the old regime can't handle. Rioting breaks out, but troops sent to crush it desert to the rioters. The anti-regime people easily take over power amidst popular rejoicing.

- Moderates initially seize power. They opposed the old regime but as critics rather than as revolu-

tionaries. They want major reform rather than total revolution. Extremists accuse them of being weak and cowardly, and true enough, they are not ruthless enough to crush the extremists.

- Extremists take over because they are more ruthless, purposeful, and organized than the moderates. In what Brinton likened to a high fever during an illness, the extremists whip up revolution to a frenzy, throwing out everything old, forcing people to be good, and punishing real or imagined enemies in a reign of terror. In France, this stage came with Robespierre; in Iran, with Khomeini.

- A "Thermidor," or calming-down period, ends the reign of terror. Brinton named Thermidor after the French revolutionary month—the revolutionaries even devised a new calendar—in which Robespierre fell. Every revolution has a Thermidor, which Brinton likened to a convalescence after a fever, because human nature can't take the extremists and their revolutionary purity for too long. Power usually then falls into the hands of a dictator, who restores order but not liberty—a Napoleon.

Brinton's theory became a classic and has largely stood the test of time. Revolutions do seem to pass through stages, although their timing cannot be predicted with accuracy. Iran, for example, has followed the Brinton pattern, but we still await Iran's Thermidor.

THE BOURBON RESTORATION

Europe breathed a sigh of relief once Napoleon was packed off to a remote island in the South Atlantic and the brother of Louis XVI was restored to the French throne as Louis XVIII. In what was called the Bourbon Restoration, exiles from all over Europe returned to France to try to claim their old rights.

The France they found was badly split. Most aristocrats hated the Revolution, while most commoners supported at least a version of it. The Catholic church was reactionary, for the Revolution had confiscated church lands and ended its fiscal privileges. French Catholics for generations hated the anticlericalist republicans and democrats, who in turn mistrusted the church. Remnants of the clerical-anticlerical split persist to this day. But France had also changed quite a lot in the quarter-century since the Revolution. Parliaments now counted for something; kings could no longer rule without them. The civil reforms of Napoleon were preserved. People insisted on equality before the law.

Great French Expressions: "They Learned Nothing and They Forgot Nothing."

Frenchmen who favored the Revolution considered the Bourbons arrogant fools. When the Bourbons and their aristocratic helpers returned with the Restoration, some Frenchmen said they were as bad as ever, that they had learned nothing from the revolutionary upheaval and had forgotten none of their old privileges. A related expression: *Quand Dieu a voulu punir la France, il a fait retirer les Bourbons.* ("When God wanted to punish France, he brought back the Bourbons.")

At first the French, tired from upheaval and warfare, accepted the Bourbons. But by 1830 the Bourbons proved to be as pig-headed as ever, and rioting broke out. In a semilegal switch, the liberal Duc d'Orleans, Louis-Phillipe, replaced the last Bourbon, Charles X. He too proved inept, and a small uprising in that revolutionary year of 1848 brought the Second Republic. This didn't last long either.

The French people tend to turn from tumultuous democracy to authoritarian rule. In 1848 they overwhelmingly elected Napoleon's self-proclaimed nephew, Louis Napoleon, as president. Using plebiscites, in 1852 he turned the Second Republic into the Second Empire with himself as Emperor Napoleon III. This brought two decades of peace and progress until Louis Napoleon allowed himself to be goaded into war with Prussia in 1870. Bursting with overconfidence, the French were quickly trounced. The Germans surrounded Paris and shelled it daily, but there was no French government that could surrender. In

Paris itself, a revolutionary take-over by workers brought the short-lived Paris Commune, which conservative French troops crushed, killing some twenty thousand Parisians. Karl Marx saw the Commune as the first proletarian uprising, and among leftists the Commune grew into a legend of worker power.

THE THIRD REPUBLIC

Amidst near anarchy, the Third Republic was born. It was a republic not because its founders were enthusiastic republicans—they were mostly monarchists—but because they couldn't agree on a monarch. Their first task was a humiliating peace with Germany that cost France the province of Alsace (which has many German-speaking people) plus a billion dollars in gold. The enraged French ached for revenge and transferred their traditional hatred of Britain to Germany.

Curiously, the accidental Third Republic turned out to be the longest-lasting French regime since the ancien régime. The Third Republic was basically fairly conservative and bourgeois. France was not healed during its long tenure; indeed, social tensions mounted. A reactionary Catholic right dreamed of an authoritarian system, while the left organized Socialist and later Communist parties. Economic and population growth was slow, and France slipped further behind the rapidly growing Germany.

Still, the Third Republic staggered through the ordeal of World War I. At first the French were delighted with a chance for revenge against Germany, but soon the appalling losses—a million and a half French lives—turned France bitter and defeatist even though they were on the winning side. France regained Alsace but had no stomach to fight again.

The defeatism played right into the hands of Nazi Germany, which swept easily through France in May–June 1940. Only one French tank column fought well; it was commanded by an obscure colonel named de Gaulle, who had been warning for years of the need to develop a better French armored force. The French thought they could prevent a repetition of the World War I bloodshed by hiding behind the Maginot Line, a supposedly invulnerable network of tunnels facing Germany. But fixed defenses can't move; the Germans simply went around them on the north.

The Dreyfus Affair

Nothing better illustrates the deep division of French society in the late nineteenth century than the trial of Captain Alfred Dreyfus, a Jewish officer on the French general staff. In 1894, accused of selling secrets to the Germans, Dreyfus was given a rigged military trial with fake evidence and sent to the infamous penal colony of Devil's Island for life. It soon became clear that Dreyfus could not possibly have been the culprit; he had been chosen by the bigoted military simply because he was a Jew, a handy scapegoat.

France split in two. Those defending Dreyfus—the *Dreyfusards*—felt they were defending the republican traditions of equality. These tended to be people on the left. Novelist Émile Zola published his famous letter *J'accuse!* (I accuse!), charging the government with covering up for the military. The *Antidreyfus-ards*—reactionary aristocrats, army officers, fanatic Catholics, and anti-Semites—grew equally passionate in defense of their prerevolutionary values. Virtually all French people took one side or the other; there was even street fighting.

Finally, in 1906, Dreyfus was exonerated. But his trial had left deep scars. It showed how underneath the beautiful, civilized veneer of *belle époque* France lurked the primitive passions of reaction and anti-Semitism. The lesson was not lost on one Viennese journalist covering the trial. Theodore Herzl was so shocked by the anti-Semitism he had seen in France that he immediately organized a world Zionist movement to save Jews from what he feared would be other, similar outbursts.

VICHY: FRANCE SPLITS AGAIN

The Germans largely let Frenchmen run occupied France. Named after the town of Vichy in central France where it was set up, the Vichy government was staffed by the same sort of reactionaries who earlier had reviled Dreyfus, people who hated democracy and admired the authoritarian Germans. The aged Marshal Pétain, hero of World War I, became chief of state, and an opportunistic politician, Pierre Laval, became premier without benefit of elections. Many French people thought Vichy was an improvement over the Third Republic which had permitted a left coalition, the Popular Front, to come to power in 1936. "Better the Nazis than the Communists," muttered Vichy supporters. French SS units fought in Russia. French police rounded up Jews for deportation to death camps. French workers volunteered to work in Germany. Although most French people today are loathe to admit it, many collaborated with the Germans and even liked them.

Other Frenchmen, however, hated the Germans and Vichy. Some joined the *Résistance*, a loosely knit underground network that sabotaged and spied on the Germans, rescued British and American airmen, and occasionally killed collaborators. Again France split. The Vichy period was, in the words of political scientist Stanley Hoffmann, "a Franco-French war."

The Resistance attracted French people of many political persuasions, but the left predominated. The Communists, who refused to attack Germans until the 1941 invasion of Russia, became the most effective *maquisards* (underground fighters) and emerged from the war with prestige and a good organization. The rallying point of the Resistance was Charles de Gaulle (promoted to general in the last days of the Third Republic), who broadcast from London: "France has lost a battle. But France has not lost the war!" Organizing French-speaking people around the world—France had sizable colonies, and thousands of able-bodied men fled from France—de Gaulle declared a provisional government comprised of "Free French" expatriates. Participating in military action in North Africa, the Normandy landings, and the liberation of Paris in 1944, the Free French Army was of considerable help to the Allies. During the war de Gaulle came to think of himself as the savior of France, a modern Joan of Arc.

THE FOURTH REPUBLIC

~1958

From 1944 to early 1946, de Gaulle headed a provisional government. A newly elected constituent assembly, dominated by parties of the left, drafted a constitution for the Fourth Republic that gave great power to the legislative branch. De Gaulle opposed the new constitution and resigned with the warning that the Fourth Republic would have the same institutional weaknesses as the Third. He retired to the small town of Colombey-les-Deux-Eglises, not to return to power until the people called him back to save France again late in the next decade.

He was right about the Fourth Republic resembling the Third: from its inception the Fourth was plagued by a weak executive, a National Assembly paralyzed by small squabbling parties, and frequent changes of cabinet. The result was, as before, *immobilisme*, the inability to solve big problems. Politicians played games with each other; they were good at wrecking but not at building

Still, like the Third Republic, the Fourth might have endured had it not been for the terrible problems of decolonization, problems the fractious parliamentarians could not solve. The first problem was Indochina, a French colony for nearly a century that was occupied by the Japanese in World War II and then reclaimed by France. War with the Communist-led Viet Minh broke out in 1946 and dragged on until the fall of the French fortress of Dienbienphu in 1954. (The United States came close to jumping into the Vietnam conflict that year but backed off.)

Indochina was a bad experience for France, but Algeria was worse. The French had been there since 1830, at first to vanquish pirates but later to settle. Close to a million Europeans dominated Algerian economic, social, and political life; Algeria was even declared a part of France. The revolt of Algerian nationalists started in 1956 with urban terrorism. This time the French army was determined to win. They hunted down nationalists and tortured them. When the civilian politicians in Paris got cold feet about the Algerian War, the French army in Algeria started to carry out a coup d'état in 1958. Paratroopers were ready to drop on their own country; France tottered on the brink of civil war. At the last minute both sides agreed to call back General de Gaulle. The army assumed he would keep Algeria French. (He didn't.) De Gaulle, acting as if he had known all along that history would recall him to lead France, demanded as his price a totally new constitution, one that would cure the ills of the Fourth Republic. He got it. In the next chapter, we explore the institutions of the Fifth Republic.

VOCABULARY BUILDING

ancien régime	chauvinist	Huguenots	Reign of Terror
anticlericalism	collaborator	*immobilisme*	Resistance
authoritarian	Commune	*intendants*	Restoration
Bastille	coup d'état	Jacobins	Sun King
belle époque	decolonization	*maquisards*	Thermidor
Bourbon	Dreyfus Affair	mercantilism	Third Estate
bourgeois	Estates-General	paternalism	Third Republic
Cartesian	Free French	plebiscite	Versailles
Charlemagne	general will	Popular Front	Vichy

FURTHER REFERENCE

Arendt, Hannah. *On Revolution.* New York: Viking, 1963.

Brinton, Crane. *The Anatomy of Revolution.* New York: Vintage Books, 1965.

Brogan, D.W. *The French Nation: From Napoleon to Pétain, 1814–1940.* New York: Harper & Row, 1957.

Cobban, Alfred. *A History of Modern France: III. 1871–1962.* Baltimore: Penguin Books, 1965.

Kohn, Hans. *Making of the Modern French Mind.* New York: Van Nostrand Reinhold, 1955.

Shirer, William L. *The Collapse of the Third Republic: An Inquiry into the Fall of France in 1940.* New York: Simon & Schuster, 1969.

Tocqueville, Alexis de. *The Old Regime and the French Revolution.* New York: Doubleday, 1955.

Williams, Stuart, ed. *Socialism in France: From Juarès to Mitterrand.* New York: St. Martin's Press, 1983.

Wright, Gordon. *France in Modern Times: 1760 to the Present.* Chicago: Rand McNally, 1960.

8

THE KEY
INSTITUTIONS

SEVENTEEN CONSTITUTIONS

The English constitution grew piecemeal and has never been formalized into one document. French constitutions—and there have been seventeen of them since the Revolution—are always spelled out with logic and clarity. Whereas the Americans regard their Constitution with an almost religious awe, not to be touched in its basic provisions, the French, and most other European countries, have seen constitutions come and go and are not averse to rewriting the basic rules of their political game every few decades.

By 1958, many French citizens agreed that the Fourth Republic was inherently flawed and unable to settle the ghastly Algerian War. The chief problem, as defined by de Gaulle, lay in the weakness of the executive, the premier. The president was simply a figurehead, typical of European republics. The premier (or prime minister) depended on unstable coalitions; faced with controversial issues, one or more coalition parties would usually drop out, vote against the government in a "vote of no-confidence," and thereby bring it down. In all, there were twenty cabinets, or "governments," in less than twelve years. Personal jealousies sometimes played a role; if a premier was too effective, other politicians sometimes voted against him out of resentment. Pierre Mendès-France, for example, settled the Indochina War in 1954, but that made him too popular and effective, and the National Assembly voted him out a few months later.

The Fourth Republic embodied all the weaknesses of a multiparty parliamentary system that still plague Italy. Such a system can work well and with stability, as in Sweden, but it depends on the *party* system and the national political style. Given French parties and political style, however, it is doubtful that a pure parliamentary system could ever work well. Accordingly, the French may have made a wise choice in going to a presidential system (see box).

A PRESIDENTIAL SYSTEM

Some define the Fifth Republic as a hybrid, or "quasi-presidential," system because of the ability of the National Assembly to censure a cabinet. But in most other areas the powers of the president are so overwhelming that we may safely call France a presidential or even "superpresidential" system. Some go so far as to label the French president an elected monarch or presidential dictator.

The French president is elected directly for seven years. In the original 1958 constitution the president was selected by an electoral college of parliamentarians and local office holders. But de Gaulle wanted nothing—certainly no politicians—to stand between him and the people, so in 1962, by means of a plebiscite, he changed the constitution to provide for direct election. There is no limit on the number of presidential terms.

Virtually all foreign and defense affairs are in the president's hands. Most legislation originates with the executive, the case worldwide now. As we shall see, in key areas the executive can *force* the National Assembly to vote on executive proposals in a simple yes-or-no manner. But de Gaulle had something greater than political dominance in mind when he constructed the French presidency. To de Gaulle the president should also be a "guide" for the nation's des-

Parliamentary Versus Presidental Systems

Most European governments are parliamentary; that is, they depend on votes in parliament to put a cabinet into executive power and keep it there. The cabinet is usually composed of members of parliament and can be seen as a sort of parliamentary steering committee that also guides the ministries or departments. If no party in parliament has a majority, a coalition of parties is necessary, and this may be unstable. In policy splits, a "vote of no-confidence" ousts the cabinet. Where a single party dominates the parliament—which is mostly the case in Britian—the system can be very stable.

A presidential system, such as the United States, does not depend on parliamentary support, for here the chief executive is elected more or less directly for a fixed term. The parliament can do what it wants, but it cannot oust the president in a vote of no-confidence. (In the United States, of course, Congress can impeach the president.) The advantages of a presidental system is its stability and certainty: there will always be a president to lead. The disadvantage is that the president and the legislature may deadlock, producing the same *immobilisme* that plagues parliamentary systems.

The French system has been called "quasi-presidential," for the cabinet still has a certain parliamentary connection. The cabinet is named by the president but can be censured and forced to resign by the National Assembly. If that happens—and it has occured only once, in 1962—the president can dissolve the legislature and hold new elections.

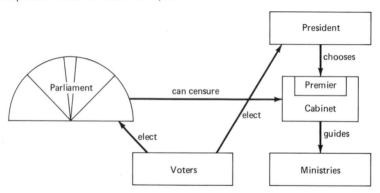

The French System. Compare with the parliamentary and presidential systems shown on p. 8.

tiny, an "arbiter" among its many interests. Under de Gaulle, who served as president from 1958 to 1969, the office took on almost mystical connotations, which it has since shed as less charismatic figures have occupied it.

One important power which de Gaulle especially liked to use is the calling of plebiscites or referendums. You'll recall that such mass votes on issues are alien to British tradition but very much a part of French usage, especially by Napoleonic figures who believe they embody the general will and communicate directly with the people, bypassing the politicians.

Another potentially Napoleonic power at the disposal of the French president is the prerogative to invoke "emergency powers" in time of danger to the nation. While many democracies have such an emergency provision, there is always the fear that it can be abused, as Hitler used Article 48 of the German constitution to snuff out freedom. Article 16 of the French constitution seems to place no limits on what a president can do during an emergency, a situation that is up to the president to define. During such an emergency the National Assembly must meet, but it has no power to veto presidential decisions. The emergency clause has been invoked only once—in 1961, when the same generals who put de Gaulle into power tried to overthrow him for pulling out of Algeria—and many agreed that it was a genuine national emergency. All one can say about the emergency-powers clause is that it hasn't been abused yet.

PREMIER AND CABINET

French ministers, including the prime minister, have been reduced to messenger boys for the president. Strictly speaking, a premier's main function now is legislative liaison to push presidential measures through parliament. Unlike the British cabinet, which contains fairly powerful politicians, the French cabinet is mostly staffed with experienced administrators, often apolitical technicians.

The French president chooses a premier and cabinet, who do not have to be approved by the National Assembly but usually are. The president picks whomever he wishes. A premier or cabinet member does not need to be a member of parliament as in Britain. Indeed, once named to the cabinet a minister must resign his or her seat. De Gaulle wanted to make sure his ministers wouldn't run back to parliament to protest his policies; by making them resign from the National Assembly he took away their political base and forum. De Gaulle picked as one of his premiers Georges Pompidou, a man who had absolutely no political experience.

The French cabinet, like the British, can be remade to suit the policy of the president and the personnel available. Ministries are not quite the same as U.S. departments, which are firmly fixed by statute and change only after great deliberation. Paris ministries are almost ad hoc combinations of existing French agencies and bureaus, which change as the president wishes. When Mitterrand came to power in 1981, for example, he named a cabinet of more than two dozen to carry out an ambitious program of Socialist change. With the French economy awry in 1984, he named a smaller cabinet with many combined portfolios (ministerial assignments) to carry out his new policy of retrenchment and lower expectations. In addition to the prime minister, there were only sixteen ministers (plus several subcabinet portfolios):

> Planning and Territorial Development
> Economy, Finance, and Budget
> Foreign Affairs
> Interior and Decentralization
> Industrial Redeployment and Foreign Trade
> Social Affairs and National Solidarity
> Town Planning, Housing, and Transport
> Trade, Crafts, and Tourism
> European Affairs

A Socialist Romantic for President

For its first twenty-three years, conservatives presided over the Fifth Republic: de Gaulle, Pompidou, and Giscard d'Estaing. But in 1981 France elected a Socialist president, François Mitterrand, and a National Assembly dominated by his Socialist party. But it was a pre-Marxist, very French, sort of socialism, one stressing humane and romantic values rather than economics. Symbolically, the elections of 1981 represented a swing back to the leftist and revolutionary half of France's longstanding political split. In practice, *hélas,* Mitterrand's presidency was a disappointment for most French. He promised more than the French economy could possibly deliver.

Mitterrand was born in 1916 in the Cognac region of southwest France, one of eight children of a Catholic and *petit bourgeois* family. As a student in Paris, he witnessed the 1936 triumph of the Popular Front; the mass enthusiasm rubbed off on him, and he turned to politics and away from the conservative Catholic church. In World War II, Sergeant Mitterrand was wounded in the chest and captured but escaped to the Resistance. Under the alias Morland, he supplied forged papers to fellow Resistance members. In the Fourth Republic he was repeatedly elected to parliament as a leader of several small centrist parties and served in eight cabinet posts, including the important position of interior minister under Pierre Mendès-France.

As de Gaulle consolidated his Fifth Republic, Mitterrand—who already hated de Gaulle for his haughty ways during the war—moved to the left. His plan was to strengthen the non-Communist left but to use the Communists when necessary to win elections. Mitterrand made a strong showing against de Gaulle in the 1965 presidential race. In 1971 he simultaneously joined and became the leader of the Socialist party, whose electoral fortunes were at a low ebb. Patiently building the PS, Mitterrand came in a close second to Giscard in 1974. In 1981, after France had had seven years of Giscard's aristocratic arrogance, Mitterrand won the presidency at age 64.

For a winning politician, Mitterrand is almost antipolitical. He prefers literature to politics. A shy intellectual, he has written eleven books, some of them conveying an almost mystical attachment to France and its revolutionary values. Said Mitterrand: "The soul of France lives in me."

(French Embassy Press & Information Division)

Labor, Employment, and Job Training
Research and Technology
Justice
Defense
Agriculture
Education
Environment

It was, doubtless, not Mitterrand's last cabinet structure: new policy, new cabinet.

Great French Expressions:
"Plus ça change, plus c'est la même chose."

The French, used to seeing cabinets come and go with no substantive change taking place, developed the cynical expression: "The more things change, the more they stay the same." The phrase perfectly sums up the contempt many French citizens felt toward the institutions of the Third and Fourth Republics.

By American standards the French cabinet is large and specialized. For Europe, where chief executives make and unmake ministries to suit their policy emphases, it is typical. Notice how many ministries are concerned with economic matters—at least six. The paternalism of the French government toward economic activity is a heritage of the *ancien régime*. Notice the mininstry that underscored Mitterrand's socialist emphasis on promoting equality: social affairs and national solidarity.

The interior ministry is especially important, for unlike the U.S. Department of the Interior, which deals with federal lands, a European interior ministry *controls* the entire interior of the contry. In France, for example, the national police force is under the interior minister, as are the agents of the Paris government in the ninety-six *départements* into which France is divided. When Mitterrand decentralized French politics, he gave the task to the interior minister.

THE NATIONAL ASSEMBLY

During the Third and Fourth Republics the National Assembly was dominant. Making and unmaking cabinets, the parliament controlled the executive. Some say this sort of parliamentary system has a weak executive and strong legislature. That's not quite accurate. In this case the legislature wasn't strong either. Divided into several quarrelsome parties that were unable to form stable coalitions, the French National Assembly was no more able to govern than were the cabinets.

To Americans this sounds like complete chaos. The government "fell" every few months on the average. This is not quite so horrendous as it sounds.

When a government in a parliamentary system "falls," it does not mean the entire structure of government collapses; indeed, little changes. It just means there has been a policy quarrel among the parties so that the cabinet coalition no longer commands a majority of the parliament. The cabinet then either resigns, is ousted in a vote of no confidence, or limps along as a minority government. After several days or even weeks of negotiations, another cabinet is put together that wins majority approval. Often this cabinet is composed of the same ministers in the same jobs as the previous cabinet. Instead of too much change, parliamentary systems often suffer from too little. Premiers have their hands so full just keeping the coalition together they are often unwilling to risk doing anything that might make it come apart. The result is *immobilisme*.

Meeting in the windowless Palais Bourbon, members of parliament, or deputies, prior to 1958 tended to play politics with each other and ignore what was happening outside. In a massive avoidance of responsibility, deputies concentrated on getting into the cabinet or, when unsuccessful, bringing it down. Things changed with the Fifth Republic; the legislators' paradise came to an abrupt end.

The National Assembly no longer makes cabinets; today that power belongs to the president who can name a new cabinet at will. Indeed, the relationship between the cabinet and legislature has been deliberately weakened; as noted earlier, a deputy named to the cabinet must resign his or her seat. One link does remain: the National Assembly can censure a cabinet. When that happens the president can dissolve (send home) the National Assembly for new elections before the end of its normal five-year term. The president is limited to one dissolution a year.

The president, not the legislature, now holds key powers of legislation. Most bills originate with the government. The government sets the agenda. If the government specifies, its proposals must be considered without amendments on a take-it-or-leave-it basis called a "blocked vote." That is to prevent parliamentary dilution of legislation. The National Assembly no longer has the time or structure to consider legislation closely: its sessions are limited to five and a half months a year; it has only six committees; and a bill cannot be bottled up in committee but must be reported out.

Comparing: The Italian Parliamentary System

Italy is the way France used to be: a weak executive dependent on a shaky coalition of parties elected by proportional representation. De Gaulle ended the Fourth Republic's parliamentary system and founded the Fifth's presidential. Italy stays classically parliamentary.

Italy's lower house, the 630-member Chamber of Deputies, is elected by proportional representation, a system that permits many parties to have at least a few seats in parliament. Italy has eight parties, none of them with a majority of deputies. Thus every Italian government since World War II has been a coalition and prone to breakup when the parties in it quarreled. There have been more than forty Italian cabinets since the war; the average life of each is ten months. As in Fourth Republic France, Italy suffers immobilism in the face of major problems.

A Senate That Fights Back

Most parliaments are composed of two chambers, and most don't know what to do with the upper chamber. Sweden simply abolished its upper house. The greatest value of an upper house is in representing territorial subunits, as the U.S. Senate represents the states. Where the system is unitary (Britain, France, Sweden) rather than federal (the United States, West Germany, Yugoslavia), an upper chamber doesn't have much use.

France's main legislative body, comparable to the British House of Commons, is also the lower house, the 491-member National Assembly elected every five years (or sooner in case of dissolution). The upper house, the *Sénat,* has 316 members elected for nine years each—with elections for about a third every three years—by a gigantic electoral college made up of National Assembly deputies plus more than 100,000 regional and municipal councilors. De Gaulle thought that these councilors, because they would disproportionately represent rural and small-town France, would produce a conservative Senate amenable to Gaullist direction.

Rural and small-town France is not necessarily conservative; it looks out for farming. Above all, the *Sénat* represents farmers' viewpoints; it has been called the agricultural chamber. The French Senate has critized and amended numerous government bills. *Sénateurs* aren't under pressure like lower-house assembly members to pass what the government wants. The French Senate is listened to by the government on farm matters, for when French farmers get mad they can create havoc. Still, when the government wants a measure passed, it can override Senate objections by a simple majority in the National Assembly.

The French Senate, although not equal in power to the National Assembly, cannot be dissolved by the government. Apparently de Gaulle came to regret that he had allowed the Senate an autonomous existence, for in 1969 he tried to dilute its power by means of another plebiscite. The French people, annoyed by de Gaulle, supported their Senate, the last area of French parliamentary freedom, and rejected the referendum.

The government is able to pass many laws by simple decree. The 1958 constitution specifies the types of laws that must go through parliament; all others presumably don't need to. While most decrees concern details, the power of government decree also extends to the budget. Here the legislature has lost its original, most fundamental, power—the power of the purse. Any parliamentary motion to either decrease revenues (for example, a tax cut) or increase spending (for example, a new program) are automatically out of order. And if the parliament can't settle on the budget within seventy days, the government may make it law by simple decree.

THE PARTIES

Parties can make or break a political system. Britain's stability and efficiency would diminish if instead of one party with a solid majority in Commons there were half a dozen parties of about equal size. Much of what was wrong with the Third and Fourth Republics was not government institutions but the parties that tried to operate them.

We must avoid evaluating all two-party systems as good and all multiparty systems as bad. Americans especially are disdainful of multiparty systems and often cite Italy and the Fourth Republic as examples of the ills they create. But several multiparty parliamentary democracies with institutions not too different from Italy's and the Fourth Republic's are stable and effective: Sweden, Switzerland, Holland, and Belgium. At least as much depends on the way the parties behave as on how many parties there are.

By the same token, the Fifth French Republic wouldn't have worked the way it did had not the Gaullist party ballooned into the largest of all French parties. Indeed, if the Fourth Republic had been preserved but with Gaullists occupying a large slice of the National Assembly, the most troublesome problem of that system—*immobilisme*—would have disappeared, for de Gaulle would have had a stable majority at his disposal. If one day the president is of one party while opposition parties dominate the National Assembly, the Fifth Republic may deadlock between executive and legislature, as sometimes happens in another presidential system, the United States. Some observers fear this deadlock will occur in the legislative elections due in 1986: a Socialist president facing a conservative National Assembly.

France has at present four important parties and several small ones. We could call France a "four-plus" party system. Two of the big parties are on the right—the Gaullists and Republicans—and two are on the left—the Communists and Socialists. Some small parties are on the extremes of the political spectrum— Trotskyists and racists—but only occasionally do they get elected to parliament. In the center, a couple of small parties have long managed to get a few deputies into the National Assembly, but now they rarely play an important role.

The electoral system of the Fifth Republic is actually taken from the Third Republic. Like English and American systems, the French have single-member districts for the 491 seats in the National Assembly. But unlike the Anglo-American systems, where a simple plurality is all that's required to win, the French victor needs a majority (more than 50 percent). If the candidate doesn't get it on the first ballot—and that is usually the case—the contest goes to a run-off election a week later, this time with parties that got under 12.5 percent eliminated and only a simple plurality needed to win. (see box, "The Two Elections of 1981").

Following up on a 1981 campaign pledge, the Mitterrand government brought back proportional representation (PR) for the 1986 National Assembly elections. Instead of single-member districts with run-offs, the new PR system— actually a return to the system of the Fourth Republic—has multi-member districts and only one round. Voters cast a ballot for a party, not an individual, and seats are awarded according to the percentage won by each party. Critics charged Mitterrand with changing the rules to favor his Socialist party, which had been sliping in the polls. Some predicted a return to the chaos of the Fourth Republic.

The return to PR could reverse the tendency of the French party system to coalesce into two big blocs. PR takes away the incentive for small parties to combine into bigger ones. One expected result of PR was the entry of the small, racist, National Front party into the legislature.

A DECENTRALIZED UNITARY SYSTEM

Both Britain and France are unitary systems, concentrating power in the capital. France used to be more strongly unitary than Britain, where cities and countries

The Two Elections of 1981

The back-to-back elections of 1981—the first for the presidency, the second for the National Assembly—illustrated the working of the French electoral system. Both were conducted in two rounds. The first round of the presidential election on April 26 produced the following results:

Valéry Giscard d'Estaing (Republican)	28.3%
François Mitterrand (Socialist)	25.8%
Jacques Chirac (Gaullist)	18.0%
Georges Marchais (Communist)	15.3%
Brice Lalonde (Ecologist)	3.9%

All but the top two were eliminated for the second round two weeks later, on May 10, which produced the following result:

François Mitterrand	51.8%
Valéry Giscard d'Estaing	48.2%

Immediately upon his inauguration as president on May 21, Mitterrand dissolved the National Assembly and ordered new elections. The old parliament was dominated by parties of the right—Republicans and Gaullists—and Socialist Mitterrand knew they would not pass his program of major reforms. The first round of elections for the new legislature, on June 14, gave these results:

Socialists	37.5%
Gaullists	20.8%
Union for French Democracy (Giscardians)	19.2%
Communists	16.2%
Ecologists	1.1%

In this first round, 136 candidates won actual majorities, leaving the remaining 355 seats to be decided in the second round a week later on June 21. In each district, candidates who polled less than 12.5 percent were dropped. By prearrangement, Socialist or Communist candidates withdrew where they were weaker and urged supporters to vote for the stronger left party. In most constituencies this meant the Communist candidate withdrew and instructed Communist voters to vote for the Socialist in the run-off. Gaullists and Giscardians had a similar but weaker trade-off arrangement. The results of the final round and the number of seats each party won:

Socialists (and allies)	49.0%	289
Gaullists	22.4%	83
Union for French Democracy (Giscardians)	18.3%	61
Communists	6.9%	44

The Socialist landslide gave Mitterrand an absolute majority in the National Assembly to work with and enabled him to return to proportional representation for the 1986 National Assembly elections.

enjoy a certain autonomy. Under Mitterrand, though, France decentralized, rolling back a tradition that started with Louis XI. French monarchs tried to erase regional differences but sometimes only worsened local resentments. Napoleon perfected this centralizing and homogenizing pattern. He abolished the historic provinces and replaced them with smaller, artificial units called *départements,* many named after rivers. The *départements* were administrative conveniences to facilitate control by Paris. Each *département*—there are now ninety-six—was administered by a *prefect,* a lineal descendant of Richelieu's old *intend-*

ant, now an official of the interior mininstry. It got to be pretty absurd; towns had to ask Paris if they could put in a new traffic light or pave a street. Prefects, very bright and highly trained, monitored laws, funds, and mayors with Olympian detachment.

In 1982, Mitterrand approved a law that reduced the domain of prefects to little more than police and fire departments and retitled them "commissioners of the Republic." Elected councils in the *départements* and regions (there are twenty-two regions, each comprising two to eight *départements*) won policy-setting and taxation powers in education, urban and regional planning and development, job training, and housing. In short order, French local and regional government became more important, and elections to their councils were hotly contested. Ironically, Mitterrand's conservative opponents won most of these elections. France in no sense became a federal system—indeed, its decentralization didn't go as far as Spain's during this same period (see box)—but it was probably Mitterrand's most important and lasting contribution to the French political system.

Comparing: Spain Tries Regional Autonomy

Over the centuries, Spain copied France in trying to impose a tightly centralized system on a country that didn't always like it. The Spanish kings never succeeded in crushing feelings of regionalism as well as the French kings did. Across the north of Spain, Catalonia, the Basque country (which also spills over into France), and Galicia preserve their distinctive languages and cultures. During the brief First Spanish Republic (1873) and Second Republic (1931–36), regions set up their own governments, both times crushed by the army. Under the authoritarian Franco, these areas were treated like conquered provinces, and this created all the more resentment against rule by Madrid. A Basque terrorist group, ETA, emerged in the 1970s to fight for independence by murdering dozens of policemen and officials.

After Franco's death in 1975, the democratic governments of Spain moved to defuse the issue by granting the various regions far-reaching autonomy, if they asked for it. Because this autonomy is voluntary it has been uneven. Catalonia and the Basque country set up their own regional governments with considerable powers in education, police, and taxation. Other areas with less regional consciousness were slower to take advantage of autonomy. Although not a federal system, the Spanish experiment greatly alters Spain's centralized, unitary system. And there's the rub: if the Spanish army feels regional autonomy is getting out of hand, it might pull a military coup, as it has done many times and attempted in 1981. As in France, the habits of a centralized state are hard for many to surrender.

VOCABULARY BUILDING

apolitical	*department*	liaison	Republican
blocked vote	deputy	multiparty	run-off
center	emergency powers	parliamentary	Socialist
coalition	Gaullist	system	technician
Communist	interior ministry	prefect	unitary
decree	left	presidential system	

FURTHER REFERENCE

Blondel, Jean. *The Government of France.* New York: Harper & Row, 1974.

Hayward, J.E.S. *Governing France: The One and Indivisible Republic,* 2d ed. New York: W.W. Norton, 1983.

King, Jerome. "Valéry Giscard d'Estaing and the French Government," in *Governments and Leaders: An Approach to Comparative Politics,* ed. by Edward Feit. Boston: Houghton Mifflin, 1978.

MacShane, Denis. *François Mitterrand: A Political Odyssey.* London: Universe Press, 1983.

Pickles, Dorothy. *The Government and Politics of France: I. Institutions and Parties.* London: Methuen & Co., 1972.

Pierce, Roy. *French Politics and Political Institutions,* 2d ed. Lanham, Md.: University Press of America, 1983.

Safran, William. *The French Polity,* 2d ed. New York: David McKay, 1985.

Williams, Philip M. *The French Parliament: Politics in the Fifth Republic.* New York: Praeger, 1968.

9

FRENCH POLITICAL ATTITUDES

LOVE AND HATE

An older Frenchman I knew in Toulouse told me of one of his World War II comrades, a Communist who used to rail against French capitalists, the crooked government, and the rotten system. Why then was he fighting in the war, my acquaintance asked him? "Why, for France, of course!" The Frenchman who loves France but hates other Frenchmen illustrates a kind of schizophrenia that runs generally through French society and French psyches.

This French Communist was making a distinction—as do most French people—between the real and the ideal. He hated the real, unjust, day-to-day France in which he lived, its capitalists and its crooks. But the ideal France, a beautiful land of liberty, equality, and fraternity, he loved. The English, stodgy pragmatists, do not suffer from such a split in their thinking about England; they live in the real world. The Germans, on the other hand, are capable of even greater idealism, often dreadfully misplaced, than are the French.

"La Marseillaise"

Possibly the world's greatest national anthem is the French *"Marseillaise."* Dashed off in a single night in 1792 by a 32-year-old army officer, Rouget de Lisle, to accompany volunteers from Marseille headed north to defend the Revolution, the *"Marseillaise"* soon became the Revolution's and then France's anthem.

Extremely stirring and bloodthirsty, it is the perfect song for fighting for a nation. The refrain:

Aux armes, citoyens, formez vos bataillons!

Marchons! Marchons!
Qu'un sang impur abreuve nos sillons!

If you've never heard it sung, try to catch the movie *Casablanca* the next time it's on television.

Like the French flag, the *"Marseillaise"* became a controversial political symbol. Part of the Revolution, it was banned by Napoleon and the Bourbons, accepted by the liberal Orleans monarch in 1830, banned again by Napoleon III, and made permanently the national anthem in 1879.

France has a mystique, a kind of strange drawing power that can attract equally conservatives such as de Gaulle and Socialists such as Mitterrand. The conservatives are drawn to French civilization, its Catholic roots, and its *grandeur* (greatness). Liberals and leftists, on the other hand, are drawn to the ideals of the French Revolution—liberty, equality, and fraternity—and see France as the repository of these ideals. Some French envision their land as a person, a princess, or even a Madonna. They have a reverence for their country that few Americans or Britons can match. The dramatic and stirring French national anthem, *"La Marseillaise"* (see box), gives one a feeling of the depth of French patriotism.

French patriotism in the abstract, however, does not carry over into the real, grubby, daily life of French politics. The French are usually far more cynical about politics than Britishers or Americans. France in the abstract is glorious; France in the here and now is shabby. This is why de Gaulle said France needs national greatness, for only with a vision of something great can French people rise above the sordid reality and pursue the mythical ideal.

Mitterrand was elected in part because of his ability to project an idealistic vision of France with a leftist twist. "It is natural for a great nation to have great ambitions," he proclaimed. "In today's world, can there be a loftier duty for our country than to achieve a new alliance between socialism and liberty?" The French liked the sentiment, but once Mitterrand was in power they grew quickly disillusioned with the reality.

HISTORICAL ROOTS OF FRENCH ATTITUDES

Where did this French political schizophrenia come from? Part of the problem is historical, traceable to the centralization of French kings, who implanted an omnipotent state, a state that tried to supervise everything. In theory, a centralized system should be excellent, capable of planning and building rationally. In practice, it often falls far short of the goal. Frenchmen, trained to expect a powerful government to help them (the ideal), are always disappointed when it doesn't (the real).

French paternalism also stunted the development of a voluntary do-it-ourselves attitude, something that is common in the United States. France simply has no tradition of voluntary groups of neighbors undertaking local governance. When local groups take responsibility and something goes wrong, you can only blame yourselves. In France, with all responsibility until recently in the hands of the central government, the people blame Paris.

Centuries of bureaucratized administration also left the French used to living by uniform, impersonal rules—and lots of them. This creates hatred, the hatred of the little citizen on one side of the counter facing the cold, indifferent bureaucrat on the other.

Centralization and bureaucratization are the products of the "order and reason" approach to governance that has been practiced in France for centuries. Order and reason, unfortunately, are mere ideals. Since they are always deficient in practice, the French become unhappy with a reality that always falls short of ideals.

A CLIMATE OF MISTRUST

In personal relations French people are often distant and mistrustful to anyone outside their family. Indeed attitudes of mistrust are widespread throughout Latin Europe—they are extremely pronounced in Italy—while trustful attitudes are more common in Northern Europe. The American scholar Laurence Wylie found villagers in the Vaucluse, in the south of France, constantly suspicious of *les autres,* "the others," those outsiders who talk behind your back, blacken your name, and meddle in your affairs. The best way to live, people there agreed, was to not get involved with other people and to maintain only correct but distant relations with neighbors.

Foreigners notice how shut off the French family is. Typical French houses are surrounded by high walls often topped by broken glass set in concrete. Shutters aren't just for decoration; they bang shut as if to tell the world to mind its own business. Traditionally, French people do not entertain friends at home—they'll go to a restaurant instead, for inviting outsiders to your table is an invasion of family privacy. This attitude, however, is changing; I have been invited into several French homes for superb meals.

Great French Expressions:
"L'enfer, c'est les autres."

French philosopher and playwright Jean- Paul Sartre voiced a very French feeling about interpersonal relationships when he wrote, "Hell is other people." He meant, in his play *No Exit,* that having to get along with other people was his idea of hell. But it was a peculiarly French vision of hell, and Sartre could have more accurately said, "Hell is other Frenchmen."

Special mistrust is reserved for the government. In Wylie's village it was taken for granted that all government is bad, a necessary evil at best. The elaborate duties of a good citizen that schoolchildren memorize in their civics course are lovely ideals, but in the real world government is corrupt, intrusive, and ineffective. French children learn to love *la patrie* in the abstract but to disdain politics in the here and now. Politics are also best kept private and personal; discussing politics with others only leads to arguments. Besides, it's none of their business.

THE NASTY SPLIT

Catholic countries have a serious problem that Protestant countries don't have to worry about: the role of the Church. When Britain and Sweden broke with Rome and established national churches, they also subordinated churchmen to the state. The Anglican church in Britain and the Lutheran church in Sweden depended strictly on London and Stockholm for support; they could not turn to Rome. As a result, in these societies the church no longer played an independent political role.

French and American Party Identification

In a famous study, Philip E. Converse and Georges Dupeux compared French and American party identification. What they found was startling. Most Americans were able to quickly identify which party they preferred; most French people could not. Where did this difference come from? Converse and Dupeux also found that 76 percent of Americans could name their *father's* party while only 25 percent of the French could even specify their father's general political tendency (left or right). Many French respondents reported that their fathers had never talked about politics.

The Converse-Dupeux study illustrates that in French families, politics is not a fit topic for conversation. This lack of political guidance from the old generation to the young contributes to political confusion in France, for example, the rather rapid shift in votes between parties and the quick rise and fall of "flash" parties. People who have not been socialized by their family toward one party or another are like ships without anchors, easily moved from one party to another.

In Latin European countries—France, Italy, Spain—the Roman Catholic faith retained its political power, supporting conservative regimes and getting special privileges such as control of education, tax exemption for church lands, and a considerable say in government policy. Because of this temporal power, many people in Latin Europe developed antichurch attitudes. Their most brilliant spokesman was Voltaire (see chapter 7). "Anticlericalism," as it was called, was not necessarily antireligion; it rather sought to get the church out of government, what Americans call the separation of church and state. Anticlericalism spread in Latin Europe, especially among intellectuals, so that after the French Revolution and later Italian unification many people wanted a purely secular state, that is, one with no church influence in government. That was easy to do in America, where there was no single established church, but it was hard in France, Italy, and Spain, where church and state were intertwined. To separate them required drastic surgery: sale of church lands, banning of some Catholic orders such as the Jesuits, and state rather than church control of schools. The reaction to this was predictable. Just as the Republic was anticlerical, the church turned anti-Republic. Church sentiment went from conservative to reactionary, and the Roman Catholic faith became a pillar of monarchical restoration because that meant a return of church privileges.

Comparing: The Instability of Split Societies

Unlike the stable and settled countries of northern Europe, such as Britain and Sweden, the countries of Latin Europe continued to experience political upheavals well into our century. In France, Italy, and Spain, regimes have tended to be personal creations (e.g., those of de Gaulle, Mussolini, and Franco) that often end with the demise of their creator.

The underlying factor in this instability seems to be the split quality of French, Italian, and Spanish political life that is rooted in their histories. Roughly half the population of each country is Catholic and conservative and favors strong executive leadership; the other half is anticleical and liberal or radical and favors a strong parliament. The center is very small; people in Latin Europe tend to identify with either the left of right camp, each severely mistrusting the other. When the right is in power—historically, most of the time—the left denounces the government with shrill Marxist rhetoric as the tool of the capitalists. When the left is in power—curiously, in the mid-1980s the heads of government of France, Spain, Portugal, Italy, and Greece were all socialists—the right denounces them as dangerous incompetents, possibly serving Moscow's interests. At any given time, roughly half the country regards the government as illegitimate, and this stunts feelings of legitimacy about government in general. In Latin Europe, few take pride in their nation's governmental institutions.

In the absence of shared values and underlying consensus, political difficulties can lead to violence, coups, and even civil war which in turn leads to authoritarian rule. In the 1930s, Spain split into left and right camps and exploded into a vicious civil war won by the Catholic and conservative forces of General Franco. Disgruntled rightists in the Spanish military attempted a coup as recently as 1981. Portugal had a coup in 1974. France in 1958 very nearly had a military coup. In opposition, François Mitterrand referred to the Gaullist constitution as a "permanent coup." (In office, he found the powers it gave him as president really weren't so bad.)

In this way conservative France retained its Catholic viewpoint, while revolutionary France became strongly anticlerical. The battle raged for more than a century. At one point the Vatican instructed faithful Catholics to steer clear of any political involvement with the "Jacobin" Republic. During the Dreyfus affair, French clericalists and anticlericalists lined up neatly on opposing sides. Finally, in 1905 the National Assembly completed the separation of church and state; France no longer had an established church.

The political traditions that grew out of this split were extremely lively. Until this century, to be in favor of the Republic meant to be anticlerical. The great premier during World War I, Georges Clemenceau, *le tigre,* was a passionate republican and supporter of Dreyfus. He recalled how his father used to tell him: "There's only one thing worse than a bad priest—and that's a good one."

French Elections:
The Persistence of Religion

The second ballot of the 1974 French presidential election provides a graphic illustration of how religion is still part of politics in France. With other candidates eliminated in the first ballot, the race was between Socialist François Mitterrand on the left and Republican Valéry Giscard d'Estaing on the right. A poll showed the more religious were also the more conservative.*

	PERCENT FOR MITTERRAND	PERCENT FOR GISCARD D'ESTAING
Catholic (devout)	23	77
Catholic (practicing a little)	49	51
Catholic (nominal)	74	26
No religion	86	14

*SOFRES survey reproduced in Howard R. Penniman, ed., *France at the Polls: The Presidential Election of 1974* (Washington, D.C.: American Enterprise Institute, 1975), 203.

Even to this day, the parties of the French left—Socialist and Communist—draw their supporters most heavily from the anticlerical tradition. The parties of the right—Gaullist and Republican—attract mostly people from the prochurch tradition. Indeed, in all of Latin Europe—Italy, Spain, and Portugal as well as France—if you know how often a person goes to Mass you can usually predict his or her vote; strongly Catholic almost automatically means politically conservative.

Some 90 percent of French babies are baptized into the Catholic faith, but less than one-quarter of French people regularly attend Mass. Wide areas of France are considered "dechristianized," and the Catholic church has adopted missionary tactics to try to reclaim these lost souls. After World War II, the French church sent "worker priests" into factories to work beside and win over such people. The experiment had to be called off, however, when the worker priests started picking up the leftist attitudes of their fellow toilers; some priests even expressed sympathy for the Communists.

Although the great battles between clericalists and anticlericalists have subsided, some issues are capable of reawakening the old quarrel. The abortion controversy in France split people along the old lines, as did the question of state control of church schools. Once established, social and political cleavages have tremendous staying power.

French Elections:
The Persistence of Region

In 1936 the leftist Popular Front won in the shaded *départements* (map left). In 1981, Socialist François Mitterrand won the presidency with a very similar pattern (map right). Region, as well as social class and religion, often produces distinct and durable voting patterns.

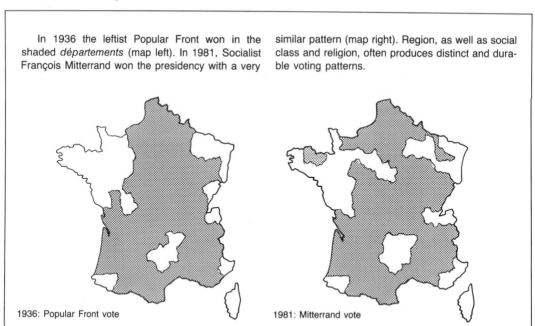

1936: Popular Front vote

1981: Mitterrand vote

SCHOOL FOR GRINDS

Another contributor to French political attitudes is schooling. The curriculum was set generations ago and is changed only slowly and reluctantly. Heavy on rote memorization, French education tends to produce diligent grinds rather than lively intellects. Even small children lug home briefcases bulging with books. A "good" child is one who puts in long homework hours.

Until recently, everywhere in the country French children learned the same thing, as established by the ministry of education in Paris, with no local input. One legendary story has it that some decades ago an education minister looked at his watch and told an interviewer what Latin verb was being conjugated all over France. Since then, the French school curriculum has become less centralized and less classical.

The curious thing about the standardized, memorized French education, however, is its deeply humanistic and individualistic content. Outwardly, French schoolchildren appear to be mechanically digesting the inflexible, unimaginative curriculum; inwardly, they are exposed to ideas that would be banned in many American schools. This tension between outward conformity and inward freedom gives rise to privatistic attitudes and occasional eruptions of rebellion. It encourages young French people to keep their thoughts to themselves. In this way, a set, rigid educational pattern may actually contribute to French individualism.

The French pride themselves on the equality of educational opportunity their system offers. "No English-style private schools for the rich here," they seem to say, "with us, everybody has the same chance." This picture is not quite accurate. While the French school system on paper is open to all, the lofty *content* of French education is tilted toward the children of middle- and upper-class homes. Working-class and peasant children, not exposed at home to correct speech—and the French are maniacs on their language—or abstract, intellectual thoughts, start disadvantaged in the school system and are often discouraged from staying in school beyond age 16.

The great gateway to social, economic, and political power in France is the *lycée,* the elite high school. Napoleon developed them with an eye to training army officers. *Lycées* are state-run. Admission is competitive, and the curriculum is demanding. Not all communities have *lycées,* which are concentrated in cities. A successful student completes the *lycée* with an examination at age 18 and gets a *baccalauréat,* which entitles the student to automatic university admission. About 25 percent of French young people earn the "*bac,*" and they tend to be from better-off families.

How Would You do on the "Bac"?

In about twelve hours of nationwide essay exams spread over a week, France's 17-or-18-year-old *lycéens* face questions like these, from the philosophy section of a recent *baccalauréat* exam. How would you do? Choose one. Spend no more than two hours.

• Why defend the weak?

• Comment on Rousseau's declaration that "one must have societies where inequality is not too great, where the tyranny of opinion is moderated and where voluptuousness reigns more than vanity."

• What is it to judge?

• Is it reasonable to love?

To put it mildly, the education one receives at a *lycée* is quite different from that of an American high school.

THE "GREAT SCHOOLS"

Just as Oxford and Cambridge tower over other English universities, the *grandes écoles* of France are the elite of French higher education. French universities, which stress the "impractical" liberal arts, have long been regarded as unimportant. To get into a French university is not hard; indeed, so many have flooded the lecture halls that standards have dropped and graduates have trouble getting jobs. The Great Schools are something else. Skimming off the brightest and most motivated French youths by means of rigorous entrance exams, the schools train (rather than "educate") them in the practical matters of running a country and then place them in top civil-service and managerial positions.

The Great Schools form the people who run France. No other country has anything quite like them. It would be as if West Point produced not army officers but leading administrators instead. Some denounce the *grandes écoles* as elitist and undemocratic, but few suggest abolishing them. Indeed, their stanglehold on French leadership seems to grow stronger.

Although there are several Great Schools, the three most important are all in Paris. The *Ecole Polytechnique* was used by Napoleon to train military engineers. Called *X* for short, *xiens* have their pick of technology and management jobs when they graduate. The *Ecole Normale Superieur,* founded by Napoleon to create loyal *lycée* instructors, still produces many of France's leading intellectuals—among its graduates have been Jean-Paul Sartre, Raymond Aron, and President Georges Pompidou. The newest Great School, founded just after World War II, is the *Ecole Nationale d'Administration* (ENA), which quickly became the most important. Many of the country's top civil servants are "enarchs," as they call themselves.

Like all Great Schools, the ENA is extremely selective. This means that the best *lycée* background is necessary, which in turn means that a working-class youth doesn't have much of a chance. Only about 10 percent of the three hundred ENA students are from working-class families. Even after a year or two of cramming for the entrance *concours,* usually less than one applicant in ten passes to join the entering class of a hundred or so. Once in, ENA students get about $600 a month during their three-year program; about half of their time is spent interning in government ministries.

Upon graduation, rewards are great. At age 25, the average ENA graduate obtains a high position in government or diplomatic service. About one-third of France's prefects and ambassadors are ENA graduates. The current prime minister, Laurent Fabius, graduated from both the *Ecole Normale Superieur* and ENA.

Training in a Great School epitomizes the best and the worst of French education. You have to be very smart and hard working. But you also have to be cold, logical, and removed from ordinary people. Products of the *grandes écoles* may be brilliant, but they often lack common sense and humanity. Some critics call them, pejoratively, "technocrats," people who rule by technical skills.

THE FEAR OF "FACE TO FACE"

Whatever the educational institution—*lycée,* university, or Great School—the teaching style is similar: cold, distant, uninvolved. Class discussion is discouraged. Questions are from the instructor, not the students. When I taught at the University of Toulouse I was determined to break this pattern; I urged and demanded that my students ask questions and participate in discussion. The result was stony silence; what I requested was totally outside the experience of French students.

Rule of the Enarchs

In 1981 the outgoing conservative cabinet of Valéry Giscard d'Estaing had seven graduates of the elite *Ecole Nationale d'Administration* (ENA), including Giscard himself (class of 1951). The new incoming Socialist cabinet of François Mitterrand had eight ENA graduates. In 1984 Mitterrand named ENA graduate Laurent Fabius ('73) as prime minister. Paris governments may come and go, but the "enarchs" seem to be always in command.

By the time they are teenagers, French adolescents have picked up one of the basic characteristics of French culture, what sociologist Michel Crozier called *"l'horreur du face-à-face."* Aside from family and intimate friends, French people feel uncomfortable with warm, cozy, face-to-face relationships. Sometimes tourists say the French are unfriendly to foreigners. They really aren't; they are simply distant and formal to everyone, including other French people. The French style is opposite that of the American, which places a premium on informality and friendliness. In the United States everyone is supposed to be outgoing, call others by their first names, smile, and say, "Have a nice day." Such behavior—much of it shallow—boggles the French mind.

To avoid face-to-face relationships, the French prefer a highly structured system with clear but very limited areas of competence and set, impersonal rules. That way people know exactly where they stand and nobody butts into another's private domain. British-style pragmatism and "muddling through" are definitely not the French style.

FREEDOM OR AUTHORITY?

The points discussed so far—the lack of trust, fear of face-to-face relationships, rigid and rote education—all contribute to a French political personality that can't quite make up its mind whether it wants freedom or authority. Actually, it wants both, the abstract *liberté* extolled by philosophers and the controlled hierarchies built for centuries by French bureaucrats. What happens is compartmentalization: the private French person loves freedom, while the public French person—in school, on the job, facing the bureaucracy—knows he or she needs reason, order, and formal, impersonal rules. The typical Frenchman has been described as an anarchist who secretly admires the police, but it would be equally valid to call him a policeman who secretly admires the anarchists.

The result of this mental split is a continual longing for freedom and a perfect society but an almost equally continual surrender to authority and a highly imperfect society. The balance is unstable; from time to time the quest for liberty bursts out as in 1789, 1830, 1848, the Paris Commune of 1871, and the Events of May of 1968. We will explore this pattern more fully in the next chapter, but it is interesting to note that each of these outbursts ended with a surrender to authority. French political culture has been described as limited authoritarianism accompanied by potential insurrection.

Legitimacy in France is weaker than in Britain. Rather than a strong feeling of the rightness of institutions and authority, many French accord their system only half-hearted support. A few, on the extreme left and right, hate it.

SOCIAL CLASS

At least as much as Britain, France is a class society. The gap between working and middle class is substantial and—with the educational system slanted in favor of middle-class children—there is not a great deal of social mobility. In France, as in Britain, if you're born into the working class you'll probably stay there. Dis-

French and American Press Conferences: A Study in Contrasts

A French presidential press conference offers a quick insight into French political style. A rare event—maybe once or twice a year—the press conference takes place in an imposing salon of the Elysée Palace, the French White House. The president is seated. On the wall behind him is either a brocade or tapestry. In keeping with the elegant setting, the president is attired in a conservative suit and plain tie.

The journalists sit quietly taking notes. The president expounds abstractly on progress, national greatness, reason, and order, like a professor giving a lecture. He speaks beautiful French, slowly and clearly, with utter confidence and literate, witty phrases, for he is the product of an elite education. Then, if there's time, the president takes a few questions from the reporters. The questions are polite, even timid, for no one dares try to catch or embarrass the president. The president in return treats the journalists like small children who do not understand the logic and clarity of his policies. The president is, in keeping with French political style, magisterial, rational, and aloof.

The American presidential press conference, held more frequently, takes place against a plain blue backdrop. The president stands at a lectern. He is wearing an indifferent suit and striped tie. The president is nervous and ill at ease, for he knows that the newspeople are out to get him, just as they have been out to get every president. As they see it, that's their job. Little beads of perspiration break out on his brow. He offers a few opening remarks in an almost defensive tone to explain his recent actions. Then, with a forced smile, he throws the conference open to questions from the floor. The journalists descend like a wolf pack, clawing at the air with their upraised hands, each one demanding attention.

The newsperson called upon—often by name, as the president wants to show he cares about them personally—gives a little lecture setting the background for his or her question. The question itself—on how the president's policies contradict themselves or on his political enemies—is hostile in tone, trying to catch the president in an uncomfortable situation. The president replies in stammering, ungrammatical English, for he is the product of an American college. After a half-hour or so of this ordeal, the dean of the White House press corps lets the victim off the hook with the prearranged, "Thank you, Mr. President." The president, in keeping with the democratic American style, tries to treat the journalists as his equals, but his smile and handshakes as he leaves can scarcely conceal his adversary relationship with the media.

President Mitterrand prepares to instruct journalists at a press conference in the Elysee Palace. (French Embassy Press & Information Division)

tribution of income in France is more unequal than in Britain or even Spain. A 1976 study found that the richest 10 percent of French households got 30.5 percent of the country's after-tax income, while the poorest 10 percent got only 1.4 percent. The rich live superbly in France; the poor scrape by.

Class differences tend to reinforce other cleavages in French society—clerical-anticlerical, urban-rural, radical-conservative, even to a certain extent North-South. That is, these factors tend to line up on one side—never perfectly, of course, but enough to produce a major left-right split in French voting. Very broadly, here are the typical characteristics of French voters for the left and the right:

LEFT VOTER	RIGHT VOTER
working class	middle class
anticlerical	prochurch
urban	rural or small town

Great French Expressions:
"The heart is on the left, but the billfold is on the right."

Nothing better explains French ambivalence over voting for leftist candidates. Their ideals say vote left, but self-interest often pulls the other way.

A CHANGING INTELLECTUAL CLIMATE

French intellectuals, some of them from the same *grandes écoles* as the governing elite, were for a long generation attracted to Marxism. Observing the huge gap between the ideal of equality and the reality of gross inequality, many highly educated and middle-class French turned to Marxist explanations and sometimes to membership in the Communist party. Philosopher Jean-Paul Sartre backed every leftist cause he could find and urged other intellectuals to become likewise *engagé*. Another *normalien,* his adversary Raymond Aron, disparaged Marxism as "the opium of the intellectuals," a play on Marx's famous statement that "religion is the opium of the masses."

Under Mitterrand, if not before, this changed. French intellectuals became disillusioned with Marxism, communism, and traditional leftist positions. There seem to be several reasons for this major shift, which has long-term implications for French political life. A group of "New Philosophers" (see box) emerged who scathingly criticized the Soviet Union and communism. In the early 1980s, many West German intellectuals turned anti-American over how to deal with the Soviets and especially over the stationing of new U.S. missiles on German soil. There is no love lost between French and German intellectuals, and the French were happy to repudiate what they regarded as naive German pacifism. French intellectuals became, in contrast, pro-American, an unusual position for them. The Soviet-supervised takeover of Poland by a Polish general chillingly reminded many French of the takeover of France by Marshal Pétain in the service of Germany during World War II.

But most important, with the election of a Socialist government in 1981, the left was in power. It was one thing to criticize a conservative government but quite another to run a government yourself. French intellectuals and leftists saw how difficult it was to run an economy, assume a role in world affairs, and transform French society. Clever slogans do not translate into effective policy, and many French intellectuals became middle-of-the-roaders. "Obviously", said Régis Debray, onetime darling of the French left and companion of Che Guevara who became a Mitterrand advisor, "It's a bit less chic than before to be on the left." The Mitterrand presidency, if it serves no other purpose, will have contributed a lot if it matures the French intellectual left and teaches them that theory is not reality.

France's "New Philosophers"

French intellectuals had a long-term addiction to Marxism but in the 1970s a countertrend emerged that rocked French politics. A group of young intellectuals, all of them former Marxists, denounced Marxism as a system that inherently leads to tyranny. Many French Marxists had denounced Soviet communism before, but they had depicted it as a Russian aberration, a good idea gone wrong because it was applied in bad circumstances and fell into the hands of a dictator, Stalin. The young critics—who were called the "New Philosophers" because nobody could think of a better name—said on the other hand, "No, the Soviet Union is not a bad example of socialism in practice. It's a *good* example."

Intellectuals play an important role in French politics; many people follow their lead. And French intellectuals had been heavily Marxist for decades. The anti-Marxist challenge of the New Philosophers had political ramifications that extended far beyond cafés and intellectual magazines.

The revelations of Alexander Solzhenitsyn about Soviet slave-labor camps had a profound impact on the New Philosophers. One of the main New Philosophers, young, handsome Bernard-Henri Lévy, rattled the French left with his book, *Barbarism with a Human Face,* his description of communism. The real problem, according to Lévy, goes back to the great French Enlightenment thinkers of the eighteenth century (see chapter 7), who launched the idea of remaking the world into something perfect, under the leadership, naturally, of intellectuals, those who knew what people really needed. In comparison, some New Philosophers conclude, Western-style democracy and capitalism really are not so bad.

The New Philosophers are not the last word in what is probably a perpetual debate on the French left, the debate between liberty and equality. If you go for equality, as the Marxists do, you'll lose liberty. If you go for liberty, you may not be able to solve the problem of gross inequality. There's no solution to this dilemma, but the New Philosophers, by injecting a sober appraisal of Marxism, shoved the emphasis back to the side of freedom.

VOCABULARY BUILDING

anticlericalism	Elysée Palace	intellectuals	*normalien*
baccalauréat	ENA	*liberté*	*patrie*
bureaucratized	grande école	*lycée*	privatistic
class bias	*grandeur*	"La Marseillaise"	schizophrenia
	inequality	New Philosophers	worker priests

FURTHER REFERENCE

Aron, Raymond. *France: Steadfast and Changing.* Cambridge, Mass.: Harvard University Press, 1960.

Converse, Philip E., and Georges Dupeux "Politicization of the Electorate in France and the United States," *Public Opinion Quarterly (1),* Spring 1962.

Crozier, Michel. *The Bureaucratic Phenomenon.* Chicago: University of Chicago Press, 1964

DeGramont, Sanche. *The French: Portrait of a People.* New York: Putnam, 1969.

Ehrmann, Henry W. *Politics in France,* 4th ed. Boston: Little, Brown, 1983.

Hoffmann, Stanley. *Decline or Renewal? France Since the 1930s.* New York: Viking, 1974.

———— , ed. *In Search of France.* New York: Harper & Row, 1965.

Wylie, Laurence. *Village in the Vaucluse.* Cambridge, Mass.: Harvard University Press, 1957.

10

PATTERNS OF
INTERACTION

PARTIES IN CONFUSION

In contrast to Britain, party image and voter identification with parties are not highly developed in France. Many French people do not have long-term party preferences, and French parties are always coming and going and changing their names, blurring the images they have built up. The result is a good number of voters not firmly attached to one party who shift parties from one election to another. In most of West Europe, elections show only small swings of a few points from the previous contest. In France, whole new parties rise and fall within a few years. French parties sometimes gain ten to twenty percentage points from their previous showing. French voting is volatile.

Few French parties haven't changed their names at one time or another. Founded in 1905, the Socialists originally called themselves the French Section of the Workers International, or SFIO. In 1969, merging with some smaller left groups, they changed the name to the *Parti Socialiste* (PS). In 1981 the PS under Mitterrand won both the presidency and National Assembly.

The Gaullists seemed to have a new name for each election. From 1947 to 1952 they called themselves the Rally of the French People (RPF). With de Gaulle's coming to power in 1958 it became the Union for the New Republic (UNR), then in 1967 the Democratic Union for the Fifth Republic (UDV^e), in 1968 the Union for the Defense of the Republic (UDR), in 1971 the Union of Democrats for the Republic (with the same initials, UDR), and in 1976 the Rally for the Republic (RPR).

The Republicans, now one of the four large parties, was formed as a parliamentary grouping only in 1962 and first ran in elections in 1966. In 1974 its leader, Valéry Giscard D'Estaing, was elected president. The rapid rise of the Republicans was due at least in part to the demise of several small parties in the center that had changed their names so often we won't bother listing them.

One French party does not play around with name changes—the Communists (PCF)—although they too have trouble with their party's image, as we shall explore.

To make things even more confusing, parties often run jointly as the Union of the Left or Common Program (Socialist and Communist), the "Majority" (Gaullists and Republicans), or the Union for French Democracy (Republicans plus the small Social Democrat and Radical parties). Sometimes these joint tickets last no longer than one election; they come up with a new name for the next contest.

THE TWO BLOCS

The French party system is not as complex as it used to be; it is down from ten relevant parties in 1958 to four today. Smaller parties have been dropping out, larger ones consolidating and forming into two blocs—one left and one right—composed of two parties each. Schematically it looks like this:

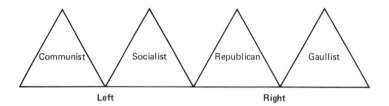

The two blocs are by no means internally harmonious. As we shall see, the Communists are always feuding with the Socialists and the Republicans constantly striving for predominance with the Gaullists. In terms of voter appeal, however, the two blocs fit into two great French "tendencies" of which we spoke earlier. The left favors ways to make people more equal, by taxing the rich, controlling or nationalizing some industries, and providing more welfare benefits. The right also claims to be for change, but much more cautiously, based on capitalistic economic growth and modest reforms. When it comes down to election day, the left usually appears to favor rather radical change and the right to favor the status quo.

THE SOCIALISTS AND THE COMMUNISTS

In most countries, Socialist and Communist parties are natural enemies, partly because they both claim to be ideologically correct. Typically, when one is strong the other is weak. Britain, Sweden, and West Germany all have large Socialist parties and small Communist parties. In Italy a large Communist party overshadows the Socialists. In France it used to be that way, but during the 1970s the Socialists grew and the Communists shrank so that now the PS is the largest party in France.

The two parties have common roots. In fact, the PCF is a 1920 offshoot of the Socialists. In a battle that has raged all this century, the Communists claim the Socialists aren't militant enough, that they have abandoned revolutionary Marxism to settle for gradual, pragmatic reformism. Since its founding, the PCF has been faithful to Moscow. For example, the French Communists didn't join in the Resistance until Germany attacked the Soviet Union in 1941. Since Stalin's time, however, the PCF has been gradually becoming more moderate. It denounced the 1968 Soviet invasion of Czechoslovakia and claimed to favor "Eurocommunism," a doctrine developed by the Italian Communists that swears independence from the Kremlin and acceptance of democratic norms. French voters can't trust the Communists, though, for old Stalinist tendencies reappear, as when the party expels a dissenting intellectual, supports the growth of Soviet power, or stabs fellow leftists in the back.

The result is an unstable alliance of Socialists and Communists. The two parties hate each other but know they need each other. The second round or run-off of a French election—as in the Anglo-American system—placed a great

The French Left: Smother Thy Brother

When François Mitterrand took over the shrunken and demoralized Socialist party in 1971, it was overshadowed on the French left by the Communists, who regularly won a fifth of the vote. Given France's peculiar electoral system—single-member districts with run-off—Mitterrand knew the PS couldn't grow on its own. His plan was to embrace the Communists, use them, win away some of their supporters, and then discard them. He did that, and it worked.

In 1972 the PS and PCF worked out their Common Program, spelling out what they would do in power: some nationalization of banks and industry, wage increases, and more welfare funding. They agreed to support each other in the second round of parliamentary and presidential balloting. The Socialist vote grew, in part at the expense of the Communists. Many French on the left don't trust the Communists but found Mitterrand and the reinvigorated PS attractive. By 1977 the PCF was getting worried and sabotaged the Common Program by making it more radical—something the Socialists refused to go along with. This effectively lost the 1978 National Assembly elections for the left, even though public-opinion polls foresaw them beating the Gaullist and Republican "Majority."

But it was too late for the PCF to dominate the left; the PS was bigger, and the Communists were discredited for wrecking the Common Program and for applauding the Soviet invasion of Afghanistan. In 1981 they went into the first round of the presidential elections denouncing the Socialists but did so poorly—they lost a quarter of their vote—that they meekly supported Mitterrand on the second round. Mitterrand had them where he wanted them: junior partners on whom he depended not at all, for the Socialists held an absolute majority of the National Assembly. Why then did Mitterrand bring the PCF into his cabinet with four rather minor ministries?

The United States was upset with this move that brought Communists into a West European government: Vice President Bush went to Paris to protest. He needn't have worried; Mitterrand knew what he was doing. The Communists in the cabinet (1) kept them from criticizing the government, (2) held down strikes by the largest, Communist-led union, and (3) humiliated the PCF by making it follow Mitterrand's policies, which included a pro-American tilt to build Western defenses against the Soviets. In 1984 a shrunken, demoralized PCF left the cabinet. Mitterrand no longer needed them.

premium on combining parties, for in the French run-off a simple plurality won. If the Communists and Socialists ran separately on the second ballot they would lose badly to the combined Gaullists and Republicans. Accordingly, the left parties, the PS, PCF, and sometimes leftist splinter groups, pledged to support the strongest left candidate, regardless of party, on the second ballot. It was the French electoral system that drove two rivals on the French left together.

Their alliance, or misalliance, seldom lasts, however. The Communists are disciplined and doctrinaire, always citing the "correct" Marxist interpretation of events. The Socialists are loose and sloppy, home to a wide variety of people ranging from Marxists to moderate Social Democrats. The PS even permits the organization of factions within its ranks, something no Communist party ever allows.

The two parties speak to different electorates. The Communists concentrate on the urban proletariat; some of their greatest strength is in the industrial "Red belt" around Paris. The Socialists typically try to reach the more middle-class civil servants and skilled workers; they have been called "the party of schoolteachers." Indeed, 58 percent of the Socialists elected to the National Assembly in 1981 were teachers or professors. The leadership of the PS is composed almost completely of intellectuals; that of the PCF is heavily working class.

Factions Within the Socialists

Some observers counted four factions within France's ruling Socialist party:

- A mainstream around President Mitterrand that was fairly radical in tone but moderate in practice and far from the Communists' revolutionary dreams; estimated to be home to about half the Socialist deputies in the National Assembly elected in 1981.

- A more centrist or social-democratic faction around Michel Rocard, who quit the cabinet in protest at the shift to PR for the 1986 election;

perhaps a fifth of Socialist deputies were Rocardians.

- A Marxist study group named CERES, the left wing of PS, headed by Education Minister Jean-Pierre Chevènement, favored by only about an eighth of Socialist deputies.

- A moderate, grass-roots labor approach linked to the CFDT union, which has little time for ideological hairsplitting; home to about one Socialist deputy in seven.

THE GAULLISTS AND REPUBLICANS

While the French left bloc is unstable, the French right bloc is in no better shape. For the right, doctrine is much less important; they essentially want to keep things the way they are. The Gaullists and Republicans differ little on their main goals. They also tend to speak to much the same electorate. On the right—and this is true of many countries—personality becomes the leading issue.

Here the shadow of de Gaulle still looms large. The French right is torn between those who want to keep his image alive and those who favor more traditional center-right politics. De Gaulle, curiously enough, never aimed at founding a political party. Like Franco, Mussolini, and Latin American military dictators, de Gaulle hated parties, blaming their incessant squabbles for all the troubles of the Third and Fourth Republics. De Gaulle didn't even much care for the Gaullist party; he never formally headed or endorsed it. His attitude seemed to be: "All right, if you must, go ahead and worship me." During his long reign (1958–69), the Gaullist party was simply a tool for his control of the National Assembly. In the legislative elections of 1968, the Gaullists won 46 percent of the popular vote and an outright majority of National Assembly seats. With de Gaulle no longer the party's rallying point, however, Gaullist electoral fortunes declined. In 1981, Gaullists were well behind the Socialists.

A single charismatic figure leading a national movement is a tough act to follow. A charismatic leader doesn't tolerate other important personalities around him; he prefers obedient servants and yes-men. As a result, when de Gaulle departed in 1969, he left a vacuum that no one in the Gaullist party could really fill. His former premier Georges Pompidou won the presidency that year, but by the time Pompidou died in 1974 the Republican candidate, Valéry Giscard d'Estaing, was more attractive than another Gaullist ex-premier, Jacques Chaban-Delmas. Because de Gaulle disdained parties, he never bothered institutionalizing his movement into a durable party. The real genius in politics is the one who builds lastingly; de Gaulle didn't.

Backstabbing on the Right

Valéry Giscard d'Estaing and his challenger Jacques Chirac follow closely parallel patterns. Both come from well-connected families, both are extremely bright, both graduated from the elite ENA, both became high-level government officials and cabinet ministers quite young, and both were fired by their respective presidents. When Giscard was finance minister in 1966, de Gaulle fired him. Then Giscard went out and organized his Republican party, which in 1974 brought Giscard to the presidency. Chirac served as Giscard's first premier from 1974 until their venomous relations led to Chirac's departure in 1976. Chirac immediately reorganized the Gaullists into a tool to enable him to eclipse Giscard.

While the French left concentrates on ideology and doctrine, the French right focuses on personality and ambition. It seems as if in rightist cabinets there are one or more eager ministers who dream of replacing the boss.

In the 1981 presidential elections, Chirac got his revenge against Giscard. In the first round of voting Chirac won 18 percent and Giscard 28 percent. Instead of urging his supporters to transfer their votes to Giscard on the second ballot, Chirac said nothing, and only about 75 percent of Chirac voters did so. In contrast, an estimated 90 percent of Communist first-round voters obeyed party dictate and transferred their votes to Socialist François Mitterrand on the crucial second ballot. The result: Mitterrand won the presidency, 52-to-48 percent. Giscard was furious; he stalked off to his country home muttering that Chirac had committed "premeditated treason." The two so hated Mitterrand, however, that they agreed to cooperate again in the 1986 legislative election.

Trying to fill the vacuum, Jacques Chirac in 1976 reorganized the moribund Gaullists into the Rally for the Republic, which some called the "neo-Gaullists." A slick performer who alienated many French people by his high-handedness, Chirac alternately quarreled and made up with Giscard and the Republicans.

The relationship of the two French right parties is similar to that of the two French left parties: they hate each other but need each other. The difference is that the hatred is largely personal, a struggle between two bright, ambitious party leaders who both want to be president. Just plain jealousy plays a role here.

THE STALEMATE CYCLE

French politics seems to run in a roughly cyclical pattern. "Normal" politics in France usually means a stalemate in which political groups, constantly feuding among themselves, block major change. This is punctuated every decade or two by an explosion, a crisis the stalemated system can't handle. To get out of the fix, the French people have repeatedly turned to a hero, a charismatic figure who hasn't been sullied by "status quo" politics. French politics seems to require a Napoleon from time to time.

After a dozen years of revolutionary turmoil, France welcomed the first Napoleon as a hero who would end chaos. Half a century later, they turned to Louis Napoleon for the same reason. In 1940 the French parliament actually voted dictatorial powers for the aged Marshal Pétain. Pierre Mendès-France was the thinking-person's hero in 1954 when he got France out of Indochina, but he lacked the charisma of the outsider who is above ordinary politics. That figure arrived in 1958 in the person of de Gaulle, who saved France from civil war over Algeria.

De Gaulle believed he had put an end to France's recurrent stalemates and crises by constructing a Fifth Republic with a strong president. But did the Fifth Republic really transcend French history? At first it appeared to. France withdrew from the Algerian debacle, streamlined its party system, and surged ahead economically. In 1968, however, all hell broke loose—see box—and people began to wonder if the Fifth Republic wasn't suffering from some of the same ills that had plagued predecessors.

Mitterrand also found that the transformation of French politics was not as complete as de Gaulle believed. De Gaulle's personal popularity insured not only his election as president but a large Gaullist party in the National Assembly. This made it easy to govern; any law or budget de Gaulle wanted was rubber-stamped in the Palais Bourbon. The Fifth Republic did not depend on the unstable coalitions of the Third and Fourth to govern. But how much did it depend on the same party maintaining control of both the executive and legislative branches?

The Events of May 1968

Just ten years after the near civil war over Algeria that brought de Gaulle into office, his regime suffered another explosion almost as powerful, the "Events of May," as it was euphemistically called. A month of student and worker strikes and battles with the police revealed that under the law-and-order surface of Gaullist France throbbed the old revolutionary tradition. The great split that had plagued France for generations had not completely healed; the cleavage still ran through French society like an earthquake faultline in California—ready to crack open without warning.

Trouble began at the University of Nanterre in a suburb of Paris. Students—fed up with overcrowded facilities, a rigid curriculum, and complete lack of student input—staged a strike. The students' immediate grievances were real and specific. But the strike spread like wildfire because it also appealed to the revolutionary dreams of left-wing students in general. Soon most universities in France were occupied by students playing at revolution. Slogans went up on campus walls: "Be realistic, demand the impossible." "I am a Marxist—of the Groucho tendency." For the students, the Events of May was a cross between the Paris Commune and Woodstock.

It wasn't quite so funny when the student protests spread to workers. With some seven million workers on strike, France virtually shut down. Workers' complaints were more concrete: low wages and long hours. In several occupied factories, workers put up the red flag. *Lycéens* and professional employees joined in the strike. The Communist reaction to all this illustrates how far the party had come from its revolutionary origins. The PCF and its CGT trade union *opposed* the strikes! Fearing a loss of their dominant position on the French left, the Communists denounced the strikers as adventurists who thought they could change society overnight. In some respects the Communists have become a conservative force in French politics, anti-left leftists.

The police waded into protesters with tear gas and truncheons. Special riot police, the Republican Security Companies (CRS), seemed to enjoy cracking student skulls. De Gaulle quietly conferred with the French army stationed in Germany, and troops and tanks could be seen around Paris.

But then the revolution—if that's what it was—burned out, like many previous uprisings in French history. De Gaulle went on television with soothing words; he had heard the demand for more participation and would submit himself to the voters' approval in a referendum. De Gaulle changed his mind about a plebiscite and held parliamentary elections instead. The 1968 elections showed, once again, that only half of France was revolutionary, for a majority of the voters supported conservative candidates; Gaullists won an actual majority of seats in the National Assembly.

France seemed about to find out in 1986. With Socialist popularity in decline, it seemed possible that Republicans and Gaullists could win control of the National Assembly, leaving a Socialist president with two years remaining to face an uncooperative legislature. One possible result could be a U.S.-style deadlock between executive and legislature. In France, it could be more complicated, for the National Assembly can censure the cabinet. The President would have to name a new premier and cabinet, or dissolve parliament and hold new elections, or try to govern without a formal cabinet, or resign.

It was to try to avoid these unpleasnt alternatives that Mittterrand reintroduced proportional representation for the 1986 parliamentary election; he calculated it would enable the Socialists to retain more seats and perhaps govern in coalition with some small parties. In any case, the Fifth Republic was not working the way de Gaulle thought it would; it began to resemble the Fourth. (One possible solution: completely sever the connection between cabinet and legislature and go to a straight U.S.-style presidential system.)

THE PLEBISCITE GAME

One technique French leaders revert to is the plebiscite or referendum. This poses major questions directly to the people without going through elected representatives in parliament. The referendum, almost unknown in Britain, has since 1793 been used seventeen times in France. It fits neatly into a very French tradition: Rousseau's idea of the general will. On the surface, nothing could be more democratic than consulting the people directly on their wishes.

In reality, plebiscites can be very tricky, an authoritarian tool that manipulates the masses rather than serving them. The key power in a referendum is the one who writes the question. The question can be posed in such a simplified way that one almost has to vote yes. Furthermore, a referendum often comes after the decision has already been made and the leader just wants popular endorsement.

De Gaulle played the plebiscite game to the hilt. For de Gaulle, the purpose of a referendum was not merely to gain mass approval for a given policy but to reinforce his personal rule. After every plebiscite he could turn to his old enemies, the traditional politicians and say, "You see, the people understand and support me. Who needs you?" In French political theory, again derived from Rousseau, a nation run by a leader who stands in direct communication with the people—without parties, parliaments, politicians, or interest groups getting in the way—is the ideal democracy. Some, however, see in this model the seeds of dictatorship.

De Gaulle attached his personal prestige to each referendum. "If the nation rejects the measure," he in effect told France, "it also rejects me, and I shall resign." This blunt approach worked every time until the last. In 1958 people were glad to see a new constitution. In 1961 and 1962 they were delighted to see Algeria become independent and French troops come home. But de Gaulle's second referendum of 1962 raised some questions. De Gaulle had made a mistake in the 1958 constitution by having the president chosen by a gigantic electoral college composed of local office holders, who he assumed would be conservative and pro-de Gaulle; they weren't. So in October 1962, bypassing the National Assembly, he asked the voters to amend the constitution to allow direct election of the president. The referendum passed with a 62 percent yes vote, but this represented only 46 percent of the total electorate, far less than de Gaulle expected.

The Five Plebiscites of de Gaulle

YEAR	QUESTION	PERCENT "YES"
1958	New constitution for Fifth Republic	79
1961	Self-determination for Algeria	75
1962	Approve Algerian independence	91
1962	Direct election of president	62
1969	Reform of Senate and regions	47

The hint was clear—the French people were happy to get out of Algeria but not so happy with their president's tinkering with the constitution—but de Gaulle ignored it. In 1969, after riding out the 1968 Events of May with resounding electoral success, de Gaulle once again sought to demonstrate that the people were behind him. He picked a rather technical issue that didn't require a plebiscite: the reform (that is, weakening) of the Senate and the setting up of regional subunits. The French people said no, and true to his word, de Gaulle resigned. He went back to Colombey-les-Deux-Eglises, where he died the following year.

Since then, there has been only one referendum, held by Pompidou in 1972, on enlarging the Common Market to include Britain, Ireland, and Denmark. Mitterrand proposed a referendum in 1984 on expanding the scope of referendums to include questions of personal freedom. The French Senate rejected the move, and Mitterrand dropped the project. In neither 1972 nor 1984 were referendums really needed to solve a political impasse, and neither instance aroused much popular passion. Rather, both presidents tried to use a referendum to bolster mass support and deflect attention away from more serious matters. The 1984 Senate rejection suggests that France has finally tired of plebiscites.

FRAGMENTED LABOR UNIONS

In Britain we saw how interest groups were well organized and powerful, especially big labor and big business. This pattern is true of Northern Europe in general, as we shall consider when we come to West Germany. In France and in Latin Europe in general there are also plenty of interest groups, but they are usually splintered along party lines.

In Britain (and West Germany and Sweden), for example, there is one big labor federation. In France (and Italy and Spain) there are several labor unions, the largest Communist, with smaller Socialist, Catholic, and independent unions competing against each other. The Communist-led CGT (*Confédération*

Generale du Travail) is considered powerful in France, but on a comparative basis it isn't very powerful at all. It speaks for perhaps 10 percent of the French work force. Indeed only about a fifth of French labor is organized into unions, a weak level of unionization comparable to that of the United States.

French unions also quarrel among themselves. In 1983 when the Talbot car plant wanted to trim its work force, the CGT agreed, but the smaller, Socialist-oriented CFDT *(Confédération Française Democratique du Travail)* refused. Opposing unionists hurled nuts and bolts at each other; fifty-five were injured. Finally, the CFDT called in the riot police. Labor's voice in France is weak and divided. Accordingly, French unions are strong neither in bargaining with management nor in making an impact on government. There are many strikes in France, but they tend to be short because unions lack strike funds.

Part of the problem with French unions is their political slant. Since the largest union, the CGT, is led by Communists, the other parties, especially those who control the government, ignore their demands. French unions engage in political strikes, actions aimed at government policy rather than bread-and-butter demands. In the 1980s French unions often protested closures or layoffs at state-owned industries, much as in Thatcher's Britain. Few French unions take the American view that a union is a device for negotiating better terms with management, not a political tool.

Comparing: Latin Europe's Divided Unions

	FRANCE	ITALY	SPAIN
Communist	CGT	CGIL	CO
Socialist	CFDT	—	UGT
Catholic	—	CISL	—
Other	FO	UIL	CNT
	(centrist)	(soc. dem.)	(anarchist)

The relative weakness of French unions has an important side effect: it makes them more, rather than less, militant and ideological. Feeling that the government has turned its back on them, French workers are more bitter than the workers of West Germany and Sweden, where strong unions have an important voice in government. In those two countries, large and well-organized unions have become moderate and pragmatic.

BUSINESS AND THE BUREAUCRACY

French business is perhaps less fragmented than labor, for business people rarely dabble in ideology if the present system suits them. The National Council of French Employers *(Conseil National du Patronat Français)* speaks mostly for large firms and generally enjoys good relations with the government, for both are committed to economic growth. Indeed, the state sees its role as guiding and helping industry, a pattern of paternalism going back centuries. At first, Mitterrand thought he could ignore business interests and pursue a leftist economic program. This worried businesses, and they cut investment in France; some French firms invested in the United States. Mitterrand backed off and tried to make peace with French business.

The *Patronat* is probably not as influential as the CBI in Britain because of the French tendency toward individualism. A French firm may belong to the *Patronat,* for example, but rely only on its own resources for discreet contacts with the bureaucracy.

The big advantage business has over labor in dealing with government contacts is that the French business executive and civil servant are the same kind of people, often graduates of the same *grand école,* who move back and forth between top jobs in government and industry. Such connections give France's major firms "structured access" to the machinery of administration, something small-business people, farmers, and labor unionists don't enjoy. This builds up bitterness and frustration in the latter groups that explode from time to time in flash parties such as the *Poujadists,* in produce dumping by farmers, and in wildcat strikes. The political-bureaucratic systems of Northern Europe, by providing access for all major groups, generally avoid such outbursts.

But neither do French business people dominate government decision making. French political tradition is stacked against it. In the Anglo-American tradition, pluralism is respected, sometimes even celebrated. *Pluralism* is the open and welcome interplay of interest groups with government. When farmers, business people, trade unionists, and ethnic groups lobby in Washington, it is considered perfectly normal. In Britain's Commons, "interested members" make no secret of the fact that they represent certain industries. French political theory, however, still devoted to Rousseau's notion that interest groups are immoral—because they represent partial wills rather than the overall general will—tends to view such groups as illegitimate. The French tradition is *étatisme,* "statism," the national government firmly in control, ignoring interest-group demands, and doing what it deems best for French power and prestige. This gives great power to bureaucrats.

"Putting on the Slippers"

The movement of top civil servants to the executive suites of industry is so well known in France that they even have a word for it, *pantouflage,* or "putting on the slippers." This means that a graduate of the Ecole Polytechnique or the ENA, after a few years in a Paris ministry, can slip into a cushy, high-paying management job, often in a firm he or she used to deal with as an official. *Pantouflage* is an important connecting link between French business and bureaucracy.

THE ETERNAL BUREAUCRACY

France has been developing its bureaucracy for five centuries. Almost every change of regime has led to growth in the number and functions of French bureaucrats. During the revolving-door cabinets of the Fourth Republic, people used to say that the fall of governments didn't really matter that much because the bureaucracy ran the country anyway.

In France, civil servants oversee a great deal more than do their counterparts in most non-Communist countries. France has several nationalized industries—aircraft, automobiles, coal mines, banks, steel, gas, and electricity—in addition to the areas that are state-run throughout Europe, such as the "PTT" (post, telephone, and telegraph) and the railroads. Workers in these industries are not considered civil servants, but top management people are. Every French teacher, for that matter, from kindergarten to university, is a civil servant.

The bureaucrats we are concerned with, however, are the several thousand who staff the Paris ministries. Most are graduates of one of the Great Schools. Even more powerful than their British counterparts, French civil servants of the administrative class (about the top 20 percent) run France. If anything, the bureaucrats' power was enhanced with the coming of the Fifth Republic, for de Gaulle so hamstrung the National Assembly that it could no longer provide a policy counterweight to, or check on, the actions of the top civil servants. Furthermore, under de Gaulle and his successors, including Mitterrand, many of those named ministers were themselves civil servants, often graduates of the ENA or of other *grand écoles.*

This is not to say that French bureaucrats run things badly; often they do their jobs very well. It's the bureaucratic attitude that alienates their countrymen: aloof, arrogant, cold, logical, and rigid. It's not that they don't meet and interact with other Frenchmen; civil servants sit on some fifteen thousand committees and councils all over the country with representatives of business, labor, and farming. The highest of these is the national Social and Economic Council, but even it has a purely advisory capacity, and often advice is ignored as "unobjective." The composition of many of these consultative bodies is increasingly bureaucratic; some 30 percent of the Social and Economic Council is named by the government, for example. The French bureaucratic approach is expressed in their term *tutelle* (tutelage), for they act far more as protectors or guardians than as equals, much less as true "servants" of the public.

GOVERNMENT BY BUREAUCRACY

More than in Britain, the civil service in France constitutes a powerful governing body uncontrolled by elected officials, who sometimes denounce the bureaucracy as an "administrative labyrinth" or even as "adminstrative totalitarianism." But they can't seem to do much about it.

We should not think France is unique in this regard, for no country has devised a way to keep its bureaucracy under control. France, with a longer history of bureaucratization and the Great Schools' monopoly over the top civil service, merely reveals the pattern more fully. If you look closely at your own country, you will find much the same thing: government of the bureaucrats, by the bureaucrats, and for the bureaucrats.

In trying to reform, trim, or democratize a bureaucracy we run into a problem underscored by Yale political scientist Joseph LaPalombara: almost any solution we can think of entails *adding* more bureaucrats. In France, for example, ministries now have special offices for the reform of administration—still more bureaucracy.

We can see here why the French people, faced with an unresponsive, undemocratic bureaucratic maze, turn frustrated and bitter. Where bureaucracy thrives, democracy shrivels. In trying to fix this, Mitterrand stepped in a contradiction. Socialism needs lots of bureaucracy—to run welfare programs, supervise industry, and plan the economy. But decentralization means loosening bureaucratic controls and returning power to local decision-making bodies. It took Mitterrand about three years to realize he had been working at cross purposes; he turned away from socialism and continued with decentralization.

VOCABULARY BUILDING

bloc	Events of May	*Patronat*	reformism
CFDT	factious	PCF	RPR
CGT	fragmented	plebiscite	stalemate
charismatic	Gaullism	pluralism	Stalinist
Common Program	Majority	PS	*tutelle*
étatisme	*pantouflage*	referendum	UDF
Eurocommunism			UDR

FURTHER REFERENCE

Andrews, William G., and Stanley Hoffmann, eds. *The Fifth Republic at Twenty.* Albany: State University of New York Press, 1981.

Bell, David Scott, and Bryon Criddle. *The French Socialist Party: Resurgence and Victory.* New York: Oxford University Press, 1984.

Charlot, Jean. *The Gaullist Phenomenon: The Gaullist Movement in the Fifth Republic.* New York: Praeger, 1971.

Frears, J.R. "The French National Assembly Elections of March 1978," *Government and Opposition* 13, no. 3 (Summer 1978), 323–40.

Hartley, Anthony. *Gaullism: The Rise and Fall of a Political Movement.* New York: Outerbridge & Dienstfrey, 1971.

LaPalombara, Joseph. "Bureaucratic Pathologies and Prescriptions," chap. 8, in *Politics Within Nations.* Englewood Cliffs, N.J.: Prentice-Hall, 1974.

Macridis, Roy C. *French Politics in Transition: The Years after De Gaulle.* Cambridge, Mass.: Winthrop, 1975.

Penniman, Howard R., ed. *France at the Polls, 1981.* Durham, N.C.: Duke University Press, 1985.

Pickles, Dorothy. *The Government and Politics of France: II. Politics.* London: Methuen, 1973.

Suleiman, Ezra N. *Elites in French Society: The Politics of Survival.* Princeton, N.J.: Princeton University Press, 1978.

Wilson, Frank L. *French Political Parties Under the Fifth Republic.* New York: Praeger, 1982.

Wright, Vincent. *The Government and Politics of France,* 2d ed. New York: Holmes & Meier, 1983.

11

WHAT THE FRENCH QUARREL ABOUT

FROM STAGNANT TO DYNAMIC

In some ways, the state of the French economy has been the opposite of the British. Britain has suffered a long-term economic decline, dropping further and further back in the front rank of industrialized countries. France, whose economy grew only slowly in the nineteenth and early twentieth centuries, awoke as if from a slumber after World War II and zoomed ahead economically. With growth rates reaching 6 percent a year—more recently, however, much lower—France became the fourth industrial power in the non-Communist world (after the United States, Japan, and West Germany). The French experience illustrates that decline need not be permanent and that a country, with the right policies and the right spirit, can turn its economy from stagnant to dynamic.

What did the trick? The typical French business firm prior to the Second World War was a small family affair. Growth was not emphasized; keeping it in the family and earning just enough for a good living was all that mattered. This meant lots of little companies and stores rather than a few big ones. Rather than compete by cutting prices or offering better goods and services, the French, with their *bourgeois* mentality, sought to hide behind a protective government that would set prices and keep out foreign competition by high tariffs. It was a cozy arrangement for French business families, but it kept France economically backward.

World War II produced quite a jolt. The French elite, smarting from the German conquest and eager to restore France to world leadership, realized the economy had to change. A Planning Commission issued what were called "indicative plans" to encourage—but not force—French business people to expand in certain sectors and regions. Quite distinct from Communist-style centralized planning, indicative planning in effect said, "Look, everything is favorable for a new widget factory in the southwest. If you build one you'll probably make a lot of money." As we saw in the last chapter, there are warm connections between French bureaucracy and business, and it didn't take business people long to get the hint. The French Planning Commission provided the business community with economic research and gentle nudges to push it along what are deemed desirable paths.

Foreign competition was another jolt. First the European Coal and Steel Community starting in 1952, then the Common Market starting in 1957, dismantled France's protective tariffs. At first French business people were terrified, sure that more aggressive German industry would swamp them. But gradually they learned that French firms could be quite competitive and enjoy the enlarged sales opportunities afforded by the Common Market. French business firms changed, becoming bigger, more modern, and expansion-oriented. But success brought its own problems.

BIG GUYS VERSUS LITTLE GUYS

On a street where the author lived in Toulouse, in the space of a few blocks, there were not only pharmacies, dairy shops, bakeries, houseware shops, furniture and vegetable stores, butchers, cafés, and tobacco shops, but at least three of each type of store. Perhaps two miles distant, in a suburb, was a mammoth

Nukes, French Style

The French complain and quarrel about many things, but, curiously, nuclear energy isn't one of them. The French accept nuclear energy, and none of the four major parties is against it. The small anti-atom Ecology party won only 1 percent of the first-round vote in the 1981 legislative elections.

The French, lacking other energy sources, have gone all-out for nuclear-generated electricity and have made a success of it. In 1984 half of France's electricity was from nuclear power plants; in 1990 it will be 70 percent. In comparison, less that one-eighth of U.S. electricity is nuclear, a level unlikely to rise in the face of astronomical cost overruns in power-plant construction. Some U.S. plants have been scrapped before they were finished. Overall, French nuclear-generated electricity costs less than half America's, and New Hampshire's problem-plagued Seabrook reactor could have been built by the French for one-sixth its cost.

How do the French do what Americans can't? Here we see some of the occasional advantages of centralized, technocratic rule. The state-owned utility, Electricité de France, developed a single type of reactor and stuck with it. Competing U.S. manufacturers proffer a variety of designs, some not well tested. When Paris gives the word to build a reactor, the political, financial, regulatory, and managerial sectors mesh under central direction, and the project gets done on time. In the United States, those sectors quarrel, with no central guidance, and the project takes years longer than it should. Environmentalist groups in France—not very big anyway—have no legal power to block or delay projects. The centralized French system is also better able to train personnel; there have been no Three Mile Islands in France. Nuclear power plants are an important and growing part of France's export trade. The very strengths of the American system—decentralization, competition, light regulation, and pluralist interplay—tripped up the U.S. nuclear industry.

The "other" nuclear question—nuclear weapons—also drew relatively little attention in France. Whereas British and West German peace marchers mightily protested the installation of new U.S. missiles, the French did not. In the first place, no U.S. missiles were put on French soil; de Gaulle had kicked out all American bases in 1966. Second, most French, including President Mitterrand, saw the need for a greater West European counterweight to growing Soviet strength. Third, ever since de Gaulle, the French have had an independent nuclear *force de dissuasion* of which they are proud. Accordingly, banning the bomb may be an issue in Britain and West Germany, but it isn't in France.

single-stop shopping center named, ironically, *Mammouth*. There, under one roof, were a combined supermarket (offering perhaps a hundred different cheeses), discount house (everything from clothes to auto parts), and cafeteria. Not only was the selection bigger at *Mammouth* than among the myriad neighborhood stores, but prices were lower, too.

Such developments have been going on throughout France for years. Some call it the Americanization of France, but it's really just the modernization of an old-fashioned economy. The impact on the small shopkeepers is predictable: they are squeezed out, screaming all the way. What they regarded as their birthright—the small, family-owned, uncompetitive shop—is being destroyed. As Marx put it: "One capitalist kills many."

A parallel problem hits French farmers; there are also too many small farms. French peasants, for a variety of reasons, became overly attached over the years to their holdings and lifestyle. With few jobs in the cities anyway, almost 40 percent of French people stayed on the family farm through World War II. France remained a nation of peasants for an unusually long time. With postwar industrialization, this has changed; now only 9 percent of the labor force works on the land (still high for an advanced country). Many small farms have disappeared; they either lie fallow or have been swallowed up by larger, more mechanized farms. Still, French agriculture, like its U.S. counterpart, frequently overproduces foodstuffs, and from time to time French farmers dump produce on highways to protest what they regard as inadequate price supports. The Paris government, like most governments, is extremely protective of farmers, and French insistence on subsidizing many farm products has been one of the Common Market's main stumbling blocks.

The small shopkeepers and farmers who are being squeezed out contribute to France's electoral volatility. They shift allegiances rapidly, to whoever seems to promise their survival. The Gaullists have been a major beneficiary, but the frightened little shopkeepers have also contributed to the French tendency for "flash parties" to suddenly appear on the scene, sparkle for a few years, and then fade to oblivion. There is no nice solution to the problem of too many small shops and farms; they've got to go and it hurts. Attempts to retain them are hopeless and even reactionary, the stuff demagoguery is made of.

The Poujadists: A Classic Flash Party

In 1953 Pierre Poujade founded the Union for the Defense of Shopkeepers and Artisans (UDCA) to protect small-business people from the bigger, more efficient department stores and supermarkets that were driving many of them out of business. Tinged with reaction and anti-Semitism, *Poujadism* caught fire, and in the parliamentary elections of 1956 won 12 percent of the popular vote; some thought it was the coming party. It fell as quickly as it rose, however; *Poujadism* disappeared in 1958 when de Gaulle took over the French right.

THE NATIONALIZATION QUESTION

About 29 percent of French business and industry is state owned, more than double the percentage of any other West European country. More than half of this state ownership occurred under Mitterrand's Socialist government in 1982. Some nationalization of French industry took place right after World War II.

Louis Renault, founder and owner of the auto firm, had collaborated with the Germans, so the Free French seized his empire in 1944. Other industries, such as steel, were taken over by the state because without government subsidies they'd go under, creating unemployment. Still other areas, such as aviation, are prestige industries aimed at boosting France's world standing.

The left in France demanded more nationalization, including all big banks and industries. They argued that under state control big industries would pay workers more, hire more workers, and produce what French people really need rather than capitalist luxuries only a few can afford. The more conservative parties insist nationalization guarantees inefficiency, which in turn requires subsidies and tariff protection, a step backward in France's economic history.

Under President Giscard d'Estaing, the conservatives got their chance. His premier, economist Raymond Barre, instituted a "new revolution" that aimed to give France a free economy for the first time. Barre scrapped the government price-control system (consisting of over thirty thousand decrees) that France had used for decades to try to hold down the cost of living. (It didn't work: manufacturers would go to their friends in the bureaucracy and get them to raise price ceilings.) Barre, as a professor of economics, recognized that a free market in the long run would restrain prices better than decrees. In the short run, however, the French economy behaved like the British economy under the first few years of Thatcher's very similar program: inflation and unemployment increased. This contributed to the Socialists' electoral victories of 1981. Good economics is sometimes bad politics.

Within two years, however, Mitterrand discovered that good politics—promising growth and greater equality—can be bad economics. Mitterrand, fol-

The Concorde: A Prestigious Dinosaur

The Concorde supersonic aircraft illustrates what can go wrong with nationalized industries: they can build the wrong product for the wrong reason and cost taxpayers a fortune. The Concorde's development began in 1962 as a joint Anglo-French enterprise to give their lagging aircraft industries a technological jump on the Americans. They thought the graceful bird would be purchased by airlines all over the world.

Things didn't work out that way. Huge overruns boosted development cost to $4.28 billion and the price per plane to $92 million, close to ten times what had been estimated. The Concorde consumed three times the fuel per passenger mile of a Boeing 747. Only British and French airlines purchased Concordes and then only because the nationalized air carriers were required to by law. Because they seldom filled their one hundred seats, the airlines lost money on Concorde runs. Only twenty-one Concordes were ever finished before production shut down in 1978.

Why did Britain and France do it? A nationalized industry often has different priorities than a normal commercial venture. In this case "technological nationalism" was a factor, that is, their need to show the world how advanced they were. Employment was another factor; both Britain and France created thousands of jobs with the Concorde. Once the project was underway and the cost overruns mounting, neither country wanted to admit it had made a mistake. Because the aviation companies building the supersonic plane had access to their national treasuries, they did not have to undergo the discipline of raising capital in the marketplace.

This is not to say that nationalized industries always do things wrong. Aerospatiale of France, once it made the decision to drop Concorde and concentrate on the more conventional Airbus (purchased by Eastern Airlines and Pan Am among others), started doing much better. Nationalized industries can prosper if they are run like private industries, the way Renault is run.

lowing a Keynesian policy of pumping money into the economy, generously increased welfare benefits, raised the minimum wage, shortened the work week to thirty-nine hours, and added a fifth week of paid vacation. In 1982 the Socialists nationalized five giant industrial groups and thirty-nine banks. The governmental deficit led to increased inflation, and the franc slid to ten to a dollar. Increased purchasing power in the hands of the public sucked in a prodigious amount of foreign goods and gave France a gigantic international debt. Unemployment rose. The newly nationalized firms, which the Socialists had naively believed were making profits, turned out to be mostly money losers that had to be propped up with government funds. By 1983, observers were calling the Socialist economic policy a debacle.

The Gaullists promised to denationalize if they came to power. Mitterrand did no such thing but, greatly sobered, backed down on his economic dreams. In 1983 Mitterrand fired some of his more leftist ministers and replaced them with moderates. In particular, he demoted Industry Minister Jean-Pierre Chevènement, who had been trying to restructure French industry over the protests of leading industrialists and replaced him with brainy Laurent Fabius, the former budget minister, who was less *dirigiste* (directing things from above, the longstanding French technocratic style) than Chevènement. Fabius was more in favor of private industry, including small- and medium-size firms. In 1984 Mitterrand named Fabius, 37, his prime minister, the youngest French head of government in a century.

Mitterrand also administered a strong dose of austerity to the French economy—or "Socialist rigor," as he called it. The Socialists increased taxes, implemented a "forced loan" equal to 10 percent of an individual's income tax, and reduced public spending to bring down inflation. To help curb France's balance-of-payment deficit, French tourists were limited to $275 for foreign vacations. The measures worked, but the French people turned angry at the belt tightening; one affected group after another staged noisy demonstrations.

For a Socialist who had promised to use state power to correct all wrongs, it was an incredible reversal. "You don't want more state?" asked Mitterrand in 1984. "Me neither." On letting a giant engineering firm go into receivership: "The state's jobs don't include creating industries or rushing to the rescue of failing companies." On Bastille Day in 1984: "I say, no promises, no commitments, no dazzling perspectives." Thatcher or Barre couldn't have said it better.

Comparing: The Spanish Socialists Do It Better

Just a year after the French Socialists, the Spanish Socialists swept to power in 1982 with a resounding 46 percent of the vote and a majority in parliament. Young, attractive Felipe González became Spain's first Socialist prime minister since the 1930s. Unlike Mitterrand, though, González stayed popular. The secret of his success: Unlike Mitterrand, González had turned his PSOE (*Partido Socialista Obrero Español*) into a moderate, center-left party *before* the election, not after. Mitterrand whipped up leftist phra-seology and promised a socialist France with prosperity and equality. González earlier overcame Marxists within PSOE to rededicate the party to merely consolidating democracy—an important enough task in a Spain only recently emerged from Franco's authoritarianism. González promised no quick improvements in the economy and had little interest in nationalizing industry. The result: few disappointments or policy backdowns. The moral: Don't promise too much.

THE WEALTH GAP

As we considered in chapter 9, income differences in France are among the largest in Europe. This by itself is a political issue. Indeed, the 1976 report on income differences in Europe, showing France more unequal than Spain, confirmed precisely what the Socialists and Communists had been saying.

The wealth gap in France—and in most countries—is even wider than the income gap. Wealth and income are not the same: *income* is what you acquire (wages, dividends, etc.), and wealth is what you own or have saved (houses, stocks, etc.). Wealthy French people often have a chateau in the country as well as a house or apartment in Paris. Giscard d'Estaing, who was raised in a chateau, has at least three country houses. Even Socialist President Mitterrand has a nice country home.

At the bottom of the French socioeconomic ladder, an estimated two million French people form a "subproletariat" of unemployed, illiterate, despairing people. Giscard made a point of visiting such people and promised to make all French citizens more equal. He didn't, and Socialist François Mitterrand won the presidency in 1981 with the same promise. He too made little progress.

It's easy to promise, but the question is how to accomplish this goal. Taxes are supposed to provide one classic way: soak the rich and distribute the revenue to the poor. In few countries has this worked out, however, for most taxation systems have loopholes that help the rich stay wealthy. In France, as in America, the tax burden falls most heavily on wage and salary earners, lighter on those with "unearned" income from financial wheeling and dealing. And trying to collect taxes in France is a difficult task. The French, like the Italians, are masters at deceiving tax collectors. Wealthy French put their money in diamonds, gold and paintings (goods that can be hidden out of sight), agricultural or forest land (taxed at only one-fourth its value), and even government bonds, which because they don't list the owners' names are advertised as a "convenient and exceptionally discreet investment."

To make up for its tax shortfall, France—following Common Market policy—has a "value-added tax" (VAT), a large, hidden sales tax that doesn't show on the purchaser's receipt. Like sales taxes generally, the VAT penalizes poorer people more than rich; economists call it a "regressive" tax. But the French government relies on it for over 40 percent of its revenue because, since it is hidden, people don't complain too much.

Unequal income and wealth and unfair taxation remain a Communist and left-Socialist battle cry in France. The mainstream Socialists now realize how difficult it is to correct these imbalances.

FRANCE'S RACIAL PROBLEM

The worst-off among France's subproletariat are immigrant workers. And the poorest of these are workers from the former French colonies in North Africa and Black Africa. Like Britain, France is paying a delayed price for imperial grandeur: a race problem.

There are about two million foreign workers in France, 20 percent of the manual work force. With their families, immigrants number some 4.3 mil-

Is There a VAT in Your Future?

Throughout Western Europe, governments raise a good part of their revenues through value-added taxes (VAT) that make up some 10 to 20 percent or more of the prices of goods. But VAT is invisible; it's calculated into the price tag. Accordingly, European governments reason that it's not so painful as income taxes.

VAT makes some economic sense, too. By making prices higher, it channels money from consumption to savings. This helps contain inflation and makes more money available for loans that encourage economic expansion and new employment.

For these reasons, U.S. Presidents Nixon and Reagan have considered VAT for the United States. In the 1980s, especially, with massive budget deficits, VAT is an appealing possibility as Congress considers how to raise revenues without increasing income taxes. VAT has at least one drawback: as soon as people hear it is coming, they rush out to buy anything they can think of, and that's inflationary.

lion, about 8 percent of France's population. Those of European origin—Italian, Spanish, and Portuguese—suffer relatively little discrimination, for they are white, Catholic, and assimilable.

Tens of thousands of brown and black immigrants, however, are subjected to a kind of racism that French intellectuals used to think existed only in America. From Algeria, Morocco, Tunisia, Senegal, and Mali, Moslem immigrants—some of them illegal—take the hardest, dirtiest, lowest-paid work, tasks French citizens won't do anymore. They collect garbage, clean sewers, carry bricks, and labor on assembly lines. For housing they have shantytowns or barracks.

Worst of all, most French people fear and hate them. The French, like the British, don't like to admit their racism, but eruptions in recent years make the charge hard to deny. Algerians have been murdered. Brown-skinned people are subject to racist abuse. Signs say: "Stop the Brown Threat." A new political party sprang up in the 1980s with the avowed aim of ridding France of the immigrants (see box). Leftists founded a movement against racism to try to counter the increasing hatred. It was very much like Britain. In France, too, the working class can be quite racist, especially in times of high unemployment. As in Britain, France has cracked down on immigrants, expelling illegal ones and paying legal ones to return home. This is harder than in Britain, for illegals can sneak across France's land borders.

The conservative parties—Gaullist and Republican—have no trouble promising to stem the brown tide. For the parties of the left—Communist and Socialist—it is a sticky issue. Their ideology says equality, but many of their voters say get rid of the immigrants.

CONTROLLED NEWS MEDIA

Like many other aspects of life in centralized France, the news media are also under a certain degree of government control. Especially with the Fifth Republic this has become a political issue, the parties of the left charging the ruling conservatives with rigging the news for political ends. There is a good deal of truth to the charge.

The National Front: Another Flash Party

Very much like the Poujadists of the 1950s, the National Front sprang from out of nowhere in the 1980s to capture—at least for a while—a sizeable chunk of the French vote. The National Front's leader is Jean-Marie Le Pen, a former Poujadist deputy, who preaches a racist and nationalist line against France's resident foreigners. His 1984 book: *Les Français d'Abord* (*The French First*). In municipal and parliamentary by-elections, the National Front did well, especially in localities with a substantial immigrant population. Many Republican and Gaullist activists, having lost in 1981, transferred to the National Front.

It is improbable that the Front, which is also anti-Semitic, will win much of anything, but it is a measure of the rootlessness and confusion among French voters that explode from time to time in flash parties. Like the Poujadists, the National Front derives its main support from the petty bourgeoisie; it favors lower taxes and more law and order. Recall that Britain, facing the same immigrant problem, also produced a National Front.

De Gaulle was fascinated by television. During his self-imposed exile from 1946 to 1958, the general became a TV addict, especially of news programs. He was convinced that here was the ideal way to rule a country. Control of television would give a heroic leader the direct contact with the people Rousseau had dreamed about. De Gaulle was an impressive TV performer: attired in military uniform, with his sonorous voice and dramatic gestures, he put down two rebellions by televised calls for loyalty. Each of de Gaulle's five plebiscites was preceded by his televised calls for support.

Television, far from independent in France, is controlled by a government agency. News supportive of the regime is played up, critical items played down. Matters came to a head during the 1968 Events of May, when French TV news people, angered by a government that wanted to portray the striking students and workers as dangerous fools, went on a strike that lasted several weeks; many were fired. French people know their TV news is slanted and do not completely trust it; a majority told a poll they would prefer private television networks.

The Mitterrand government freed up French television, but not completely. In 1982 a nine-member High Commission for Television was set up that was supposed to be politically neutral. But the president and presiding officers of the National Assembly and Senate name three members each, and the first two of these were Socialist and named pro-Socialist people, enough to dominate the commission. Supervision of TV is something no French government—either of the right or left—is likely to give up. The main hope for French TV—which besides being biased is of a lower cultural level than British or West German television—is its gradual professionalization.

Newspapers are not under government control, but even here the government has an influence, through the state-subsidized *Agence France Presse* (AFP) wire service. Unlike the American AP virtually all European news services are government subsidized and usually government supervised. While legally autonomous, AFP's fifteen-member board has five government people on it, enough to make sure it doesn't become independent and critical. Much of the news in French newspapers comes from AFP. In any case, French newspaper readership is very low.

The French climate of mistrust described in chapter 9 extends to French news media. One result is that millions of French radio listeners and TV viewers tune to stations beyond France's borders. From Monaco and Luxembourg often come more objective news and livelier entertainment than from French stations. During election campaigns, many French politicians prefer to debate on Luxembourg television, where more people are liable to watch and take it seriously, than on French.

RESTIVE REGIONS

For centuries, Paris has been proud that France is a thoroughly unified country. Some regions, however, have kept alive a sense of their individuality, much as Scotland and Wales have in Britain.

One French problem comes from the ancient Britons who fled the Anglo-Saxons more than a millennium ago. Some eight hundred thousand Bretons still speak their ancient tongue, which is related to Welsh. Many long for a cultural identity separate from France. They want Breton taught in schools. Like Scottish and Welsh nationalism, much of the appeal of Breton nationalism is romantic. A Breton Liberation Front was formed in 1966 to press for Brittany's independence. Treated as a joke for years, the movement turned grim in 1978 when a Breton bomb demolished numerous art treasures in Versailles Palace, now a national museum.

Corsican nationalism has also appeared. A part of France only since 1768, the year before Napoleon's birth, Corsicans still generally speak their own dialect of Italian in addition to French. In 1975 there were riots on Corsica demanding autonomy for the island; several persons were killed. An illegal Corsican National Liberation Front stages hundreds of bombings a year and extracts a "revolutionary tax" from professional people to fund its campaign for independence. Corsica is much poorer than the rest of France and, even though it is heavily subsidized, some Corsicans feel it suffers from a colonial status. As part of Mitterrand's decentralization, Corsica got its own elected Corsican Assembly, but local nationalists consider it an ineffectual sham. Corsica probably does not have the explosive potential of Ulster or Spain's Basque country, but like them it is a problem that defies a cure.

Decentralization introduced a new controversy to French politics. While some like decentralization, other thought it would undermine national unity. A future conservative government may some day modify Mitterrand's innovation back toward the centralized pattern.

CHURCH AND STATE AGAIN

The old split between clerical and anticlerical forces has never completely died out in France. Under Mitterrand, it flared up again in the two-century-old dispute over Catholic schools. Just as British Labourites have long wanted to abolish "public" schools, the French left has long wished to end the anomolous status of private schools—mostly Catholic—that get state subsidies but stay free of state control. About 15 percent of French children go to Catholic schools.

Is Seven Years Too Long?

One factor in French elections, working to the disadvantage of incumbent presidents, is the seven-year presidential term. As a presidency wears on, many French people come to wonder if seven years isn't too long. As you may have noted, the French love to grumble, and seven years gives them plenty to grumble about. During this time scandals are bound to occur. The president's grandiose plan to redo France comes to little. The president's personality appears increasingly cold and aloof. And there's nothing the French voter can do about it, except vote for the opposition in the next legislative or municipal elections. After a few years of one president, the French feel stuck with a leader they no longer like. The above describes the feelings that developed under both Giscard d'Estaing (1974–81) and Mitterrand.

De Gaulle designed the 1958 constitution to give stability, and it did, maybe too much. From time to time U.S. political figures suggest going to a single six-year term for the U.S. president instead of two four-year terms. They argue that the present setup ties a president's hands for the first term: the president worries so much about getting reelected that he is unwilling to undertake difficult, bold, and important new policies. Before Americans amend the Constitution to make the president's term six years, however, they should consider the French experience.

Draft bills in 1983 and 1984 proposed gradually turning the teachers in Catholic schools into civil servants, as in regular schools. Catholics and conservatives saw this as a state take-over, and the howl of protests shook Paris. One demonstration drew a million who viewed the bills as robbing French parents of the freedom to choose what kind of education to give their children. The French left, long the champions of personal freedom, found themselves accused of limiting that freedom for others. Mitterrand fumed: "They're saying, 'Freedom! Freedom!' when they're really just defending their privileges." We are reminded once again that only about half of France is leftist and revolutionary; the other half is still conservative and Catholic.

The big clerical-anticlerical quarrel of the 1970s was abortion, illegal in France until 1975. Many women and the left in general argued that plenty of abortions were being performed illegally anyway. The Catholic hierarchy and many conservative politicians denounced the law. On a 1980 parliamentary vote confirming the law, Socialist and Communist deputies voted for it; most Gaullist and about half the Republican deputies voted against. French Catholics would still like to repeal the abortion law.

CAN THE COMMUNISTS BE TRUSTED?

A major quarrel in French politics is over the French Communist party. Can they be trusted? If they came to power would they preserve democracy? Have they really repudiated their radical and revolutionary origins?

In the 1970s *Eurocommunism* became a fashionable word. Applied to the Communist parties of France, Italy, and Spain (see box), it meant communism with a West European twist: democratic, independent of Moscow, ready to compromise with other parties, nonrevolutionary, and fit partners for a ruling coalition. The word was perhaps overused, for all Communist parties are different and have to be analyzed in relation to their country's political system.

Three "Eurocommunist" Parties

PARTY	PARTY CHIEF	MEMBERS	PERCENT WON LAST ELECTION
Italian (PCI)	Alessandro Natta	1,700,000	30
Spanish (PCE)	Gerardo Iglesias	60,000	4
French (PCF)	Georges Marchais	67,000	16

The giant Italian Communist party (PCI), which wins close to a third of the Italian vote, for years bent over backward to be moderate and advocated a "historic compromise" with the ruling Christian Democrats. The Spanish Communist party (PCE) emerged from the underground after Franco's death forswearing any revolutionary intentions; PCE wanted only to "consolidate democracy." PCE worked cooperatively with other Spanish parties in establishing a new constitution and even dropped the name Leninist from party descriptions. The French Communist party (PCF) does not present such a clear commitment to moderation and democracy. As we considered in chapter 10, in 1978 the PCF deliberately sabotaged their joint Common Program, with the Socialists, who they feared would dominate the government coalition. The French Communists tolerate little criticism or independent thinking in party ranks; every now and then leading party intellectuals resign or are expelled. The PCF is hostile to the European Common Market and even tried to keep Spain out. Grumbled one old Spanish Communist: "We knew Chauvin was French. We didn't know that he was also Communist." In response to the PCF's anti-European stance, the PCI and PCE snubbed their erstwhile allies.

If the Italian and Spanish Communist parties don't trust the French Communists, why should French voters? In most elections of the Fifth Republic, conservatives campaigned and won on fear of the Communists. In the 1980s this fear was to a certain extent overcome. Mitterrand demonstrated how he could use and discard the Communists. PCF chief Georges Marchais, who presided over a decline in party electoral strength, came under sharp criticism and was marked for replacement. Even with new leadership, though, chances are the PCF will stay in its self-constructed ghetto on the French left.

VOCABULARY BUILDING

Agence France Presse	Corsica	*petit bourgeois*	tariff
autonomy	decontrol	Planning Commission	technocrat
Breton	flash party	Poujadism	technological
Brittany	income	regressive tax	nationalism
chateau	indicative planning	subproletariat	value-added tax
Common Market	nationalization	subsidy	wealth

FURTHER REFERENCE

Ardagh, John. *France in the 1980s.* New York: Penguin Books, 1982.

Ashford, Douglas. *Policy and Politics in France: Living with Uncertainty.* Philadelphia: Temple University Press, 1982.

Estrin, Saul, and Peter Holmes. *French Planning in Theory and Practice.* Winchester, Mass.: Allen & Unwin, 1983.

Flower, J. E. *France Today,* 5th ed. New York: Methuen, 1984.

Freiberg, J. W. *The French Press: Class, State, and Ideology.* New York: Praeger, 1981.

Hoffmann, Stanley. "Year One," *New York Review of Books,* 12 August 1982.

Lange, Peter, and Maurizio Vannicelli, eds. *The Communist Parties of Italy, France and Spain.* Winchester, Mass.: Allen & Unwin, 1981.

Lauber, Volkmar. *The Political Economy of France: From Pompidou to Mitterrand.* New York: Praeger, 1983.

Wright, Vincent, ed. *Continuity and Change in France.* Winchester, Mass.: Allen & Unwin, 1983.

—— "Socialism and the Interdependent Economy: Industrial Policy-Making Under the Mitterrand Presidency," *Government and Opposition* 19 (summer 1984) 3.

part three

WEST GERMANY

12

THE IMPACT OF THE PAST

GERMANY'S UNCERTAIN BORDERS

Britain has natural borders. France claims to have natural borders, but one of its six sides (the northeast) has been disputed. Germany, however, has natural borders only on its north and south (the Baltic Sea and Alps), and this fact has contributed to its tumultuous history. Germany has expanded and contracted over the centuries, at times stretching from Alsace (now French) to East Prussia (now Polish and Russian). After World War II its eastern wing was chopped off, and the country was divided into eastern and western occupation zones. The area we are studying, the Federal Republic of Germany, is half that of the mighty Second Reich at the turn of the century.

Germany's location in the center of Europe and the flat, defenseless North German Plain imposed two unhappy options on the nation. If Germany was divided and militarily weak—its condition through most of history—it was Europe's battleground. On the other hand, if Germany was united and militarily strong enough to deter any combination of potential attackers, it was also strong enough to beat all its neighbors one at a time. When Germany unified in the last century, it automatically became a threat to the rest of Europe; it was big, populous, and strategically located.

Some Germans still dream of the reunification of their land, now divided into an East and a West Germany. The matter is not merely a question for Germans, however. The rest of Europe, especially the Soviet Union, fears a united Germany. Although some of Germany's West European neighbors won't say so publicly, the partition of Germany suits them fine. Geography, in making a united Germany a threat, has been unkind to Germany.

WHO ARE THE GERMANS?

Contrary to Nazi race theory, the Germans are as much an ethnic mixture as any people in Europe. The original Germans identified by the Romans were a collection of several barbarian tribes, some of which became Romanized. The invasion of the Huns in the fourth century set off gigantic migrations throughout Europe as everyone fled from their advance. Many Germans sought refuge in Roman territory, and soon Germanic tribes were roaming through and destroying the Roman Empire, eventually settling in various parts of it.

Since that time Germans have presented one face to the West and another to the East. To the West, to France and Italy, the heirs of Rome, they were awed and respectful of the superior culture, which they tried to copy. To the East, however, they saw barbarians—first Huns, then Slavs—whom they either Germanized or pushed back. Whole Slavic- or Baltic-speaking areas were Germanized, and many of today's Germans are of East European descent. Some Germans hate to admit it, but they are a combination of Celts, Romans, several Germanic tribes, Slavs, Balts, and even Jews. When the Nazis introduced their model of the perfect nordic specimen, some Germans quietly chuckled, for practically none of the Nazi leaders matched the tall, athletic, blond, blue-eyed image.

The Changing Shape of Germany

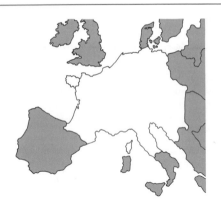

800: Charlemagne's Holy Roman Empire

1648: After Westphalia

1815: The German Confederation

1871: The Second Reich

1919: The Weimar Republic

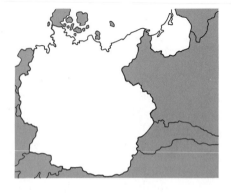

1939: Hitler's Third Reich

1945: Occupied Germany (four zones)

1949: Two Germanies

THE FRAGMENTED NATION

The Germanic tribes were so impressed by Rome—whose empire they were inadvertently destroying—that they pretended to preserve and continue the empire. When in 800 the Frankish king Charlemagne was crowned in Rome, he called his gigantic realm the Holy Roman Empire. Although it soon fell apart, the German wing continued calling itself that until Napoleon ended the farce in 1806.

In England, as we saw, power between king and nobles was kept in balance, resulting in a constitutional monarchy that moved in spurts toward civil liberty, limited government, and rule by Parliament. In France, absolutism upset the equation, and the French kings amassed more and more power leading to a centralized, bureaucratic state. Germany went the other way: the nobles gained more and more power until by the thirteenth century the emperor was a mere figurehead while princes and leading churchmen ran ministates as they saw fit. Germany was not one country but a crazy-quilt of hundreds of independent principalities and cities.

The split between Roman Catholic and Protestant accentuated Germany's fragmentation. Protestant reformer Martin Luther reflected the feeling of much of northern Germany that the Roman church was corrupt and ungodly. The North German princes especially didn't like paying taxes to Rome and found Lutheranism a good excuse to stop. South Germany stayed mostly Catholic. A predominantly Protestant north and Catholic south still characterize modern Germany.

Two wars resulted from the religious question. In the first, the Schmalkaldic War (named after the town of Schmalkaden where Protestant princes formed a coalition) of 1545 to 1555, the Habsburg Emperor Charles V nearly succeeded in crushing Lutheranism, when the Protestants allied with Catholic France to beat Charles. Trying to decide which parts of Germany should be Catholic and which Protestant, the Religious Peace of Augsburg in

1555 came up with the formula *cuius regio eius religio*—"whoever reigns, his religion." Thus the religion of the local prince decided an area's religion, a point that deepened the disunity of Germany and the power of local princes.

The peace proved shaky, though, and in 1618, as the Habsburgs again tried to consolidate their power, a much worse war broke out, the Thirty Years' War. Again, at first the Catholic Habsburgs won. By 1631, help from other countries arrived. Cardinal Richelieu of France saw Habsburg might encircling his country, so he sided Catholic France with the Protestants. In international relations, power and national interests are a lot more important than religious or ideological affinity. A strong Swedish army under Gustavus Adolphus battled in Germany for the Protestants. Germany suffered terribly, losing a third of its population, many by starvation. Until World War I, the Thirty Years' War was the worst war in human history. The Treaty of Westphalia in 1648 confirmed *cuius regio eius religio* and left Germany atomized into 360 separate political entities.

Impressive German Words: Obrigkeit

One of the offshoots of the Protestant Reformation and breakup of Germany into ministates was the exaltation of the power and authority of each prince. *Obrigkeit,* "authority," was preached by Luther in defending princely rule against rebellious peasants. While Luther's religious doctrines aimed at making people free, his political doctrines aimed at making them obedient to authortity. Blind obedience to authority became a German characteristic, and a German thought of himself or herself as an *Untertan,* a "subject," someone who is under *(unter)* authority.

Consider the political impact of religion on the three countries we have studied so far. In Britain, there was a nearly clean break with Rome; the return of Catholic kings merely confirmed the power of Parliament. In France, the Catholic Church and *ancien régime* stayed loyal to one another while many French turned anticlerical, leading to a division of French society into conservative Catholics and anticlerical radicals. Germany didn't split into clerical and anticlerical factions but into Catholic and Protestant. The result was ghastly: a long and ruinous war, further breakup of an already fragmented country, and centuries of ill will between Germans of different faiths. To this day, you can to some extent predict how a West German will vote if you know his or her religion: Catholics are more conservative, Protestants more liberal or left.

THE RISE OF PRUSSIA

One German state eventually came to dominate the others. Brandenburg, later known as Prussia, situated in North Germany around Berlin, during the eighteenth century expanded greatly, taking over the eastern German conquests of the Middle Ages along the Baltic and adding Silesia and parts of the Rhineland. In the eastern Baltic regions a type of nobility had developed, descended from the old Teutonic knights, that had a major impact on German history. The *Junkers* (from *Junge Herren,* "young gentlemen") held great estates worked by obedient serfs. Unlike the English lords, however, they did not retain their independence and act as a counterweight to the king but became a state nobility, dependent on the government and controlling all the higher civil-service and military positions. Famous for their discipline and attention to detail, the *Junkers* contributed to modern Germany a passion for excellence in both military and civil administration.

Prussian kings, with potential enemies on all sides, became obsessed with military power, leading to the wisecrack that "Prussia is not a country with an army but an army with a country." In the early eighteenth century, King Frederick William acted as drillmaster to his entire people, demanding military obedience and Prussian efficiency not only on the parade ground—where he personally marched his hand-picked corps of oversize soldiers—but in civilian life as well.

His son, Frederick the Great, who ruled from 1740 to 1786, like France's Louis XIV, perfected what he inherited. In Frederick's case this inheritance was the Prussian army which he kept in such a high state of readiness that it frightened the monarchs of larger states. Administering his kingdom personally, Frederick became known as the "enlightened despot" who brought art and culture (Voltaire stayed at his court for a while) as well as military triumphs and territorial expansion to Prussia. A brilliant commander and daring strategist, Frederick served as a model for expansion-minded German nationalists. Trying to identify himself with Frederick the Great, Adolf Hitler in 1933 announced the founding of the Third Reich from Frederick's tomb in Berlin.

Impressive German Words: Machtstaat

Prussia was the prime example of a *Machtstaat*, a state *(Staat)* based on power *(Macht*, a cognate of might). Prussia expanded by means of *Machtpolitik* (power politics), using a strong army and tricky diplomacy. Prussia also grew into a *Soldaten und Beamtenstaat*, a state run by soldiers and bureaucrats. Its characteristics were passed on to a unified Germany in the nineteenth century.

GERMAN NATIONALISM

At the time of the French Revolution, there were still over three hundred German states. Prussia and Austria were the strongest of them, but they too were pushovers for Napoleon's conquering legions. German liberals, fed up with the backwardness and fragmentation of their country, at first welcomed the French as liberators and modernizers. Napoleon consolidated the many German ministates—but not Prussia or Austria—into about thirty, calling them the Confederation of the Rhine, and introduced new laws to free the economy and society from the accumulated mire of centuries.

The French brought with them more than liberalism, however; everywhere they went they infected conquered lands with the new idea of nationalism, the exaggerated belief in the greatness and unity of one's country. Nationalism is the most contagious -ism of all; when one country catches it, the fever soon spreads to neighboring lands. In short order Germans, Russians, and Spaniards were fired with anti-French nationalism. Napoleon, without realizing it, had let an imp out of the bottle; the push he gave to German nationalism indirectly led to three German invasions of France. Great historical events have highly unpredictable aftereffects.

As we saw in the case of France's borrowing English and American notions of freedom, ideas conceived in one country often become warped, exaggerated, or distorted when applied to another. This happened with German nationalism. The French already had a unified country and secure national identity; the Germans didn't. French nationalism was first and foremost a defence of *la patrie,* then a desire to spread liberalism throughout Europe. There was little racist about French nationalism. German nationalism was emotional, hate-filled, racist, and conservative. The French loved reason; the German nationalists were romantics, harkening back to the primitive tribal passions still lurking in the German soul. Hitler plugged into exactly the same theme.

Germany looked to Prussia for leadership in throwing off the French yoke, and Prussian troops did contribute to Napoleon's downfall. Like France, Germany after Napoleon was not the same. Caught up in nationalism and liberalism—more of the former than the latter—German thinkers wanted a unified and modernized nation. The ultraconservative Austrian Prince Metternich, who hated both nationalism and liberalism, helped create a German Confederation of thirty-nine states, which he thought would contribute to European stability after Napoleon.

Impressive German Words: Volksgeist

A combination of *Volk* (people) and *Geist* (spirit), German nationalist intellectuals of the nineteenth century used "spirit of the people" in a racist sense, meaning that the spirit of the German people was superior to all others. German professors and writers attributed mystical qualities to the German *Volk,* a term that came to mean *race* and was heavily used by the Nazis.

In 1848 revolution broke out all over Europe as discontented liberals and nationalists sought to overthrow the Metternichian system. In the midst of urban uprisings German liberals met in Frankfurt to set up a unified, democratic Germany. They sent a delegation to Berlin to offer the king of Prussia leadership of a German constitutional monarchy, but he contemptuously refused it with the remark that he "would not accept a crown from the gutter." The army cleared out the National Assembly in Frankfurt, and German liberals either converted to pure nationalism or emigrated to the United States. The first big tide of German immigrants to America was in 1848–49.

THE SECOND REICH

In contrast to the attempts of liberal nationalists in 1848, German unification came not from the people but from above, from the growth of Prussia. Neither was it the work of liberals but rather of a staunch conservative, Otto von Bismarck, who had seen the liberals in action in 1848 and thought they were fools. Bismarck, who became Prussia's prime minister in 1862, wasn't really a German nationalist; he was first and foremost a loyal Prussian servant of his king who saw German unification under Prussian leadership as the only way to preserve and defend Prussia. As such, Bismarck's goals were quite limited; he had no intention of turning a united Germany into a military, expansionist state.

For Bismarck, armies and warfare were simply tools. In 1862 when the Prussian parliament was deadlocked over whether to increase the military budget, Bismarck ordered new taxes and spent the money without parliamentary approval. He declared: "Not by speeches and majority decisions will the great questions of the time be decided—that was the fault of 1848 and 1849—but by iron and blood."

Bismarck used his military tools to solve the great question of his day— who was to lead a unified Germany, Prussia, or Austria? In a series of three limited wars—in 1864 against Denmark, in 1866 against Austria, and in 1870 against France—Bismarck first consolidated the many German states behind Prussia, then got rid of Austria, then firmed up German unity. The new Second Reich (Charlemagne's was the first) was actually proclaimed in France, at Versailles Palace, in 1871.

The Second Reich, lasting from 1871 to 1918, was not a democracy. The legislature, the *Reichstag*, had only limited power, namely, to approve or reject the budget. The chancellor (prime minister) was not "responsible" to the

Bismarck's Dubious Legacy

Otto von Bismarck, Germany's chancellor from 1871 to 1890, was a Prussian *Junker* to the bone, and the stamp he put on a unified Germany retarded its democratic development for over half a century. Bismarck and Disraeli knew and liked each other, and many compared them as dynamic conservatives. English and German conservatism, however, are two different things. Disraeli's Tories widened the electorate and welcomed a fair fight in Parliament. Bismarck barely tolerated parties and parliaments. Bismarck left Germany an antidemocratic and one-man style of governance that was overcome only by Allied occupation following World War II.

Bismarck's most dangerous legacy to Germany, however, was in his foreign policy. To *Machtpolitik* Bismarck added *Realpolitik,* the politics of realism, and with these he manipulated first his own Prussia and then the rest of Europe to produce a unified Germany. War for Bismarck was just a tool. Cynical amorality was another pattern Bismarck bequeathed to Germany.

Bismarck's real problem, as Henry Kissinger has pointed out, was that he was a tough act to follow. Bismarck used cynical power politics for very limited

ends—the unification of Germany. His successors picked up the amoral *Machtpolitik* but forgot about the limits, the *Realpolitik.* Bismarck, for example could have easily conquered all of Denmark, Austria, and France, but he didn't because he knew that would bring dangerous consequences. Bismarck used war in a very controlled way, to unify Germany rather than to conquer Europe. Once that was done, Bismarck spent the rest of his career making sure potential enemies would not form a coalition against the Reich.

Bismarck cautioned that a tight alliance with Austria, supporting Austrian ambitions in the Balkans, could eventually lead to war. "The entire Balkans," he said, were "not worth the bones of one Pomeranian grenadier." Curiously, his prediction came true. That was precisely the way World War I came about. Bismarck's successors, men of far less ability and far greater emotion, let Austria pull them into war over the Balkans. The real tragedy of Bismarck is that he constructed a delicate balance of European power that could not be maintained without himself as the master juggler.

parliament—that is, he couldn't be voted out—and hand picked his own ministers. The German *Kaiser* (from Caesar) was not just a figurehead but a working executive. The individual states that had been enrolled into a united Germany retained their autonomy, a forerunner of the present federal system.

Germany, which had been industrially backward compared to Britain and France, surged ahead, especially in iron and steel. The once-pastoral Ruhr became a smoky workshop. With the growth of industry came a militant and well-organized German labor movement starting in the 1860s. In 1863 Ferdinand Lassalle formed the General German Workers' Association, partly a union and partly a party. In 1875 the group became the *Sozialdemokratische Partei Deutschlands* (SPD), now the oldest and one of the most successful social-democratic parties in the world.

Bismarck so hated the SPD that he suppressed it in 1878 and tried to take the wind out of the Socialists' sails by promoting numerous welfare measures himself in the *Reichstag.* In the 1880s Germany became the first country with medical and accident insurance, a pension plan, and state employment offices. Germany has been a welfare state ever since.

Impressive German Words: Kulturkampf

Bismarck, following Prussian tradition, put the state ahead of any church. There could be nothing higher than *der Staat,* held Bismarck, and Germans should have no other loyalties. The many German Catholics saw things differently, namely, that in questions of faith and morals they should turn to Rome, not Berlin. Bismarck's efforts to break the German Catholic church of this attitude took the name *Kulturkampf,* meaning culture struggle. Between 1871 and 1875 Bismarck had the Jesuits expelled, broke diplomatic relations with the Vatican, made civil marriage compulsory, and did everything he could to harass the church into giving in. It didn't, and Bismarck finally backed down. The *Kulturkampf* left a sense of Catholic differentness within Germany, of resentment of Catholic south against Protestant north, and led to the formation of the Catholic Center party.

THE CATASTROPHE: WORLD WAR I

The Second Reich might have evolved into a democracy. Political parties became more important. After Bismarck was fired in 1890, the SPD came into the open to win a million and a half votes that same year. By 1912 it had won more than four million votes and almost a third of the *Reichstag's* seats; it was Germany's largest party. Gaining responsibility in elected offices, the German Socialists slowly grew moderate, turning away from their Marxist roots and toward "revisionism," the idea that socialism can come gradually through democratic means rather than by radical revolution. So domesticated had the SPD become that in 1914, when the emergency war budget was placed before the *Reichstag,* SPD deputies forgot about the "international solidarity of all workers" and voted like good Germans—for it.

After Kaiser Wilhelm II dismissed Bismarck in 1890, Germany's foreign policy lost its sense of limits. Wilhelm placed more and more generals in his cabinet and started seeing Germany as competing with Britain. A program of naval armament, begun by Germany in 1889, touched off a race with Britain to build more battleships. Wilhelm supported the Boers against the British in South Africa and the Austrians who were coming into conflict with the Russians over the Balkans. By the time the shots were fired in Sarajevo in 1914, Germany had managed to surround itself with enemies, exactly what Bismarck had worked to prevent.

The Germans, with their quick victories of half a century earlier in mind, marched joyously off to war. In early August of 1914 Kaiser Wilhelm told his troops: "You will be home before the leaves have fallen from the trees." All of Europe thought the war would be short, but it took four years and ten million lives until Germany surrendered.

Many Germans couldn't believe they had lost militarily. They had done so well: in 1914 they'd almost reached Paris, and in 1917 they'd knocked Russia out of the war. Fed nothing but war propaganda, Germans didn't understand that the army and economy had given their utmost and could give no more. The war ended before there was any fighting on German soil, so civilians didn't see for themselves how their troops were beaten. Making matters worse was the Versailles treaty, which unjustly placed total blame for the war on Germany and demanded an impossible $33 billion in reparations. Germany was stripped of its few colonies (in Africa and the South Pacific) and lost a chunk of Prussia to make a "Polish corridor" to the Baltic. Many Germans could think of nothing but revenge. If a treaty is to be judged on what it produces, then Versailles was a supercatastrophe, for it led straight to Hitler and World War II.

Impressive German Words: Dolchstoss

Surprised by Germany's surrender in 1918, right-wing Germans darkly muttered the word *Dolchstoss* (stab in the back) to explain the Reich's defeat. According to the *Dolchstoss* myth, Germany had not lost militarily but had been betrayed on the home front by democrats, socialists, Bolsheviks, Jews, and anyone else right wingers could think of. The *Dolchstoss* legend contributed to Hitler's rise and to German willingness to again march to war.

REPUBLIC WITHOUT DEMOCRATS

Looking back, we can see how the Weimar Republic—which got its name from the town of Weimar, where its federal constitution was drawn up in 1919—started with three strikes against it. In the first place, Germans had no experience with a republic or democracy; yet suddenly the nation became a democratic republic when the Kaiser fled to Holland at the war's end. Second, for many Germans, the Weimar Republic lacked legitimacy; it had been forced upon Germany by the victorious allies and "back stabbers" who had betrayed the Reich. Third, the Versailles treaty was so punitive and its demands for payment so high that Germany was humiliated and economically hobbled.

It has been estimated that only about one German in four was a wholehearted democrat. About another quarter hated democracy. Other Germans went along with the new republic until the economy got rough and then shifted their sympathies to authoritarian movements of the left or right. Weimar

Germany, it has been said, was a republic without republicans and a democracy without democrats.

The German government, in a crisis with France over reparations, printed money without limit. The result was a "hyperinflation" so insane that by 1923 it took a wheelbarrowful of marks to buy a loaf of bread. Especially hard hit were middle class families who saw their businesses and savings wiped out; many of them became eager recruits for the Nazis. The period left an indelible mark on Germans, and to this day the Bonn government places great emphasis on keeping inflation low. Inflation is a frightening word in Germany.

By the mid-1920s the economy stabilized and things looked better. Cabinets changed frequently: twenty-six in fourteen years. The Social Democrat, Catholic Center, and Conservative parties were the largest; the Nazis were tiny and considered something of a joke. Then the world depression started in 1929,

The Horrors of Polarized Pluralism

Italian political scientist Giovanni Sartori has described what happens when a multiparty system such as Weimar's or Spain's in the 1930s gets terribly sick. The leading parties in the center face nasty opposition on both their right and left. In competing for votes in a highly ideological atmosphere, extremist parties try to outbid each other by offering radical solutions. Votes flee from the center to the extremes, to parties dedicated to overthrowing the system. Sartori called this syndrome "polarized pluralism," and the last years of Weimar are a good example of it. Compare the percentage of votes parties got in 1928 with what they got in 1933, and the "center-fleeing" tendency is clear:

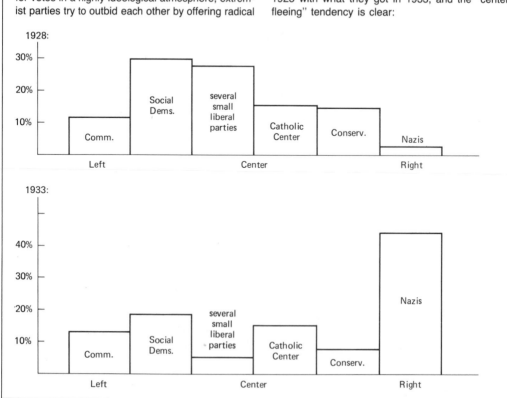

and German democracy went down the drain. Moderate parties declined, and extremist parties—the Nazis and the Communists—grew (see box). Unemployment was the key: the more people out of work, the higher the Nazi vote.

One combination might have blocked the Nazis' rise to power. If the Social Democrats and Communists had forgotten their differences and had formed a united front, the Weimar system might have been saved. But the German Communists, who split off from the SPD after World War I, reviled the Social Democrats as nonrevolutionaries who had sold out to the capitalists. Under Stalin's orders, the German Communists rejected a joint program with the Socialists on the theory that Hitler would be a passing phenomenon and when Germany collapsed the Communists would take over. This was one of Stalin's greatest blunders, and Communists and Socialists alike paid for it with their lives.

By late 1932, the Nazis had won a third of the German vote, and the aged President Hindenberg, a conservative general, named Hitler as chancellor the following January. The Weimar Republic, Germany's first try at democracy, died after a short life of fourteen years (1919–33).

THE THIRD REICH

Nazi was the German nickname for the National Socialist German Workers party. Nazism, like other forms of fascism, had a pseudosocialist component that promised jobs and welfare measures. Many Germans were delighted to get work on government projects, such as building the new *Autobahns*. Although the Nazis never won a majority in a fair election, by the late 1930s it is certain a majority of Germans supported Hitler, whom they saw as restoring prosperity.

Since most Germans had not been enthusiastic about democracy, relatively few protested the systematic growth of tyranny. Some Communists and Socialists went underground, to prison, or into exile, and some old-style conservatives disliked Hitler, who, as far as they were concerned, was nothing but an Austrian guttersnipe. But most Germans got along by going along. Centuries of being taught to keep their place and obey authority led them to accept Nazi rule.

For opportunists, membership in the Nazi party offered better jobs and sometimes snappy uniforms. Many ex-Nazis now claim they joined only to further their careers, and most are probably telling the truth. You don't need true believers to staff a tyranny; opportunists will do just as well. The frightening thing about Nazi Germany was how it could turn normal humans into cold-blooded mass murderers.

Among the first and worst to suffer were the Jews. Exploiting widely held racist feelings, Hitler depicted the Jews as a poisonous, foreign element who aimed to enslave Germany in the service of international capitalism, international communism, or both. Logical consistency was never the Nazis' strong point. Jews were deprived, one step at a time, of their civil rights, their jobs, their property, their citizenship, and finally their lives.

Few Germans were aware of it, but Hitler ached for war. At first he seemed to be merely consolidating Germany's boundaries, absorbing the Saar in 1935, Austria and the Sudetenland in 1938, and Bohemia, Moravia, and Memel in 1939. And it was so easy! Germany's enemies from World War I, still war weary, did nothing to stop the growth of German power and territory. Hitler's generals, it is now known, were ready to overthrow him if the British had said no to his demands at Munich in 1938. It looked as though Hitler could amass victories without even fighting, and the German generals suppressed their doubts. Finally, when the Germans conquered Poland in September 1939, Britain and

Impressive German Words: Gleichschaltung

The Nazi style of running an economy and a country was not to nationalize everything like the Communists but rather to "coordinate" things by placing loyal Nazis in all the key positions in industry, the army, civil service, news media, education, and the justice system. *Gleichschaltung* (coordination) signified leaving the existing institutions pretty much in place but "coordinating" their function so as to serve party ends.

Impressive German Words: Lebensraum

In Nazi race theory, the "superior" German nordics deserved more space in which to live—*Lebensraum,* literally "living space." The natural area for expansion, Nazis argued, was eastward, like the old Teutonic knights had pushed along the Baltic. This *Drang nach Osten* (push to the east) would lead to a gigantic German Reich in which some of the Slavic inhabitants (Poles, Russians, Czechs, and others) would be exterminated and the rest enslaved. Such was Hitler's dream and motivation for his invasion of Poland and Russia.

France declared war. France was overrun, Britain was contained beyond the Channel, and by the summer of 1940 Germany or its allies ruled virtually all of Europe.

The following year Hitler ordered that his "final solution" to the Jewish question begin: extermination. Death camps killed some six million Jews and a large number of inconvenient Christians (Poles, gypsies, and others). A new word was added to mankind's vocabulary: genocide, the murder of an entire people. To this day, some Germans claim they didn't know what was going on, but neither did they show any inclination to find out.

Hitler—just a week before he attacked Poland in 1939—had completed a nonaggression pact with Stalin. In the summer of 1941, however, Hitler assembled the biggest army in history and gave the order for "Barbarossa," the conquest and enslavement of the Soviet Union. Here, at last, Hitler's dream totally parted company with reality. The Russian winter and surprising resistance of the Red Army devoured whole German divisions. From late 1942 on it was all downhill for Germany. The end result of Hitler's attack on Russia can be seen on any map in Europe: the eastern half of Europe under Soviet control, Germany broken up, its easternmost territories lost for good, and its central portion a separate state (East Germany) that cannot in the foreseeable future rejoin West Germany.

Another Tale of Two Flags

Like France, Germany's divided loyalties have been symbolized by its flag's colors. The German nationalist movement flag was black, red, and gold; colors of a Prussian regiment that fought against Napoleon. By 1848 it symbolized a democratic, united Germany. Bismarck rejected it. For the Second Reich's flag he chose Prussia's black and white plus the white and red of the medieval Hansa commercial league.

The Reich's collapse in 1918 and founding of the Weimar Republic brought the democratic black, red, and gold back to the German flag. Hitler, a fanatic on symbols, insisted on the authoritarian black, red, and white colors. Finally the Bonn republic designed the present West German flag with the original democratic colors:

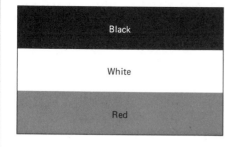

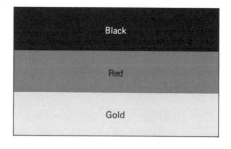

Might Have Been: The Plot To Kill Hitler

On July 20, 1944, a group of high-ranking German officers tried to kill Hitler. Had he not stepped away from the map table, the briefcase-bomb under it would have surely succeeded. More than two hundred anti-Nazi Germans were cruelly executed for their part in the plot. They came from all walks of life: generals, diplomats, Weimar politicians, trade unionists, scholars, theologians of both Christian confessions, and students. They were united in their opposition to totalitarianism, mass murder, and the war, which they would have ended as quickly as possible. Although they failed, they left a valuable legacy: the symbol that Germans fought Hitler, a moral statement for present-day West Germany.

THE OCCUPATION

This time there could be no *Dolchstoss* myth; Germans watched Russians, Americans, British, and French fight their way through Germany. German government ceased to exist, and the country was run by foreign occupiers. At Yalta in February 1945 the Allied leaders agreed to divide Germany into four zones for temporary occupation; Berlin, inside the Soviet zone, was similarly divided.

The Cold War grew in large part out of the way the Soviets handled Germany. The Soviets, having lost some twenty million people in the war, were intent on looting the conquered nation. They dismantled whole factories, shipped them home, and flooded the country with inflated military currency. The British and Americans, on the other hand, distressed at the brutal Soviet take-over of East Europe, decided to revive German economic and political life in their zones. The U.S. Marshall Plan and other aid programs pumped $3.5 billion into German recovery. In 1948 the British and Americans introduced a currency reform and a new Deutsche mark, which effectively cut out the Soviets from further looting the western zones. In retaliation, the Russians blockaded Berlin, which was supplied for nearly a year by an incredible British-American airlift. The Cold War was on, centered in Germany.

In 1949, the Western allies decided to give governing power back to Germans in order to insure West German cooperation against Soviet power. Accordingly, the present West German regime is a child of the Cold War with the Americans acting as godfathers. Although nobody was quite sure it would work, it did—spectacularly. To examine how, let us turn to West Germany's institutions.

VOCABULARY BUILDING

Alps	hyperinflation	principality	*Staat*
Baltic	*Junker*	Prussia	Versailles
Barbarossa	*Kaiser*	*Reichstag*	*Volk*
Dolchstoss	Marshall Plan	reparations	Weimar
final solution	nordic	revisionism	Westphalia
Gleichschaltung	opportunist	Second Reich	Yalta
Habsburg	polarized pluralism		

FURTHER REFERENCE

Bracher, Karl Dietrich. *The German Dictatorship: The Origins, Structure, and Effects of National Socialism.* New York: Praeger, 1970.

Bullock, Alan. *Hitler, A Study in Tyranny.* New York: Harper & Row, 1962.

Craig, Gordon A. *Germany, 1866–1945.* New York: Oxford University Press, 1978.

Kissinger, Henry. "The White Revolutionary: Reflections on Bismarck," *Daedalus* 97 (1968), 888–924.

Lepsius, M. Rainer. "From Fragmented Party Democracy to Government by Emergency Decree and National Socialist Takeover: Germany," in *The Break-*

down of Democratic Regimes: Europe, ed. by J. Linz and A. Stepan. Baltimore: Johns Hopkins University Press, 1978.

Merkl, Peter H. *The Origin of the West German Republic.* New York: Oxford University Press, 1963.

Pinson, Koppel S. *Modern Germany: Its History and Civilization.* New York: Macmillan, 1966.

Sartori, Giovanni. *Parties and Party Systems: A Framework for Analysis.* New York; Cambridge University Press, 1976.

Shirer, William L. *The Rise and Fall of the Third Reich: A History of Nazi Germany.* New York: Simon & Schuster, 1960.

13

THE KEY
INSTITUTIONS

A TRUE FEDERATION

West Germany, founded in 1949, reverted back to an old pattern in German history: giving its component parts plenty of local autonomy. West Germany is a true federation; its ten *Länder* (states) have at least as much power as American states, maybe more. Education, medical care, police, and many other functions are the province of the *Land* government. Part of the reason for this strong federalism was to repudiate the centralization of the Nazi period and to make sure that such power could never become so concentrated again.

West Berlin presents a unique situation. Located 110 miles (180 kilometers) inside East Germany, Berlin is still nominally governed by the four occupying powers. The Soviet sector, however, has become the capital of East Germany, and the American, British, and French sectors have become nearly a part of West Germany. Bonn counts West Berlin as the eleventh *Land,* but the three Western allies do not recognize it as such, and all four agree that it is safer under Allied protection than if it were officially part of the Federal Republic. So legally West Berlin is not a part of West Germany, but in practice it is. West German currency, laws, and passports apply in West Berlin, but the city sends only nonvoting representatives to the Bonn parliament.

THE PRESIDENT

West Germany's federal president *(Bundespräsident)* is the classic type of European president, a figurehead with few political but many symbolic duties. Like the monarchs of Britain and Scandinavia, the German president is an official greeter and ambassador of good will rather than a working executive. The French president of the Third and Fourth Republics and the Italian president today are other examples of highly forgettable presidencies. De Gaulle, of course, totally transformed the French presidency.

Impressive German Words:
Bundesrepublik

In West Germany today almost everything associated with the federal government in Bonn bears the prefix *Bundes-*, meaning "federal." Thus:

- *Bundesrepublik Deutschland* is the Federal Republic of Germany.
- *Bundestag* is the lower house of the federal parliament.
- *Bundesrat* is the upper house.
- *Bundeskanzler* is the federal chancellor (prime minister).

- *Bundeswehr* is the army.
- *Bundesbahn* is the national railway system.
- *Bundesministerium* is a federal ministry.
- *Bundesregierung* is the federal government.

The prefix *Bundes-* is new, stemming only from the founding of West Germany in 1949, and has a modern, democratic ring to it. The old prefix to many of the same words, *Reichs-*(imperial), has a slightly sinister, discarded connotation. In Germany, "federal" has become synonymous with "democratic."

Impressive German Words:
Grundgesetz

In 1949, the founders of West Germany were hopeful that the east and west sections of their country would be reunified. Accordingly, they called their founding document the Basic Law *(Grundgesetz)* rather than constitution *(Verfassung),* which was to come only when Germany was reunified. They meant to indicate that the Federal Republic was temporary and operating under temporary rules. By now the name is a legal quibble, for the Basic Law is the Federal Republic's permanent constitution and an excellent one at that.

The president is the "head of state" rather than "head of government" (for the distinction, see chapter 3), and as such receives new foreign ambassadors who present their credentials to him rather than to the people they will actually be working with, the chancellor and foreign minister. In addition, the president proclaims laws (after they've been passed by parliament), dissolves the *Bundestag* (upon the chancellor's request), and appoints and dismisses the chancellor (after the leading party has told him to). In short, the West German president is, to use Bagehot's terms, a "dignified" rather than "efficient" part of government.

The president is elected by a special Federal Assembly composed of all *Bundestag* members plus an equal number from state legislatures. The president serves five years and may be reelected once. The dead-end job is usually given as a reward to distinguished politicians about to retire. In 1984, the courtly Richard von Weizsäcker, the Christian Democratic mayor of West Berlin, was elected president with the overwhelming support of both major parties.

THE CHANCELLOR

West Germany has a weak president but a strong chancellor. Unlike the changing chancellors of the Weimar Republic, the Bonn chancellorship has been a stable and durable office. Part of the reason for this is that the Basic Law makes it impossible to oust the chancellor on a vote of no-confidence unless the Bundestag simultaneously votes *in* a new chancellor. This reform ended one of the worst problems of parliamentary (as opposed to presidential) governments, namely, their dependence on an often-fickle legislative majority.

The West German reform is called "constructive no-confidence" because parliament has to offer something constructive—a new chancellor—rather than a mere negative majority to get rid of the old one. This has happened only once, in 1982, when the small Free Democratic party abandoned its coalition with the Social Democrats in midterm and voted in a new Christian Democratic chancellor. Constructive no-confidence makes ousting a chancellor a rarity.

Another reason the chancellor is strong stems from the first occupant of that office: Konrad Adenauer, a tough, shrewd politician who helped found the Federal Republic and served as chancellor its first fourteen years (1949–63). First occupants, such as Washington in the American presidency, can put a stamp on the position, defining its powers and setting its style for generations. As

Der Alte: Adenauer

Arrogant, high-handed, crusty, obstinate, authoritarian, and maybe a little senile. All of these complaints were made about Konrad Adenauer (1876–1967), but even his critics admit that *der Alte* (the Old Man) more than any other German contributed to the founding of democracy in West Germany.

The most amazing thing about Adenauer was that his career really didn't begin until he was 70 years old. Trained in law, Adenauer became mayor of Cologne in 1917 and lasted until the Nazis kicked him out in 1933. Vaguely implicated in the 1944 plot to kill Hitler, Adenauer was arrested and held in jail for two months.

A devout Catholic, Adenauer was active in the prewar Center party. After World War II, people like Adenauer decided not to revive a Catholic-only party but to form a larger center-right grouping, the Christian Democratic Union, which welcomed both Catholics and Protestants. In 1946 Adenauer became chairman of the CDU's Rhineland branch and in 1948 president of the parliamentary council in Bonn. Some say Bonn was chosen as West Germany's capital because it was near his home on the banks of the Rhine.

In 1949 the first *Bundestag* elected him chancellor. Adenauer's choice of coalition partners had a major and positive impact on Bonn's democratic stability. Instead of a "grand coalition" with the Social Democrats, Adenauer formed a small coalition of the CDU and other conservative parties, some of which the CDU eventually absorbed. This polarized politics in a healthy way. The SPD in opposition had to rethink its program and patiently build electoral support before finally entering the cabinet in 1966. The wait did both major parties good and contributed to the present "two-plus" party system in Germany.

In foreign relations, Adenauer pointed the Federal Republic decisively westward. As a Catholic Rhinelander, Adenauer didn't have to think twice about whether to integrate Germany with the West or with Protestant Prussia. In 1952 Stalin hinted that Germany could be reunified if it were neutral. Adenauer would have none of it; he cemented Germany into NATO, the European Coal and Steel Community, the Common Market, and a special relationship with France. The price was the permanent division of Germany.

Some say that Adenauer was never a German nationalist but rather a West European Catholic. It's a good explanation of his foreign policy. A symbolic high point came in 1962 when Adenauer and de Gaulle knelt together in prayer in the ancient French cathedral of Reims, the two old enemy nations united at last in the arms of the church. Bismarck must have turned in his grave: the Catholics had finally won the *Kulturkampf*.

Symbolizing German-French ties, Adenauer and de Gaulle celebrated Mass together in the Reims cathedral in 1962. *(German Information Center)*

may be judged from German history, Germans respond more to strong leadership than to democratic principles. With Adenauer, they got just that. In the Bismarckian tradition, Adenauer made numerous decisions without bothering parliament or his cabinet too much. This is not to say that Adenauer was anti-democratic; rather he understood that to lead Germans, especially in founding a new republic out of the rubble of the past, he had to show strength. Chancellors ever since Adenauer have been measured against him. His successor, for example, the amiable and intelligent Ludwig Erhard, was found wanting precisely because he couldn't exercise firm leadership.

Partly thanks to the style Adenauer set, the West German chancellor is approximately as powerful as the British prime minister, which is to say pretty powerful. The chancellor picks his own cabinet—with political considerations in mind, like the British PM. He is responsible for the main lines of government policy and has to defend them before the *Bundestag* and the public. As such, he is implicitly held responsible for what his ministers say and do.

THE CABINET

The typical Bonn cabinet is somewhat smaller than its Paris or London counterpart, but it too changes over the years as specialized ministries are created and other ministries are combined or split apart. In the 1980s the West German cabinet was staffed by the following officials:

> Chancellor
> Foreign Minister
> Interior Minister
> Justice Minister
> Finance Minister (that is, treasury)
> Economics Minister
> Minister for Food, Agriculture, and Forestry
> Minister for Labor and Social Affairs
> Defense Minister
> Minister for Youth, Family, and Health
> Transport Minister
> Minister for Urban Planning and Construction
> Minister for Intra-German Relations
> Minister for Research and Technology
> Minister for Post and Telecommunications
> Minister for Education and Science
> Minister for Economic Cooperation

In addition, sometimes the head of the chancellery (which organizes the workings of the cabinet) and the chief spokesperson are counted as cabinet-level officials.

The German cabinet has some interesting features. The minister for intra-German relations is in charge of Bonn's contacts with the German Demo-

Helmut Kohl: Drift and Scandal

When Christian Democrat Helmut Kohl became chancellor in 1982 no one called him a charismatic personality, but all agreed he was avuncular and moderate, a good choice for the job. By 1985, however, Kohl was accused of indecisiveness and involvement in a payoff scandal that rocked Bonn. Germans could look wistfully back to the strong figures who put their stamp on the chancellor's office: Adenauer, Brandt, and even Kohl's immediate predecessor Helmut Schmidt. In comparison, Kohl seemed to be lacking in leadership qualities.

A Catholic Rhinelander—like Adenauer—Kohl was put into uniform at age 15, but the war ended before he faced combat. Kohl never had any liking for the Nazis. While earning his doctorate in law during the 1950s, Kohl worked his way up the Rhineland-Palatinate CDU party organization, becoming its chairman in 1966 and *Land* minister-president in 1969. Most of his political experience has been at the state level; he was elected to the *Bundestag* only in 1976 but immediately headed his party in an unsuccessful bid for the chancellorship in the 1976 election. Kohl knows how to wait, and when the So-

cial Democrat-Free Democrat coalition split in 1982, the *Bundestag* voted him in as chancellor. In 1983, he called a new election and won resoundingly.

But things started going wrong for Kohl. Faced with difficult questions of high unemployment and Germany's position between the United States and the Soviet Union, he offered platitudes instead of policy; he reacted instead of acted. Making matters worse was the Flick scandal which partially paralyzed his government. The giant and secretive Flick holding company, which decades earlier helped bankroll Hitler, admitted to making illegal political "donations," mostly to the Christian Democrats and their smaller allies, the Free Democrats. Some of the money had gone into private pockets, and leading politicians resigned in shame. Kohl himself was grilled seven hours by a parliamentary committee.

Earlier, Kohl had been compared to fellow conservatives Ronald Reagan and Margaret Thatcher. But in office, Kohl did relatively little; he offered no conservative vision of the future and no firm leadership. Germany likes a strong chancellor, and Kohl did not measure up.

German Chancellor Kohl, right, clasped hands with French President Mitterrand at the cemetery of Verdun, site of a dreadful World War I battle, to symbolize Francó-German friendship. (*German Information Center*)

cratic Republic, a delicate and controversial topic, for Bonn still claims to theoretically represent the entire German nation. There are two ministries concerned with science and research. (The United States has none.) Notice how the
Labor Ministry also deals with social questions, including health insurance and
social security. As we well shall see, the labor movement and welfare state are
closely linked in Germany.

As in Britain (but not in France), practically all German cabinet ministers
are also working politicians with seats in the *Bundestag.* Like their British counterparts, they are rarely specialists in their assigned portfolio. Most are trained as
lawyers and have served in a variety of party and legislative positions. The job of
parliamentary state secretary serves as a training ground for potential cabinet
ministers. Below cabinet rank, a parliamentary state secretary is assigned to each
minister to assist in relations with the *Bundestag,* in effect a bridge between executive and legislative branches, as in Britain.

The Grand Coalition: A Dangerous Experiment

From 1966 to 1969 West Germany was ruled by a joint Christian Democrat-Social Democrat govern-ment, a so-called "grand coalition" because it in-cluded both the large parties and left only the small Free Democrats, who had but 6 percent of the *Bundestag* seats, to oppose and criticize. The ad-vantage of a grand coalition is obvious: it has such an overwhelming majority in parliament that it can't be ousted and can pass any laws it likes.

The negative side became more obvious with time: people came to feel that nobody could criticize the government, that politics was a game rigged by the powerful, and that democracy was a sham. An "extraparliamentary opposition" of leftist bent began to grow and criticize the government in radical terms. Some of West Germany's terrorists first became ac-tive in disgust at the wall-to-wall grand coalition. A grand coalition is probably useful only for emergen-cies; if it stays in office too long it starts undermining faith in democracy. A good democracy requires a lively interaction between "ins" and "outs" rather than collusion between the two.

THE BUNDESTAG

Konrad Adenauer, the authoritarian democrat, did not place great faith in the
lower house of the German parliament, the *Bundestag.* Germany never had a
strong parliamentary tradition. Bismarck all but ignored the *Reichstag.* During
the Weimar Republic the *Reichstag,* unprepared for the governing responsibilities thrust upon it, could not exercise power. Then in 1949 came Adenauer who,
like most Germans, had never seen an efficient, stable, responsible parliament
and so tended to disdain the new one. Since Adenauer's time, the *Bundestag* has
been trying to establish itself as a pillar of democracy and as an important branch
of government. Success has been gradual and incomplete. Many West Germans
still do not respect the *Bundestag* very much.

The *Bundestag's* 496 members (temporarily enlarged to 498 in 1983 due
to a fluke in the electoral law) are elected for four years. Under a parliamentary
(as opposed to presidential) system, the legislature can never be a severe critic of
the administration in the manner of the U.S. Congress. After all, the *Bundestag's*
majority parties produce the government; they can't very well criticize it too
harshly. Neither is the *Bundestag* the tumultuous assembly of the French Third

and Fourth Republics; the Bonn legislature can unmake a government only when it makes a new one. Nor is the *Bundestag* the docile rubber stamp that de Gaulle made of the French National Assembly. Still less is it the colorful debating chamber of the House of Commons where brilliant orators try to sway the public for the next election. On balance, the *Bundestag* has less independent power than the U.S. Congress but more than the French National Assembly and possibly even the British House of Commons.

The *Bundestag's* strong point is its committee work. Here, behind closed doors (most sessions are secret) *Bundestag* deputies, including opposition members, can make their voices heard. German legislative committees are more important and more specialized than their British counterparts. German party discipline is not as tight as the British so that deputies from the ruling party can criticize a government bill while opposition deputies sometimes agree with it. In the give and take of committee work, the opposition is often able to get changes made in legislation. Once back on the *Bundestag* floor—and all bills must be reported out; they can't be killed in committee—voting is on party lines, with occasional defections on matters of conscience.

There are nineteen standing Bundestag committees:

Foreign Affairs
Interior
Justice
Finance
Economics
Food, Agriculture, and Forestry
Labor and Social Affairs
Defense
Youth, Family, and Health
Urban Planning and Construction
Intra-German Relations
Research and Technology
Transport, Post, and Telecommunications
Education and Science
Economic Cooperation
Credentials, Immunity, and Agenda
Petitions
Budget
Sport

Notice how all but the last four committees are exactly the same as the cabinet ministries listed earlier in this chapter. The system was designed that way: each cabinet minister can deal directly with a parallel, relevant *Bundestag* committee. The ministers, themselves *Bundestag* members, sometimes come over from their executive offices to explain to committee sessions what the government has in mind with a proposed piece of legislation.

The composition of the *Bundestag* membership is interesting: its membership is heavily composed of civil servants. German law permits bureaucrats to take a leave of absence to run for and serve in the *Bundestag*. Another important category is people from interest groups—business associations and labor unions. Together, these two groups usually form a majority of the *Bundestag* membership. While we can't be sure that this does any harm to German democracy, it does contribute to a public feeling that parliament is a place where the powerful meet to decide matters with little reference to popular wishes.

THE CONSTITUTIONAL COURT

In very few countries is the judiciary equal in power to the legislative or executive branches. The United States and West Germany are two; both allow the highest court in the land to review the constitutionality of laws. The Federal Constitutional Court (*Bundesverfasungsgericht*, BVG) located in Karlsruhe, was put into the Basic Law partly on American insistence. The American occupiers reasoned that something like the Supreme Court would help prevent another Hitler, and many Germans agreed with what was for Germany (and indeed all of Europe) a new concept.

The Bundesrat: A Useful Upper House

Neither Britain nor France really needs an upper house because Britain and France are unitary systems. The West German federal system has a useful upper house, the *Bundesrat*. Not as powerful as the U.S. Senate—an upper house that powerful is a world rarity—Bonn's *Bundesrat* represents the ten *Länder* (plus observers from West Berlin) and has equal power with the *Bundestag* on legislation that will affect state affairs. On other issues the *Bundesrat* can veto a bill, but the *Bundestag* can override it with a simple majority.

The *Bundesrat* consists of forty-one members.

Every German *Land*, no matter how small, gets at least three. More populous *Länder* get four, the most populous get five. Each *Land* has the right to appoint its delegates, and in practice this has meant delegations of the leading state-level politicians, officials elected to the *Landtag* who become cabinet members in the *Land* government. This often means that members of a state's delegation will all belong to one party. Each *Bundesrat* delegation must vote as a bloc, not as individuals. The theory here is that they represent states, not parties or themselves.

The Karlsruhe court is composed of sixteen judges, eight elected by each house of parliament, who serve for nonrenewable twelve-year terms. Completely independent of other branches of German government, the court decides cases between *Länder*, protects civil liberties, outlaws dangerous political parties, and otherwise makes sure that statutes conform to the Basic Law.

The Constitutional Court's decisions have been important. It has declared illegal both the neo-Nazi and the radical-left parties, on the grounds that they sought to overthrow the constitutional order. It found that a 1974 abortion bill collided with the strong right-to-life provisions of the Basic Law and thus ruled the bill unconstitutional. In 1979 it ruled that "worker codetermination" in the running of factories was not unconstitutional. In 1983 it found that Chancellor Helmut Kohl had acted within the constitution when he arranged to lose a *Bundestag* vote of confidence so he could hold elections early (which he won).

Judicial review has worked well in Germany, although the *Bundesverfa-sungsgericht,* because it operates in the context of the more rigid Roman law, does not have the impact of the U.S. Supreme Court, whose decisions literally *are* law within the U.S. Common Law system.

THE PARTIES

Much of the reason the Bonn government works rather well is the party system that has evolved since 1949. The Weimar *Reichstag* was bedeviled by a dozen parties, some of them extremist, that made forming a stable coalition difficult. West Germany today, like Britain, has a "two-plus" party system, that is, two big parties and two small ones, plus a handful of tiny parties that seldom win elections. A two-plus party system decreases the difficulty of coalition formation; governments consist of two out of the four parties. A single party has seldom had a majority of the *Bundestag,* and thus "monocolor" (one-party) cabinets have been rare.

Most of the time the largest party has been the Christian Democratic Union *(Christlich Demokratishe Union,* CDU) with its Bavarian branch, the Christian Social Union. Sometimes the party is designated CDU/CSU. The original core of the CDU was the old Catholic-related Center party, one of the few parties that held its own against the growth of Nazism in the early 1930s. After World War II, Center politicians like Adenauer decided to go for a broader-based center-right party, one in which Protestants would feel welcome. This was largely successful, and the CDU now draws nearly equal portions of Protestant and Catholic voters. The CDU/CSU has been West Germany's largest party in every election except 1972 (when the SPD edged it out). In 1983 it drew 48.8 percent of the national vote.

The Social Democratic party *(Sozialdemokratische Partei Deutschlands,* SPD) is the grand old party of socialism and the only party in West Germany that antedates the founding of the Federal Republic. Originally Marxist, the SPD gradually became more and more "revisionist" until, in 1959, it dropped Marxism altogether. It was then that its electoral fortunes grew as it expanded beyond its traditional working-class base and into the middle class. A middle-class German today is almost as likely to vote SPD as CDU. Now a center-left party, the SPD's socialism amounts basically to support for welfare measures. It won 38.2 percent of the national vote in 1983.

Impressive German Words:
Regierungsfähig

Meaning "able to form a government," the term *regierungsfähig* has both a numerical and psychological connotation for Germans. It means not only that a party has enough parliamentary seats to build a cabinet but that it is mature enough to carry out the responsibilities of governing. Before 1959, when the Social Democrats were still rigid and somewhat Marxist, they were not considered *regierungsfähig.*

When the SPD shifted toward the center in the 1960s, they came to be seen as more and more *regierungsfähig,* a serious party capable of ruling. Invited into a grand coalition in 1966, they proved they were responsible people and went on, in 1969, to govern Germany quite well in coalition with the small FDP. *Regierungsfähig,* in other words, means that a party has graduated to adult tasks.

The small Free Democratic party (*Freie Demokratishe Partei*, FDP) is a descendant of the classic liberal parties that tried to stick to a center ground between socialists and conservatives. Now the FDP has trouble defining itself and at times has dropped to under 10 percent of the vote. In 1983 it won 6.8 percent. Like Britain's Liberals, the FDP offers a vague middle way to voters mistrustful of the two big parties.

In 1983, a new ecology-pacifist party, the Greens, made it into the *Bundestag* with 5.6 percent of the vote. Several small leftist and rightist parties, including Communists and neo-Nazis, have enjoyed no electoral success.

A SPLIT ELECTORAL SYSTEM

Both Britain and the United States use single-member districts in their parliamentary elections. The advantage with this system is that it anchors a deputy to a district, giving the representative an abiding interest in his or her constituents. The disadvantage is that the system does not accurately reflect votes for parties nationwide; seats are not proportional to votes. The alternative, proportional representation (PR), makes the party's percentage of seats almost exactly proportional to its votes. Weimar Germany had a PR system, and it was part of its undoing. PR systems are theoretically the fairest but in practice often lead to difficulties. They permit many small parties in parliament, including antidemocratic extremist parties. They make coalitions hard to form and unstable because usually several parties must combine. Italy and Israel (see box) suffer these consequences of proportional representation.

Comparing: Israel's PR Electoral System

Ironically, Weimar's proportional-representation (PR) system is alive and well in present-day Israel. The 120-member Israeli *Knesset* is elected by pure proportional representation with the entire country as one district. A party need win only one percent of the vote to qualify for a seat, an extremely low threshold that permits many small parties to exist. In 1984, twenty-seven parties ran for election, fifteen made it into the *Knesset,* some with only one seat. The two largest parties were nearly equal in strength, but neither had a majority. The Labor party, after weeks of bargaining, finally put together a grand coalition; however, it seemed likely to stalemate.

Even Israel's first prime minister, David Ben-Gurion, recognized the difficulties of a system that tried too hard to reflect all shades of opinion. He tried—as have later political leaders—to modify Israel's PR in a way that would produce fewer but bigger parties; however, the existing parties have blocked such change. Weimar never did change its electoral system; it collapsed first. On paper, pure PR systems are the fairest and most democratic. In practice, they often cannot create and sustain stable governing authority.

The West German system combines both approaches, single-member districts and proportional representation. The voter has two votes, one for a single representative in one of 248 districts, the other for a party. The party vote is the crucial one, for it determines the total number of seats a party gets in a given *Land*. Some of these seats are occupied by the party's district winners; additional seats are taken from the party's *Landesliste* to reach the percentage won on the second ballot. This *Landesliste* is a list of persons who will become deputies, starting with the names at the top of the list. The "party list" is the standard

"You Have Two Votes": A West German Ballot

Stimmzettel

für die Wahl zum Deutschen Bundestag im Wahlkreis 63 Bonn am 6. März 1983

Sie haben 2 Stimmen

hier 1 Stimme
für die Wahl
eines Wahlkreisabgeordneten
(Erststimme)

hier 1 Stimme
für die Wahl
einer Landesliste (Partei)
(Zweitstimme)

1	**Prof. Dr. Ehmke,** Horst Professor für öffentliches Recht **SPD** Sozialdemokratische Bonn Partei Am Römerlager 4 Deutschlands	◯	◯	**SPD**	**Sozialdemokratische** **Partei Deutschlands** Brandt, Wischnewski, Frau Huber, Schmidt, Frau Renger	1
2	**Dr. Daniels,** Hans Notar **CDU** Christlich Bonn Demokratische Union Schmidtbonnstr. 7 Deutschlands	◯	◯	**CDU**	**Christlich Demokratische** **Union Deutschlands** Dr. Barzel, Dr. Blüm, Frau Dr. Wilms, Vogel, Frau Hürland	2
3	**Rentrop,** Franz Friedhelm Steuerberater u. Wirtschaftsprüfer **F.D.P.** Freie Bonn-Bad Godesberg Demokratische Langenbergsweg 72 Partei	◯	◯	**F.D.P.**	**Freie Demokratische** **Partei** Genscher, Dr. Graf Lambsdorff, Frau Dr. Adam-Schwaetzer, Dr. Hirsch, Möllemann	3
4	**Rohde,** Volker August Wilhelm Fritz Journalist **DKP** Deutsche Bonn-Beuel Kommunistische Stroofstr. 15 Partei	◯	◯	**DKP**	**Deutsche Kommunistische** **Partei** Mies, Frau Nieth, Frau Bobrzik, Bublitz, Frau Buschmann	4
5	**Dr. Skupnik,** Wilfried Bruno Beamter **GRÜNE** DIE GRÜNEN Bonn Clausiusstr. 21	◯	◯	**GRÜNE**	**DIE GRÜNEN** Vogel, Frau Dr. Vollmer, Stratmann, Frau Nickels, Schily	5
			◯	**EAP**	**Europäische** **Arbeiterpartei** Frau Zepp-La Rouche, Cramer, Frau Cramer, Schiele, Vitt	6
			◯	**KPD**	**Kommunistische Partei** **Deutschlands** **(Marxisten-Leninisten)** Brand, Detjen, Frau Schnoor, Voß, Frau Lenger-Koloska	7
			◯	**NPD**	**Nationaldemokratische** **Partei Deutschlands** Schultz, Gerlach, Frau Krüger, Siepmann, Aengenvoort	8
			◯	**USD**	**Unabhängige** **Soziale Demokraten** Bönnemann, Vorhagen, Thränhardt, Bartz, Stahlschmidt	9

technique for a PR system. Leading party figures are assigned high positions on the list to insure that they get elected; people at the bottom of the party list don't have a chance.

The West German system works like proportional representation—percentage of votes equals percentage of *Bundestag* seats—but with the advantage of single-member districts. As in Britain and the United States, voters get a district representative. More than in straight PR systems, personality counts in West German elections; a politician can't be just a good party worker but has to go out and talk with voters to earn their confidence on a personal basis. It is a matter of considerable pride among Bonn politicians to be elected from a single-member district with a higher percentage of votes than their party won on the second ballot. It means that voters split their tickets because they liked the candidate better than his or her party.

Just as the British and American systems tend to be two-party, the partially single-member West German system has slowly cut down the number of parties from Weimar days until it is two-plus. Small parties seldom have a chance in the single-member districts; their best hope is for a showing on the second (PR) ballots of over 5 percent. This is another electoral innovation of the Federal Republic: a party must win at least 5 percent nationwide to gain admittance into the *Bundestag*. The "threshold clause" is designed to keep out splinter and extremist parties. The German modifications of the old PR system seem to have cured its ills: Italy should take note.

VOCABULARY BUILDING

Basic Law	center-right	federation	*regierungsfähig*
Bundes-	chancellor	grand coalition	Rhineland
Bundesrat	constructive no-confidence	*Land*	SPD
Bundestag	extraparliamentary	party list	threshold clause
CDU	opposition	proportional	
center-left	FDP	representation	

FURTHER REFERENCE

Conradt, David P. *The German Polity,* 2d ed. New York: Longman, 1982.

Goldman, Guido. *The German Political System.* New York: Random House, 1974.

Johnson, Nevil. *State and Government in the Federal Republic of Germany: The Executive at Work,* 2d ed. New York: Pergamon Press, 1983.

Loewenberg, Gerhard. *Parliament in the German Political System.* Ithaca, N.Y.: Cornell University Press, 1967.

Norpoth, Helmut. "The German Federal Republic: Coalition Government at the Brink of Majority Rule," in *Government Coalitions in Western Democra-* cies, ed. by Eric C. Browne and John Dreijmanis. New York: Longman, 1982.

Pinney, Edward L. *Federalism, Bureaucracy, and Party Politics in Western Germany: The Role of the Bundesrat.* Chapel Hill: University of North Carolina Press, 1963.

Sontheimer, Kurt. *The Government and Politics of West Germany.* New York: Praeger, 1972.

Schweitzer, Carl-Christoph, et al., eds. *Politics and Government in the Federal Republic of Germany: Basic Documents.* New York: St. Martin's Press, 1984.

14

WEST GERMAN POLITICAL ATTITUDES

ACHTUNG! YOU VILL BE DEMOKRATIC!

A German woman once recounted to the author how the Americans, in the last days of World War II, had bombed her hometown, a charming North Bavarian place with a splendid church and no military value. The town was a mess: bodies lay unburied, water and electricity were out, food supplies were unmoved. What did the people of the town do to meet this emergency? "Oh, nothing," she shrugged. "We waited for the Americans to come and tell us what to do."

Such were the beginnings of democracy in West Germany: a foreign implant grafted onto a people who were used to being told what to do. Can democracy be transplanted? Has it in fact taken in West Germany? This is the really bothersome question. The institutions are fine; in some ways the Federal Republic's Basic Law is better than the U.S. Constitution. But, as we saw with Weimar, good institutions aren't worth much if people don't support them. Are liberal-democratic values sufficiently strong and deep in West Germany to withstand economic and political hard times?

Historically, there has long been a liberal tradition in Germany, an outgrowth of the Enlightenment, as in France. In Britain, liberalism gradually triumphed. In France, liberalism and reaction seesawed back and forth, finally reaching an uneasy balance. In Germany, on the other hand, liberalism was overwhelmed by authoritarian forces. In 1848 the German liberals were driven out of the Frankfurt cathedral. In Bismarck's Second Reich they were treated with contempt. In the Weimar Republic they were in a distinct minority position, a pushover for authoritarians. Until the Bonn Republic, the liberal strand in German politics was a losing tradition.

THE MORAL VACUUM

In addition to a lack of democratic tradition, Germany faced a more subtle problem after World War II. A liberal democracy requires certain moral foundations. If you are entrusting ultimate authority to the people through their representatives, you have to believe that they are generally moral, perhaps even a bit idealistic. When this belief vanishes, a democracy loses some of its legitimacy. People may go along with it, but without deep faith.

The Nazi period left a kind of moral vacuum, and filling it has been a long, slow process, one still not complete. One problem that hindered the development of West German democracy was the persistence of ex-Nazis in high places. Every time one was discovered it undermined the moral authority of the regime. People, especially young people, thought, "Why should we respect democracy if there are still the same old Nazis running it?"

Immediately after the war, the Allied occupiers tried to "denazify" their zones. Party members, especially officials and the Gestapo (secret police), lost their jobs and sometimes went to prison. Henry Kissinger, then a U.S. Army sergeant, had a neat trick for rounding up Gestapo agents in the town he was running. He just put an ad in the newspaper for experienced policemen; when they showed up he slapped them in the klink. Still, aside from the 177 war criminals

Impressive German Words: Gehorsamkeit

Obedience is the counterpart of authority. Germans have been *gehorsam* (obedient) for centuries, an attitude not conducive to democracy. A working democracy requires a certain amount of speaking up, of criticizing, of participation, and until after World War II these qualities were generally lacking among Germans. In one possibly apocryphal incident, Marxist revolutionaries rushing government buildings in 1918 Berlin still wouldn't step on the grass: there was a sign forbidding it. Lenin is said to have wondered, "How are you going to make a revolution with people who won't even step on the grass?"

tried at Nuremberg (25 sentenced to death), denazification was spotty, and many Nazis got away, to Latin America or to new lives within Germany. Many sinister Nazis succeeded in covering their tracks and working their way into business, politics, the civil service, and even the judicial system.

It is this last-mentioned group that kept Nazi mass murderers from coming to trial. There are laws on the books against such people, but curiously, Nazi criminals were rarely brought to trial until the 1960s. By then younger people had worked their way up the judicial ladder and were willing to prosecute cases their elders preferred to let pass. This helps explain why Nazi criminals were still being tried in the 1980s.

Two presidents of the Federal Republic, Walter Scheel of the FDP and Karl Carstens of the CDU, and one chancellor, Kurt Kiesinger of the CDU, were once Nazi party members. All pointed out that they were nominal rather than active members, "just opportunists" out to further their careers during a time when the Nazis controlled many paths to success. True, none were charged with any crime, but what kind of moral authority did "just an opportunist" lend to the highest offices of a country trying to become a democracy?

Who Likes the USA?

Germans have long seen the United States as their benefactor (Marshall Plan aid), teacher (of democracy), and protector (from the Soviets). The West Germans are the most pro-American of all Europeans, as this 1982 poll demonstrated in asking, "All in all, what is your opinion of the USA?"

Among the German respondents, those who feel warmest to the United States are older people—who have memories of CARE packages and the Berlin airlift—and Christian Democratic voters. Social Democrats like the United States a little less, and the Greens the least.

	VERY GOOD	FAIRLY GOOD	FAIRLY POOR	VERY POOR
West Germany	14%	59%	19%	5%
France	5	50	25	7
Britain	10	36	31	13
Belgium	11	42	16	6
Denmark	9	37	27	12
Italy	18	45	15	6

FORGETTING THE PAST

Can a society experience collective guilt? Was it realistic to expect Germans as a whole to feel remorse for what the Nazis did? The West German response was mostly to flush the Nazi era down the memory hole, to say in effect, "Past, go away!" German fathers were reluctant to say much about what they had done. German history textbooks stopped at 1933 and picked up again in 1945. The result has been appalling ignorance among young Germans about Hitler, the Nazis, and what they did. In survey after survey, some German high-schoolers identify Hitler as a CDU politician, the leader of Germany in World War I, or as "the man who built the *Autobahns*" (express highways). This attempt to forget the past was not merely an oversight; it reflected the inability of the German elite—including education officials—to come to grips with the past and with themselves.

Can a society simply forget its past, blot it out? West Germans tried. Climbing out of the ruins of World War II, Germans threw themselves with single-minded devotion into work, making money, and spending it conspicuously. The results were spectacular; the economy soared, and the German archetype became the *Wunderkind*, the wonder child, the businessman who rose from rubble to riches in the postwar boom. His symbols: a fat body, a fat cigar, and a fat Mercedes.

But material prosperity could not fill the moral and historical void. Many young Germans were profoundly dissatisfied with the emphasis on materialism that seemed to be a sort of cover-up for a lack of deeper values. Some of them turned to far-left and later "green" politics.

Nothing else explains the growth of radical and sometimes violent politics among young Germans in the 1970s and 1980s. Certainly it wasn't because they were poor; their society was prosperous, and often they were from wealthy families. Prosperity and materialism, in fact, rubbed them the wrong way. Said one rich girl: "I'm sick of all this caviar gobbling." Then she joined the terrorists and helped murder an old family friend, a banker. The Baader-Meinhof gang committed murder and bank robbery in the name of revolution, and some young Germans sympathized with them. The terrorists, in their warped, sick way, put their finger on the German malaise: German society, avoiding its past, had developed a moral void with nothing to believe in but "caviar gobbling." The past, it seems, doesn't stay buried; it comes back to haunt the society trying to forget it. In the words of American philosopher George Santayana, "Those who cannot remember the past are condemned to repeat it."

THE GENERATION GAP

As a guest in a German home once, the author saw how the family reacted when one of the daughters found, in the back of a china closet, an old poem, *"Die Hitlerblume"* (the Hitler flower), comparing the *Führer* to a lovely blossom. The three college-age children howled with laughter and derision. "Daddy, how

The Rise of "Postmaterialism"

One of the trends among rich nations—especially pronounced in West Germany—is the feeling of some young people that modern society is too focused on material goods. Starting in the late 1960s, "countercultures" sprang up in every advanced country. Young people rejected the work-and-buy ethic of their parents and turned instead to beards, blue jeans, and "quality of life" questions. This caught on strongly in the Federal Republic as young Germans sought to repudiate the supermaterialism of their parents.

Postmaterialism underlies the Federal Republic's Marxist, antinuclear, ecology, and pacifist movements, much of which came together in the Greens. Postmaterialism also plugged into German romanticism and nationalism.

Will postmaterialism last or decline? One of its causes was the prosperity of the 1960s and 1970s. By the 1980s, the FRG was experiencing economic difficulties; unemployment was at a postwar high. The scramble for jobs may persuade the upcoming generation that materialism isn't so bad after all. That is what happened in the United States: the job-oriented young people of the 1980s think the hippies of the 1960s were weird.

could you go along with this kind of garbage?" they asked. The father, an old-fashioned authoritarian type, grew red in the face and stammered, "You don't know what it was like. They had everybody whipped up. The times were different." He was quite embarrassed.

The incident underscores the very real generation gap in German political attitudes: simply put, the younger the generation, the more democratic it is; the older, the more authoritarian. It is the younger Germans who are more willing to come to grips with the past—partly because they were not personally involved—and to give unqualified allegiance to democracy.

The younger generation has also freed up German society a great deal. No longer are German women confined to *Kinder, Küche, Kirche* (children, kitchen, and church); many work outside the home and even participate in politics. German youngsters are not as obedient as they once were, and German fathers no longer beat them as in the old days. If democracy starts in the home, Germany now has a much better foundation for democracy.

The typical German of today is far more democratic in attitudes than the typical German of 1949 when the Federal Republic was founded. Those who would support another Hitler, trade civil rights for "security," or think a one-party system is best have steadily dwindled, while those who think democracy and civil rights are worthwhile values in their own right have steadily increased. German attitudes are now at least as democratic as any of their European neighbors.

Is the change permanent, though? Political scientist Sidney Verba drew a distinction between "output affect" and "system affect" in his discussion of German political culture. The former means liking the system for what it produces (jobs, security, and material goods), the latter, liking the system for its own sake. Verba thought Germans showed more of the first than the second; that is, they liked the system while the going was good—they were "fair-weather democrats"—but had not yet become "rain-or-shine democrats" the way Britons or Americans are. Verba's point was made in the early 1960s. Since then, system affect among Germans has increased as the younger generation has come of age.

The FRG survived the economic downturn of the early 1980s unscathed, even though unemployment topped 10 percent.

Germany Watches "Holocaust"

Not everyone in West Germany welcomed the American-made TV miniseries "Holocaust." The country's two nationwide channels declined to show it. The smaller regional channels proved braver; they showed the four-part series in 1979, expecting to get about 15 percent of the viewing audience. Instead, "Holocaust" broke all previous German TV viewing records: 36 percent tuned in the first night, 41 percent for the final part.

Reactions to the broadcast were intense. The stations' telephone lines were jammed with calls. About a third said "Holocaust" should never have been shown because it "reopened old wounds." But a greater number said they had been moved by the grim story of a Jewish family destroyed by the Nazis. "How could it have happened?" was a frequent query. Some observers noted that West Germany was incapable of making such a movie; it had to come from a foreign country.

"Holocaust" triggered an overdue interest in the crimes of the Nazi era. German television put on a tough documentary, "Europe under the Swastika," which concluded on the fiftieth anniversary of Hitler's coming to power. The Federal Center for Political Education in Bonn received some seventy thousand inquiries from schoolteachers alone following "Holocaust," which was repeated in 1983. Other TV documentaries on the anti-Nazi resistance, Nazi propaganda, why Germans voted for Hitler, and economic conditions under the Third Reich were soon broadcast, almost as if Germany was trying to make up for lost time.

A NEW GERMAN DEMOCRACY

In a sense, democratic attitudes have taken root too well in West Germany. Now one of the FRG's big problems is young people, schooled in freedom and democracy, who want to see more of it applied in practice. They want to be able to criticize and participate without their elders or the Americans telling them to hush up. The younger generation brings with them new concerns, about war and the environment, that the older generation didn't worry about and didn't like being reminded of.

A certain distance developed between many young Germans and the mainstream political parties. In the German party system, newcomers must slowly work their way up party ranks, starting at the local and state levels, before they can have a say at the national level. By the time they can, they are no longer young. In the meantime, they are expected to obey party dictates and not have much input. Some youth organizations of both the Social Democrats and Free Democrats became so rambunctious that they had to be disowned by their parent parties. For many young Germans, the Christian Democrats and Social Democrats who alternated in power looked a lot alike, staid and elderly, and neither was responsive to young people.

Belatedly, some German politicians recognized the problem. President Richard von Weizsäcker worried openly about "the failure of my generation to bring younger people into politics." Young Germans, he noted, "do not admire the moral substance of the older generation. Our economic achievement went along with a very materialistic and very selfish view of all problems."

Young Germans also developed resentment of the United States. In the

1950s and 1960s, young Germans nearly worshiped the United States; it was their model in politics, lifestyles, and values. Then things happened that shook this. The assassination of President Kennedy—who had recently proclaimed "Ich bin ein Berliner" at the Berlin Wall—horrified Germans and made them wonder about the United States. The Vietnam War was worse; some young Germans compared it with Hitler's war of aggression. Finally, rising tensions between East and West and the warlike posture of President Reagan convinced many young Germans that the United States would be willing to incinerate Germany. A minority began to see Washington rather than Moscow as the source of tension. Some wanted the Americans out of Germany. It was ironic that the United States—which had tutored Germans to repudiate militarism—found itself the object of West German antiwar feeling.

The above attitudes fed the Green party. In the 1983 elections, the Greens did three times better among young voters than among the total population. These attitudes also contributed to a new German nationalism that no longer liked following in America's footsteps. Instead of automatically looking west, a minority of young Germans began to look east, to a reunified Germany with neither Americans nor Russians encamped on their soil. At present, of course, most Germans are still pro-U.S., pro-NATO, and anti-Soviet. If tensions rise, however, and the United States fails to recognize that many Germans are justifiably nervous about nuclear or any other kind of war, the West could lose Germany.

Impressive German Words:
Angst

The German word *Angst* is richer in meaning than its English cognate, "anxiety." *Angst* is a subtle thing, a slow, clammy feeling that things are going wrong. It can be used in an individual, psychiatric sense, as Freud used it, but currently it is more applied to the societywide "cultural pessimism" some observers detect in the Federal Republic of Germany.

Explanations for German *Angst* are many. The end of the postwar economic miracle and increase in economic uncertainty may contribute. The fear that the world is on the brink of nuclear war—in which Germany will be the main battlefield—is a major fac-

tor. Some believe *Angst* is a reflection of Germans' loss of identity. "Who are we? What is our mission in the world?" young idealists ask themselves.

The West German newsweekly *Der Spiegel* carried a four-part series on "Angst—the German Depression" and concluded: "The majority of citizens feel alone, helpless and threatened . . . . The direction is not clear. 'Where are we going?' has become a standard phrase." British, French, and Americans have complaints, unrest, even anger, but only the Germans have *Angst*.

THE END OF SHELL SHOCK

Many Germans, especially the older generation who had gone along with the Nazis, felt so damaged by political involvement that they swore never to take an active part in politics again. To appreciate how an older German might feel shell-shocked and cautious about politics, imagine a German born at the turn of the century who was raised under a conservative monarchy and taught to obey authority. All of a sudden a republic comes that expects its citizens to be good

Willy Brandt: A German Mr. Clean

One of the more optimistic signs that democracy had taken root in Germany was the 1969 election that made Willy Brandt chancellor of the Federal Republic. It would not have been possible even a few years earlier, for Brandt represented a repudiation of German history and society that few Germans could have then tolerated. First, Brandt was an illegitimate child, and in a society as stuffy as Germany's that was a black mark. Adenauer, in fact, had used it against Brandt in election campaigns. Second, Brandt was a Socialist, and in his youth in the North German seaport of Lübeck had been pretty far left (although never Communist). No Socialist had been in power in Germany for decades; the CDU kept smearing the SPD as a dangerous party, and many Germans believed it. Third, and most damaging to Brandt, was the fact that he had fled to Norway in 1933 and become a Norwegian citizen and hadn't reclaimed his German nationality until 1947. Some even unjustly accused him of fighting Germans as a Norwegian soldier.

With a record like that, it seemed Brandt was starting into German politics with three strikes against him. But Brandt also had appeal for many Germans, especially younger ones. He was "Mr. Clean," a German who had battled the Nazis— literally, in Lübeck street fights—and who had never been "just an opportunist" who survived by going along. Brandt seemed to represent a newer, better Germany as opposed to the conservative, traditional values of Adenauer and the CDU.

As mayor of West Berlin from 1957 to 1966, Brandt showed how tough he was by standing up to Soviet and East German efforts at encroachment; he also demonstrated to the West German public that he was anti-Communist. A leading figure in the SPD, Brandt supported the 1959 move away from Marxism. In 1964 he became the SPD's chairman, and this lent a boost to the party's electoral fortunes.

In 1966 the SPD was invited into the cabinet in a grand coalition with the CDU. As is usual in coalition governments, the head of the second largest party is

Kneeling at the tomb of the Unknown Soldier in Warsaw, Poland, in 1970, West German Chancellor Brandt showed genuine regret for the past and a hope to improve relations through his *Ostpolitik*. *(German Information Center)*

given the position of foreign minister. Here Brandt showed himself to be a forceful statesman. Under his leadership, the foreign ministry began its efforts to improve relations with East Europe *(Ostpolitik).* By 1969 the SPD had enough *Bundestag* seats to form a small coalition with the FDP, and Willie Brandt became the Federal Republic's first Socialist chancellor. The event was a symbolic breakthrough: Germany looked more democratic under an anti-Nazi than an ex-Nazi (Brandt's predecessor, Kiesinger).

The story, however, does not have a happy ending. In 1974 it was discovered that one of Brandt's closest assistants was an East German spy. (The Federal Republic is riddled with East German spies.) Brandt, regretting his security slip, resigned the chancellorship to become the grand old man of not only German but also West European social democracy.

democrats (they weren't). Then comes a dictatorship that demands the enthusiastic, unquestioning complicity of all Germans. After that come Allied occupiers telling the bewildered citizenry that they must now forget all that and become democratic again. No wonder that in the first decades of the Federal Republic many Germans said *ohne mich* (without me) to politics.

In their famous book, *The Civic Culture,* Almond and Verba described the German attitude of 1959 as one of detachment. Germans were often well informed about politics but didn't want to participate in much more than voting. They were pragmatic and sometimes cynical about politics. If the system worked it was okay, but there was no point in getting personally involved. Germans showed low levels of social trust or of willingness to discuss politics with others. In the decades since, however, this attitude has receded so that now Germans are among the most democratic and participatory in the world. Every decade there are fewer and fewer of the skeptical generation and more and more of the postwar generation. Ironically, the United States has gotten along best with the party that most embodies the older, less-participatory values (the CDU) and not as well with the parties that embody the newer, participatory virtues (the SPD and Greens).

THE REMADE SOCIETY

The tremendous changes Germany has gone through in this century have had some good effects too. While the shifts in regime made older Germans cautious about political involvement, the upheavals also freed German society from some of its old traditions and patterns. The cumulative effects of the successive collapses of the old monarchy, the Weimar Republic, and the Third Reich, followed by the postwar American influence, had the effect of a social revolution. Much of Germany changed.

One of the best changes was the disappearance of Prussia. Divided among Russia, Poland, and East Germany, its *Junkers* displaced from their great estates, Prussia and its authoritarianism can no longer crush German democracy. Also gone is the Prussian concept of the state—something to be worshiped—replaced by the more British and American pluralist conceptions of the state as reflection and integrator of diverse, conflicting interests and viewpoints. Pluralism, you will recall, is the attitude that interest groups and their interplay are good; this was an alien idea in traditional German political thinking but one now widely accepted. The shift of capitals from Berlin to Bonn symbolized the move away from Prussian authoritarianism to Western pluralism.

Accompanying the Communist take-over of the eastern parts of Germany was one of the most massive exoduses in human history. Close to ten million Germans fled westward in the late 1940s. Another three million fled from East Germany before the Berlin Wall went up in 1961. In the 1950s about one West German in five was from outside the Federal Republic. This flood had the effect of breaking up the narrowness and provincialism of German society. The refugees, granted instant West German citizenship, integrated themselves rather quickly into their new homes. While the older generation harbors some nostalgia for their old home regions—now lost forever—most of their children couldn't care less and have become West Germans.

There was change among the German elites too. While some of the old family fortunes stayed intact (Krupp, for example), much of the West German economic elite consists of new-rich *Wunderkinder,* often from humble backgrounds. The old military elite, at one time virtually a caste, disappeared with the Nazis' defeat and never revived. The West German military is under firm civilian control. The old nobility—people with *von* before the family name—no longer have the position they once had. Although there are Bonn politicians with *von* in their names, probably as many are in the SPD as the CDU.

THE GERMAN POLITICAL ELITE

Where then does West Germany's political elite come from? One of the strong points of West German democracy is that its elite recruitment is quite mixed, more like that of the United States than Britain or France. There is no German equivalent of Oxbridge or the Great Schools. The three German political collapses of this century left a relatively clean slate for bright talent to achieve political office. Some (such as Brandt) were not even university graduates, although practically all politicians now are. There is no single university or institute in West Germany that serves as a training ground for a political elite; rather, one university is considered just about as good as another.

As in America, the typical German politician has studied law, although in Germany this is done at the undergraduate rather than the postgraduate level. German (and other European) legal systems produce different attitudes than the Anglo-American Common Law system. Continental law is Roman law—often in the updated form of the Napoleonic Code—and it emphasizes rather rigid adherence to fixed rules. The Common Law, on the other hand, is judge-made law that focuses on precedent and persuasion; it is more flexible. The former system produces lawyers who tend to go by the book; the latter, lawyers who negotiate and make deals. Consequently, German politicians with their legal background are heavily law oriented rather than people oriented.

Impressive German Words: Rechtsstaat

Literally a "state of laws," the term *Rechtsstaat* has both a positive and negative connotation in German. *Recht* can be translated as both "law" and "right," as in civil rights. Obviously such a state is better than a dictatorship. In a negative context, however, *Rechtsstaat* may imply a state with too many laws, where behavior is too narrowly supervised. People used to joke that in Germany "everything not prohibited is mandatory," clearly no longer the case. A *rechtsstaatlich* mentality connotes a by-the-book, strait-laced application of laws and regulations.

Much of the work of the *Bundestag,* for example, is devoted to the precise wording of bills, making that house a rather dull, inward-looking chamber that has failed to win a great deal of admiration from the German public. Likewise cabinet ministers conceive of their role heavily in terms of carrying out laws. Half of Kohl's cabinet were lawyers.

The German political elite is not all lawyers. A smaller group has had a disproportionate role in German politics: economists. In few other countries have professional economists achieved the stature they have in Bonn. One German chancellor had a Ph.D. in economics: Ludwig Erhard. Under Adenauer, the rotund, jolly Erhard (nicknamed *der Gummilöwe,* the rubber lion), as economics minister, charted Germany's rise to prosperity; later he became chancellor. Helmut Schmidt, an economics graduate, succeeded Brandt as SPD chancellor and managed to keep both inflation and unemployment low in Germany while much of the world went through a major recession. In Germany, economists are not just advisors but often become important politicians themselves.

THE GERMAN SPLIT PERSONALITY

The French, as we discussed, often seem split between demanding impersonal authority and rebelling against it. The Germans have a sort of split personality too, but it's between romanticism and realism.

Most of the time Germans are workaday realists: hard working, thrifty, clean, orderly, cooperative, family oriented. But a persistent romantic streak exists in German history that comes out every now and then: the nineteenth-century intellectuals (such as composer Richard Wagner) who reveled in the *Volksgeist,* the Nazi youth who really believed they were building a "thousand-year Reich," and in the 1970s the far-left terrorists who thought they could build utopia by means of assassination and kidnapping. The latest German romantics are the Greens, who long for an imaginary pastoral idyll free of atoms and industry.

German romanticism manifests itself in other ways too, in the continual striving for perfection, for example. This leads Germans to undertake vast projects they may not have the resources to complete. Hitler's plan to conquer all of Europe, including Russia, is an infamous example. But this drive for perfection also operates on more mundane levels. As an American ski enthusiast remarked: "If you're at an international ski resort where in one day four people break a leg, three of them will be Germans. It's because even on skis they're trying too hard, pushing themselves beyond their limits."

Impressive German Words: Sehnsucht and Streben

Sehnsucht and *Streben,* or "longing" and "effort," are twin characteristics of German romanticism and appear widely in German literature and poetry. *Sehnsucht* implies a deep yearning for something impossible to attain, such as a lofty ideal (or, in Goethe's *Sorrows of Werther,* the protagonist's love for Charlotte). And *Streben* means applying utmost effort to try to get it. The twin forces lend a dynamic impulse to German life and work, but they can also lead to despair if frustrated. When Goethe's Werther didn't get Charlotte (who was married), he blew his brains out.

Germans set high store by achievement. To work harder, produce more, and proudly let others know about it seems to be an ingrained cultural trait. This helps explain Germany's rise after the war to Europe's number-one economic power. Contrast Germany's dynamic growth with Britain's limping performance. The cause lies in the work attitudes of the two peoples: the German economy works because Germans work; the British doesn't because Britons don't. That goes for management as well as labor.

Both East Germany's leader Walter Ulbricht and West Germany's Helmut Schmidt toured their respective camps giving unsolicited advice on how other countries should copy the German economic miracle. (East Germany's, although not as spectacular as the Federal Republic's, has been impressive nonetheless.) The author once told an anti-Communist West Berliner that East Berlin also looked pretty prosperous. He didn't dispute me but nodded and said, "Of course. They're Germans too."

Perhaps the archetypal German figure is Goethe's Faust, the driven person who can never rest or be content with what is already his. This quality can produce both great good and evil. Former Chancellor Helmut Schmidt, himself a stereotype of the German realist strain, once said, "Germans have an enormous capacity for idealism and the perversion of it."

VOCABULARY BUILDING

Achilles heel	Common Law	opportunist	Roman law
Angst	denazification	output affect	romanticism
archetype	detachment	postmaterialism	system affect
authoritarian	Holocaust	provincialism	terrorism
Autobahn	materialism	*Rechtsstaat*	*Wunderkind*

FURTHER REFERENCE

Almond, Gabriel, and Sidney Verba. *The Civic Culture: Political Attitudes and Democracy in Five Nations.* Boston: Little, Brown, 1965.

Böll, Heinrich. *The Lost Honor of Katharina Blum.* New York: McGraw-Hill, 1975.

Braunthal, Gerard. "Willy Brandt: Politician and Statesman," in *Governments and Leaders: An Approach to Comparative Politics,* ed. by Edward Feit. Boston: Houghton Mifflin, 1978.

Childs, David, and Jeffrey Johnson. *West Germany: Politics and Society.* New York: St. Martin's Press, 1981.

Conradt, David P. "Changing German Political Culture," in *The Civic Culture Revisited,* ed. by Gabriel A. Almond and Sidney Verba. Boston: Little, Brown, 1980.

Craig, Gordon A. *The Germans.* New York: Putnam's, 1982.

Dahrendorf, Ralf. *Society and Democracy in Germany.* Garden City, N.Y.: Anchor Books, 1969.

Edinger, Lewis J. *Politics in West Germany.* Boston: Little, Brown, 1977.

Fallaci, Oriana. "Willy Brandt," in *Interview with History.* Boston: Houghton Mifflin, 1977.

Szabo, Stephen F. "The New Generation: Protest and Postmaterialism," in *The Federal Republic of Germany in the 1980s,* ed. by Robert Gerald Livingston. New York: German Information Center, 1983.

Verba, Sidney. "Germany: The Remaking of Political Culture," in *Political Culture and Political Development,* ed. by L. Pye and S. Verba. Princeton, N.J.: Princeton University Press, 1965.

15

PATTERNS OF INTERACTION

PARTIES AND THE ELECTORATE

We saw how the Weimar Republic collapsed with the shrinking of the moderate parties and growth of extremist parties—"polarized pluralism" in action. This probably cannot happen in the Federal Republic: with only two-plus parties, they, for good political reasons, stick close to the center of the political spectrum. Political competition in West Germany tends to be center seeking, that is, the parties struggle to win the big vote in the center and neglect the relatively few votes on the extremes. This makes German politics—like American—safe but dull.

Social scientists have found that political opinion in most modern democracies resembles more or less a bell-shaped curve: a lot of people are in the center, with fewer and fewer as one moves to the left or right. If you want to sound more scientific you call this a "unimodal" distribution of opinion. In 1973, for example, citizens of the European Community (Common Market) were asked to place themselves on a one-to-ten ideological scale, one for the most left

The Shape of the German Electorate

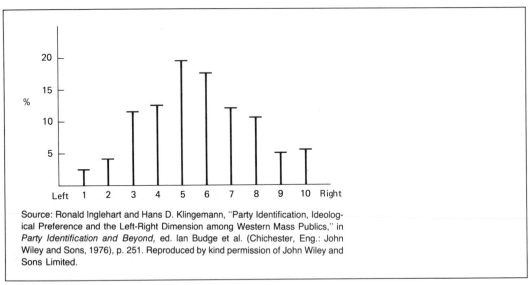

Source: Ronald Inglehart and Hans D. Klingemann, "Party Identification, Ideological Preference and the Left-Right Dimension among Western Mass Publics," in *Party Identification and Beyond,* ed. Ian Budge et al. (Chichester, Eng.: John Wiley and Sons, 1976), p. 251. Reproduced by kind permission of John Wiley and Sons Limited.

and ten for the most right. Germany came out almost a bell-shaped curve (see box).

How does this affect political parties? When party leaders come to understand the shape of the electorate, either through modern polling techniques or by losing elections, they try to modify their party image so that it appeals to the middle of the opinion spectrum. If the Social Democrats position themselves too far left—say, at one on the ten-point scale—by advocating nationalizing private industry and dropping out of NATO, they may please some of the left-wing ideologues in the party but do poorly in elections. In 1973 only 2 percent of West Germans placed themselves at the one position (most left). So the Social Democrats tone down their socialism and emphasize their commitment to democracy plus welfare measures, moving to the three or four position. Now they do much better in elections, but the left wing of the party is unhappy with the dilution of socialist gospel. Finally, sniffing the possibility of becoming Germany's governing party, the SPD virtually throws out socialism and tells the electorate that they will do a better job running the capitalist, market economy. At this point they are in roughly the five position. The party's left wingers are angry, accusing the SPD leadership of selling out socialist ideals and turning into apologists for capitalism; some left-wing socialists even quit the party. But electorally, the SPD is doing well. By emphasizing democracy and minimizing socialism, they win the support of many centrists.

Unhappy on the Left: The Jusos

The youth branch of the SPD—the *Jungsozialisten,* or *Jusos* for short—has been a continual thorn in the left side of the party. Limited to people under 35, the *Jusos* attract some young zealots ablaze with Marxist notions of socialism. Impatient and idealistic, many *Jusos* find the mainstream SPD too moderate and gradualist. Ideology among some factions within the *Jusos* verges on communism.

Periodically, the SPD has to disown its offspring. If it doesn't, it costs the party votes. In areas where *Jusos* gain control of the party machinery—in Munich and Frankfurt, for example—the SPD has lost several seats that it held for years. What the *Jusos* can't understand is that Germans as a whole are moderate in their political views and there is little support for pulling out of NATO, nationalization of industry, "cultural revolution," and massive taxes on the rich. When the *Jusos* helped move the SPD toward such positions in 1983, the party lost the election. Some *Jusos* defected to the Greens. The SPD as a whole was faced with the question of whether to try to retain young radicals—by moving leftward, or to win elections—by staying centrist.

The above, in a nutshell, is the history of the SPD. In the last century the Social Democrats started to shed their Marxism, in practice if not yet in theory. In the 1950s, seeing the CDU triumphantly win the center, they decided to break out of their left-wing stronghold. Meeting in Bad Godesberg (just outside Bonn) in 1959, they drew up a Basic Program so moderate one can hardly find any socialism in it. Marxism was *kaput;* the SPD proclaimed itself "rooted in Christian ethics, humanism and classical philosophy."

Now, while the Social Democrats are moving rightward, the Christian Democrats are moving leftward, or perhaps more accurately, since they have already carved out for themselves a broad swath of the ideological spectrum, they now claim to stand for everything, a party of all Germans, just as the British Conservatives claim to represent all Britons. The CDU downplays its conservatism, for it too understands that if the party image is too rightist it will lose the big prize in the center. The result is two large parties trying so hard to be moderate that they start to resemble each other. In the process, they rub their respective left and right wings the wrong way (see boxes).

Thunder on the Right: CSU

Bavaria is the Texas of Germany, a land with a raucous brand of politics all its own. On principle, the Christian Social Union (CSU) never let itself be absorbed into the CDU; instead it calls itself an allied party and sometimes threatens to burst out of Bavaria and set itself up in nationwide competition with the CDU. The CSU is generally to the right of the CDU, demanding a tougher anti-Soviet stance in foreign policy, a firmer crackdown on radicals, and a rollback of welfare.

The guiding force behind the CSU is beefy Franz Josef Strauss, prime minister of the state of Bavaria where they call him "der Franzl" (Little Franz). The Bavarian equivalent of Jesse Helms, Strauss is Germany's right-wing tough guy. Although he was never a Nazi, Strauss tells Germans that they should not be ashamed of their past and that Germany was not entirely to blame for World War II. An authoritarian, Strauss had two news-magazine editors jailed in 1962 for publishing alleged military secrets when he was defense minister in Bonn. In the public uproar at his abuse of power, Strauss resigned.

But Strauss is also extremely intelligent, and when he won the joint CDU/CSU nomination for the chancellorship for the 1980 election, he immediately switched to a moderate line. It didn't work. Strauss's image—which was a major part of the SPD campaign—worked to the CDU/CSU's detriment. He did not run for chancellor again, nor was he invited into the CDU/CSU/FDP cabinet in 1983.

THE CHANCELLOR AND THE ELECTORATE

In Germany, as in many countries, personality has become more important than ideology in the mind of many voters. With the decline of *Weltanschauung* parties (see box) and the move of most large parties to the center of the political spectrum, the personality of candidates is often what persuades voters. This has long been the case in the United States and is now becoming the European norm as well. Some call it the Americanization of European politics, but it is less a matter of copying than it is of reflecting the rise of catchall parties. Throughout Europe, election posters now feature the picture of the top party leader, the person who would become prime minister. Although voting may be by party list, citizens know that in choosing a party they are actually electing a prime minister.

West German campaigns, for example, are conducted almost as if they were for the direct election of a president—as in the United States and France. Officially there is no "candidate for the chancellorship," but in practice the leading figures of the two big parties are clearly identified as such—in the press and in the public mind—so that much of the campaign revolves around the personalities of the two leading candidates.

Impressive German Words:
Weltanschauung

In prewar Europe, many political parties used to try to imbue their supporters with a "view of the world" (or *Weltanschauung*) corresponding to the party's ideology and philosophy. This was especially true of parties on the left, particularly in Weimar Germany. Today this insistence on a particular world view implies ideological narrowness and intolerance. After World War II most of the *Weltanschauung* parties disappeared as they broadened their appeal or merged into bigger parties. The Communist parties of West Europe preserve some of the old *Weltanschauung* style—party newspapers, a tight organization, a rather firm set of beliefs—but even they have toned down and diluted their ideology.

The "Catchall" Party

Noting the demise of the prewar *Weltanschauung* parties, German political scientist Otto Kirchheimer coined the term "catchall party" to describe what was taking their place: big, loose, pluralist parties that have diluted their ideologies so they can accommodate many diverse groups of supporters. His model of a catchall party was the CDU, a veritable political vacuum cleaner, drawing in all manner of groups: farmers, business people, labor, women, Catholics, Protestants, white-collar workers, blue collar, you name it.

For a while, under crusty Kurt Schumacher, the SPD tried to stay a *Weltanschauung* party, defining itself in rigid and ideological terms that turned away many middle-of-the-road voters. Since 1959, the SPD too has become a catchall party, appealing to Germans of all classes and backgrounds.

Indeed, by now the catchall party is the norm in modern democracies. Almost axiomatically, any large party is bound to be a catchall party, for example, the Italian Christian Democrats, Canadian Conservatives, Spanish Socialists, Japanese Liberals, and of course both major U.S. parties.

A German candidate for chancellor must project strength and level-headedness. In a country obsessed with fear of inflation, the candidate's economic background plays a bigger role than in most nations. Two of Germany's postwar chancellors have been economists. The candidate's adherence to democratic rules also plays a role, and Franz Josef Strauss's authoritarian streak contributed to his defeat in the 1980 race.

Personality contributed to the results of the 1983 election, too. The CDU/CSU was no longer encumbered by the negative image of Strauss; instead,

Newly elected Chancellor Kohl addresses his party's victory celebration. Theoretically, West German elections are for parties, but in practice they now focus on top personalities, almost like U.S. presidential contests. (*German Information Center*)

it had the pleasant, reliable image of Helmut Kohl. The SPD's Helmut Schmidt, the former chancellor, was personally popular—polls showed him well ahead of his party—but, feeling a little age and with a pacemaker in his heart, he decided not to run again. His place was taken by the lesser-known Hans-Jochen Vogel, who came across as a bit cold and intellectual. Further, Vogel had to preside over a split SPD, part of which was moderate, upholding welfare and U.S. missiles in Germany, and part of which was more radical and pacifist. Much of postwar German politics can be described as parties groping for the right leader to bring them to power in the *Bundestag* and chancellor's office. When they find the right one—Adenauer of the CDU and Schmidt of the SPD—they stick with him.

Movable Mayors

As in Britain, West German political figures are not anchored to one spot. They move around as their party places them in higher and higher positions. Hans-Jochen Vogel, for example, the SPD's chancellor candidate in 1983, was born in Göttingen, in the north, but climbed through the ranks in Munich, in the south. He was elected mayor of Munich in 1960 and then to the *Bundestag* in 1972. The SPD government made him minister of planning and urban development, then minister of justice. In 1981 they moved him to Berlin to become mayor. To be the mayor of two different cities is unthinkable in the United States, but it's quite normal in Germany where party counts for more than local roots. The German parties use municipal and state offices as training grounds for national office.

THE BUNDESTAG AND THE CITIZEN

One reason German elections have turned into chancellery elections is the murky status of the *Bundestag* in the mind of many voters. They know what the chancellor does but aren't too clear on what the *Bundestag* does. Part of the blame for this is the concept *Bundestag* deputies have of their role. As noted in the previous chapter, the *Rechtsstaat* tradition is focused on laws. The *Bundestag*, staffed heavily by lawyers and civil servants, has become a law factory.

But isn't a legislature supposed to legislate? Not entirely. By confining their activities to law books and committee meetings, *Bundestag* deputies have failed to grasp the less obvious but still very important function of a legislature. Actually, the most important role of a legislature is probably in overseeing the activities of the national government, catching corruption and inefficiency, uncovering scandals, threatening budget cuts, and otherwise keeping bureaucrats on their toes. The harsh glare of publicity is often the best medicine for governmental wrongdoing. The overly cozy client relationships between bureaucracy and business thrive only in the dark. It is in this area that the *Bundestag* has been weak. Although there are commissions of inquiry and a question hour, the former are not pursued as thoroughly as on Washington's Capitol Hill—where televised committee hearings are a major preoccupation—and the latter is not carried out with as much verve as in the House of Commons—where baiting the government is a great sport that sometimes yields political results. In functioning as little but lawmakers, German legislators have undermined their own stature in the eyes of the electorate.

One function the *Bundestag* has failed to develop is that of education.

The way a legislature operates, the arguments that are presented, the manner in which members of parliament conduct themselves, these are great teachers of democracy. Instead, *Bundestag* activity seems calculated to put observers to sleep. The *Bundestag* doesn't generate good press because it's a dull story. Capitol Hill and Westminster attract much more public interest because they do interesting things.

Another function an effective parliament must perform is to represent people in a way that they feel someone speaking for them really understands their point of view. In this the *Bundestag* suffers from a problem common to all elected legislatures: it isn't representative of the voters. The average *Bundestag* deputy is close to 50 years old, male, trained as a lawyer, and employed as a civil servant, party leader, or interest-group official. Fewer than 10 percent are women, and they are elected only because the party places them on *Land* election lists; only a handful have ever won in a single-member district.

Impressive German Words:
Sachlichkeit

Sachlichkeit, "objectivity" or "factualness," is highly respected among German legislators. A person who knows the facts and sticks to them is esteemed by members of the *Bundestag*. The trouble, though, is that such a legislator is also bound to be a bit dull and unimaginative. Too much *Sachlichkeit* and not enough boldness in legislative style is one reason the *Bundestag* is not as admired as it might be.

The strong German party system means that people must slowly work their way up in party ranks before they will be put on a ballot. Accordingly, candidates tend to be older, seasoned, party loyalists rather than bright, fresh, new faces. Unlike the American system, a German candidate cannot "come from out of nowhere" and win an election on his or her own. You're either a piece of the party machine or you're nothing. The result is unrepresentative representatives. As one German newspaper put it: "This gap between electorate and elected has become too wide." Many Germans do not feel represented; they feel that the *Bundestag* is the arena where the powerful interests of society work out deals with little reference to the common citizen, the little guy. Such feelings contributed to the Green vote.

THE UNION-PARTY LINKUP

One characteristic of Northern European political systems—and here we include Britain and Sweden along with West Germany—is the close relationship between labor union and political party, specifically the social-democratic parties. In these countries unions are large and cohesive; most blue-collar workers are organized, and their unions in turn form a single, large labor federation. Such federations support the social-democratic parties with money, manpower, and influence with the rank and file. Often union leaders actually run for office on the party ticket.

Compare this pattern with the Latin European systems. Labor is not as well organized and is fragmented into several federations. The biggest labor unions are Communist led and encourage members to vote Communist (with imperfect success). Socialist and Christian unions, supporting other parties, have difficulty cooperating with the large Communist-led unions. The fragmentation reduces the effectiveness of a working-class voice. American unions face a similar problem. They too are fragmented into several federations and historically have not tied themselves to one party. U.S. labor does not have the same kind of political input as North European labor.

Impressive German Words:
Spitzenverbände

Spitzenverbände (literally, "peak association") is the German term for a federation of like-minded special-interest groups. For example, most labor unions are organized into one *Spitzenverbändl* (the DGB), and all big businesses into another (the BDI). The interactions of *Spitzenverbände* (the plural) among themselves and with government bespeaks the high degree of interest-group organization in Germany.

In Britain, the TUC is an actual constituent member of the Labour party. In Sweden, the gigantic LO is so close to the Social Democrats that some of their top personnel are the same. The West German Basic Law forbids a formal union-party tie, but here too everyone knows that labor support is an important pillar of SPD strength.

In France and the United States, only one fifth of the labor force is unionized; in West Germany a hefty 36 percent is. There are seventeen West German unions—the biggest is the metalworkers *(IG Metall)*—but they are federated into a "peak" or "roof" organization, the *Deutscher Gewerkschaftsbund*, DGB for short. With nearly eight million members, the DGB's voice is heeded by the Social Democrats; its leader, Ernst Breit, is regularly consulted by SPD chiefs. Although they don't dictate party policy, unions get a good deal of what they want: an elaborate welfare system, support for a shorter work week, and even directors' seats on the boards of large companies (more on this, next chapter). About one-third of the SPD's *Bundestag* deputies have union ties.

But the catchall nature of the SPD prevents its being dominated by any

Variations on a Theme:
Union Party Links in Three Countries

COUNTRY	UNION	PARTY LINKAGE
Britain	TUC	Labour
Sweden	LO	Social Democrat
West Germany	DGB	SPD

one group. The more the SPD seeks votes in the center of the political spectrum, the more it has to turn away from one-on-one cooperation with the DGB. The British Labourites face the same problem with the TUC; if they let the union component dominate they lose votes. Accordingly, in the 1970s the SPD and DGB found differences developing between them, something that had never happened before. Helmut Schmidt, representing the SPD right, was a better democrat and economist than he was a socialist. DGB relations with the SPD grew a little cool. Still, the DGB is locked into supporting the Social Democrats for the simple reason that no other party will treat them as well.

On the management side, there is a similar but weaker pattern. The powerful *Bundesverband der Deutschen Industrie* (Federation of German Industries, BDI) has warm connections with the CDU, but not as close as those of the DGB with the SPD. When the Social Democrats came to power, the BDI found it could get along with them quite well too. As in Britain and France, big business doesn't need to get closely involved with one party; it's to their interests to be able to work with all parties. The major focus of business is the bureaucracy, not the parties. Providing information to the relevant ministry, explaining to civil servants why a given regulation should be modified, going along with government economic plans—in these and other ways business quietly cements ties with government.

Interest Groups: "Family" versus "Client" Relationships

Yale political scientist Joseph LaPalombara used the Italian words *parentela* and *clientela* in his groundbreaking study of Italian interest groups. The terms caught on and now refer to the two distinct ways interest groups interact with government.

In a *parentela* (family) relationship, a large, conspicuous interest group has close ideological ties to a party or candidates, works to get them elected, and has a say in the formation of policy. Catholic Action in Italy, for example, has this sort of relationship to the Italian Christian Democratic party. Likewise, the big West German labor federation, DGB, has a *parentela* relationship with the SPD.

In a *clientela* (clientelistic) relationship a government works closely but usually quietly with an interest group such as a business or industry, viewing it as a natural constituency, fighting for its interests, and relying on information and ideas it supplies. The government agency, in effect, develops a lawyer-client relationship with the special interest. The BDI has a *clientela* relationship with various sectors of the Bonn bureaucracy.

THE LÄNDER AND BONN

Britain and France are unitary systems that have attempted devolution and decentralization. West Germany is a federal system that some people would like to make a little more centralized. The interesting thing here is that in both unitary and federal systems there are pressures to move toward a middle ground. Centralization in France is rigid, inefficient, and time consuming and ignores local wishes and regional pride. Federalism in Germany is often uncoordinated, powerless, and deadlocked and encourages federal-state squabbles. In some ways the distinctions between unitary and federal systems are overdrawn; if you look closely, you see elements of centralization in federations and elements of federalism in unitary states.

West Germany was founded as a federal republic for at least two reasons: (1) Germany has a long history of particularism and regional pride; (2) the occupying powers, fearful of a resurgence of German might in a centralized state, wanted it that way. The French in particular would have been delighted to see Germany broken up into several independent states that could never again threaten France. Postwar German politicians themselves, aware of the abuses of power of Hitler's centralized Reich, were mostly committed to a federal structure.

Germany is probably more federal than the United States; that is, its *Länder* run more of their own affairs and get a bigger portion of taxes than do American states. For example, individual and corporate income taxes are split between Bonn and the *Länder* in equal 40 percent shares; the cities get 20 percent. The *Länder* also get a third of the value-added tax, the large but hidden sales tax used throughout Europe. The result is that, while some additional funds are transferred from Bonn to the *Länder* and cities, the *Länder* do not have to go begging the way American states and cities do in their repeated pleas to Washington for bail-out money.

Germany's federalism has some drawbacks. For example, there's really no nationwide police force (aside from the Border Police), so law enforcement is a *Land* affair. Terrorists who committed their crimes in one *Land* could flee to another, counting on communication and coordination foul-ups to delay police. The cleaning of the seriously polluted Rhine River until recently lacked a central authority because such matters were controlled by the states, and each state saw its environmental responsibilities differently. The decentralized nature of education has made it impossible for federal authorities to insist on the nationwide study of the Nazis and their crimes in schools.

Many Germans would like Bonn to have a little more control over things. But the German *Länder,* like American states, stoutly resist moves that would erode the powers of *Land* officials, and they have the perfect weapon to do so: the *Bundesrat.* Not popularly elected, *Bundesrat* delegations are designated by *Land* governments, which usually means the state's political chiefs also sit in Bonn. The *Bundesrat* must concur on any move that would alter the balance of powers between federation and state. In the late 1970s a strange situation developed. The CDU ran most *Land* governments; therefore the *Bundesrat* came under CDU control while the cabinet, chosen by the *Bundestag,* was an SPD-FDP coalition. The *Bundesrat* and the cabinet were frequently at loggerheads, a legislative stalemate not unlike that faced by many American presidents. With the 1983 election, this situation corrected itself so that both chambers were in the hands of the CDU/CSU.

As to the preferability of unitary versus federal systems, there is no simple answer. If you have one system, you usually want a little of the other. On balance, the West German federation works pretty well. Further, in founding a new democracy it was probably wise to give people a smaller unit to focus on, to serve as a building block for developing nationwide democratic loyalties.

How Germans Voted: The 1983 Elections by Land

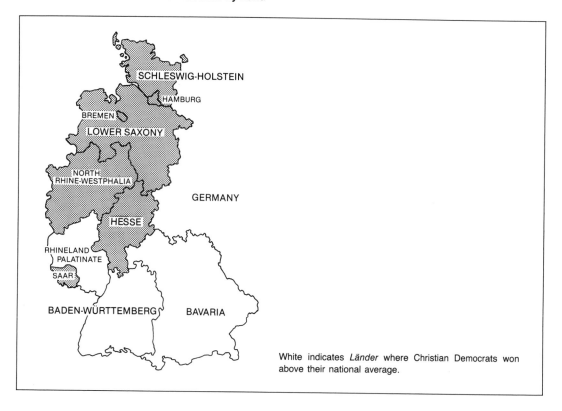

White indicates *Länder* where Christian Democrats won above their national average.

GERMAN VOTING PATTERNS

In Britain, as we saw, the vote is structured at least in part along lines of social class and region. That is, Labour usually wins much of the working class plus Scotland, Wales, and large industrial cities. French voting is similar, with the added factor of religious attitude—clerical or anticlerical. German voting patterns also tend to follow class, region, and religion, but here religion means Catholic or Protestant. A German Catholic is more likely to vote CDU, a Protestant slightly more likely to vote SPD, although it was never the intention of either party to develop a religious basis.

By the same token, the heavily Catholic *Länder* tend to elect Christian Democrat deputies. The CSU, for example, has long had Bavaria sewn up. In the large cities people tend to the left, a universal pattern. In Germany as elsewhere, the rural and small-town vote goes conservative. German workers, especially those belonging to a labor union, are more loyal to the SPD than British workers are to the Labour party. There are fewer "working-class Tories" in Germany than in Britain. Accordingly, an ideal-typical SPD voter is a Protestant worker in a large North German city. His CDU counterpart is a middle-class Catholic in a small South German town.

VOCABULARY BUILDING

authoritarian	catchall party	electoral punishment	*Spitzenverbändl*
Bavaria	*clientela*	*parentela*	unimodal
BDI	DGB	representative	*Weltanschauung*

FURTHER REFERENCE

Beyme, Klaus von. *The Political System of the Federal Republic of Germany.* New York: St. Martin's Press, 1983.

Braunthal, Gerard. *The West German Social Democrats, 1969–1982: Profile of a Party in Power.* Boulder Colo.: Westview Press, 1983.

_____ *The Federation of German Industry in Politics.* Ithaca, N.Y.: Cornell University Press, 1965.

Budge, Ian, Ivor Crewe, and Dennis Farlie, eds. *Party Identification and Beyond: Representations of Voting and Party Competition.* New York: Wiley, 1976.

Downs, Anthony. *An Economic Theory of Democracy.* New York: Harper & Row, 1957.

Hennis, Wilhelm. "Reform of the Bundestag: The Case for General Debate," in *Modern Parliaments: Change or Decline?* ed. by Gerhard Loewenberg. Chicago: Aldine, 1971.

Kirchheimer, Otto. "Germany: The Vanishing Opposition," in *Political Oppositions in Western Democracies,* ed. by Robert A. Dahl. New Haven, Conn.: Yale University Press, 1966.

Kolinsky, Eva. *Parties, Opposition and Society in West Germany.* New York: St. Martin's Press, 1984.

Lehmbruch, Gerhard. "Party and Federation in Germany: A Developmental Dilemma," *Government and Opposition* 13 (spring 1978), 151–77.

Merkl, Peter H. "Factionalism: The Limits of the West German Party-State," in *Faction Politics: Political Parties and Factionalism in Comparative Perspective,* ed. by Frank Belloni and Dennis Beller. Santa Barbara, Calif.: ABC-Clio, 1978.

Paterson, William E., and Gordon R. Smith, eds. *The West German Model: Perspectives on a Stable State.* Totowa, N.J.: F. Cass, 1981.

Penniman, Howard R., ed. *West Germany at the Polls, 1980/1983.* Durham, N.C.: Duke University Press, 1985.

Reuter, Konrad. *Many States but One Country: On the Structure of the Federal Republic of Germany.* Bonn: Inter Nationes, 1981.

Smith, Gordon. *Democracy in Western Germany: Parties and Politics in the Federal Republic,* 2d ed. New York: Holmes & Meier, 1982.

16

WHAT
WEST GERMANS
QUARREL ABOUT

THE ECONOMIC MIRACLE

Only one word can describe West Germany's economic performance in the third of a century after World War II: Wow! Americans and Britons touring the Federal Republic sometimes got the feeling it was the Germans who won the war. Paradoxically, it was precisely because Germany lost much of its industrial plants and the equipment was new. Some was destroyed by Allied bombing; more was ripped out and shipped back to Russia by the vengeful Soviets. While the British and Americans patched up their old industries, the Germans often started from scratch with new, more efficient equipment.

The war had other beneficial aftereffects. Almost everybody was poor; food and fuel were barely sufficient for minimal survival in the years after the war. This meant a kind of rough equality among Germans; income distribution was more equitable in Germany (and Japan) than in the victorious countries. Consequently the bitter class antagonisms found in Britain and France did not develop in postwar Germany. Everyone started from a similar low level, and, most Germans feel, everyone got a share of the economic growth. Further, defeat in the war and empty stomachs in the postwar years left Germans with more modest expectations than Britons or Americans, who expected to be handed some kind of postwar paradise.

People used to joke that Germans don't work to live but rather live to work. This is no longer the case, but it fairly describes German attitudes toward their ruined country: "Get to work and fix it." Further, the human skills and much of the infrastructure (roads, railroads, electricity) were still there. After Hitler, economic growth was about the only outlet for German national pride.

Under the conservative leadership of the CDU and Economics Minister (later Chancellor) Ludwig Erhard, the Bonn government pursued a nearly laissez-faire policy. While Britain turned to Labour's welfare state and France to *planification* after World War II, West Germany relied mainly on market forces. It worked. By 1955 Germany had surpassed its prewar levels of production. By 1980 it was one of the richest countries in the world, with a per capita GNP that nearly matched that of the United States.

Impressive German Words:
Wirtschaftswunder

"Economic miracle," or *Wirtschaftswunder,* is how West Germans proudly describe the transformation of their country in the 1950s. After the awesome devastation of World War II—in which entire German cities were made hills of rubble—Germans labored like dogs to produce the modern, spanking new Federal Republic. There is no miracle about where the *Wirtschaftswunder* came from: not from heaven but from the right attitudes toward work.

No miracle lasts forever, though, and by the early 1980s the West German economy was in trouble—although not in as much trouble as its neighbors. The oil shocks of 1973 and 1979 had impacted not only directly on the FRG economy but indirectly, in weakening demand for its exports. West Germany, concentrating on metal-working, fell behind the Japanese and Americans in high-tech areas. Unemployment topped 10 percent, the worst in living memory. For two years, the German economy registered negative economic growth. The Christian Democrats won in 1983 with the slogan, "Vote for recovery!" Chancellor Kohl implemented an economic policy closer to that of Reagan than of Thatcher, and the German economy improved. Still, what direction to go in economic policy is a major West German political quarrel.

Impressive German Words: Sozialmarkt

Ludwig Erhard's phrase for his economic policies, "social market," describes what he was trying to do in laying the basis for the *Wirtschaftswunder.* The German economy should be that of a free market, he urged, with individuals and firms deciding for themselves what to produce, invest in, and spend on. But the whole thing should be aimed to socially useful ends—cleaning up the ruined cities, settling refugees, providing a welfare floor, and insuring full employment. You might call Erhard's *Sozialmarkt,* "capitalism with a conscience." Tax breaks and government control over investment banking pointed the German market economy toward filling in the gaps left by the war (for example, apartment-house construction). When the Social Democrats took power in 1969 their economic policies were basically the same.

ROLE OF UNIONS

German workers and their labor unions have stood in marked contrast to their British counterparts. German unions are as powerful as British unions but don't strike as much (see box). German labor leaders, like Germans in general, emerged from World War II badly burned. They had seen what economic instability—inflation and unemployment—can lead to and were determined not to let it happen again. Owners and managers felt much the same way. West German industry, accordingly, revived in a spirit of labor-management cooperation rather than conflict, the norm for Britain and France.

German labor leaders saw that asking for too much too soon would choke off the capital growth needed to finance reconstruction. Their attitude was: "First let the pie grow, then we'll get our slice." The DGB, in a move highly unusual for unions, practiced wage restraint, not going to the mat for every *pfennig* they could squeeze out of the boss and rarely going out on strike. By restraining their wage demands, German workers ended up among the best paid in the world, with wages and fringe benefits surpassing those of American workers.

German labor unions were psychologically prepared to accept wage restraint. In the first place, Germany always had an extensive welfare system, and even the conservative CDU under Adenauer reinforced and supported it. German workers had a welfare floor under them that provided medical care, unemployment insurance, and a job-finding service. They didn't feel insecure. Second—and this is very important—German workers felt they had access to political power. Not only the SPD, which has a long history of union alliances, but the CDU too listened to what workers had to say. Although generally bourgeois in orientation, the Christian Democrats took pains to bring blue-collar workers

*Comparing: Annual Average
Working Days Lost in Strikes
Per 1,000 Employees, 1970–82*

Italy	1403
Britain	512
United States	443
France	184
Sweden	139
West Germany	42
Netherlands	38
Austria	9
Switzerland	2

Source: Institute of German Industry.

into the party and even sponsored a labor section within their party (whose members, however, mostly belong to the DGB). German workers did not develop the bitter, alienated feelings of British and French workers.

Growing out of their political access, the German labor movement gained an important, innovative tool: codetermination, the right to participate in the big decisions of their companies (see box). German workers, far from feeling totally helpless before an all-powerful management, know their worker representatives are directly involved in management questions of expansion, layoffs, and working conditions.

During the 1970s, codetermination was a major political quarrel. Owners and managers fought it, arguing that it would infringe upon their property

Impressive German Words: Mitbestimmung

Sometimes known by its longer name, *Arbeitermitbestimmung* (worker codetermination), labor participation in basic management decisions has been part of the coal and steel industry since 1951. It was expanded in 1976 after decades of discussion. Basically it means that large firms—those with over 2,000 employees—must have a supervisory board with half the directors chosen by labor and half by shareholders. The chairperson, elected only by the shareholders, can cast the deciding vote in case of a tie. Smaller firms have less stringent codetermination rules, and companies with less than five employees have none.

How does *Mitbestimmung* work in practice? When a Ruhr steelworks wanted to cut its 7,200-person work force by 300 jobs, it had to negotiate and compromise with worker representatives on the supervisory board. Early retirement, job retraining, and income guarantees cushioned the impact of the cuts. Worker councils throughout the factory discussed the proposals and agreed to them before the labor representatives voted yes. No strikes, no anger, no feeling of powerlessness.

When Volkswagen wanted to set up a U.S. plant, the union was understandably hostile: it sounded as if the company was exporting jobs. When it was pointed out that high German wages were making it hard to sell Volkswagens in the United States and that the main components would still be made in Germany, labor went along with the move and hasn't regretted it.

Codetermination doesn't mean that the unions run everything. But it does mean that on the general thrust of company policy—the decisions that affect the livelihood of employees—labor has a nearly equal say.

rights. In 1979, in one of its most important decisions, the Constitutional Court decided there was nothing unconstitutional about worker codetermination. The issue is not settled. Owners and managers would like to roll back *Mitbestimmung,* whereas unions would like to take it further. Union chiefs point out that with a shareholder-elected chairperson casting the deciding vote, unions are still less powerful than management on the supervisory boards. Codetermination is a creative if imperfect attempt to solve one of the long-standing problems of industrialized democracies: how to extend democracy from the voting booth into the workplace. The rest of the world should be studying *Mitbestimmung.*

SHORTENING THE WORKWEEK

With the high unemployment of the early 1980s, German workers rallied to a new cause: shortening the workweek—without any cuts in pay—so as to provide more jobs. The giant metalworking union, *IG Metall*—with 2.5 million members the largest union in the world—staged a selective seven-week strike in 1984 to demand a 35-hour workweek. Rippling out to other industries, at one point 350,000 workers were idle. It was the biggest strike in postwar German history. The SPD supported the 35-hour week, and other unions voiced similar demands.

The union's management counterpart, *Gesamtmetall,* would have none of it, arguing that less production for the same pay would wreck German industry and cause inflation. The CDU agreed; Chancellor Kohl called the union demand "silly and dumb." The strike was finally settled when a Social Democratic politician was called in to mediate. He proposed an average 38.5-hour week with some small pay adjustments. The union accepted but vowed this was just the beginning, that they would keep pushing for 35 hours.

Would it work? Would a shortened workweek help lower unemployment? Economists doubted it; maybe it would help if workers were willing to accept less pay. The mediated compromise was actually in line with what had been happening to the German workweek for decades: it got shorter with mostly moderate pay hikes. The industrial workweek dropped from nearly 50 hours in 1955 to under 40 in 1983.

Some unions, managers, and CDU politicians suggested the way to handle the problem was not by shortening the workweek but by lowering the retirement age. This too would open up jobs but at a more moderate cost. Actually, Germans now retire at an average age of 59 anyhow, earlier than in most other industrialized countries.

The point is that, with either a shorter workweek or earlier retirement, Germans don't like to work as much as they used to. Gone is the old zest to labor that raised the FRG from the ashes; now Germans value their vacation and leisure time, almost like the British. Is this civilized or potentially dangerous? The world market is a highly competitive place, and resource-poor Germany exports about a third of its production. If the price of German goods rises too high, consumers in other countries buy fewer of them and switch to other products. The Volkswagen car was eagerly sought by Americans in the 1960s; by the 1980s it had nearly disappeared, its place taken by Japanese imports. Germany's highest areas of unemployment were in the "smokestack industries," where it was no longer competitive—a parallel to the United States.

Had German workers grown fat and lazy? Had they held back in the 1950s and then overshot the mark in the 1980s? Perhaps the beneficial aftereffects of World War II are wearing off. If so, we can look forward to a more troubled West Germany that will more closely resemble its neighbors in problems of economics and how to deal with them.

FOREIGN WORKERS

Like Britain and France, West Germany too finds that foreigners from poor countries are attracted to its better jobs and higher pay. But in Germany the numbers—and the problems—are bigger. There are 4.4 million foreigners in Germany, mostly from Mediterranean nations (Turkey, Yugoslavia, Greece, Italy, Spain). About 2 million are workers; the rest are spouses and children. All together, they comprise over 7 percent of the population of the Federal Republic.

The trend started in the late 1950s when the "economic miracle" had absorbed all working Germans and was still short of labor. Italians and later Spaniards were allowed into West Germany, eager for the plentiful jobs. Soon Germans began abandoning dirty, dangerous, and unskilled lines of work for better positions, leaving their old jobs to foreigners. At first the impact seemed temporary: the immigrant workers, it was assumed, would stay for a year or two, amass some savings, and return home. But the "guest workers," faced with unemployment at home, often decided to remain and to send for their families. Large numbers began arriving from Turkey, where unemployment is especially high. There are now over 1.4 million Turks in the Federal Republic; whole neighborhoods have turned into Turkish ghettos. The "guests" had come to stay.

Germans began to have second thoughts about the influx. They were not only importing labor but importing problems as well. As in Britain and France, antiforeign feeling grew among all social classes. Germans perceived foreign workers as crime prone, lecherous, and disorderly. A new racism appeared in Germany.

With the economic difficulties of the early 1980s, many Germans were delighted to see foreign workers sent home. Work and residence permits are tightly controlled in Germany, as in most European countries, and can be revoked. As in Britain and France, in 1984 the Bonn government offered to pay foreign workers to go home—cheaper than unemployment compensation and other social insurance, Bonn calculated—and about 300,000 accepted the deal and left. Sending home a few hundred thousand foreign workers had no impact on German unemployment rates. Expelling foreign workers was, rather, a symbolic and psychological move to ease the German public's economic fears. "Too many *Gastarbeiter*," thought some Germans.

Impressive German Words: Gastarbeiter

Garstarbeiter, or "guest worker," was initially meant to have a nice ring to it, meaning that the many Turks, Yugoslavs, and others who came to work in the Federal Republic were welcome guests. In time, though, *Gastarbeiter* came to mean the shifty-eyed foreigners who were taking the lowest jobs available. In effect, the *Gastarbeiter* (it's the same spelling in the plural) had turned into a subproletariat that lived within but was not part of German society nor wanted by it. In German cities appeared the graffito *Turkenraus* (Turks out).

They reasoned that if the two million foreign workers were sent home, the job vacancies would nearly eliminate German unemployment. But Germans wouldn't take those jobs any more than Americans would take the work done by undocumented Mexican workers.

The really serious problem the Gastarbeiter presented was their families, especially the Turks. Originally it was thought only single workers would come, and no provision was made for educating children. But the Turkish families have about three times as many babies as do Germans. The result is a growing mass of underprivileged youth in Germany with inadequate schooling—most drop out before finishing—inadequate command of German, no job skills, and no work permits even if they could find a job. The situation has been called a social time bomb: seven hundred thousand foreign children, many of whom are candidates for juvenile delinquency and drugs. Germany became Europe's number-one drug country; pure heroin from Turkey's poppy fields flowed in with Turkish *Gastarbeiter.*

Now, what to do with the immigrant workers and their families? Many German politicians, especially the more conservative ones, have tried to pretend it isn't Germany's problem: if the foreigners aren't happy in the Federal Republic, they should leave. They see no reason to hire foreign-language teachers and social workers to help immigrant youngsters. In fact, many Germans do not wish to make the *Gastarbeiter* feel at home or to integrate them into German society; they are just temporary guests. (South Africa's *apartheid* system is based on the same fiction.)

Liberal and leftist Germans, on the other hand, recognize that the immigrants aren't just temporary and that the problem will be helped only by integrating them into German society. They recommend that fees for kindergarten be abolished, that foreign children receive remedial German instruction in school, and that they have the option of assuming German nationality at age 18. All this would cost money, but they point out that *Gastarbeiter* have been paying taxes and social security for years.

The irony of the immigrant workers and their families is that postwar Germany, which had overcome much of its old class antagonisms and differences, is creating the problem anew. The German economic miracle brought with it a new underclass of poor foreigners; it solved one problem and created another. That is the nature of economic growth: it leads to new sets of problems that were earlier unforeseen.

Running Out of Germans

While foreigners have been coming to the Federal Republic, Germans have been leaving—by dint of the world's lowest birthrate. From a peak population of 62.1 million in 1973, the FRG has dropped to under 61 million—and less than 57 million of them are ethnic Germans. From the mid-1960s to the mid-1980s, the number of births in West Germany fell from more than 1 million a year to 600,000. This brings problems. It means that fewer working-age Germans will have to support more retired people. At present rates, the ratio will be an impossible 1:1 by 2030. It also sharpens ethnic animosities, as foreign workers, especially Turks, have large families. Some Germans fear their country will be swamped by foreigners, the same fear felt in Britain and France.

HOW MUCH WELFARE?

In Britain, as we saw, the welfare state is a major political question. Labour wants to expand it; Conservatives want to roll it back. In Germany, the world's first welfare state, the issue is not as volatile, for both main parties support welfare measures.

But there are differences between them. The SPD would like to cautiously expand the welfare system, while the CDU/CSU tries to tighten it. In a modern country it is very difficult to cut back welfare measures: too many recipients protest. Even conservatives like Margaret Thatcher weren't able to make a dent in the British welfare system. The real debate is between a little more and a little less.

German benefits are impressive. If you lose your job in Germany, you get 63 percent of your last year's income for a whole year. Then for another three years you get 56 percent. (Kohl cut these from 68 and 58 percent to save money.) All the while a *Land* or city employment office is looking for a suitable job for you (if they find one, you must take it or lose your benefits). All Germans have medical insurance, most governmental, some private. Pensions are hefty and indexed to the cost of living; when it goes up so does your retirement check. Germans get monthly allowances for each child they have—$25 for the first, $60 for the second, and $120 for each additional. Even so, Germany's birthrate is the world's lowest (see box).

Kohl trimmed these benefits in the Reagan manner. New mothers now get only $182 a month instead of $268, when they take time off from work. Retired people have to pay 5 percent of their previously free medical insurance. Scholarships for low-income students have been turned into loans. Almost a third of Germany's GNP had been going for social spending, and this had led to a government deficit that Kohl was determined to cut. As in the United States, the trims hit poorer Germans harder. At the same time, Kohl introduced tax breaks for middle-income families, who bear a heavy burden.

The SPD reaction was predictable and the same as the charges Democrats in the United States directed against President Reagan: you have let holes develop in the social safety net and have helped rich people get richer. Like Americans, Germans were mostly so pleased with the economic recovery that they did not immediately pay much attention to the opposition argument.

The CDU/CSU and FDP argue that the tax burden of the welfare state is too high. As we saw in chapter 6, taxes in both West Germany and Britain take about 37 percent of the GNP (compared to about 30 percent in the United States). In 1960 the average German worker saw taxes and social security take 16 percent of his or her paycheck. By 1985 that had doubled. Germans are also hit with a 14 percent value-added tax on most of their purchases. Welfare states cost a lot of money, argue the conservatives, and just how much are you willing to *pay* for these benefits? For the 1980s, it looks like the conservatives have the better of the debate, but it is an argument without end.

REUNIFICATION

The Federal Republic's dream is reunification of all German territory. To some, this means reunification not only with East Germany but with the Oder-Neise territories and East Prussia, which were taken over by Poland and the Soviet Union after the war. Being for reunification has become in West German politics like being for baseball, mother, and apple pie in the United States. But chances are slim for reunification anytime soon.

The Poles and the Russians, murdered by the millions at the hands of the Nazis, are not about to give back one square centimeter of the German territory they seized. Neither do they (or any other European country) look kindly on the prospects of reunifying East and West Germany. From time to time the Kremlin drops hints that it might go along with German reunification provided the Federal Republic drops out of NATO, but Bonn knows precisely what that means: the "Finlandization" of Germany, that is, becoming neutral and lightly armed under Soviet supervision. The West Germans will make no such deal.

Berlin Wall, started in 1961, has now become a virtually impassable death strip that underscores the division of Germany. East German soldiers, like those in the watchtower, make sure none of their fellow citizens leaves for the West. (*German Information Center*)

West German politicians instead have taken a hard line. The Adenauer regime developed the "Hallstein doctrine" (named after foreign ministry official Walter Hallstein) by which Bonn refused to have diplomatic relations with any country that recognized East Germany. Only West Germany, argued Bonn, was the real Germany, and it alone spoke for all Germans. The Hallstein doctrine, however, by turning a cold shoulder to East Germany, gave the Communist regime there exactly what it needed: time to consolidate its shaky hold. Increasingly, Germans came to recognize that the hard-line approach was getting them nowhere. In fact, the Federal Republic in 1955 had to repudiate its own doctrine when it recognized the Soviet Union.

With the CDU-SPD grand coalition of 1966, things began to change. Willy Brandt, new SPD foreign minister, advocated building bridges to East Europe. When he became chancellor in 1969 he launched a full-blown program of normalizing relations with Eastern Europe, leading in 1972 to Bonn's diplomatic recognition of East Germany.

What impact did this have on German hopes for reunification? Although the Hallstein doctrine had accomplished little, it had given Germans the comfortable illusion that they were being firm in defending Germany's rights. Brandt's *Ostpolitik* implied there would be no reunification, so Germans might as well accept things as they were. Many West Germans were furious. This is what qualifies Brandt as brave: he faced his own people and told them that reunification of Germany was nothing they could hope for in the near future.

It was a bitter pill for many Germans to swallow. Some muttered that Brandt was a traitor who had "sold out Germany." The same kind of German nationalists who spoke of *Dolchstoss* after World War I hated Brandt's *Ostpolitik*. Large sections of the Christian Democrats, especially former refugees from the east and Strauss's Bavarian CSU, denounced the treaties Brandt had arranged with the Soviet Union, Poland, and East Germany.

Impressive German Words: Ostpolitik

Chancellor Willy Brandt's "eastern policy" soon took on connotations that made the word *Ostpolitik* Germany's hottest political topic in the early 1970s. Many Germans didn't relish admitting that their eastern territories, in the hands of Russia and Poland, were gone. Brandt came right out and said it; in 1970 it was enshrined in treaties with the two lands. His *Ostpolitik* aimed at building bridges to East Europe and drawing the German Democratic Republic out of its isolation and into a dialogue with the Federal Republic. It worked: in 1972 the two Germanies recognized each other, and in 1973 both joined the United Nations. The fact that Brandt's *Ostpolitik* could be accepted by a majority of West Germans testifies to their political maturity and willingness to live with reality. Brandt's moves calmed and normalized the situation in Central Europe—long the focal point of the Cold War—and for this he was awarded the 1971 Nobel Peace Prize.

By 1972, however, most Germans agreed with Brandt. It's better to have contact with East Germany than to pretend it doesn't exist, many reasoned. In the 1972 elections the SPD advanced while the CDU shrank. The treaties were ratified by the *Bundestag*.

Most Germans now believe that normalization with Eastern Europe, including East Germany, was a good step. It gave West German tourists and business people a chance to penetrate East Germany. The smaller German Democratic Republic, initially regarding its recognition by Bonn as a triumph, came to have some regrets. Western visitors brought in their rock-solid Western Deutschmarks, and soon East German workers were clamoring to be paid in part with "Westmarks," with which they could buy imported goods at special shops. Brandt's *Ostpolitik* did something the Hallstein doctrine never accomplished: it undermined the stability of the East German regime by increasing popular discontent. Thousands of East Germans clamored to leave for the West.

This helped reawaken the longing in West Germany for reunification. The CDU/CSU, back in power in 1983, played on this theme. Chancellor Kohl proclaimed, "We Germans do not accept the division of our fatherland," and "The unity of our nation lives on." Instead of *Ostpolitik*, the key phrase became *Deutschlandpolitik* (see box).

But Kohl faced some very real limits in encouraging Germans to think about reunification. The Soviets aren't about to budge from East Germany, the keystone that locks in their East European satellites. The use of force to reunify Germany is out of the question. How then can Bonn promote reunification? Kohl suffered acute embarrassment in 1985 when Germans from Silesia—taken over by Poland after the war—demanded return of "our stolen homeland" and berated Kohl for not doing anything to get it. Kohl's crowd-pleasing rhetoric had been taken too seriously by some. Like his predecessors, Kohl realized that reunification is a distant goal; he basically continued the Brandt and Schmidt policies of drawing the GDR closer by trade and loans. Although in practice little changed, the upsurge of the German Question illustrated that it still lingers under the surface of FRG politics.

Impressive German Words: Deutschlandpolitik

"Germany policy" is to the 1980s what "eastern policy" was to the 1970s in the politics of the FRG. The CDU offered its *Deutschlandpolitik* as a reply and corrective to the SPD's *Ostpolitik*. The two terms are not, however, opposites, for both envision drawing the two German states closer together. *Ostpolitik* normalized relations with the east, including East Germany, and then stopped. *Deutschlandpolitik*, would go farther. In the words of Heinrich Windelen, Bonn's minister of intra-German affairs, it seeks "to enable the German people to exercise their right of self-determination." Windelen foresees a Germany reunited in peace and freedom but proposes no major departures to implement such a goal.

THE MULTICOLORED GREENS

In 1983 a new party entered the *Bundestag,* the Greens, a strange amalgam of anti-atom environmentalists, utopian socialists, and anti-NATO pacifists. In the elections, they had just cleared the 5 percent hurdle (with 5.6 percent) to win twenty-seven seats in Bonn. The Greens were in part the political manifestation of the postmaterialism we discussed in chapter 14. Germans joked that there are "green Greens," who are mostly interested in ecology, and "red Greens," who use the movement to promote a radical anticapitalism.

The true environmentalists make some telling points. Large areas of the crowded and heavily industrialized Federal Republic are seriously polluted. About half of the beloved forests that cover a third of West Germany are threatened with death from industrial and automobile fumes and acid rain. Polls show Germans more worried about their dying forests than the arms race. Dependent on unreliable foreign energy sources, Germany turned to nuclear power. By 1984, 27 percent of Germany's electricity was generated by nuclear reactors, more than the United States but less than France. Unlike the French (see chapter 11), many Germans grew uneasy over nuclear power and staged massive protest demonstrations against it.

Impressive German Words: Waldsterben

In the 1980s Germans learned that by the turn of the century all of their forests could be dead or dying. A new word was coined to capture the immensity of the problem, *Waldsterben,* literally "forest death" but more accurately connoting a sort of genocide of entire forests. Pollution of the air by industry and automobiles was believed to be the cause. English has no precise equivalent to *Waldsterben,* but symptoms of the condition have also appeared in the United States.

The "red Greens" were largely the far-leftists of the 1970s in a new guise. At that time, a minority of German young people had turned away from the conventional parties to support extremist groups. A handful had even turned to terrorism. A government crackdown on radicals and dogged police work had contributed to the passing of the wave of radicalism, but the heavy-handed methods left a bad taste among many young Germans. The Greens were their natural political formation.

Can the Greens do good or ill? In calling attention to West Germany's environmental problems, they forced the major parties to adopt tougher antipollution policies. The Greens provided a home for many young German voters who might have otherwise dropped out of participation or thrown their votes to an extremist party. The problem is that the Greens are not *regierungsfähig*—they aren't able to form a government and don't want to. This could play hob with the formation of coalitions, if not in Bonn then at the *Land* level. The Greens' natural coalition partner is the SPD, but some Green leaders, the so-called *Fundis* (fundamentalists), refuse to compromise their demands to join a coalition. More moderate Greens, the *Reaos* (realists), indicated they might be willing to cooperate. If the Greens should become the *Bundestag's* third largest party—which is possible if the FDP slips much lower (see box)—they could not perform a balancing role like the FDP. This could leave the *Bundestag* with no party able to form a government.

Will the Greens last? Many observers doubt it. They are extremely faction-ridden and weak on organization. To prevent any leader from gaining too much power, they insist that all leaders rotate every couple of years. They

Who Needs the FDP?

With the Free Democratic party dipping dangerously close to the 5 percent threshold—they barely outpolled the Greens in 1983—some wondered if the FDP would survive. Others wondered if it should. The Free Democrats had long had trouble defining themselves; they were to the left of the Christian Democrats on civil rights but well to the right of the Social Democrats on economics. When they pulled out of their coalition with the SPD in 1982, some accused them of betraying Chancellor Schmidt. Germans had elected the SPD in 1980, but thanks to the Free Democrats' treachery, they suddenly had a CDU government. In the 1983 elections, the FDP suffered.

But enough Germans want to keep the FDP in the *Bundestag* to act as a balance against excessive tendencies in either of the two big parties. The FDP in the cabinet kept the Social Democrats from going too far with welfare measures, and in the succeeding Christian Democratic cabinet they kept out Bavaria's Strauss—a worthwhile little party to have around. So on the crucial second vote of the ballot—the one that determines the number of seats for each party—an estimated 1.6 million CDU voters, after having voted for a Christian Democrat in the first column, "loaned" their votes to the FDP. In U.S. terms, they "split their ticket" between the CDU and FDP, enough to keep the latter afloat.

But voters might not do it again. In 1984 FDP Economics Minister Count Otto Lambsdorff resigned over charges he gave illegal tax breaks in return for donations to his party. (The CDU's former candidate for chancellor, Rainer Barzel, resigned from the *Bundestag,* where he served as Speaker, when he was implicated in the same scandal.) If the CDU ticket-splitters turn sour on the Free Democrats, they could be out of the next *Bundestag,* possibly replaced by the Greens as West Germany's third party.

suffered an acute embarrassment when their oldest member of the *Bundestag* turned out to have been a fairly high Nazi government official. Another Green legislator, former general Gert Bastian, who had left the army to protest deployment of new U.S. missiles, resigned from the party because of its "intrigues and power struggles" and growing Marxist orientation. The young party seemed ready to split apart. The Greens' electoral appeal is largely limited to the young and the intellectuals. German workers and managers, oriented to industry, see environmentalism as a threat to jobs and productivity, just like their American counterparts. The Greens may turn out to be a flash party.

No Nukes, German Style

Even more than in Britain, protests over the deployment of new U.S. missiles turned into a political issue in Germany. To offset Soviet SS-20s, SPD Chancellor Helmut Schmidt in 1979 agreed to station 108 Pershing II and 96 cruise missiles on German soil. Other Germans weren't pleased, pointing out that the Pershing IIs could hit Moscow or Leningrad from Germany in less than ten minutes. This would push the Soviets to a hair-trigger "launch on warning" strategy targeted chiefly at West Germany. More than ever, Germany would be in danger of nuclear incineration. President Reagan's bellicose rhetoric alarmed Germans. Polls showed two-thirds of Germans opposed to the new deployments (although an even greater number favor remaining in NATO).

Much to Schmidt's chagrin, the SPD shifted to opposing deployment. The Greens, of course, strongly opposed the missiles, even if the Soviets have similar ones. Massive antimissile protests dotted the Federal Republic in 1983, including a seventy-mile-long human chain. A catchy antiwar song, "99 Balloons," became a hit. But the CDU government of Chancellor Kohl stood firm, and the missiles arrived, albeit under very heavy security. Once deployed, the issue faded, but many Germans are still very unhappy at the thought that they will be the battlefield if there is a World War III.

IS BONN ANOTHER WEIMAR?

By most measures the Federal Republic of Germany is an unqualified success story. Its constitution, leading parties, and economy deserve to be studied by other countries. But some observers have wondered if, under the glittering surface, democracy has taken firm root. Could the Bonn democracy go the way of Weimar's?

All survey data have said no. Decade by decade, West Germans have grown more democratic in their values. By the 1980s, they were at least as committed to a pluralist, free, democratic society as the British and French. They weathered the terrorism of the 1970s and the economic downturn of the early 1980s as well as any of their democratic neighbors. It's a good bet that they'll make it.

We should be aware of the international context of West German democracy, however. Since World War II, Germany has not really been on its own. The Federal Republic was founded with American and British help. A quarter of a million U.S. soldiers are still camped on German soil. West Germany is cemented into West Europe by NATO and the Common Market. Suppose this international context some day changes? Suppose the Americans leave and Germany assumes a more neutral position between Eastern and Western Europe? Then all bets are off, for the forces that have molded German democracy could vanish. Granted, it may never happen; the division and polarization of Europe will continue as long as a powerful Soviet Union defines Eastern Europe as its buffer zone, and that may be forever.

In a very basic sense, West Germany is a child of the Cold War, a product of the Soviet presence. Modern Germany is not easily understood without consideration of the Soviet Union and its domination of the eastern half of Europe. For such an analysis, let us now turn to the largest country in the world, the Union of Soviet Socialist Republics.

VOCABULARY BUILDING

environmentalism	Hallstein doctrine	*Mitbestimmung*	*Sozialmarkt*
Gastarbeiter	income distribution	*Ostpolitik*	*Wirtschaftswunder*
Greens	infrastructure	reunification	

FURTHER REFERENCE

Beck, Barbara. "Down to Earth: A Survey of the West German Economy," *The Economist* 4 February 1984.

Braunthal, Gerard. "Codetermination in West Germany," in *Cases in Comparative Politics,* 3d ed., ed. by James Christoph and Bernard Brown. Boston: Little, Brown, 1976.

Dean, Jonathan. "How to Lose Germany," *Foreign Policy* 55 (Summer 1984).

Eisfeld, Rainer. "The West German Elections: Economic Fears and the Deployment Debate," *Government and Opposition* 18 (Summer 1983) 3.

Federal Republic of Germany. *Documentation Relating*

to the Federal Government's Policy of Détente. Bonn: Press and Information Office, 1978.

————. *Co-Determination in the Federal Republic of Germany.* Bonn: Ministry for Labor and Social Affairs, 1978.

Markovits, Andrei S., ed. *The Political Economy of West Germany: Modell Deutschland.* New York: Praeger, 1982.

Merkl, Peter H. *German Foreign Policies, West and East.* Santa Barbara, Calif.: ABC-Clio, 1974.

Nelkin, Dorothy, and Michael Pollak. *The Atom Besieged: Extraparliamentary Dissent in France and Germany.* Cambridge, Mass.: MIT Press, 1982.

Papadakis, Elim. *The Green Movement in West Germany.* New York: St. Martin's Press, 1984.

Ross, George, et al. *Unions and Economic Crisis: Britain, West Germany and Sweden.* Winchester, Mass.: Allen & Unwin, 1984.

part four

THE SOVIET UNION

17

THE IMPACT OF THE PAST

THE BIGGEST COUNTRY IN THE WORLD

The Soviet Union is immense, stretching eleven time zones across the northern half of Asia to the Pacific. Looking at a map of the Soviet Union, you notice that only a small part of it is in Europe. (Look at a globe and you'll notice that Europe itself is only a small peninsula of Asia.) Only part of the vast Soviet Union is Russia, and ethnic Russians are just half the population. To be accurate, then, we call this land the Soviet Union, not Russia, and its people Soviets unless we mean the ethnic Russians who are indeed their leading element.

Although the Soviet Union has few natural boundaries, its very size and harsh winters make it difficult to conquer. Charles XII of Sweden, Napoleon, and Hitler discovered to their horror that Russia's size and fierce winters could swallow whole armies.

These same winters give the Soviet Union a rather short growing season. Sometimes the Soviet Union has the right temperature and rainfall to produce good crops, but agriculture is a chancy business, with crops failing on an average of one year in three. Geography has not been as kind to Soviet agriculture as it has been to the United States'.

The vast territory Siberia adds to the Soviet Union's size is problematic; its weather is hostile to settlement, and its mineral and forest wealth is hard to extract. Most of the Soviet population continues to live in the "European" part, that is, west of the Ural Mountains. Plans to settle in and develop Siberia, some of them going back to tsarist days, always fall short of expectations. Industrial projects tend to be one-shot efforts by temporary labor. The promises of Siberia remain largely unfulfilled.

Another geographic problem has been the difficulty of reaching the open sea. The first Russian states were totally landlocked; only under Peter the Great at the beginning of the eighteenth century did Russians overcome the Swedes to reach the Baltic and the Turks to reach the Black Sea. The Northern Russian ports ice over in winter, and the Black Sea is controlled by the Turkish Straits, still leaving European Russia without year-round, secure ports. One of the great dreams of tsarists and Communists alike has been for warm-water ports under exclusive Russian control.

THE SLAVIC PEOPLE

Occupying most of Eastern Europe, the Slavic peoples are the most numerous in Europe. Russians, Ukrainians, Poles, Czechs, Slovaks, Serbs, Croats, Bulgarians, and others speak languages that are closer to each other than are the Romance languages (Italian, Spanish, French) of Western Europe. It is said that a Slovak peasant can converse with any other Slavic peasant—so similar are their vocabularies and syntax.

The way the Slavic languages are written, though, has differentiated them. The Western Slavs (Poles, Czechs, and others) were Christianized from Rome; hence their alphabet is Latin. The Eastern Slavs (Russians, Ukrainians, and others) were converted by Eastern Orthodox monks from Constantinople, and their languages are written in a variation of the Greek alphabet called cyrillic after St. Cyril, one of the proselytizing monks.

Memorable Russian Slogans: "Moscow is the Third Rome"

After Constantinople fell to the Turks in the fifteenth century, Russia felt itself to be the last and only center of true Christianity. Rome and Constantinople had both failed; now Moscow would safeguard the faith. The great Soviet filmmaker Sergi Eisenstein, in a chilling portrait of Ivan the Terrible (whom Eisenstein is said to have modeled after Stalin), has the mad tyrant utter: "Moscow is the third Rome; a fourth is not to be." After the Bolshevik Revolution, Russia's new rulers felt the same way about world communism, namely, that Moscow was its capital and there could be no other.

St. Basil's cathedral recalls Moscow's former role as a center of Christianity. (Michael Roskin)

Their Orthodox Christianity (as opposed to Roman Catholicism) and cyrillic writing have contributed to the Russians' isolation from the rest of Europe. In addition to being at the geographical fringe of Europe, Russia was beyond its cultural fringe for centuries. The important ideas that helped modernize Catholic and Protestant Europe penetrated Russia only much later. Rome was a lively fountainhead of thought in Western Europe, but the headquarters of the Orthodox faith, Constantinople, was captured by the Turks in 1453 and ceased to provide intellectual guidance for its followers. At the same time that Western Europe was experiencing the invigoration of the Renaissance, which rippled outward from Catholic Italy, Russia stayed isolated and asleep. It missed the Enlightenment altogether.

A more important factor in explaining Russia's isolation and backwardness was its conquest in the thirteenth century by the Mongols, also known as the Tatars. The Mongol khans crushed the first Russian state, centered at Kiev in the present-day Ukraine, and enslaved much of the population. For two centuries, while Western Europe moved ahead, Russian culture under the barbaric Mongols declined. Some historians believe that even after the Tatar yoke was lifted, it still took five centuries for Russia to catch up with the West.

RUSSIAN AUTOCRACY

Under the Mongol khans, the duchy of Moscow came to be the most powerful Russian state, first as a tax collector for the khans, then as their triumphant enemy. It was Moscovy's Ivan the Terrible (1530-84) who had himself crowned *tsar* (from "caesar"). Ivan was both murderous and successful; his brutal use of force set a standard for later Russian and Soviet rulers. To this day, many Russians think national greatness can be achieved only by the ruthless actions of a strong leader. Under Ivan, Russian territory expanded greatly, down the Volga to the Caspian Sea and into Siberia.

When the Russian nobles (*boyars*) came into conflict with Ivan, he had them arrested, exiled, or executed. Since that time, the Russian nobility never played an autonomous role in political life. It was as if the absolutism of France was applied early and completely to a culturally backward country. The result was *autocracy,* the rule of one person in a centralized state. Unlike the countries of Western Europe, Russia never experienced the mixed monarchy of nobles, church, commoners, and king held in some kind of balance. Accordingly, Russians had no experience with limited government, checks and balances, or pluralism.

As Ivan grew older he became madder. Able to trust no one, he murdered those around him—even his own son—at the least suspicion. By the time he died he had carved out the modern Russian state, but his subjects suffered in fear.

ABSOLUTISM OR ANARCHY

One of the reasons Russians put up with autocracy—and sometimes admired it—was because they felt that without a firm hand at the top the system would degenerate into anarchy. This had happened in the early seventeenth century. Lacking a strong tsar, unrest, banditry, civil war, and a Polish invasion plagued the land; it was known as the Time of Troubles. Russians accepted the idea that they had to serve a powerful state under a strong tsar. The Russian Orthodox church transferred its loyalty from the now-defunct Byzantine Empire and became a pillar of the monarchy, teaching the faithful to worship the tsar as the "little father" who protected all Russians. Russia has been called a "service state" in which all walks of life, from nobles to peasants to priests, served the autocrat. Western concepts such as liberty and individual rights did not take root in Russia.

Russia's First Secret Police

Ivan the Terrible started the Russian tradition of a feared and powerful secret police. His *Oprichnina* rooted out suspected treason with ferocity. The *oprichniki,* marked by their black horses adorned with black dogs' heads, in time became a new aristocracy on land confiscated from the old nobles (*boyars*) whom Ivan destroyed. The force was disbanded in 1572.

In one crucial area, Russia actually moved backwards in the fifteenth and sixteenth centuries. Previously free peasants became tied to the land, to labor for aristocrats who in turn served the tsar. By the seventeenth century Russia's peasants had become serfs, to be used and discarded by their masters like cattle. While the rest of Europe outgrew serfdom, Russia found itself trapped in backwardness, the vast majority of its population poor and ignorant farm laborers.

From time to time these wretched people revolted. Some ran off and joined the Cossacks, bands of mounted freebooters who gloried in burning, looting, and killing. One Cossack leader, Stenka Razin, immortalized in ballad, led a peasant revolt that seized much of the Ukraine. In time, the Cossacks turned into semimilitary federations which the tsars enrolled as effective and ruthless cavalry.

State Plus Church: "Caesaropapism"

Historically, in European countries the leaders of the state and of the church were almost always two different people, although sometimes the king had a say in naming the church father. But in old Russia, the two offices were one; the tsar was also the head of the Russian Orthodox church, a combined function called "caesaropapism." Russians rendered not just to their Caesar but to their pope—he was one and the same.

FORCED MODERNIZATION

By the time Peter I became tsar in 1682, Russia was far behind the rest of Europe. Peter, an enormous man who stood six feet nine inches (206 cm.), was determined to modernize Russia and make it a major power. He didn't care about his people's wishes or their welfare; he would force them to become modern. Gifted with enormous energy, some of it dissipated in women and alcohol, Peter personally handled Russia's legislation, diplomacy, and technical innovation. He was the first tsar to travel in Western Europe. Admiring its industries, he ordered them duplicated in Russia. Nearly continually at war, Peter pushed the Swedes back to give Russia an outlet on the Baltic. There he ordered built a magnificent new capital, St. Petersburg (now Leningrad), to serve as Russia's window to the West.

Copying the excellent Swedish administrative system, Peter divided Russia into provinces, counties, and districts, which were supervised by bureaucrats drawn from the nobility. All male nobles had to serve the tsar from age 15 until death, either as bureaucrats or military officers. Even the bureaucrats were organized on military lines, complete with ranks and uniforms. With Peter, the Russian government apparatus penetrated deep into society. A census determined the number of males available for military conscription, and each community had a quota. Draftees served for life. Taxation squeezed everybody as Peter ordered his officials to "collect money, as much as possible, for money is the artery of war."

When Peter died in 1725, he left behind a more modern and Westernized Russia, but one that still lagged far behind the advanced countries. Peter the Great contributed a pattern of forced modernization from the top, pushing a gigantic, backward country forward despite itself. Russia paid dearly. The mass of peasants, heavily taxed, were worse off than ever. The Westernized nobility—forced, for instance, to shave for the first time—was cut off from the hopes and feelings of the peasantry. The pattern was to continue for a long time.

WESTERNIZERS AND SLAVOPHILES

After Napoleon's invasion of Russia and capture of Moscow in 1812, Russian intellectuals were painfully aware of the backwardness of their land. Many sought to bring in Western politics and institutions, including a constitutional monarchy that would limit the autocratic powers of the tsar.

Not all Russian intellectuals were Westernizers. An important minority disliked the West; they saw it as spiritually shallow and materialistic. The answer to Russia's problems, they argued, was to dig into their own Slavic roots and develop institutions and styles different from and superior to the West's. "Russia will teach the world," was their view. These Slavophiles (literally, "lovers of the Slavs"), who stressed the spiritual depth and warm humanity of Russian peasants, were romantic nationalists who painted all aspects of West European culture black rather than admit anything might be worth borrowing. In our day this pattern continues, as many Third World countries claim they wish to reject Western materialism in favor of traditional spiritual values.

For most of the nineteenth century Westernizers argued with Slavophiles. In many ways the present Communist party of the Soviet Union is a synthesis of the two views, favoring Western technology, but using it to build what they regard as a superior system.

FROM FRUSTRATION TO REVOLUTION

Despite calls for far-reaching changes in Russia, reform during the nineteenth century was largely neglected. No tsar was prepared to give up any autocratic power in favor of a parliament. Even Alexander II, the "tsar-liberator," permitted only limited reforms. In 1861 he issued his famous Edict of Emancipation, freeing all serfs from legal bondage. Most of them remained in economic bondage, however. He set up district and provincial assemblies called *zemstvos*, but gave them only marginal local power.

Premature Democrats: The Decembrists

After Tsar Alexander I died in 1825, there was a period of uncertainty over who was going to be the new tsar. Some army officers, impatient with tsarist autocracy, attempted a coup d'état in December. They favored a constitutional monarchy that would bring some democratic concepts to Russia for the first time. Easily crushed and their leaders executed, the Decembrists were ahead of their time, for Russia was too backward, and few Russians wished to change.

The reforms were meant both to modernize Russia and to improve the living conditions of the masses. Under certain conditions, however, reforms may actually make revolution more likely rather than less. Alexander's reforms, which he saw as extensive and generous, were regarded by an increasingly critical *intelligentsia* (the educated class) as not going nearly far enough. Whatever he granted, they wanted more. The reforms merely whetted the critics' appetites. Many intellectuals became bitter and frustrated.

Some tried action at the grass-roots level. In the 1870s thousands of idealistic students put on peasant clothes and tried "going to the people" in the villages to rouse them toward revolution. These *Narodniki* (from the word for "people," *narod*) made absolutely no progress; the suspicious peasants either ignored them or turned them over to the police.

Others tried assassination, believing that killing the right official constituted "propaganda of the deed," a way to arouse the inert masses. One group of committed terrorists, *Narodnaya Volya* (People's Will), made the tsar their special target and, after seven attempts, killed him with a bomb thrown into his carriage in 1881.

Actually, Russia did make considerable progress in the nineteenth century. Archaic usages were swept away, industry started with an infusion of British, French, and German capital, railroads were built, and intellectual life flourished. But in the crucial area of political reform—parliaments, parties, elections, and the sharing of power—Russia essentially stood still. Political reforms do not make themselves, and in many ways they are more basic to the peaceful evolution of society than social, cultural, or economic reforms. A ruler who modernizes his economy but not his political system is asking for trouble.

Tsarist Repression: The Okhrana

Russia's political police, the Okhrana, were instituted by the reactionary Tsar Nicholas I after the Decembrist Revolt. *Okhrana* agents, working under the interior ministry, kept tabs on everyone suspicious. Once detected, revolutionaries suffered deportation to Siberia—or worse. Because the *Okhrana* was so powerful, Lenin argued in favor of keeping the revolutionary movement small and underground to resist secret-police penetration.

MARXISM COMES TO RUSSIA

According to Marx's theory, backward Russia was far from ready for proletarian revolution. There simply wasn't much of a proletariat (class of industrial workers) in the still overwhelmingly agricultural land, where industrialization was just

A Russian Genius: Lenin

It has been said—although no one can prove it—that the dominant passion in Lenin's life was revenge against the tsarist system for hanging his older brother, Alexander; in 1887 Lenin's brother was executed for his part in a bomb plot against the tsar. It is clear that Lenin was dominated by a cold, contained fury channeled toward one goal: revolution in Russia.

Born in 1870 as Vladimir Ilyich Ulyanov, son of a provincial education official, Lenin was from the intellectual middle class rather than from the proletariat in whose name he struggled—a pattern typical of revolutionary socialist leaders. Expelled from university for alleged subversive activity after his first three months, Lenin was sent into rural exile. Nonetheless, with the incredible self-discipline that became his hallmark, Lenin taught himself all he needed to know to breeze through law exams with the highest marks.

In the early 1890s Lenin, like many who hated tsarism, converted passionately to Marxism, devoured everything Marx wrote (some in the original German, which Lenin had taught himself), and wrote Marxist analyses of the rapidly growing Russian economy. Recognized as a leading Marxist thinker, Lenin quickly rose to prominence in underground revolutionary circles.

In December 1895, while editing an illegal socialist newspaper, Lenin was arrested and sent to prison for a year followed by three years' exile in Siberia. The curious thing is, he didn't much mind it. The solitary hours gave him time to read, learn foreign languages, and write. Again, the monumental self-discipline showed: Lenin wasted not one day of prison and exile on moping or self-pity. Released in 1900, Lenin soon made his way to Switzerland where he spent most of the next seventeen years. In Zurich you can still sip tea in the Café Odeon, as Lenin used to. He would nurse a cup for hours to read the newspapers for free.

At times during his long exile Lenin despaired that there would ever be a revolution in Russia. The working class was moving more in the direction of Economism, concentrating on higher wages rather than revolution. The Russian Social Democratic Labor party was small; there were only a few thousand members in Russia and in exile.

Lenin was determined to transform this small party into an effective underground force. Size was not important; organization was everything. In his 1902 pamphlet *What Is to Be Done?* Lenin demanded a tightly disciplined party of professional revolutionaries, not a conventional European social-democratic party open to everybody. Ever since this time, Communist parties the world over have been fanatics on organization and discipline. Under Lenin the early Communists forged the "organizational weapon," and they've been using it ever since.

But how could a proletarian revolution happen in backward Russia? This was the great theoretical problem Lenin faced. In solving it, he greatly changed Marxism. First, Marx theorized revolution should come in the most advanced countries, where the proletariat was biggest. Lenin said not necessarily, revolution could come where capitalism is weakest, where it is just starting. Imperialism had changed capitalism, Lenin argued, giving it a new lease on life. By exploiting backward countries, the big imperialist powers were able to bribe their own working class with higher wages and thus keep them quiet. Where capitalism was beginning—as in Russia with heavy foreign investment—was where it could be overthrown. The newly developing countries, such as Russia and Spain, were "capitalism's weakest link," said Lenin.

Secondly, Lenin disagreed with Marx's insistence that the peasantry could never play a revolutionary role—Marx wrote that peasants wallowed in "rural idiocy." Under certain conditions, Lenin believed, they could become highly revolutionary and, throwing their weight in with the small working class, provide a massive revolutionary army. (Three decades later, Mao Zedong would pick up and elaborate on these two themes to argue that backward China, a victim of imperialism, could have a socialist revolution based entirely on the peasantry. Mao simply completed the train of thought Lenin started.)

Lenin showed himself to be not a great theoretician—you can find many inconsistencies and contradictions in his works—but a brilliant opportunist, switching doctrine this way and that way to take advantage of the existing political situation. Lenin was less concerned with preserving a pure Marxism than in using a variation of Marxism to overthrow the system he hated. And in this he succeeded, largely by the sheer force of his brilliant, disciplined, calculating personality.

beginning in the late nineteenth century. Marx believed revolution would come first in the most industrially advanced countries, such as Britain and Germany. Curiously, though, Marxism caught on more strongly in Russia than elsewhere. Marx's works were eagerly seized upon by frustrated Russian intellectuals who badly wanted change but didn't have a theoretical framework for it. Here at last they believed they had found a reason and a means to carry out a revolution.

There were several schools of Marxism in Russia. The "Legal Marxists," noting Russia's economic backwardness, thought the country would first have to go through capitalism before it could start on socialism. Marx had a very deterministic view of history and saw it developing in clear stages based on the level of economic development. Loyal to Marx's historical analysis, the Legal Marxists believed they would have a long wait for revolution and must first work to promote capitalism.

Another school of Russian Marxism was called "Economism." Stressing bread-and-butter gains (better wages and working conditions) through labor unions, the Economists thought that the immediate economic improvement of the working class was the essence of Marxism. In this they resembled the course taken by Western European social democrats, whose Marxism mellowed into welfarism.

Opposing these two gradualist schools were impassioned intellectuals who wanted first and foremost to make a revolution. They argued that they could "give history a shove" by starting a revolution with only a small proletariat, gaining power, and then using the state to move directly into socialism. Lenin made some theoretical changes in Marxism so that it fit Russian conditions (see box). Ever since then, the doctrine of Soviet Communism has been known as Marxism-Leninism.

In 1898, after several small groups had discussed Marxist approaches to Russia, the Russian Social Democratic Labor party was formed. Immediately penetrated and harassed by the *Okhrana,* many of its leaders went into exile in West Europe. Its newspaper, *Iskra* (the *Spark*), was published in Zurich, Switzerland, and smuggled into Russia. One of its editors was Lenin.

In 1903 the small party split over a crucial question: organization. Some of its leaders wanted a normal party along the lines of the German SPD, with open but committed membership that tried to enroll the bulk of the Russian working class. Lenin scoffed at this kind of organization, arguing that the tsarist secret police would make mincemeat out of an open party. Instead, he urged a small, tightly knit underground party of professional revolutionaries, more a conspiracy than a conventional party.

Lenin got his way. At the 1903 party congress in Brussels, Belgium (it couldn't be held in Russia), he controlled thirty-three of the fifty-one votes. Although probably unrepresentative of total party membership, Lenin proclaimed his faction *bolshevik* (majority), and the name stuck. The *menshevik* (minority) faction at the congress continued to exist, advocating a more moderate line.

CURTAIN RAISER: THE 1905 REVOLUTION

At the turn of the century two expanding powers, Russia and Japan, collided. The Russians were pushing eastward, consolidating their position on the Pacific by building the Trans-Siberian Railway, the last leg of which ran through Manchuria. Japan was meanwhile pushing westward, having taken Taiwan and Korea in 1895, then coveting Manchuria, which was nominally a part of China. The tsar's cabinet, certain that they could defeat the forces of an "inferior" yellow race (and hoping to shift the focus from domestic unrest), thought war with Japan might be a good idea. Said the interior minister: "We need a little victorious war to stem the tide of revolution." It was not to be. The Japanese fleet launched a surprise attack against the Russians at Port Arthur, then beat the Russians on both land and sea.

The Russo-Japanese War revealed the tsarist regime as unprepared, inept, and stupid. Moral: weak regimes shouldn't count on a "little victorious war" to paper over domestic unrest; wars may make troubles worse. In Russia rioting and then revolution broke out. Some naval units mutinied. (See Eisenstein's film classic *Battleship Potemkin*.) Workers briefly seized factories at St. Petersburg. It looked like a dream-come-true for the socialist underground.

Tsar Nicholas II, although none too bright, gave way and decreed potentially important reforms: freedom of speech, press, and assembly and the democratic election of a parliament called the *Duma*. Briefly, this 1905 October Manifesto by the tsar looked as if it would turn autocracy into constitutional monarchy.

The tsar and his reactionary advisors backed down on their promises, however. Nicholas, like his predecessors, refused to yield any of his autocratic powers. The *Duma* was dissolved when it proved too critical and turned into an undemocratic debating society without power. The *Duma* was Russia's last hope for a peaceful transition to democracy. People in modern times need to feel they participate at least in a small way in the affairs of government. Parties, elections, and parliaments may be highly imperfect ways to channel participation, but they are better than violent revolution. Since the Decembrist revolt of 1825, Russian intellectuals had been trying to tell the tsar this simple truth, but he refused to listen.

WORLD WAR I AND COLLAPSE

Communists like to speak of the Russian Revolution as inevitable, the playing out of historical forces that *had* to lead to the collapse of imperialism and capitalism. There was nothing inevitable about the October Revolution. Indeed, without the First World War, there might have been no revolution in Russia at all, let alone a Bolshevik revolution. Lenin himself, in early 1917, stated he doubted he'd live to see a revolution in Russia.

One City, Three Names

Peter the Great founded St. Petersburg on the Baltic early in the eighteenth century. When war with Germany broke out in 1914, the Russian government felt their leading city should not have a German name, so they Russified it to Petrograd. After Lenin's death in 1924 the Communist regime changed it to Leningrad.

Things were not so terrible in Russia before the war. The *Duma* struggled to make itself effective and in time might have been able to erode tsarist autocracy. Industry grew rapidly. Peasants, freed from old restrictions on land ownership, were turning into prosperous and productive small farmers.

Memorable Russian Slogans: "Bread, Land, Peace"

When Lenin got off the train in Petrograd's' Finland Station in April 1917, he knew the Bolsheviks were a small minority of the revolutionary forces seething in Russia. He also recognized—in what has become an uncanny Communist skill—that the right slogan could galvanize the masses of discontented people into action on the Communist side. Accordingly, Lenin picked out exactly the right three words, the three things that war-weary Russians wanted most: bread for the worker, land for the peasant, and peace for the soldier. The three words had little to do with Marxist theory, but the slogan was tactically brilliant and helped the Bolsheviks grow from a small party to the dominant force of the revolution. Ever since then, sloganeering has been a Communist art form.

The war changed everything. Repeating their overconfidence of 1904, the tsarist military marched happily to war against Germany in 1914, and this doomed the system. It was a large army, but badly equipped and poorly led. Major offensives ground to a halt before the more effective German forces. The Russian economy started to fall apart. Troop morale disintegrated and desertion was widespread. Peasants started seizing their landlord's grounds. The government was paralyzed, but the tsar refused to change anything. By 1917 the situation was desperate. In March of that year a group of democratic moderates seized power and deposed the tsar. Resembling Western liberals, the people of the Provisional Government hoped to modernize and democratize Russia. The Western powers, including the United States, welcomed the move, thinking it would rally Russians to continue the war. The Provisional Government, which by July was headed by moderate socialist Alexander Kerensky, tried to stay in the war, and that was its undoing. If Kerensky had betrayed the Western Allies and

Kerensky: Nice Guys Lose

In the late 1950s at UCLA the author had an eerie experience: seeing and hearing Alexander Kerensky speak. History lives. Still fit and articulate in his seventies, Kerensky recalled his brief stint (July to November of 1917) as head of the Provisional Government in Russia. One man in the audience, a Russian emigré, asked angrily why Kerensky didn't use his power to have Lenin killed. Kerensky reflected a moment and said, "Sometimes when you have power it's hard to use it."

That was Kerensky's problem. A decent man, he wouldn't have a political opponent murdered. The Western Allies begged him to keep Russia in the war, and he didn't have the heart to betray them.

What Kerensky lacked in political ruthlessness he may have gained in longevity. Living in New York City, he spent his years justifying his brief rule and denouncing both the Bolsheviks and Russian rightists who tried to bring him down. He died in 1970 at the ripe old age of 89.

made a seperate peace with Germany, the moderates might have been able to retain power.

Meanwhile, the German General Staff, looking for a way to knock Russia out of the war, thought it would be clever to send the exiled Lenin into Russia to create havoc. In April 1917 Lenin and his colleagues traveled in a famous "sealed train"—so the Bolshevik bacillus wouldn't infect Germany, where revolutionary discontent was also growing—across Germany, Sweden, and Finland to Petrograd. Without German help, Lenin might never have made it back to Russia.

In Petrograd, Lenin found a "dual authority" trying to rule the land. The Provisional Government controlled the army and foreign policy. But in the most important city, Petrograd, a council (*soviet* in Russian) of workers, soldiers, sailors, and revolutionaries ran things. Soon these councils appeared in many Russian cities. The composition of these soviets was mixed, with the Bolsheviks a small minority. Lenin pursued a double strategy: make the soviets the only effective governing power and make the Bolsheviks the dominant power in the soviets.

Memorable Russian Slogans: "All Power to the Soviets"

With councils of workers and soldiers springing up all over Russia to oppose the Provisional Government, Lenin and the Bolsheviks argued that only the soviets should have power. Gradually, as the Kerensky government weakened, that is what happened. Not only did the soviets take power—giving us the name Soviet Union, a union of worker councils—but within the soviets the Bolsheviks took power. This is what Lenin had in mind with the slogan but did not state openly.

THE REVOLUTION AND CIVIL WAR

The actual seizure of power in October (see box) was amazingly easy. In a scene exaggerated ever since by Soviet historians, soldiers and sailors loyal to the Petrograd soviet charged across a big square into the Winter Palace to oust the Provisional Government. But control of Petrograd and Moscow was one thing, control of all gigantic Russia was something else.

The tight organization and discipline of Lenin's Bolsheviks paid off. In a situation of almost total chaos, the best organized will win. By a series of shrewd moves, the Bolsheviks were able to dominate the soviets and win many converts from deserting soldiers and sailors. Lenin headed the new government and immediately took Russia out of the war, accepting a punitive peace treaty from the Germans at Brest-Litovsk in March 1918. It was a dictated treaty (*Diktat* in German) that enabled the Germans to seize large areas of Russia and redeploy nearly a million troops to the western front.

Feeling betrayed and concerned that allied military supplies would fall into German hands, the Western Allies sent small expeditionary forces into Russia. American troops actually fought the Bolsheviks in north Russia in 1918-19. This was the beginning of the Soviet view that the capitalist powers tried to strangle the infant Bolshevik regime in its cradle.

Why the October Revolution Was in November

Every November 7 the Soviet Union celebrates the anniversary of the Great October Revolution. If this sounds curious, it's because Russia in 1917 was still using the old Julian calendar, which lagged thirteen days behind the Western Gregorian calendar (which introduced leap years), in use in Catholic countries since 1582. The Bolsheviks switched to the Gregorian but in so doing had to recalculate the October Revolution into the following month.

From 1918 to 1920 civil war raged. The White Army, led by reactionary Russian generals and admirals and supplied by the Western Allies, tried to crush the Communists' Red Army. Both sides displayed incredible ruthlessness in what was for them a life-or-death struggle. Millions of Russians perished from starvation. Expecting their revolution to spread, the Red Army invaded Poland in 1920 hoping to trigger a Europe-wide socialist upheaval. Instead, the Poles threw back the Red Army and seized Russian territory. Lenin and his colleagues saw there would be no world revolution and so settled down to build the world's first socialist country.

WAR COMMUNISM AND NEP

During the civil war, the Bolsheviks tried to plunge directly into their utopian system by running the ruined economy by executive fiat. This "war communism," as it was euphemistically called, was due as much to the demands of a desperate civil war as to visionary schemes. In either case, it was a flop; starvation broke out and only the charity of American grain shipments (supervised by Herbert Hoover) held deaths to a few million.

Lenin saw that Russia was far from ready for pure socialism, so he conducted a planned retreat of state control to the "commanding heights" of heavy industry and let most of the rest of the economy revert to private hands. This period of Lenin's New Economic Policy (NEP), from 1921 to 1928, brought relative prosperity; farmers worked their own land, "nepmen" behaved like small private entrepreneurs, and things in general were relaxed. There was one catch: the NEP wasn't moving the Soviet Union any closer to socialism, and industry grew only slowly. It is likely that Lenin meant the NEP only as temporary rest

Memorable Russian Slogans: "He Who Does Not Work, Neither Shall He Eat"

In trying to motivate the population during the lean years of "war communism" (1918-20), Lenin laid down this slogan as policy; it later appeared in the 1936 constitution. Draconic as it sounds, we might remember that Lenin borrowed it from the Bible (2 Thessalonians 3:10). The expression was also used in the Jamestown colony of old Virginia, which had similar motivational problems.

before moving on to socialist construction. Among older Soviets, NEP is remembered as a happy period.

That changed when Stalin gained power in the late 1920s. In 1928 began the first of the government-enforced Five-year Plans that accelerated collectivization and industrialization (see box). Peasants resisted giving up their fields, farm production dropped, and millions starved. In new factories, workers toiled with primitive implements to boost production of capital goods. Consumer goods were deliberately neglected, and the standard of living declined. While many admit that the forced industrialization of the 1930s was brutal, some

Stalin: "One death is a tragedy. A million is a statistic."

The present Soviet system is not so much Lenin's as Stalin's. Lenin was 54 when he died in 1924, before giving definitive pattern to the Soviet system. Although capable of great ruthlessness, it is doubtful that he would have been like Stalin. Exactly who is to blame for the horrors that developed—Lenin or Stalin—is still a matter of great controversy both within and outside the Soviet Union. Some argue that if Lenin had lived, his intelligence and sophistication would have set the country on the path to "true socialism." Others say the structure Lenin created—concentrating power first in the party, then in the Central Committee, and finally in his own person—made the misuse of power inevitable.

Stalin aptly illustrates Acton's dictum that "power corrupts." Stalin lived in order to amass political power, and he was very good at it. Born Yosif Vissarionovich Djugashvili in 1879, son of a poor shoemaker, Stalin lacked Lenin's intellectual family background and education. Some of Stalin's behavior can be traced back to his family home in Georgia, part of the Caucasus, a mountainous land with a warm climate and fiery people given to personal hatred and family blood-feuds. In Georgia today, "Soso" (his Georgian nickname) is still praised as a local boy who made good.

The young Djugashvili entered an Orthodox seminary to study for the priesthood but soon became more interested in revolution. Expelled from the seminary, he joined the Georgian Marxist underground as an agitator and strike organizer. Repeatedly arrested, jailed and exiled to Siberia, he always managed to escape. Going underground, he took the name Stalin, from the Russian for "man of steel."

Never a great theoretician, Stalin attracted Lenin's attention as a non-Russian who could write the Bolsheviks' position on the nationalities question. Playing only a moderate role in the October Revolu-

tion, Stalin was named commissar for nationalities in 1918 and then, in what may have been Lenin's worst mistake, picked as the party's first secretary general in 1922. People thought the new office would be a routine job with little real power. Lenin and Stalin were never particularly close—although Stalin's historians tried to make it look that way—and toward the end of his life Lenin had an inkling of what Stalin was like. In one of his last messages Lenin urged the party to reject Stalin as "too rude."

It was too late, however. Using his position as secretary general, Stalin organized the party to his advantage by promoting to key posts only those personally loyal to him. It was this organizational spadework that gave Stalin the edge over his rival, Leon Trotsky, organizer of the Red Army and a far more intelligent Marxist. Stalin beat him in party infighting and had him expelled from the Soviet Union in 1929 and murdered in Mexico City in 1940. Reviled as a deviationist traitor ever since, Trotsky did try to organize an anti-Stalin opposition within the CPSU, a point that fed Stalin's natural paranoia and contributed to his ruthlessness in exterminating officials on the slightest suspicion of disloyalty.

Stalin, an uncanny manipulator, played one faction against another until, by the late 1920s, he was the Kremlin's undisputed master. Like Peter the Great, Stalin was determined to modernize regardless of human cost. In 1928 he instituted the first Five-Year Plan, beginning the forced industrialization of the Soviet Union. Farmers, very much against their will, were herded into collectives and forced to produce for the state, sometimes at gunpoint. Better-off farmers, the so-called *kulaks*, were "liquidated as a class," a euphemism for killed. Economic development was defined as heavy industry, and steel production became an obsession with the "man of steel."

In 1934, during the second Five-Year Plan, Stalin became obsessed with "Trotskyite" disloyalty in party ranks. Thus began the Great Purge: thousands of party comrades were killed, some after confessing to be British spies or Trotskyite "wreckers." Tens of thousands were sent to Siberian forced-labor camps. *Paranoia* means unreasonable suspicion of other people, not simply fear, and Stalin was a classic paranoid. Much of the population, especially people in positions of prominence, trembled with fear that they might be next. Stalin even had all his experienced generals murdered, a blunder that left him open for the 1941 German attack. In total, Stalin's orders led to the death of as many as twenty million people during collectivization and the purge.

Was Stalin mad? It's hard to say. There was some Trotskyite opposition to him, but he exaggera-

ted it. It was Plato who first observed that any tyrant, even one who starts out sane, must lose his mind in office because he can't trust anybody. More than a question of personality, Stalin shows what happens when one person assumes total power. The Soviets don't like to admit it, but it's their *system* that's at fault more than any particular *individual*.

During his lifetime Stalin was deified as history's greatest linguist, art critic, Marxist theoretician, engineer, agronomist, you name it. By the time he died in 1953—while preparing yet another purge—Stalin had turned the Soviet Union into *his* system, and, in basic outlines, it hasn't changed much since. Ultimate power is still in the hands of the party's general secretary and still potentially open to the same kinds of abuse.

point out that it alone gave the Soviet Union the industrial base to arm against the German invasion in 1941.

As it was, the German invasion caused some twenty million Soviet deaths. The Nazis cared nothing for Slavic lives; starvation was their standard treatment for Soviet prisoners of war. Still, it was a time when the Soviet Union pulled together. Stalin, like Lenin, recognized the force of Russian nationalism beneath the Communist surface. Reviewing troops marching from Moscow to the front, Stalin is said to have mused: "They aren't fighting for communism or for Stalin; they're fighting for Mother Russia." In the Soviet Union today, World War II is known as the Great Patriotic War.

By the time he died in 1953, Stalin had transformed a backward country into a gigantic empire and major industrial power. He had also founded a political system, to which we turn in the next chapter.

VOCABULARY BUILDING

autocracy	*Diktat*	Marxism-Leninism	Slavic
Bolshevik	Duma	Menshevik	Slavophiles
boyars	Economism	*Narodniki*	soviet
Brest-Litovsk	Five-Year Plans	NEP	Tatars
caesaropapism	Georgia	October Revolution	Time of Troubles
Cossacks	Great Purge	*Okhrana*	War Communism
cyrillic	*intelligentsia*	paranoid	Westernizers
Decembrists	*kulaks*	Petrograd	Whites
deified	Legal Marxism	Provisional Government	*Zemstvo*

FURTHER REFERENCE

Cohen, Stephen F. *Rethinking the Soviet Experience: Politics and History Since 1917.* New York: Oxford University Press, 1985.

Rigby, T.H., Archie Brown, and Peter Reddaway, eds. *Authority, Power and Policy in the USSR.* New York: St. Martin's Press, 1980.

Salisbury, Harrison E. *Black Night, White Snow: Russia's Revolutions 1905–1917.* Garden City, N.Y.: Doubleday, 1978.

Sumner, B. H. *Peter the Great and the Emergence of Russia.* New York: Collier Books, 1962.

Ulam, Adam B. *Ideologies and Illusion: Revolutionary Thought from Herzen to Solzhenitsyn.* Cambridge, Mass: Harvard University Press, 1976.

——— . *In the Name of the People: Prophets and Conspirators in Prerevolutionary Russia.* New York: Viking, 1977.

——— . *The Bolsheviks: The Intellectual and Political History of the Triumph of Communism in Russia.* New York: Collier Books, 1965.

——— . *Stalin: The Man and His Era.* New York: Viking, 1973.

Vernadsky, George. *A History of Russia.* New York: Bantam Books, 1967.

Wolfe, Bertram D. *Three Who Made a Revolution.* New York: Delta, 1964.

Yanov, Alexander. *The Origins of Autocracy: Ivan the Terrible in Russian History.* Berkeley: University of California Press, 1981.

18

THE KEY
INSTITUTIONS

THE IMPORTANCE OF THE PARTY

In our first three countries, we had to do a little detective work to learn what the key institutions were. Parliaments, executives, political parties, interest groups, and bureaucracies all played a role; it was hard to pinpoint any one as being the most important. In the Soviet Union this choice is much simpler, for all students of the subject agree that the Communist party of the Soviet Union (CPSU) dominates the political system. The Soviet constitution is very specific about the role of the party; article 6 reads:

> The Communist Party of the Soviet Union is the leading and guiding force of Soviet society, the nucleus of its political system and of state and public organizations. The CPSU exists for the people and serves the people.
>
> Armed with Marxist-Leninist teaching, the Communist Party determines general prospects for the development of society and the lines of the USSR's domestic and foreign policy, directs the great creative activity of the Soviet people, and gives their struggle for the victory of communism a planned, scientifically substantiated nature.

This is not to say the party runs things directly. The Soviet system looks, on the surface, like many other governments. There are ministries, civil servants, and a parliament. We might call these the "body" of the political system. But running through the body is a "nervous system" leading back to a central brain, the Communist party. This nervous system plays many vital roles: transmitting general policy lines, keeping tabs on economic development, reporting discontent and unrest, and, most important, selecting, promoting, and supervising the system's personnel.

Another way to look at the Communist party is as a watchdog over Soviet government. The Soviet regime consists of two systems: one is the regular government, the other the control system of the party. A government official in most cases will have two superiors, one governmental and one party. This is called "dual subordination."

There is a good deal of overlap between party and state systems. At the lowest level, some of the people who sit on local soviets are also active in the primary party organizations. The higher one goes up the party and state ladder, the more the two overlap, until, at the top, most of the government ministers are also on the party's Central Committee (see box).

At first this double system sounds cumbersome, redundant, and inefficient. But the more you think about it, the more you conclude that the "parallel hierarchies" are a clever idea and probably indispensable to the Soviet system. The Soviet Union is a society *aimed* at a certain goal (the creation of a socialist utopia). Western societies have no such clear-cut goal. To keep the Soviet system on course, they need a control and back-up network of loyal, obedient party members strategically placed throughout the society—industry, the army, arts and culture, the press, just about anything you can name. Obviously, the CPSU is quite different from Western parties, which concentrate on getting their people elected and then play a relatively minor role in the formulation and execution of policy.

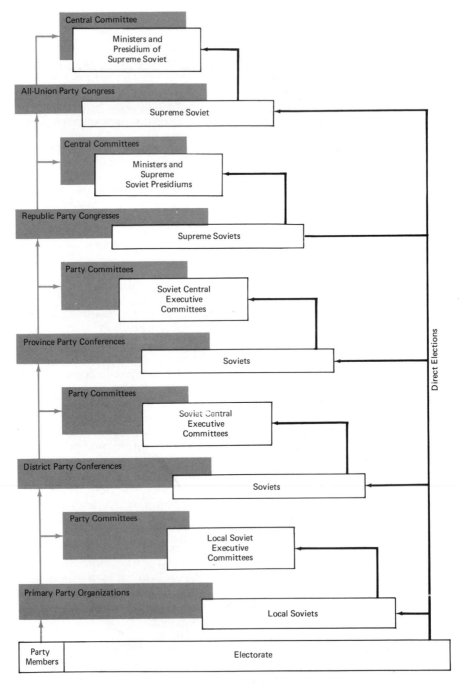

Source: Vernon V. Aspaturian, "Soviet Politics," in Roy Macridis, ed., *Modern Political Systems: Europe, 4th ed.* (© 1978) p. 405. Adapted by permission of Prentice-Hall, Inc., Englewood Cliffs, N. J.

"The Communist party is not a party like other parties."

Lenin used these words when the Bolsheviks were still a small underground party, most of whose leaders were in exile. In his fight with the Mensheviks, Lenin made it clear that the Bolsheviks were not going to play the normal political games of ordinary parties. After coming to power, Lenin again made it clear that the Communists were not to revert to a normal party role but were to stay firmly in command to guide Soviet society.

PARTY STRUCTURE

Not everyone is supposed to join the Communist party; indeed, membership is tightly controlled. At present only less than 7 percent of the Soviet population is in the party (about 18 million out of 274 million), or about 9 percent of the adult population. Applicants must have a good record as workers, students, or youth leaders. They must be vouched for by established party members, and they must serve a year as "candidate members," doing lots of volunteer work, before they can be elevated to full party-member status. The aim of the CPSU is to skim off the best of Soviet society.

The party is organized like a gigantic pyramid. At the bottom are the primary party organizations, consisting of anywhere from a handful to several hundred members. In theory, every member of CPSU, even the general secretary, must belong to one. Organized either on the basis of work (factory or office) or residence (village or city ward), a primary party organization is supposed to meet once a month. While most party members hold down regular— although often better—jobs, those who work full-time for the party are called *apparatchiki,* "men of the apparatus." They are the cement that holds the thing together.

Each level of the party is supposed to elect delegates to the next highest level. In practice, these delegates are usually designated by the higher level and then approved by the lower level. By the same token, each level has its governing committee of party officials also ostensibly elected by the larger body. The hierarchy goes from primary party organization, to district party conference, to province party conference, to republic party congress (the Soviet Union is composed of fifteen republics), to all-union party congress (the whole Soviet Union). Presiding over each of these levels is a committee.

The most important element of the party structure is the top. Theoretically the CPSU is guided by an All-Union Party Congress that meets every few years. (Under Stalin, it met rarely.) Now with some 5,000 delegates meeting for only a few days, a Party Congress is obviously no place to actually devise policies. Party Congresses are forums to ratify decisions already made, to announce new policies, and to energize party members for the great tasks of socialist construction. More important than the brief and infrequent Party Congresses is the Central Committee, ostensibly elected by the Party Congress but in practice named by the top party people. The Central Committee, consisting of some 300 full and 150 candidate members, is supposed to run the party in the long interval between congresses. It meets once every six months, usually just before its governmental counterpart, the Supreme Soviet, for the memberships of the two bodies overlap.

"Democratic Centralism"

Originally, "democratic centralism" meant that there was to be full and open discussion of all questions within the party but that once a decision was made, all members were to carry it out faithfully. Thus the party was to be both democratic and yet centralized.

In practice, the democratic element in the Soviet Union has withered and the central element has strengthened, so that there is very limited input from lower ranks and a great number of central decisions are simply handed down from the higher level.

The Top of the CPSU Structure

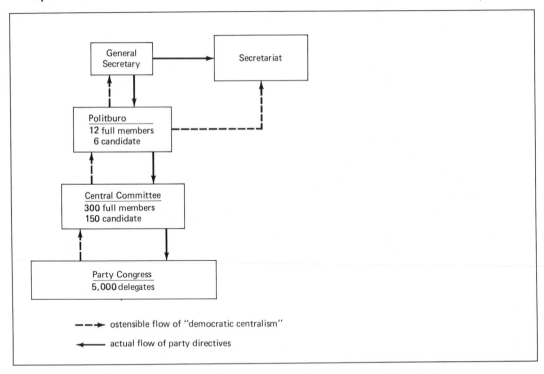

But again the Central Committee is not the real decision maker. Running things between the half-yearly Central Committee meetings is the Politburo (political bureau), a full-time decision-making body with about a dozen full and six candidate members. They are experienced, powerful, and usually old. Politburo decisions are automatically approved by the Central Committee, Central Committee decisions are automatically approved by the Party Congress, and so on down the line.

But wait, there's a still higher level. Leading the Politburo is the general secretary. Theoretically, the *gensek* is not supposed to be a one-man ruler or dictator, but in practice (as we shall explore in chapter 20) he tends to amass a great deal of personal power. If the general secretary loses control of the Politburo, and if they come to oppose his policies, they can dump him. This happened in 1964, when Khrushchev was ousted.

Backing up the general secretary and giving him considerable control over the party apparatus is a large Secretariat. It has been said that he who controls the Secretariat controls the party *apparat,* for that person has the ability to select for key assignments *apparatchiki* who will be loyal to the general secretary. In most Communist countries, the person in control of party organization is sooner or later the locus of political power.

Brezhnev: The Manager

In many ways Leonid Brezhnev was the first "normal" ruler of the Soviet Union. He was not a charismatic revolutionary like Lenin, a bloody tyrant like Stalin, nor a flamboyant "harebrained schemer" like Khrushchev. Instead, he was very much a man of the system who sought no major transformation of that system. Coming to power in 1964 after Khrushchev's ouster , Brezhnev was at the helm for eighteen years, until his death in 1982, a tenure in office second only to Stalin's.

Like Khrushchev, Brezhnev was born in the Ukraine and entered politics there. (Both, however, were of Russian parents.) Brezhnev, in fact, was a Khrushchev protégé. Born in 1906, the son of a metalworker, Brezhnev went to work in a steel mill at age 15 for a few years. Then, as a young party member, he went back to school, first in agriculture and then in metallurgy. Most of the time, however, he worked full time for the party and rose rapidly through the ranks as Stalin's purges created room at the top. In World War II, like Khrushchev, he did political work in the army. A party secretary at higher and higher levels, he was selected by Khrushchev in 1954 to oversee the Virgin Lands project in Kazakhstan. By 1956 Brezhnev was a Central Committee secretary and candidate member of the Politburo; by 1958 he was a full member.

Brezhnev was clearly a "comer"; even Khrush-chev identified him as his probable successor. That became fact, but not in the way Khrushchev imagined. Many members of the Politburo and Central Committee, including Brezhnev, grew fed up with Khrushchev's turbulent reforms, which they feared were damaging the party. After some plotting, they removed Khrushchev from office legally and nonviolently in October 1964 and sent him into obscure retirement.

Brezhnev then began to consolidate his power, at first ruling in tandem with Aleksei Kosygin but gradually eclipsing him. Kosygin remained as chairman of the Council of Ministers (roughly the prime minister) while Brezhnev not only kept the all-important job of party general secretary but also took over the chairmanship of the Presidium of the Supreme Soviet to become the equivalent of the country's president.

While Brezhnev repudiated Khrushchev's style of leadership, he continued many of Khrushchev's ideas but in ways that did not threaten the power and position of the party and its key leaders. Brezhnev did not turn the Politburo into a tool of personal rule but rather appeared to be a classic balancer of conflicting interests—between heavy and consumer industry, for example. Not a colorful character like Khrushchev, Brezhnev was a manager who steered an unimaginative but steady course.

THE SUPREME SOVIET

Far less important than the party is the legislature, the Supreme Soviet. Virtually all outside observers agree that this gigantic (1,500-member) body that meets only a few days a year is not a serious parliament. It simply rubber-stamps laws drafted higher up; there has never been one negative vote in the Supreme Soviet.

The function of the Supreme Soviet, rather, is to give people the *feeling* they are represented. To this end, the Supreme Soviet, like the U.S. Congress, has two chambers; one, the Soviet of the Union, is based on districts of equal population, the other, the Soviet of Nationalities, on the various types of republics and regions. The membership of the Supreme Soviet more closely represents the Soviet population than any Western parliament represents its country's population. Typically about half are workers and farmers, and some 30 percent are women. Still, the body is far from representative in that a majority of its members have received at least some higher education and three-fourths are party members. To increase the feeling of participation, turnover in the Supreme Soviet is high; about half the members change with each election, held every four years.

The two houses meet twice a year in Moscow, first separately then jointly, to hear reports, pass laws, and have their pictures taken by the press. Like their party counterpart, the Party Congress, the Supreme Soviet "elects" a governing body, in this case the Presidium of the Supreme Soviet, a twenty-member legislative elite whose membership overlaps with the party's Politburo. The Presidium can pass whatever decrees it likes, and these have the force of law. Then, at the next meeting of the full Supreme Soviet, these decrees are routinely turned into laws. The Presidium, not the Supreme Soviet, is the real legislature.

The Presidium also functions as a collective presidency of the Soviet Union. The chairman of the Presidium is the closest the Soviet Union gets to a head of state; sometimes he is referred to in the West as the "president" of the Soviet Union. When a foreign head of state visits or an ambassador presents credentials, the Presidium chairman is the one who receives them. In theory, then, the Presidium chairman is the head of the Soviet state, but only because the party *gensek,* since Brezhnev, has routinely taken over the post to consolidate his position. Lenin, Stalin, and Khrushchev let others occupy the ceremonial presidency, but Brezhnev grew annoyed that his party chieftainship was unrecognized as head of state in diplomatic protocol, so he took over the presidency in 1977. His successors had themselves named president within months of assuming power except for Gorbachev, who named Gromyko to the post.

Western observers dismiss the Supreme Soviet as a charade, for obviously its decisions, debates, and policy formulations take place elsewhere, in the higher reaches of the party. But to what extent is an element of artificiality true of *all* legislatures? In the first three countries studied—Britain, France, and West Germany—we saw how most of the time the legislature simply obeys the party leaders in office, the prime minister, president, or chancellor, respectively. Policies and drafts of laws come from elsewhere—from the cabinet, which in turn gets them from the bureaucracy. On a world scale, the independence and liveliness of the American Capitol Hill is quite rare. In most countries, parliaments tend to become rubber stamps of the executive. The Supreme Soviet is simply the most obvious and developed type of rubber stamp.

Government in a Fortress

> The Kremlin (from the Russian *kreml*, "fortress") is a walled city dating back centuries. (The present walls were built in 1492.) Triangular in shape and a mile and a half (2.4 kilometers) around, the ancient Kremlin houses both tsarist government buildings (now used by the Communists) and cathedrals (now public museums). Right next to the Kremlin wall is Lenin's tomb, used as a reviewing stand by the Politburo for parades in Red Square on May 1 (international workers' day) and November 7 (anniversary of the revolution). Also facing Red Square: the colorful onion-shaped domes of St. Basil's Cathedral.

THE COUNCIL OF MINISTERS

The Supreme Soviet also "elects" the functional equivalent of a cabinet, the mammoth Council of Ministers, which has some eighty-five ministers; Western cabinets typically have about twenty. This is because the Soviet system is socialist; that is, the state runs nationalized industries. Accordingly, by our standards, Soviet ministries are almost comically specialized; they include ministries for every imaginable branch of industry (see box).

Sitting on the Council of Ministers, however, are usually about half the members of the party's Politburo. If you see what position they occupy, you get a pretty good idea of which are regarded as the important ministries. Typically these ministries are reserved for Politburo members:

> Chairman of the Council of Ministers
> First Deputy Chairman
> State Security (KGB)
> Culture
> Defense
> Foreign Affairs

The Romance of Machine Building:
Some Specialized Soviet Ministries

- Electrical Equipment Industry
- Electronics Industry
- General Machine Building
- Heavy and Transport Machine Building
- Machine Building
- Machine Building for Animal Husbandry and Fodder Production
- Machine Building for Light and Food Industry and Household Appliances
- Machine Tool and Tool-Building Industry
- Medium Machine Building
- Power-Machine Building
- Pulp and Paper Industry
- Construction, Road and Municipal Machine Building
- Fish Industry

The Soviet Ministry of Medium Machine Building also builds their nuclear warheads, a function taken care of by the Department of Energy in the United States. Both countries hide their bombs behind euphemisms.

The chairman, since 1985 Nikolai Ryzhkov, is the equivalent of a Western prime minister but does not have to busy himself with legislative tasks. The Council of Ministers, which rarely meets, administers the economy. It contributes little in the way of policy; that comes from the party.

THE FEDERATION

Like the United States, Canada, and West Germany, the Soviet Union is a federation; that is, it is composed of fifteen "republics" with some local powers. Because the web of the Communist party weaves throughout these republics, they are less autonomous in practice than are the subunits of the other federations mentioned. Some observers dismiss Soviet federalism as a façade for highly centralized rule. True, all the important decisions are made in the Kremlin, but we should remember that even federations in Western democracies reserve considerable and often overriding power for the central government. The U.S. Civil War was fought to prove this point. As we discussed in chapter 15, federations and unitary systems tend to converge on a middle ground that has elements of both. The Soviet republics have taken on a certain life of their own, as competing bureaucracies.

There are two other Communist federal systems: Yugoslavia and Czechoslovakia. These three countries chose federalism because of their ethnic diversity. Czechoslovakia has two (some say three) distinct nationalities; Yugoslavia has five; the Soviet Union has some two dozen major nationalities

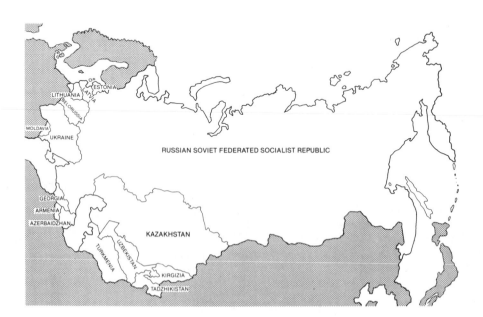

Major Soviet Nationalities, 1979

	MILLION	PERCENT OF SOVIET POPULATION
Slavs		
Russians	137.4	52.4
Ukrainians	42.3	16.1
Belorussians	9.5	3.6
Central Asians		
Kazakhs	6.6	2.5
Uzbecks	12.5	4.7
Turkmen	2.0	0.8
Kirgiz	1.9	0.7
Tadzhiks	2.9	1.1
Transcaucasians		
Georgians	3.6	1.4
Armenians	4.2	1.6
Azerbaidzhanis	5.5	2.1
Balts		
Estonians	1.0	0.4
Latvians	1.4	0.5
Lithuanians	2.9	1.1
Other		
Tatars	6.3	2.4
Moldavians	3.0	1.1
Germans	1.9	0.7
Jews	1.8	0.7
Chuvash	1.8	0.7
Bashkirs	1.4	0.5
Mordvins	1.2	0.5
Poles	1.1	0.4

and many more minor ones—about a hundred in all. Notice in the box "Major Soviet Nationalities" how ethnic Russians form a bare majority. Given the high birthrates of non-Slavic nationalities—especially the Moslem peoples of Central Asia—Russians will become a minority of the Soviet population by the turn of the century. We'll discuss Soviet nationality problems in chapter 21.

The fifteen Soviet "union republics" are:

Russian Soviet Federated Socialist Republic (RSFSR)
Ukrainian Soviet Socialist Republic
Belorussian SSR
Lithuanian SSR
Latvian SSR
Estonian SSR
Georgian SSR
Armenian SSR

Azerbaidzhan SSR
Turkmen SSR
Kazakh SSR
Kirgiz SSR
Tadzhik SSR
Uzbek SSR
Moldavian SSR

All of these "SSRs" (Soviet Socialist Republics) together make the USSR (Union of Soviet Socialist Republics).

The Russian republic is by far the biggest and is itself a federation of numerous "autonomous republics," "autonomous regions," and "national regions," designations for areas of lesser importance. Whatever the level of autonomy, the real importance of these subunits is in the preservation of language rights. While Russian is used throughout the Soviet Union, the various republics and regions can have schools (even universities), newspapers, government documents, and theaters in their local language, and this is very important to them. Stalin, who developed Soviet nationality policy, recognized that language and culture are potential political dynamite, and that it was best to let them alone while turning each region into an otherwise faithful Soviet republic. The policy has been only partly successful; some nationalities still want more than just language and cultural rights.

In some ways, the fifteen Soviet republics quarrel among themselves like the fifty U.S. states or ten West German *Länder*. Each republic has its own bureaucracies, jealous of their own powers and privileges. Further, much economic planning is at the republic level, and the republics sometimes have to battle to get scarce raw materials and capital goods to fulfill their plans.

It was claimed that a chief complaint of Brezhnev's was that the republics had too much economic autonomy, and it was said that he remedied the situation by strengthening Moscow's hand in the area of economic coordination in the 1977 constitution. What appears to us outsiders as essentially a cosmetic federalism appears to Kremlin insiders as lively and sometimes destructive competition between republics that must be curbed. The mere fact that the Soviet Union is organized as a federation and not as a unitary state (like East Germany) creates distinctive problems and patterns.

THE BUREAUCRACY

Karl Marx envisioned the "withering away of the state" after socialism was established. The state is an instrument of class repression, he argued, and when there are no more classes there won't need to be a state. The German sociologist Max Weber argued precisely the opposite: that socialism would entail much more state power and a much larger bureaucracy. Marx was wrong; Weber was right.

Memorable Russian Slogans:
"National in Form, Socialist in Content"

This was Stalin's answer (in the 1924 constitution) to the nationality issue in the Soviet Union. Stalin, himself a Georgian, understood that the ethnic groups within the old Russian empire were intensely proud of their languages and cultures and resentful of the tsarist policy of "russification"—making everyone learn Russian. So give them relatively free rein in this symbolic area, Stalin reasoned, but make sure the actual content of political and economic decisions is under the firm central control of the Kremlin. That was the theory. In practice, Stalin often favored russification as a means of crushing and controlling the non-Russian nationalities.

Three UN Seats for One Country

During World War II, while the Allies were planning a postwar United Nations, Stalin argued that it wouldn't be fair to give the Soviet Union just one seat. The USSR was the only Communist Country at the time, and with its single vote it would mean permanent capitalist dominance of the UN. To gain Stalin's acceptance of the UN idea, the Western Allies foolishly consented to give the Soviet Union three seats, one each for the Soviet Union, Belorussia, and the Ukraine, pretending the last two were independent sovereign nations. Although the balance of votes in the UN has shifted decisively against the West since then, the Soviet Union still has its three seats and three missions to the UN. Every fall the representatives of Belorussia and the Ukraine stand before the General Assembly to give basically the same speech as the Soviet representative.

The Soviet bureaucracy is monstrous, both in size and in style. Now employing some fourteen million persons, it governs every facet of Soviet life. Whereas the first three countries we studied tend toward "bureaucratism" (a pejorative word in Russian), the Soviet Union has become the bureaucratic state par excellence.

The Soviet bureaucracy builds on a tsarist tradition of powerful, arrogant, and rigid civil servants who commanded in the name of the tsar. Only Russia could produce a writer like Gogol, who brilliantly satirized officialdom in his novel *The Inspector General.* Now, with a vast economic machine to manage, Soviet bureaucracy is even worse: slow, marginally competent, inflexible, indifferent to efficiency, and immune to criticism except from party officials.

Part of the problem is that the Soviets had trouble making up their mind whether a civil servant should be a specialist in his or her field or a loyal and enthusiastic party member, in other words, whether to be "expert" or "Red." Having tried both with mixed success, they now hope for a combination of the two: Red experts.

As we mentioned before, the Communist party plays an important role in appointing, checking, and supervising this gigantic bureaucracy. Without what the party calls its *kontrol* function, things would be much worse. It's knowing that ultimately they are responsible before the party, and that the party is keeping tabs on them, that keeps Soviet officials on their toes. If they foul up, if their department or factory doesn't run right, they can be demoted or transferred to a remote area. This also tends to make them extremely cautious, going strictly by the book rather than taking a chance on something new. They also know that if they are succesful, the party takes note and can recommend them for a higher position.

The key tool in party control of the bureaucracy—and, bear in mind, the Soviet bureaucracy runs not only the government but the economy as well—is the *nomenklatura*, a list of all important positions that require higher approval to fill. Once an official, who is almost invariably a party member, is appointed to a *nomenklatura* post, he or she tends to keep this seal of approval permanently. There is nothing about the *nomenklatura* in the Soviet constitution or in statutes, but it is obviously an important control mechanism, giving the party its leading role in Soviet life. Some Western writers use *nomenklatura* as another way of saying "Soviet elite."

The KGB

Terror has been called "the linchpin of the Soviet system," the key element that holds it together. During Stalin's time there was a lot of truth to this, but since then, terror—the fear of being arbitrarily arrested, imprisoned, sent to Siberia, or shot—has largely disappeared as a means of political control. The political police, now called the Committee on State Security, or KGB, are still present and active, but their methods are more refined and subtle than the *Cheka* of Lenin's tenure or the NKVD of Stalin's.

Some half million KGB agents are everywhere: guarding the borders; in factories, hotels, universities, keeping tabs on anyone who contacts foreign tourists, handles classified materials, or dissents against the Soviet system. Millions of Soviet citizens have KGB dossiers, and some find out to their surprise that the KGB is able to recite even trivial incidents that happened years earlier. Part-time informers, called *stukachi* (squealers), are everywhere.

While the political police no longer have the power to actually try most cases—which now go to a regular court—they still have the power to frighten by selectively intimidating dissidents. Citizens can lose jobs, get sent to psychiatric clinics, be denied university entrance, have their rooms bugged, lose the right to live in a city, and generally be made uncomfortable by a word from the KGB.

GOSPLAN

The State Planning Committee, *Gosplan,* is the nerve center of the Soviet economic system, attempting to establish how much of what should be produced each year and setting longer-term targets for some 350,000 enterprises. Central planning can produce both impressive results and massive dislocations. Under Stalin, it enabled the Soviet Union to industrialize quickly, albeit at terrible human cost. But it also means chronic shortages of items the *Gosplan* forgot about or deemed unimportant. It appears that one year no toothbrushes were produced in the entire Soviet Union, a *Gosplan* oversight.

The Soviets are convinced that a planned and centrally directed economy is more rational than a Western market economy. Actual results would seem to dispute that, but the Soviets are reluctant to surrender central planning, long an article of faith of "scientific socialism." (Some Communist countries, namely China, Yugoslavia, and Hungary have scaled back central planning and have brought in varying degrees of market economy with good results.)

In *Gosplan,* the hopes, aims, fears, and sometimes caprices of the Soviet system converge and struggle. *Gosplan,* itself quite sensitive to the wishes of the Politburo, determines who gets what in the Soviet Union, whether steel will grow at x percent this year and plastics at y percent next. Now heavily computerized, *Gosplan* may be described as the steering wheel of the Soviet economy.

VOCABULARY BUILDING

apparatchik
Belorussia candidate
 member
Central
 Committee
Council of
 Ministers

democratic
 centralism
dual subordi-
 nation
Gosplan
Kremlin
nationalities
 question

nomenklatura
parallel hier-
 archies
Party Congress
Politburo
Presidium
russification

Secretariat
secretary
 general
Supreme Soviet
Ukraine
union republic

FURTHER REFERENCE

Barry, Donald D., and Carol Barner-Barry. *Contemporary Soviet Politics,* 2d ed. Englewood Cliffs, N.J.: Prentice-Hall, 1982.

Hill, Ronald J., and Peter Frank. *The Soviet Communist Party,* 2d ed. Winchester, Mass.: Allen & Unwin, 1983.

Medish, Vadim. *The Soviet Union,* 2d. rev. ed. Englewood Cliffs, N.J.: Prentice Hall, 1985.

Reshetar, John S., Jr. *The Soviet Polity: Government and Politics in the USSR.* New York: Dodd, Mead, 1971.

Rothman, Stanley, and George W. Breslauer. *Soviet Politics and Society.* St. Paul, Minn.: West Publishing Co., 1978.

Ryavec, Karl. *Soviet Society and the Communist Party.* Amherst: University of Massachusetts Press, 1978.

Schapiro, Leonard. *The Government and Politics of the Soviet Union,* 6th ed. Dover, N.H.: Longwood Publishing Group, 1984.

Sharlet, Robert. *The New Soviet Constitution of 1977: Analysis and Text.* Brunswick, Ohio: King's Court Communications, 1978.

Šik, Ota. *The Communist Power System.* New York: Praeger, 1981.

Voslensky, Michael. *Nomenklatura: The Soviet Ruling Class.* New York: Doubleday, 1984.

19

SOVIET POLITICAL ATTITUDES

LOVE-HATE OF THE WEST

A few decades ago when I spent a year at the University of Belgrade, in Yugoslavia, I met a young Russian, Ivan, who was also studying there. Just in fun, I repeated a story making the rounds of Belgrade that during a recent visit of the Soviet fleet to a Yugoslav port, Soviet seamen had bought up every shoe in the place, including old styles the stores had not been able to sell. I thought it was a funny comment on Soviet backwardness in consumer goods, but to Ivan it was no laughing matter.

I didn't realize it, but I had hit on a sore spot with Russians—they know they're backward and don't like being reminded of it. Ivan turned sullen and unfriendly at my jest, which for him was a put-down of his entire country. Later, Ivan and I became good friends. I learned never to make any comments about Soviet deficiencies. Eventually, it was he who commented on his country's problems. One day he told me: "Mikhail, Soviet consumer goods are terrible."

First lesson about Soviets, particularly ethnic Russians: national pride matters at least as much as Marxism-Leninism—although by now the two are so fused it's hard to separate them. Russians are extremely nationalistic and sensitive to criticism of their system. Accordingly, if you want to get to know Russians, do not approach them in a critical manner. They become both defensive and superior: "Don't worry. Soon we'll overtake you. You'll see."

A key component of Soviet political attitudes is Russian nationalism. Marxism-Leninism has virtually merged with traditional feelings of Russianness. Lenin himself said as much: "Scratch a Bolshevik and you'll find a Great Russian chauvinist." (This was a witty paraphrase of the old expression. "Scratch a Russian and you'll find a Tatar.")

As we discussed in chapter 17, nineteenth-century Russian intellectuals had a love-hate affair with the West. Conscious of their inferiority, some wanted to imitate the West while others sought to deny Western superiority. Marxism provided an answer to both Westernizers and Slavophiles: use the West's technological advances but in a better, Russian way. We will both follow the West and lead it, was their attitude, one that persists to this day.

Soviets still use the West—especially the United States—as the standard by which they measure their own progress. "We produce twice as much steel as the Americans!" Soviet spokesmen proudly proclaim (and it's true). When they

---

Memorable Russian Slogans: "Socialism in One Country"

Stalin, despite his Georgian origin (or maybe because of it), thoroughly appreciated Russian nationalism and made good use of it. Proclaiming "capitalist encirclement" of Communist Russia, he tapped the Russians' very old feelings of inferiority toward and fear of the West. Then Stalin offered them a way out: to start building a "socialism in one country" (Russia) that would withstand outside attack and eventually triumph over the decadent foreigners. The concept of "socialism in one country" refuted Trotsky's idea of worldwide revolution. Instead, Russia would develop socialism on its own and provide the rest of the world with a superior model.

Solzhenitsyn: Harkening to the Past

In 1963 a short, grim novel, *One Day in the Life of Ivan Denisovich,* burst on the Soviet literary scene like a bombshell. In detailing the horrors of Siberian forced labor, its author spoke from intimate experience: Alexander Solzhenitsyn had lived in such a camp from 1945 to 1953 and then in Siberian exile for another three years. His crime: as an artillery captain he criticized Stalin in a letter to a friend.

But the nightmare conditions did not break Solzhenitsyn; on the contrary, they made him stronger. Freed during Khrushchev's brief period of liberalization, Solzhenitsyn resolved to tell the whole story of Soviet repression through novels and nonfiction. But *One Day* was about as much of the truth as the regime was prepared to allow—and that was under the unusual circumstances of Khrushchev's destalinization drive—and Solzhenitsyn soon found himself expelled from the official writers' union and unable to publish.

Smuggled to the West, though, his works found a growing audience. In 1973 his monumental *Gulag Archipelago* was released in Paris. A massive compilation of the reports of 227 other camp survivors, *Gulag* (the central prisons administration) showed that capricious terror was part and parcel of the Soviet system, that by the 1940s there were from 12 to 15 million people in the Gulag at any one time, and that most had committed no crime.

That was the last straw for Soviet authorities. Against his will, Solzhenitsyn was bundled onto a plane for West Germany in early 1974. Because of his love for Russia and his belief that communism is a temporary mistake—imported from the West—that can be cured, he wanted to stay. In the classic mold of the nineteenth-century Slavophiles, Solzhenitsyn wrote a long letter to the Kremlin's rulers urging them to abandon communism, world empire, heavy industry, and domination over non-Russian nationalities and to return to the Orthodox faith, a simple agricultural life, and the tremendous spiritual roots of old Russia. The Soviet leaders did not act on Solzhenitsyn's modest proposal.

Solzhenitsyn is not merely anti-Communist. He hates anything Western: rationality, technology, materialism, legalism, even personal freedom (which, he holds, has degenerated into license). Although he has settled in Vermont, he is not particularly impressed by the United States. At the 1978 Harvard commencement he thundered:

Should someone ask me whether I would indicate the West such as it is today as a model to my country, frankly I would have to answer negatively. Through intense suffering our country [Russia] has now achieved a spiritual development of such intensity that the Western system in its present state of spiritual exhaustion does not look attractive. After the suffering of decades of violence and oppression, the human soul longs for things higher, warmer and purer than those offered by today's mass living habits, introduced by the revolting invasion of publicity, by TV stupor, and by intolerable music.

Many Russians share Solzhenitsyn's gut anti-Western feeling and mystical Russian nationalism.

admit that the Soviet Union still lags in many areas, they also retort: "But our system is better and fairer than yours. We have eliminated capitalism and its class struggles that you are still caught up in. In America the economy benefits only a few; here everybody benefits." The underlying theme is an old one: Russia will save the world.

At times Soviet nationalism becomes xenophobia—fear and hatred of foreigners. Today, as in tsarist times, foreigners are closely watched, and Soviets who come into contact with them are suspect. Over the centuries, Russians have come to feel they are beseiged in a fortress nation. Stalin utilized this feeling beautifully: he told the Soviets they were surrounded by threatening capitalists, and many believed him.

Foreign tourists often run afoul of Soviet xenophobia. Cut off from the West for centuries, Russians developed a cultural inferiority complex that can leap out in anger if they think foreigners are ridiculing or disrespectful of their system (see box).

When studying Soviet ideology, bear in mind that a lot of "Marxism-Leninism" is intense national pride masking feelings of inferiority. Marxism, by predicting the collapse of the capitalist West, tries to reassure Russians that their system is superior even though their standard of living at the moment is behind the West's. Marxism-Leninism attempts to play the role of a secular religion, promising Soviets a better life in the socialist utopia to come, something few now believe.

The Photo That Got Me in Trouble

(Michael Roskin)

The above photo, taken on an Odessa street, landed me in a police station for an hour. I was strolling around town, snapping pictures of street scenes, when three burly local citizens accosted me and demanded my camera. I'd heard of foreign tourists having their cameras smashed, but I refused to relinquish mine, keeping it tucked tightly under my elbow. The leader of the three seemed to object to the picture I'd just taken of eggs for sale on the sidewalk and demanded we go to a police station.

On reaching the station, the equivalent of a desk sergeant earnestly listened to the three citizens' complaints and was in complete agreement with them. I had done something bad—they wouldn't say what—and should surrender my film.

Then an English-speaking policeman arrived—his English wasn't much better than my Russian—who again insisted I cooperate. "But what have I done wrong?" I asked him. "Were they bad eggs?" No, came the reply. "Were the shop attendants badly dressed?" No. "Were the eggs secret, part of the Soviet arsenal?" No. "Then what did I do bad?"

"You have behaved very badly," was his only reply. Gradually it began to dawn on me that they were probably sensitive to the way the picture might be used outside their country. Because it showed people *lined up* to buy eggs, suggesting a shortage of eggs, the photo could be used as anti-Soviet propaganda, although that was the last thing on my mind. Without knowing it or meaning to, I had touched a Soviet nerve, implying that the Soviet Union was inferior in some way—in this case, in the production of eggs.

The three citizens filled out complaint forms against me. By this time I was getting irritated. "I demand to speak with my consulate in Moscow," I said. Impossible, they told me. (That may well have been true; Soviet long-distance lines are jammed.) "In which case," I said, "you are violating the provisions of the U.S.-Soviet consular convention, which gives me the right to call my embassy." They started looking confused and worried; perhaps the American was

right. Actually it was a bluff, since I knew only that most consular conventions hold that foreigners detained by police have the right to contact their consulate. But I pressed my advantage: "Wow, are you going to get in a lot of trouble. Wait till your bosses find out you've contravened the 1964 consular convention."

Unsure of themselves, they let me go. That evening, the police interpreter came around to our group's hotel to explain, defensively, that as far as they were concerned the incident was trivial and finished, and he urged me to view it the same way. The Odessa "egg flap" was the educational high point of my tour. In one hour I had had a course on both Soviet xenophobia and bureaucratism—how to avoid the former and use the latter.

OFFICIAL MARXISM

One interesting observation about the world's first Marxist country is that it seldom produces good Marxist analysis. Soviet scholarly and journalistic accounts of capitalist countries repeat without originality such Marxist clichés as "sharpening of contradictions," "increasing tempo and magnitude of crises," and "ruling circles of imperialism." Curiously, Marxism is far livelier in the West; some serious Marxists say the best thinking along Marxist lines takes place in the United States.

How could this be? Perhaps it is because when an ideology becomes an official doctrine, it dies. The invigorating elements of debate, questioning, and doubt are driven out of it. When an ideology has to struggle against other viewpoints—as Marxism must in the United States—it must keep on its toes, constantly refining and sometimes discarding its arguments. Some Soviets admit that while many mouth Marxist-Leninist slogans, few believe them. Official Soviet Marxism, like Lenin's body, has simply been embalmed for public display. Soviet students shuffle off to courses on Marxism-Leninism with the enthusiasm of American students going to compulsory chapel.

Marxism is basically a method of analysis, one that stresses social classes and their conflicts. Often it can be very useful. But it's the last type of analysis the Soviets want focused on their own society, for it would quickly reveal important class differences and even class conflict—in a system that's supposed to have abolished classes.

The problem is that Marx concentrated on analyzing capitalist society and predicting its downfall. He had practically nothing to say about the stage that was to come next, socialism. Accordingly, Communists have had to improvise as they go along; they make up whatever they want after coming to power and say it's Marxism. Yugoslav and Chinese Communists boast that they are better Marxists than the Soviets, a point that makes the Soviets extremely angry.

One of the Soviet Union's few serious Marxists is actually a dissident, historian Roy Medvedev. He looks at the Soviet system from a leftist angle, arguing that true Leninism has been betrayed by Stalin and his successors but that there is still hope for a democratic socialist Soviet Union. Kicked out of the Communist party and fired from his job (but not expelled from the country), Medvedev illustrates the moribund condition of official Soviet Marxism, which cannot tolerate discussion of basic questions. To Soviet leadership, Marxism is just as dangerous as capitalism.

The constant mouthing of a doctrine few believe creates a climate of cynicism, hypocrisy, and opportunism. Party ideologues crank out Marxist-Leninist phrases because they're paid to. People read and knit at party lectures. In private, many Soviets will tell you the system stinks, but very few will say it in public. Those who do are the dissidents. It's the old story of the emperor's new clothes with a Soviet twist: the unknowing child who speaks the truth gets spanked hard.

An Alternate Explanation: Jobs

Some scholars of the Soviet system protest that these pages do not give sufficient weight to the role of ideology in the Soviet system, that ideology was and still is quite important in Soviet decision making. Soviet agriculture, for example, is known to be defective. Why don't the Soviets permit more private farming, which is far more productive? The ideological explanation is that for the USSR's rulers that would be a step backwards from socialism and toward capitalism. An alternative explanation—which, frankly, I favor—notes that there are hundreds of thousands of Communist agricultural officials who make a good living supervising the bumbling farm system. What would happen to their jobs under private agriculture? They would be quickly unmasked as useless, so they cling tightly to their entrenched jobs and privileges, blocking any major reforms.

By the same token, Soviet industry would perform much better if decentralized to give enterprises the freedom to make their own decisions based on market considerations. Many Soviet economists understand this (and we'll consider it in chapter 21). Why then don't they decentralize? The ideological argument again is that decentralization would be unsocialist. The jobs argument is that the inefficient Soviet factories employ millions of do-nothing workers and managers who would be thrown out of work along with local, regional, republic, and all-union economic officials. A market system is a threat to jobs, not just to ideology.

Recent émigrés from the Soviet Union who were in a position to observe Soviet elites first-hand say they know next to nothing about Marxism. Their "ideology," if one can call it that, is simply to support a status quo which gives them and their families a privileged position in the hierarchical Soviet system. The next time you encounter an ideological explanation of domestic Soviet behavior, see if a jobs explanation doesn't fit as well or better.

THE SECULAR RELIGION

Moribund or not, Marxism-Leninism—usually combined with nationalism—permeates the Soviet Union. Soviet rulers believe ideology serves important purposes, that it is, in fact, indispensable. Communism in the Soviet Union has turned into a secular religion. It is used to try to motivate people, generate enthusiasm, assure the population that all is well, and foster national solidarity against foreign powers. That it actually works well is dubious.

Much Soviet architecture is aimed at giving communism a religious aura. When the Bolsheviks took over Moscow's Kremlin they cut down the crosses on each of the fortress's turrets and put up in their place electrified red stars that glow at night. In every Soviet city there is a grave to an unknown Soviet soldier who died fighting the Nazi invaders; it is bedecked with wreaths (plastic) and often an eternal flame. The greatest religious monument in Russia is Lenin's

Taking the Pledge

(Michael Roskin)

In Novgorod I happened to witness a swearing-in ceremony for Young Pioneers, a common sight in the Soviet Union where children virtually have to belong to party-directed youth groups, first the Little Octobrists from age 7, then the Young Pioneers from age 10. Whole school classes join together. Here the candidates listen to nationalistic speeches before a statue of a World War II soldier. Then, at a signal, the older members come forward to put red kerchiefs around the necks of the inductees. They give their special Young Pioneer salute and march off into the future.

The Young Communist League (*Komsomol*) is different; admission is selective for 15- to 27-year-olds. *Komsomol* is a training ground and try-out stage for admission to the party. Most university students and junior army officers are expected to be *Komsomols*. Their leadership ability is noted, and they are earmarked for party membership. Senior *Komsomols* are often also junior CPSU members.

tomb facing Red Square. People come on pilgrimages from all parts of the country to stand in line for hours to get one glimpse of what is supposed to be Lenin's preserved body. The officially atheistic Soviet Union is heavy with religiosity.

Unlike most Western societies, the Soviet Union has a goal to which all are supposed to be striving: communism. Marx envisaged communism as a stage beyond socialism, a society of equality and abundance where all citizens will have whatever they need. First, say Soviet ideologists, they must lay the "material basis" for this system by accumulating capital and reinvesting it in industry, all under centralized control. This stage is called "building socialism." When productivity is very high—the Soviets don't specify what that is but imply it's when they equal and surpass the Americans—then this socialist society will turn into a communist one.

Bear in mind that the Soviets do not claim to have a Communist society now—that's their objective, the practical utopia they are working toward. They admit that at the present "developed socialist" stage of Soviet society there are still shortages of various sorts, inequality, and uneven development. Some of this comes about because in building for the future the present generation must make sacrifices. Capital must be reinvested, not consumed. Starting from a low level after the Revolution, Soviets point out, they have become the world's second greatest industrial power by dint of hard work and sacrifice. Ideology is designed to help this process by promoting the feeling they are constructing the world's first working utopia.

Few Soviets believe this any more. In earlier decades, many tackled industrialization, the Nazi invasion, and postwar reconstruction with a certain socialist-cum-nationalist enthusiasm. Although few cared about Marxism-Leninism, some had a simple idealism. This idealism has vanished, its place taken by cynicisim, corruption, and resentment of the privileged elite. In the Soviet Union today, ideology is something of a joke.

PARTICIPATION: REAL OR ARTIFICIAL?

During the Cold War, Americans generally had the impression that the Soviet leaders ruled by pure coercion. Without the secret police, the Soviet system would collapse, many believed. Today, most political theorists argue that a system cannot be based on coercion alone; it needs at least a core of supporters and a population willing to go along. Empirically, this is what we find when we look at authoritarian systems, which often place great emphasis on generating mass support.

One way the Soviet system generates support is by fostering the feeling among citizens that they actually are participating in the great adventure of building socialism. The Soviet mass media, for example, gives a lot of attention to the democratic trappings of elections, representative bodies, and citizen complaints. A Soviet election campaign, held every four years, features almost as much hoopla as Western campaigns. "Campaign workers" get out the vote by making sure everybody in their district has cast a ballot—even in hospitals and on trains. There is a single slate of candidates with no choices—you just drop your ballot into a box. A booth is available but voters who use it come under

Agitpunkt for Agitprop

(Michael Roskin)

Scattered throughout Soviet cities are offices for agitating the population. "Agitation" in Soviet parlance means whipping up mass enthusiasm. To "agitate the masses" means to conduct oral, face-to-face political campaigns featuring slogans and simple language the common person can understand. Propaganda in Soviet usage means higher-level, more-intellectual types of persuasions. The Communists joined the two words to make *Agitprop,* short for the Department of Agitation and Propaganda of the party's Central Committee.

An *agitpunkt* (literally, agitation point) is a local *agitprop* center where party workers pick up instructions and materials. *Agitpunkti* also serve as polling stations during elections.

suspicion: they might be defacing their ballot in protest. The turnout rate—usually set in advance at 99.98 percent of the adult population—is then celebrated as an election victory by the Communist party.

Do these single-party elections really fool anybody? For the Soviets, an election is not a time to choose. They believe that only bourgeois countries need choices between opposing parties and candidates, because they still have antagonistic classes which are represented by the various parties. The Soviets, on the other hand, hold that having eliminated classes they have no need for competitive elections. Instead, Soviet elections are rituals of participation, periodic attempts to make citizens *feel* they have a say in things. While we may regard this as fraudulent, we might pause to ask ourselves to what extent elections in democratic countries perform this same function.

In addition to elections, there are frequent campaigns to "mobilize" the population to work harder, stop drinking so much vodka, turn out for flower planting and urban clean-up, or solve some local problem. For some, this is true participation. For others—probably among the more intelligent and educated—it's just an annoying game. One Leningrad engineering student told the author that the system would be all right "if only they'd shut up a little." For him, the constant mobilizations and celebrations are propaganda overkill. Although it is impossible to say how many Soviets feel this way, it is probably quite a few.

The Vodka Problem

In 1975 the Soviet Union stopped publishing key health statistics. American researchers pieced together the reason: Soviets are getting *less* healthy; infant and adult mortality rates are up. The main culprit: alcohol. Soviet figures show an increase in spirits and wine production. Some say almost as much homebrew is consumed. Workers drink on the job, even though they can be severely punished. Alcohol-related industrial accidents are common. In a relatively new trend, women are now drinking "by the glassful," like men. The effects on fetuses are terrible. An estimated one-third of the Soviet food budget goes for alcoholic beverages.

Why? Alcoholism bespeaks despair. Soviets are disappointed with the system; they no longer sense progress. Their options are limited. Serious protest gets them in trouble. Political participation is through the Communist party, and it's part of the problem. So the bottle is the easy way out.

Perhaps an even more interesting question: Why doesn't the regime, which closely controls the economy, cut alcohol production way down? The implication is that it doesn't want to, that drunkenness is better than mass anger. In chapter 9 we noted Marx's condemnation of religion as the "opium of the masses." In the Soviet Union, alcohol is the opium of the masses.

STALIN AS SYMBOL

In Germany we discussed how a moral vacuum—the inability of postwar Germany to come to grips with its Nazi past—retarded efforts to build a legitimate, democratic political culture. The modern Soviet Union has a similar problem—how to come to grips with Stalin. Until it solves this problem—which it may never do—the system will contain a permanent weakness.

The problem in a nutshell is this: For nearly a quarter of a century Stalin was officially worshiped in the Soviet Union. His name became synonymous with communism, the Soviet Motherland, and building the socialist future. Although some Soviet citizens—we don't know how many—knew this was a monstrous lie, no one who spoke out remained among the living. Soviet managers found the coercive tools of the Stalin system indispensable in keeping workers disciplined. Among the masses, Stalin exploited the old Russian tradition of the modernizing tyrant. Many admired Stalin's style: he kept people in line and got things done. There was discipline, order, and a sense of purpose.

Then all of a sudden in 1956, three years after his death, it became permissible—even praiseworthy—to criticize Stalin. Khrushchev himself had done so before the Party Congress. From out of the woodwork came people with all kinds of horror stories, of years in Siberia, of loved ones vanished without a trace, of capricious brutality. Towns and streets named after Stalin were renamed. Stalingrad, famed for its epic World War II battle, became Volgograd (before the Revolution it had been Tsaritsyn). Statues of Stalin (except in his native Georgia) came down. Finally, in 1961 Stalin's body was removed from alongside Lenin's and placed in a modest grave behind the Lenin mausoleum. The "Stalin" entry in the *Great Soviet Encyclopedia* disappeared. In Soviet parlance, Stalin became an "un-person" (*nechelovek*), someone who never existed. Books, short stories, and poems hinted that Stalin had been a fiend; in literature this period was called the Thaw, indicating the arrival of spring after an especially harsh winter.

There was one big catch, however: the system found it *needed* Stalin as a symbol. Without Stalin things started to come unstuck. Critical discussion went too far; people started doubting the system. Dissidents appeared openly. Managers had a hard time getting workers to obey without coercion. And the masses had always revered Stalin; he was their great Leader, the *vozhd*. Destalinization threw them into confusion; many harkened back to the good old days when Stalin ruled them with an iron hand.

The answer: partial restalinization, undertaken by Khrushchev's successors. This has pleased many people. An "Archie Bunker" syndrome has appeared among Soviet workers: little portraits of Stalin in trucks, buses, taxis, and workplaces. They don't know that Stalin meant terror; to them he means discipline, order, and purpose. But what about the people who know better, the more educated and sensitive people? Once again, they must be silent. To speak out can lead to loss of job, to commitment in a psychiatric clinic, to prison, and sometimes to expulsion from the Soviet Union. The tension over Stalin as a symbol remains within the heart of the Soviet system. To cover up a lie is psychologically and spiritually debilitating, as we considered in discussing West Germany.

What the System Does to People

Foreign tourists, reporters, and business people often remark on the bad temper of human relations in the Soviet Union. There's a great deal of screaming, thundering, demanding, and threatening, almost as if everyone were a New York City taxi driver. Westerners stationed in the Soviet Union for a long time find this the worst aspect of Soviet life. "It's what the system does to you," said one American newsman of my acquaintance. "It turns you into a nasty, short-tempered screamer." To get something—the hotel room you're entitled to, your reserved seat on a plane—you can't be nice; being polite will get you nowhere.

Why are Soviets like this? Their sometimes rude behavior is a sign of stress; they have been and still are under stress. Starting in the late 1920s, Stalin industrialized the country by brutal means. Managers had to get the job done or get shot. In turn, they treated employees savagely; plant conditions were inhuman. The purges made everyone jumpy; anyone might be next. Food, apartments, clothing, not to mention luxuries, were in terribly short supply. People had to stand in line for hours and connive to get necessities. You can't coerce a society the way Stalin did and produce calm, even-tempered people.

The situation isn't so bad today, but the Soviets are still jumpy and irritable, laden with fear and suspicion. Consumer goods, especially meat, are still in short supply so that Soviets have to wait in shop lines for hours each week. The manifestations of the stress of Soviet daily life can be seen in the high incidences of alcoholism, job absenteeism, wife-beating, and rude public behavior.

BLOWING OFF STEAM

In a society with as much tension as in the Soviet Union, there must be ways to blow off steam that won't hurt the system. And the Soviets have developed and institutionalized forms of criticism that do not attack the system itself.

For example, criticism and self-criticism (*kritika i samokritika*) are permitted and even encouraged in some institutions, especially at lower levels of the party. Here individual shortcomings are discussed, and people make public confessions of their own failures and wrong attitudes. *Kritika i samokritika* not only deflect criticism from the more basic problems but help cement together groups of individuals. People who share their confessions feel psychologically bound to each other.

Letters to the editor are encouraged in the Soviet press. They can be quite damning—but never directly against the system. Rather, they castigate specific problems, bureaucracies, and organizations that fail to build socialism. One can find in the Soviet press harsh words on the operations of railroads, restaurants, retail stores, and so on. You will not, however, find criticism of the party, the army, or the overall Soviet system.

When things go badly, top party leaders will single out individuals for blame, sometimes by name, otherwise by position. This is a sign that they are throwing a sacrifice to the wolves. By blaming a top agricultural official for bad harvests, for example, they hope to deflect criticism of farm policy in general and collectivization in particular. As we shall explore in the next chapter, Khrushchev was both the giver and receiver of this kind of personal attack.

"ENGINEERS OF THE SOUL"

Stalin called Soviet writers "engineers of the soul," but the expression applies to Soviet artists of all kinds: painters, composers, and filmmakers. Soviet art, like much of Soviet society, is *aimed*. It is not meant merely to entertain or explore like most Western art. The Soviet Union is building socialism, and the artist must assist in this task. Soviet art is not afflicted by self-doubt or ambiguity; its messages are simple, positive, instructive, and uplifting. Sex and violence are almost absent—the Soviets consider them examples of Western decadence.

The dominant Soviet artistic theme is "socialist realism." A work of art must be realistic so that people can understand and identify with it, but it must also have a positive twist that persuades people to get to work and build socialism. As such, it differs from American or Western European realism, which is often pessimistic and focuses on the grim struggle to survive and the permanence of human unhappiness. Soviet realism is optimistic, filled with self-sacrificing, idealistic people imbued with socialist vision.

Abstract art has had its ups and downs in the Soviet Union. The revolution unleashed tremendous creative talent, which was proud to break away from old styles and produced remarkable poetry and paintings in nonrepresentational styles. With the Five-Year Plans, however, Stalin decided that art had to

Ivan Sees Modern Art

My friend Ivan, the Russian student, had never before seen modern art. Raised on "socialist realism," suddenly in Yugoslavia he found himself surrounded by modern, sometimes surrealistic art, for Yugoslavia imposes no official artistic standards.

For Ivan, modern art was mind blowing. Westerners, used to artists painting whatever they like, usually don't pay too much attention to art galleries. Ivan, I think, saw every exhibit in every Belgrade gallery and museum. Standing in bewildered amazement before one surrealistic painting, he asked me, "Mikhail, what does this mean?" I replied that it meant whatever one wanted it to mean, that art didn't really have to have any particular meaning. Ivan was skeptical at this notion but, after some more viewing, conceded, "Perhaps you are right."

In Ivan's fascination with nonrepresentational art, I began to see why the Soviets prohibit it. If an artist can paint or sculpt whatever he or she likes, people may start thinking whatever they like, and in the Soviet Union that can be dangerous. Artistic freedom is closely connected to intellectual freedom in general, and Ivan was experiencing both for the first time.

What happened to Ivan when he went back to Russia? I don't know. I gave him my address, but he wouldn't give me his. "I'll be moving around," he said. I never heard from him. Soviet citizens, especially party members, know that they're not supposed to stay in contact with foreigners.

serve the economy, and experimentalism vanished. Some of the Soviet Union's most creative people were killed during the Great Purge. During Khrushchev's destalinization, some artists began to cautiously experiment again, but soon the regime began denouncing them for their "bourgeois formalism," that is, being obsessed with meaningless form and not producing art with a constructive content—the goal of socialist realism.

The net result of Soviet restrictions on artistic life is constant irritation on the part of creative individuals and hunger among the informed public for something new. For a while, it seemed that all great Soviet ballet stars would defect to the West. Their uniform complaint: the impossibility of doing anything new, creative, or experimental in the USSR.

Many writers feel the same way, but they have a safety valve: *samizdat* (self-publishing). These underground stories, poems, and satire are usually just carbon copies passed from hand to hand and sometimes smuggled to the West for publication. Among *samizdat* literature can be found the best Soviet writing, but when its authors are identified they are often sent into internal exile for "slandering the Soviet Motherland." Actually, many Soviet underground writers are apolitical, but the oppressive cultural bureaucracy forces them to take a dissenting stance, since those that cannot get published are automatically suspect by the KGB for writing outside of the official writers' union. Soviet official culture, like Soviet politics in general, does not take kindly to freedom.

VOCABULARY BUILDING

agitprop	consular convention	ideology	*samokritika*
bourgeois formalism	communism	infant mortality	secular
class struggle	destalinization	*Komsomol*	socialist realism
coercion	dissident	mobilization	xenophobia
collective	*Gulag*	*samizdat*	

FURTHER REFERENCE

Friedgut, Theodore H. *Political Participation in the USSR.* Princeton: Princeton University Press, 1979.

Hunt, R. N. Carew, Samuel Sharp, Richard Lowenthal, and Leopold Labedz. "Ideology and Power—A Symposium," in *Russia under Khrushchev: An Anthology from Problems of Communism,* ed. by Abraham Brumberg. New York: Praeger, 1962.

Kerblay, Basile. *Modern Soviet Society.* New York: Pantheon Books, 1983.

Medvedev, Roy A. *On Socialist Democracy.* New York: Knopf, 1975.

Scammell, Michael. *Solzhenitsyn: A Biography.* New York: W. W. Norton, 1984.

Shipler, David K. *Russia: Broken Idols, Solemn Dreams.* New York: Times Books, 1983.

Smith, Hedrick. *The Russians.* New York: Quadrangle, 1976.

Solzhenitsyn, Alexander. *One Day in the Life of Ivan Denisovich.* New York: Praeger, 1963.

——. *The Gulag Archipelago,* vols. 1–3. New York: Harper & Row, 1979.

Tumarkin, Nina. *Lenin Lives! The Lenin Cult in Soviet Russia.* Cambridge, Mass.: Harvard University Press, 1983.

Zinoviev, Alexander. *The Radiant Future.* New York: Random House, 1981.

20

PATTERNS OF INTERACTION

HIDDEN POLITICS

It used to be widely accepted that the Soviet Union had no political life in the Western sense of the word. In the absence of competitive parties, meaningful elections, and a parliament with certain powers, outside observers depicted the Soviet Union as "totalitarian," a hierarchical monolith where people simply did as they were told, more like an army than a political system.

Western systems, it was argued, are "pluralistic." As we discussed in chapter 10, pluralism does not simply mean that there are plural groups within a political system. That would be true nearly everywhere. Pluralism adds a normative component to this fact: groups and their interactions are good; lobbying and compromise between interest groups is a desirable way to run a democracy. The British and Americans celebrate pluralism; the French are somewhat skeptical; but to the Soviets, the open interplay of groups is taboo. The Soviet Communist party—like Communist parties everywhere—permits no factions. Formal interest groups do not exist.

"Totalitarian" and "Authoritarian":
Is There a Difference?

The advent of the Reagan administration reawakened an old debate in political science: Is there a difference between totalitarian and authoritarian regimes? In earlier decades political scientists had developed theories and models of "totalitarian" systems to explain Mussolini's Italy, Hitler's Germany, and Stalin's Soviet Union. Carl J. Friedrich and Zbigniew Brzezinski (who later served as President Carter's national security advisor) held that totalitarian dictatorships have these six points in common:

An official ideology

A single, disciplined party

Terroristic police control

Party monopoly of the mass media

Party control of the armed forces

Central direction of the economy

Widely accepted for years, the totalitarian model gradually came under criticism as unrealistic and oversimplified. Far from total, the systems of Mussolini, Hitler, and Stalin were quite messy. Many citizens knew the regimes were frauds, and plans were often just improvisations. The dictators liked their systems to *look* total. *Totalitarianism* fell into disuse, replaced by *authoritarianism,* meaning a system with little mass input.

Some Reagan supporters—including political scientist Jeane J. Kirkpatrick, who became ambassador to the United Nations—thought, however, that there was still a useful distinction to make between the two words. An authoritarian system, they argued, is a much looser and less-permanent regime. Most of the above six points are absent. An authoritarian regime, such as Argentina, is open to change (it returned to democracy in 1983); a totalitarian regime, such as the Soviet Union, is not. Reaganites held we should be less critical of the former than the latter.

Anti-Reaganites denounced and ridiculed the distinction between authoritarian and totalitarian. When people are being unfairly imprisoned, tortured, and denied basic human rights, what difference does it make if a regime is authoritarian rather than totalitarian? In practice, critics charged, the distinction would be used to justify U.S. aid to any anti-Communist regime, no matter how bloody its human-rights record.

It's hard to draw a clear line between totalitarian and authoritarian. The more we learn about individual systems, the harder it is to place them into one category or the other. Where, for example, would we put Poland? Under the rule of a general, most points of the above six would be open to question in Poland. Where would we put a China that has turned friendly to the West and decentralized its economy? The debate may be a futile one.

But under the surface, there's plenty of politics. Interactions, although veiled, take place between the party and the people, within the party, between unofficial interest groups and the government, and among national groups. These Soviet interactions, though harder to uncover than in Western countries, often resemble politics in more open societies.

MOTIVATING A SOCIETY TO BUILD SOCIALISM

Revolutions usually begin with popular joy at the ouster of the old regime. Life can start anew; all things seem possible. But after a time enthusiasm flags; the new regime finds it must motivate people to work hard and produce the coming millennium. The Soviet Union has used—and still uses—three approaches to motivate people: (1) slogans, (2) fear, and (3) incentives.

The first is an ideological or propagandistic approach, tapping the idealism present in all of us. The basic message is: "We are building the Future, so let's get to work, comrades!" All over the Soviet Union there are billboards urging people to work harder, to fulfill the latest economic plan, to move society into communism. Top workers may be named "Heroes of Socialist Labor." As anyone who has worked on a volunteer project knows, however, idealism doesn't last long. The voluntary spirit wanes. Exhortations in the mass media after a while fall on deaf ears.

The Stalin approach to motivation was fear, what psychologists call "negative reinforcement." Applying massive amounts of coercion, the Stalin system achieved impressive growth in the 1930s. The Great Purge of the late 1930s seems to have actually helped the growth rate: managers were so frightened of the random arrests and executions that they doubled their exertions to meet or exceed quotas. In time, however, even terror becomes an ineffective motivator. Police control strangles everything. Able-bodied workers are shipped off to grossly inefficient slave-labor camps, wasting their labor. The Soviet secret police under Stalin actually arrested people just to keep their *Gulag* projects supplied with manpower. Managers become ultracautious, afraid of attracting attention to themselves. And workers, starved for the necessities of life—enough food, a decent room, a pair of shoes—grumble at their miserable rewards and refrain from exerting themselves. Productivity slumps; the growth rate stalls.

In this way, Soviet citizens do have a certain input into the political system. When the system doesn't deliver some rewards, they drag their heels. Since Khrushchev, Soviet leaders have taken this factor into account, in effect, entering into a dialogue with the citizenry along these lines: "Look, comrades, I know you want a bigger plate of goulash and you're going to get it. Just work a little harder and I'll make sure you're rewarded." Khrushchev used such a line on Hungarian workers (goulash is a Hungarian stew), and the approach became known as "goulash communism."

Memorable Russian Slogans: "Glory to Labor!"

(*Michael Roskin*)

Western countries motivate people to work by advertising; the message is: work, earn money, and buy this product. The Soviet Union, with little need to advertise products because they are often in short supply anyway, tries to motivate people more directly by telling them that work is inherently good. One common slogan is "*Slava trudu*," which can be roughly translated as "Glory to Labor" or "Hurrah for Work." Whether it motivates many Soviets to work harder is doubtful.

This incentive approach, or "positive reinforcement," is, in the long run, the most effective. Soviet incomes are not equal. There are considerable differentials to reward the more productive and valuable people. Workers and managers get fat bonuses for exceeding their quotas. Much work is on a piece rate rather than an hourly rate, something Western labor unions won't stand for. Consumer goods are more abundant than they were, although buyers may have to wait years to get a car. People now have some incentive to work. The problem with this approach, though, is that it resembles undesirable old capitalism. Soviet leaders are reluctant to commit themselves to a consumer-oriented economy—for reasons we'll explore in the next chapter—so they are unable to meet consumer demand. As any Western tourist in the Soviet Union knows, there's more money than there are products. Soviet youths constantly approach tourists with rolls of rubles, offering to buy their jeans, sunglasses, wristwatches, and so on.

For the Kremlin to provide real incentives, they'd have to offer more consumer goods, but their heavy military spending makes that impossible.

Accordingly, the motivation game in the Soviet Union is a combination of all three approaches we've discussed: a fair amount of incentive, plus much sloganeering, backed up by a coercive apparatus that can still send people into internal exile on charges of "parasitism" (that is, not working). It is not, however, a particularly effective mix, and the Soviet leaders' number-one economic problem is still how to motivate their citizens.

Memorable Russian Slogans: "Communism in Our Generation"

The program of the 1961 CPSU congress proclaimed that by 1980 "the material and technical basis of communism will be created and there will be an abundance of material and cultural benefits for the whole population. . . . Thus, *a Communist society will on the whole be built in the USSR.*" (Emphasis in original.)

The goal was not reached. Khrushchev, the party chief at that time, tried to fire up Soviet workers to produce more by promising them the millennium in two decades. The slogan grew out of his address to the congress. Khrushchev, an enthusiastic, effusive personality, was mistaken in at least two ways:

First, the Soviet economy has not grown as fast as projected.

Second, communism, a utopia in which everyone gets whatever he or she needs regardless of work performed, keeps receding into the future. The Soviets call their present stage "developed socialism." Like a mirage, Soviet communism dissolves when approached only to reappear on the distant horizon.

MOTIVATION BY OPPORTUNISM

One way to motivate the brightest Soviet citizens is to offer them a chance to join the Communist party. Left outside the party, intelligent, energetic people could turn into dissidents (some do). By dangling both material and psychological rewards in front of young talent, the CPSU controls a large part of potential dissent by coopting it. Materially, party members are eligible for higher and better-paying positions. The highest stratum of party officials have access to special shops (where they can even get imported articles), medical clinics, and summer cottages. Psychologically, party members may feel, even vicariously, that they are their country's leaders and share in power.

A Communist party out of power is one thing; in power it is something else. Out of power, Communists are often dedicated idealists, living underground, hunted by the police. Once in power, the party often attracts an entirely different breed: the opportunist. Just as ambitious young Germans flocked to the Nazis, so do ambitious young Soviets enter the CPSU. This means that the party loses its original idealism; its members become self-serving careerists. Motivation by opportunism is thus a double-edged sword: it works—that is, it motivates the talented to serve the regime—but it also undermines the long-term goal of reaching communism. The CPSU members become the fat cats of a state-capitalist system. Dissident physicist Andrei Sakharov calls the Soviet Union "a deeply cynical caste society."

The Soviet Communist party controls most elite positions. Some gifted scientists and musicians may get to the top on sheer talent, but industrial managers, agriculture officials, army officers, and of course political leaders at all levels are almost all party members. About one-third of all Soviet university graduates are party members. In general, the higher the education level of a Soviet citizen, the more likely he or she is to be a party member. Further, the soviet elite tends to pass on its position to its children by arranging to get them into the best schools and universities. This is what Sakharov meant by a "caste" society.

"The New Class"

Milovan Djilas (pronounced *Gee-lass*) could have been Tito's successor. Until 1954 he was right-hand man to Yugoslavia's Communist chief and a dedicated Communist himself. After the Yugoslav Communists established themselves in power, however, Djilas began to notice that their vision of a happy society of equal brothers was fading. While the Communists had eliminated capitalists as a class, he wrote, they simultaneously created a "new class" of bureaucrats, party officials, secret police, and army officers, who rigged the system to favor themselves.

Socialism brought no real improvement over capitalism; both were ruled by a social class out for its own interests; bureaucrats had replaced capitalists. Additionally, Djilas said, communism brought with it tyranny over the mind and economic stupidity far worse than capitalism. For his candor, Djilas served ten years in Yugoslav prisons.

Still, Djilas's book *The New Class,* published in 1957, has become a classic analysis of why communist parties can never lead societies into communism. Once the New Class is in power, it likes things to stay pretty much the way they are, with themselves at the top. In this way, revolutionaries turn into conservatives.

What the Soviet system aims for is a siphoning off of the best and brightest of Soviet society into the party. This brings some problems, though. A party that continually skims off the cream of citizens for itself turns into an elite party, yet the CPSU prides itself on being a worker party, fulfilling Marx's dictum that the workers will lead society into the future. While the party does recruit many workers into its ranks, they tend to move upward and become foremen, managers, and even government and party officials, changing their blue collars for white collars. Accordingly, over time, the CPSU—and every other Communist party in power—becomes less and less a party of workers and more and more a party of educated white-collar people (*intelligentsia*). This causes some embarrassment in party-membership statistics, and the CPSU, like most East European Communist parties, fudges the social class of its members by listing their class when they *first* entered the party. Many thus listed as "workers" haven't dirtied their hands at labor in decades.

CPSU, because it monopolizes the elite positions of Soviet society, has become a conservative party. There are, to be sure, forces for change within the party—often among younger and more idealistic members—but, in the main, party members know that their task is simply to support the existing system. Members who advocate change and reform may be viewed as troublemakers.

Young, idealistic party members gradually become cynical; instead of trying to change the system, they decide to join it. Opportunism, loss of idealism, and status-quo party conservatism contribute to the tendency of the Soviet system to petrify, to become frozen in existing patterns.

In and Out of the Party

During its history, the CPSU has experienced membership fluctuations that indicate high-level shifts in the purpose of the party. Lenin believed in a small, tightly organized party, but after coming to power he realized that it would have to be much enlarged to penetrate a country as big as the Soviet Union. Membership growth, usually fostered by relaxing entrance requirements, has accompanied periods of mobilization, when the Kremlin wanted to generate mass enthusiasm to storm industrial targets or win World War II. Following these periods of expansion, however, usually come "purges"—the Russian is *chistka,* "cleansing"—by which the Kremlin tightens its control over the loyalty and obedience of party members.

Stalin's Great Purge of the 1930s was the most dramatic of these, but there have been others. In the 1950s, Zbigniew Brzezinski opined that purges were a permanent feature of Soviet politics, that they were a necessary part of the control system.

Since that time, however, there have been no bloody purges in the Soviet Union. Instead, expulsions have become the norm, and these are confined to lower-level party members who aren't active enough. Out of eighteen million CPSU members, some 30,000 to 40,000 are expelled each year. Occasional "exchanges of party documents," requiring members to turn in their cards for new ones, give party officials a chance to review members' qualifications and commitments. Some don't get new cards. At higher levels, practically no one is expelled from the party.

ARE THERE SOVIET INTEREST GROUPS?

In Britain, France, West Germany, and the United States, we are able to identify much in their politics as stemming from the clashes, relative strengths, and persuasiveness of interest groups. Interest-group politics are partly public and partly concealed. While most groups are organized and have official headquarters (usually in the nation's capital), only part of their activities are open and above board; most important work involves quiet contact with key elements in the bureaucracy.

Many Soviet observers believe there are competing Soviet interest groups, which act in approximately the same way. There is a very big difference, however: the public phase is missing. There is no Soviet Medical Association publicly advocating changes in Soviet health care. There is no Soviet Farm Bureau demanding help for farmers. There is no National Association of Soviet Manufacturers urging sound economic policies.

Instead of public and *voluntary* interest groups, as in the West, the Soviet union has *institutional* interest groups, that is, groups growing out of the way things are organized by the Soviet government. There are, for example, various health and agricultural ministries and dozens of ministries supervising manufacturing. Western (especially American) students of Soviet politics argue that each ministry develops a point of view and entrenched interests and that it battles for them with opposing ministries to win a bigger slice of the budget or funding of its favorite program.

We should be careful in equating interest-group activity in Soviet politics with such politics in the West. Our biggest problem here is scarcity of data. Western articles on Soviet interest groups are full of surmises, "probablys," and conjecture. One can't drop in on an interest-group office in Moscow to pick up their brochures or interview their officers. Instead, scholars must read between the lines of the Soviet press, notice which key personnel are transferred where, and calculate changes in budget and industrial organization to infer that interest-group politics are taking place.

We still don't know the importance of interest groups in the decisions of the Politburo. The ruling level of the party is doubtless influenced by the interests represented on it (military, secret police, light and heavy industries), but the Politburo rarely splits over a decision. Rather, British-style cabinet responsibility seems to be the rule. Here we are considering people who are dedicated to building up the Soviet Union and don't like other considerations to intrude.

Further, we must recognize that any interest-group activity takes place within the biggest and most powerful interest group of all, the Communist party, and that nothing that may weaken party control is apt to come out of interest-group conflicts. One of the charges against Khrushchev was that his economic and party reforms undermined party control; it was a damning accusation. Probably the second most important interest group is the military; what they want they usually get.

In sum, while it seems safe to say that there are Soviet interest groups, they are not as important as their Western counterparts. Soviet politics disdains pluralism and celebrates unity. We know there are conflicts within the Soviet leadership from time to time because we see losers periodically demoted or retired from office. But we can't be sure whether these conflicts are based on competing interests or are personal power struggles in which the participants *use* competing interests for political leverage. The way Stalin and Khrushchev consolidated their power was on the latter pattern; they used one coalition to come to power and then betrayed it.

If Soviet interest groups are allowed to become more autonomous and public in their viewpoints, it will mark a major relaxation of the Soviet political system. Hopes that this will happen soon, however, have been repeatedly disappointed.

Khrushchev: The Destalinizer

Faced with a Soviet Union that had petrified under Stalin, Nikita Khrushchev attempted to revitalize the system and get it moving down the road to communism again. He was only partly and briefly successful, for wide areas of the Soviet party and bureaucracy resisted him. We now realize that Khrushchev was far from the undisputed master of the Kremlin, the way Stalin was, and that he in fact had to balance many conflicting forces. Viewed in this way, Soviet political leadership resembles Western political leadership: both are balancing acts.

Born in 1894 of an ethnic Russian family living in the Ukraine, Khrushchev joined the Bolsheviks shortly after the revolution and worked his way up through party jobs. A protégé of Stalin, Khrushchev did some of the dictator's dirty work in the 1930s, which earned him a full Politburo membership in 1939. During the war he was made a political general and sent to the Ukrainian front. After the war he organized party work in the Ukraine and then the Moscow region, and carefully packed the party leadership with his supporters, the key to success in Soviet politics.

Stalin's death in 1953 opened a period of jockeying for power. All the Politburo was aware that Stalin had been a monster; they longed for stability and personal security. Accordingly, one of their first steps was to have the head of the secret police, Lavrenti Beria (like Stalin, a Georgian), arrested and shot. Ever since then, the KGB has been under party control. At first, the premier was Georgi Malenkov, who advocated relaxing the Stalin system and producing more consumer goods. But Khrushchev was made party first secretary, a post that has always been more powerful.

Khrushchev, who later adopted Malenkov's policies, craftily built a coalition against him. Malenkov was depicted as weak, nothing more than a "clerk," and was deposed in 1955. But it was not a Stalin-Trotsky type of struggle; Khrushchev merely had Malenkov demoted to minister for power stations. The Soviet leadership seems to have agreed that violent death is no way to run a political system; after all, anybody might be the next loser.

To consolidate his power, Khrushchev resorted to perhaps the most dramatic incident in CPSU's history: he denounced Stalin at a party congress. Khrushchev did this not so much to set the record straight or to clear his conscience but rather to trounce his enemies within the party. A party that was still Stalinist was immobile, incapable of reform or innovation. The productive potential of the Soviet Union lay under a blanket of fear and routine. To storm through, Khrushchev chose the direct route: get rid of the symbol of the whole system, Stalin.

At the Twentieth Party Congress in February 1956, Khrushchev delivered a stinging, hours-long tirade against the "crimes of Stalin," who, he said, had murdered thousands of party comrades and top military officers. Khrushchev neglected to mention his own role in the purges or the *millions* of nonparty people killed. The problem, claimed Khrushchev, was that Stalin had built a "cult of personality," something that must never be allowed again. The supposedly "secret" speech did have dramatic impact but not precisely in the intended way. Communist parties the world over had based themselves on Stalin-worship, and when the speech leaked out, all hell broke loose. A Hungarian uprising was crushed by Soviet tanks; a similar insurrection nearly happened in Poland. In the West, many long-time Communists resigned from the party. Most ominous of all, in China, Mao Zedong decided he couldn't trust someone who was undermining the Communist camp by denouncing its symbol.

Next, to revitalize the Soviet economy, Khrushchev proposed a sweeping decentralization. Outvoted in the Politburo, Khrushchev called a Central Committee meeting in 1957, packed with his supporters and backed up by the army, which forced his opponents to resign. They were designated the "antiparty group," but none were persecuted.

Unfortunately for Khrushchev, though, party leaders increasingly became irritated at his "hare-brained schemes" to boost production (especially of consumer goods), eliminate class differences (everyone would have to work before college, even the children of big-shots), and outfox the Americans by placing missiles in Cuba. To the West, at that time, Khrushchev appeared as simply another dictator, the "butcher of Budapest," and the man who banged his shoe on the table at the UN. His opponents in the Kremlin, however, considered him a reckless experimenter and liberalizer. In retrospect, the Khrushchev era brought major changes in both domestic and foreign policy.

In October 1964 the hitherto unthinkable happened: the leader of the Soviet Union was *voted* out of office by a majority of the Politburo who didn't like his economic and party "adventurism."

Khrushchev was a flamboyant, can-do character, who promised too much and delivered too little. The first Soviet leader to visit the United States, he saw in the Midwest the wonders of corn production and ordered wide regions of the USSR to convert to corn, even areas not suited to it. In his Virgin Lands program in Kazakh SSR, he ordered ploughing and planting. But rainfall is unreliable there, and after a few good harvests, much of the land turned into a dust bowl. By stressing consumer goods, he downplayed the traditional emphasis on heavy industry, and this infuriated both managers and the military. Culturally, he permitted the publication of anti-Stalin works (including Solzhenitsyn's *One Day*), then backed off when he felt things were getting out of hand.

We now see that Khrushchev was thrusting his bold ideas up against the ingrained conservatism of party *apparatchiki,* sometimes giving way to them and finally defeated by them. Politics is alive and well in the Soviet Union, even though it is not our brand of democratic politics.

THE PETRIFICATION PROBLEM

For a number of reasons we've discussed—police terror, the opportunism of the "new class," the status quo attitude of the party, and the muted interaction of interests—the Soviet Union has become an extremely conservative society, one governed by people who simply don't like change. Paradoxically, this society that boasts of its great revolution is conspicuously lacking in mechanisms for change. Consider the avenues for change that exist in Western countries: internal party revolts, elections that replace ruling parties, interest-group influence, public-opinion polls, and last but not least, the need for politicians to sound as if they're offering something new. These factors operate weakly or not at all in the Soviet political system. There are quiet expressions of group interest, the party constantly monitors public opinion (but keeps its findings secret), and an enthusiastic figure like Khrushchev may occasionally make extravagant promises of rapid improvement.

But outweighing everything is the bald fact that the Soviet Union is a gigantic bureaucracy, and bureaucracies are notoriously resistant to change. Bureaucracies work on the basis of established routines and have a tough time handling innovation.

This fact helps explain why so much of the Soviet Union is old-

Andropov and Chernenko: The Temporaries

Between the death of Brezhnev in 1982 and the installation of Gorbachev in 1985, the Soviet Union had two short-lived rulers: Yuri Andropov for 15 months and Konstantin Chernenko for 13 months. The two had some characteristics in common. Both were *apparatchiki* who had slowly worked their way up through the party under the patronage of powerful figures. Both came into the top job of party general secretary old and infirm—Andropov was 68 and Chernenko was 72—and both were medically incapacitated for much of their tenure. (An interesting point: doesn't the Soviet system have any way to retire or replace an incapacitated leader? Apparently not.)

But the two were rather different, and their differences may give a clue of things to come. Andropov was to some extent a protégé of Nikita Khrushchev; he was advanced to high positions under Khrushchev and was his ambassador in Budapest at the time of the 1956 Hungarian uprising. Later, as head of the KGB, he firmly crushed a budding dissident movement. But, like Khrushchev, he knew something had to be done about the flagging Soviet economy. During his brief tenure, he launched a fierce crackdown on the corruption and goofing off that plagued the economy and let circulate some ideas on economic decentralization to improve efficiency. Not a liberal, Andropov might be called a reformer or shaker-upper. As such, many young and liberally inclined Soviets welcomed Andropov and his efforts and were sorry to see him depart so soon.

Chernenko, on the other hand, was Brezhnev's protégé, and was a much more steady-as-she-goes figure than Andropov. Since their days together in Moldavia (next to Romania), Chernenko was rarely anything more than Brezhnev's assistant. He seemed to have been picked by the Politburo to succeed Andropov only as an interim figure; apparently Gorbachev was marked as the real comer. Chernenko let the anti-corruption drive continue, but did little else. There was no talk of reforms under Chernenko.

Do the two figures represent different tendencies within the Soviet leadership? Andropov was ready for change; Chernenko wasn't. Andropov—assisted by his protégé, Gorbachev—replaced one-fifth of the party's regional secretaries and nine of twenty-three Central Committee department heads. Chernenko left the party leadership untouched. The Soviet Communist party—or indeed any Communist party—permits no factions within its ranks, but tendencies are detectable.

fashioned: the organization of stores, clothing styles, industrial priorities, art, literature, and films.

Operating on the basis of rigid instructions, Soviet bureaucrats seldom dare to go beyond them or to apply them flexibly or creatively. "No instructions" is the typical answer Soviet officials give in facing new situations; that is, they do nothing. The result has been paralysis in many sectors of Soviet life.

To fight this tendency toward petrification, Soviet leaders in the past (especially Stalin) resorted to "storming," marshaling major economic resources to achieve one important project (build a dam, steel mill, or railroad), which was then called a "breakthrough." The technique was capable of generating temporary enthusiasm and innovation, but it invariably led to economic dislocations, and, once the project was finished, routine took over again. The Khrushchev era can be seen as a gigantic effort to "storm" the entire Soviet economy and break through to communism. The resentment this caused among the status-quo bureaucrats and *apparatchiki* led to Khrushchev's ouster.

The Brezhnev years represented a return to a kind of normalcy, but it is possible that a future Soviet leadership will again feel a need to shake up the conservative system and achieve breakthroughs. Yuri Andropov shook up the system by combating corruption during his brief tenure, but he, too, was incapacitated for most of the time. We may yet see another Khrushchev at the Soviet helm one day, for as long as petrification threatens the Soviet system, there will be periodic efforts to crash through it.

THE PERSONALITY CULT

Another recurring pattern in Soviet politics is the tendency to form a personality cult around the top leader. Stalin brought this to an absurd point during his lifetime—his portraits and statues were everywhere—and when Khrushchev denounced Stalin's "cult of personality" it seemed likely that such a thing would never happen again. Khrushchev refrained from building such a cult, but his successor, Brezhnev, allowed himself to be heroicized. While falling far short of the mass adulation of Stalin, Brezhnev was extensively quoted and praised in the Soviet media, his portraits were widely displayed, and he had made it clear he had no equals in the Soviet leadership.

The personality cult may be built into Communist systems. Leadership does not stay collegial for long; inevitably one person emerges as the top figure. Lenin wanted more obedience than consultation from his co-workers. Further, he found it convenient to let himself be turned into the symbol of the revolution. That way he could more easily mobilize and direct the masses to do his bidding. Mass worship helps silence critics and opponents within the ruling elite. Lenin, and later Stalin, began to resemble the tsars they overthrew; they claimed both temporal and spiritual infallibility and created a new caesaropapism. Not only were their policies the "correct" ones, but they were also "right" in their theoretical formulations on the decline of capitalism and growth of socialism.

Most Communist regimes manifest at least some personality cult, ranging from the godlike Kim Il Sung in North Korea to the grandfatherly Tito in

Yugoslavia. Such cults seem to be natural outgrowths of a personal rule that has no checks and balances to curb it. Power corrupts, and the power of the CPSU general secretary tends to become absolute. If a given party general secretary either cannot make his power absolute or chooses not to, then he may be vulnerable to ouster by opponents, as Khrushchev was. The moral of that 1964 episode seems to be that a Communist chief who fails to enshrine himself with a personality cult is making a mistake. Within days of taking power in 1984, for example, Chernenko's portrait, statements, and collected speeches adorned the Soviet Union.

Once in power—and buttressed by a personality cult that makes criticism of the leader out of bounds—Communist leaders tend to have lifetime tenure. Few retire before their deaths. In effect, they lock themselves in power and throw away the key. In so doing, they contribute to the tendency toward petrification.

SCAPEGOATING

Another seemingly permanent pattern in Communist politics is scapegoating, blaming an individual or group for the system's ills. Like personality cults, scapegoating seems to be built into the system. Unable to admit that their system itself generates problems (only capitalist systems do that), Communist leaders frequently vent their frustration on real or imaginary "saboteurs," "deviationists," "traitors," and "wreckers."

Stalin went through a gamut of scapegoats, including Trotskyites, *kulaks,* imperialist agents, "rootless cosmopolitans" (Jews), and various "enemies of the people" as his whim dictated. In what might be called historical justice, Khrushchev used the deceased Stalin as a scapegoat for everything that had gone wrong in the Soviet Union, from the purges to costly mistakes in the war. By 1961 Khrushchev had whipped up such an anti-Stalin frenzy that the party congress demanded removal of Stalin's body from the tomb where it lay next to Lenin's. In 1957, Khrushchev identified an "antiparty group" and had them expelled from the Politburo and party; they too were to blame for things going wrong.

It may be that the leaders of Communist countries never retire while still alive because they fear becoming the next scapegoat. Out of power they would be an irresistible and defenseless target that successors might use to deflect discontent from themselves and from the system. Because criticism of the overall system is not allowed, scapegoating is a regular phenomenon in Communist countries.

SOVIET LIBERAL AND CONSERVATIVE POLITICS

Some observers see two very general political viewpoints within the Soviet Union, the liberal and the conservative. No one is allowed to organize a faction or group to represent these viewpoints, of course, and they are not systematically articulated. Still, very roughly, Soviet political opinion can be divided along the following lines:

A Soviet liberal is more pragmatic; that is, he or she is willing to use whatever works, including ideas and techniques borrowed from the West, to move Soviet society forward. A liberal is willing to reinterpret Marx and Lenin, apply them flexibly. A Soviet conservative is more nationalistic, cautious about adapting anything from the West. A conservative sees ideology as a prop to the regime and to his position; changing or loosening it could have dangerous consequences.

Liberal and conservative attitudes spill over into foreign policy. The liberal, because he or she wants to borrow Western ways, is interested in *détente*, the relaxation of tensions between the Soviet Union and the West. The conservative would use détente only in a very limited way—to give the Soviet Union an advantage—while still pursuing a tough line toward the West. Soviet liberals see nothing wrong with Western contacts and encourage tourism and scientific and cultural exchanges. Conservatives still frown on Western contacts and would use them only to score propaganda points; Soviet citizens too eager for Western contacts are suspect.

Soviet liberals would loosen censorship, believing that honesty—for example, the revelations of Stalin's crimes—contributes to the building of socialism. To them a system that suppresses literature such as Pasternak's *Dr. Zhivago* is simply parading its fears, and the Soviet Union has no reason to be afraid. Conservatives, on the other hand, see danger in literary and artistic honesty; they might awaken discontent. Accordingly, conservatives would tighten censorship.

Along this same line, liberals tolerate some dissent, including the nationality question, seeing it as essentially harmless and perhaps even good that Soviet citizens can discuss questions as mature socialists. Conservatives would punish all dissent, especially on the nationality question, fearing that even mild criticism can undermine the system.

In economic terms, the liberal is interested in possible change from the present system, intrigued by ideas on decentralization, a partial market economy, and more emphasis on consumer goods. The conservative despises such suggestions as dangerous experimentation and would stick strictly to a centralized economy focusing on heavy industry. With economic reforms come political unraveling, he fears, pointing to Czechoslovakia's brief liberalization, which the Soviets crushed in 1968.

The figure who symbolizes the Soviet conservative viewpoint best is Stalin. That is why Stalin is still alive and well as a symbol in Soviet politics. The liberals lack a corresponding symbolic figure. Khrushchev was a halfway liberalizer; although he opened the door a little, he was afraid to open it all the way. With his forced retirement, his value as a liberal symbol evaporated.

The interesting thing about these liberal/conservative traits is that they hang together, although never perfectly. A Soviet liberal may still prefer a centralized economy, believing that with computers and scientific management techniques it can be made to produce what people need. A conservative may want détente with the West while preserving a firm hand in domestic matters.

Liberal and Conservative in Soviet Politics

LIBERALS	CONSERVATIVES
pragmatic	ideological
reinterpret Marx	orthodox Marxism
détente with West	tough toward West
encourage Western contacts	discourage Western contacts
loosen censorship	tighten censorship
permit some dissent	punish all dissent
decentralize economy	keep economy centralized
market economy	"command" economy
consumer goods	heavy industry
lighter military spending	heavier military spending
dislike Stalin	like Stalin

But in the main, Soviets are consistent in clinging to most or all of the liberal or conservative characteristics (see box).

This gives us a means of interpreting Soviet foreign and domestic policy. If a Soviet leader makes a sincere effort to increase consumer goods, some other policies logically follow. It means the economy must be decentralized and attuned to the market. It also means cutting military spending and borrowing some technology from the West; consequently there must be détente. With increased Western contacts it's impossible to keep a tight lid on dissent, so censorship recedes. Further, since this whole process raises eyebrows among Soviet conservatives, liberal leaders find that they must reinterpret what Marx and Lenin said in a pragmatic and flexible fashion.

Let us now turn in chapter 21 to some of the areas of disagreement in the Soviet Union.

VOCABULARY BUILDING

authoritarian	détente	motivation	scapegoating
careerism	incentives	New Class	storming
cult of personality	institutional interest group	petrification	totalitarian

FURTHER REFERENCE

Breslauer, George W. *Khrushchev and Brezhnev as Leaders: Building Authority in Soviet Politics.* Winchester, Mass.: Allen & Unwin, 1982.

Byrnes, Robert F., ed. *After Brezhnev: Sources of Soviet Conduct in the 1980s.* Bloomington: Indiana University Press, 1983.

Carrere D'Encausse, Helene. *Confiscated Power: How Soviet Russia Really Works.* New York: Harper & Row, 1982.

Colton, Timothy J. *The Dilemma of Reform in the Soviet Union.* New York: Council on Foreign Relations, 1984.

Dallin, Alexander. "Soviet Foreign Policy and Domestic Politics: A Framework for Analysis," in Erik P. Hoffmann and Frederic J. Fleron, Jr., eds., *The Conduct of Soviet Foreign Policy.* Chicago: Aldine, 1971.

Djilas, Milovan. *The New Class: An Analysis of the Communist System.* New York: Praeger, 1957.

Friedrich, Carl J., and Zbigniew Brzezinski. *Totalitarian Dictatorship and Autocracy.* New York: Praeger, 1961.

Hammer, Darrell. P. *The USSR: The Politics of Oligarchy,* 2d ed. Boulder, Colo.: Westview Press, 1986.

Harasymiw, Bohdan. *Political Elite Recruitment in the Soviet Union.* New York: St. Martin's Press, 1984.

Hough, Jerry F. "The Soviet System: Petrification or Pluralism?" *"Problems of Communism* (March–April 1972).

_____ **and Merle Fainsod.** *How the Soviet Union Is Governed.* Cambridge, Mass.: Harvard University Press, 1979.

Kelley, Donald R., ed. *Soviet Politics in the Brezhnev Era.* New York: Praeger, 1980.

Khrushchev, Nikita S. *Khrushchev Remembers,* trans. and ed. by Strobe Talbott. Boston: Little, Brown, 1970.

Matthews, Mervyn. *Privilege in the Soviet Union: A Study of Elite Life Styles Under Communism.* Winchester, Mass.: Allen & Unwin, 1979.

Medvedev, Roy. *Khrushchev.* New York: Doubleday, 1983.

Ryavec, Karl W. "Nikita Khrushchev and Soviet Politics: Reform or Revisionism?" in Edward Feit et al., eds., *Governments and Leaders: An Approach to Comparative Politics.* Boston: Houghton Mifflin, 1978.

Skilling, H. Gordon, and Franklyn Griffiths, eds. *Interest Groups in Soviet Politics.* Princeton, N.J.: Princeton University Press, 1971.

Wesson, Robert. *The Aging of Communism.* New York: Praeger, 1980.

21

WHAT
THE SOVIETS
QUARREL ABOUT

THE ECONOMY: SUCCESS OR FAILURE?

In absolute terms, the Soviet economy has performed impressively, transforming a backward country into the world's second-greatest industrial power (after the United States). The standard of living, while low for a major industrial power, is adequate and better than Russians have known before. Illiteracy has almost disappeared. Incomes are more nearly equal than in the United States.

But in relative terms—relative to other countries and most important to their aspirations—the Soviet economy has fallen short. Other countries have industrialized as fast or faster than the Soviet Union and without as much coercion. The standard Soviet reply to comments on their economic progress is to invoke the devastation of World War II: "If it hadn't been for the Hitler invasion, we'd be much further ahead today." After several decades, this excuse began to wear thin, especially as other war-devastated countries showed strong growth (Yugoslavia, East and West Germany, Finland).

The worst Soviet failure is in terms of their own promises and projections. The Soviet economy almost always falls short, and the targets of most Five-Year Plans have to be lowered in the third or fourth year. Khrushchev rashly promised the achievement of communism in twenty years; Soviet leaders avoid such promises now, but they still speak of economic growth.

Soviet consumers know better. They must stand in line for nearly everything. Some Soviets automatically get in any line that forms, figuring there must be something desirable at the end. Some will buy what they don't need in order to sell or swap it later. Depending on the season and luck of the harvest, Soviet housewives may spend several hours a week (in addition to a full-time job) waiting in food lines.

Earlier, the Soviet Union registered impressive gains. Why? Backward economies have certain advantages in terms of rapid growth. They can simply borrow foreign technology. They benefit from the statistical quirk that, starting from a low base, any gains show up as relatively large percentage increases. Goals are clear-cut and uncomplicated: push heavy industry, forget about everything else. But later, the situation becomes more complicated.

The first two Five-Year Plans brought major industrial growth. And for the postwar period, Soviet annual economic growth continued to average 5 to 6 percent, a very respectable performance. During the 1970s, however, it slowed, and in the early 1980s, some sectors showed negative growth. Energy and manpower shortages plus poor labor productivity had set some grim limits and hard choices before Soviet economic planners.

TO CENTRALIZE OR DECENTRALIZE?

The Stalinist economic system could be characterized as crude centralization. All major decisions were made in Moscow but with little more than guesswork, hopes, and bargaining with factory managers to go on. Data were incomplete and inaccurate. Managers downplayed their plants' abilities so they could more easily fulfill their targets. Raw materials were often misallocated, and managers had to employ *blat* (influence or connections) and unofficial "pushers" to arrange swaps with other factories. Beneath the façade of rational, centralized planning lurked a mess of wheeling and dealing, bad investments, and chronic production bottlenecks.

Memorable Russian Slogans: "Communism Is Soviet Power Plus the Electrification of the Whole Country"

Lenin's formula for communism, shortly after the Bolsheviks took over, simplified for mass consumption the idea that industrial growth under party supervision would lead to a utopia. It gave people something tangible and optimistic to focus on.

Khrushchev, who inherited the mess, was determined to clean it up and get the Soviet economy moving toward communism. Under him, an important and lively public debate started over which direction the Soviet economy should turn, toward stricter and more scientific centralization or toward some kind of decentralization. From time to time, the debate reappears, as it did in 1983 with the circulation of a memo by a group of economists associated with the prestigious Academy of Sciences that urged reducing the powers of bureaucrats and increasing plant-level initiative.

Marx never specified whether the economy of the socialist state should be centralized or decentralized. Marx expected that eventually the state would "wither away" as its coercive power would no longer be needed in the absence of social classes. That seems to imply he foresaw decentralization. It has been a general socialist predilection, though, for the state to supervise the economy through nationalization and planning. Marxist thinkers have never been able to say conclusively which is the correct Marxist approach, to centralize or decentralize the socialist economy.

The great question within Communist countries is, "How much centralization?" The centralist argument can be stated like this: Only by strict control and planning can we achieve socialist goals, prevent a revival of capitalism, and direct resources into key sectors. This is the course followed by Soviet Union and several of its satellites.

The decentralist argument might be the following: A modern economy is so complex that it cannot be centrally controlled without creating more confusion than solutions. Futhermore, centralization gives rise to Stalinist-type abuses of power. By decentralizing, by giving individual factories the power to make their own choices based on profit and market, we not only get better growth but are following Marx's idea on the "withering away" of the state. This is the course taken by Yugoslavia. Some other East European countries and China have introduced decentralizing moves.

The Soviet Union also considers decentralist notions (see box, "The Liberman Proposals") but has generally stayed well on the centralist side, albeit with changes. Soviet economics has become a lot more scientific. Under Stalin, and even for years afterward, Soviet leaders sneered at capitalist economic techniques involving input-output tables, linear programming, mathematics, and computers. But these are precisely the tools needed to run a centralized, socialist economy.

Comparing: Socialism, Hungarian Style

The Czechoslovaks made the mistake of reforming too fast in 1968, giving the Soviets the impression they were abandoning socialism. The Soviets invaded and crushed the "Prague spring." At about this same time, slow and sneaky, the Hungarians were implementing wide-ranging reforms that make the small land the most pleasant of Eastern Europe.

Under Hungary's New Economic Mechanism, collective farmers run their enterprises like businesses, for profits. Industries too must earn a profit and can fire unproductive workers (impossible in the Soviet Union). Restaurants and other small businesses can be private. Explained a top Hungarian banker, "Marx never talked against profit but only against who got the profit." Soviet leaders, impressed by Hungarian food shops, sometimes mention learning some of the techniques used in Hungary.

Gradually a new breed of Soviet economists has emerged willing to borrow Western techniques and computers in order to better direct the Soviet economy. Especially hungry for American computers, the new Soviet managers are probably as schooled in econometrics—the application of math and statistics to economics—as their MBA counterparts in the United States. They have an almost mystical faith in the power of computers to propel Soviet industry forward.

For the time being, these scientific centralizers are in the ascendancy, but the economic debate is not settled. On the one side are still party *apparatchiki* who fear the erosion of their power by economic technicians. The larger Soviet hierarchy is still conservative and skeptical of borrowing Western-style management techniques. On the other side are decentralizers who think that even with computers a totally centralized economy is clumsy. With poor Soviet economic performance in the 1980s and bitter citizen complaints about consumer goods and food, the debate is likely to show renewed life.

INVEST OR CONSUME?

Economists draw a distinction between capital goods and consumer goods. Capital goods are those which produce other things—such as lathes, steel mills, and tractors. Consumer goods are those which are simply used for themselves—such as apartments, clothes, and bicycles. For a developing country, choosing between the two can be agonizing. If they put their limited funds into consumer goods, they may make people happy in the short run but fail to produce enough in the long run. If they put their money into capital goods, although laying the basis for future prosperity they deny their people what they need right now. Countries that choose to emphasize the former may be easygoing and relaxed, but they may also fall behind countries that choose the latter.

Stalin had no trouble making the choice. Seeing a backward Russia surrounded by enemies, he ordered maximum formation of capital with minimum

The Liberman Proposals

In 1962, amidst Khruschev's efforts to reform and re-invigorate the Soviet system, an economics professor, Yevsei Liberman, was permitted to voice his ideas in the pages of *Pravda* (the daily newspaper of the CPSU). His proposals were startling: Soviet factories should start using profit and marketability as a basis for economic calculations. What seems normal to us set off a three-year public debate in the Soviet Union, where "profit" has been considered dirty capitalist exploitation.

Instead of profit, Soviet factories had been using *gross output* as their measure. For example, if *Gosplan* called for so many tons of nails, nail factories tried to produce that many tons. They did this by making mostly large nails, so they could more easily reach their tonnage target. It didn't matter what consumers wanted; the plan specified only how many tons. If the plan called for so many million pairs of shoes, shoe factories tried to crank out that many and were indifferent to style or comfort. (For years Soviet shoes were distinguishable by their loud squeaks.) The factory had to pay no attention to customer wishes; it didn't even care whether the shoes sold as long as the plan was fulfilled.

The result was poor-quality products, outmoded designs, and no attention paid to sales or service. Liberman's proposals would have changed all that. By making profit the basis, factories would have to produce what people wanted. A market system would emerge. Factories making their own decisions would mean economic decentralization. Liberman's proposals would have brought a major reorganization of the Soviet economic system.

Some Soviet economists liked these ideas that sought to borrow the best of capitalism and use it to build socialism. Some of the East European satellites (East Germany and Hungary) quietly implemented reforms along the lines Liberman suggested. East Germany's New Economic System became a big success.

But many Soviets, especially party people, detested the notion of reform. In the first place, it threatened to undermine the guiding role of the party and its bureaucrats. If profits and marketability determined production, what role would they have? Futher, party people said the proposals were un-Marxist and would contaminate Soviet socialism. The directors of heavy industry feared the reforms would take away their privileged position within the Soviet economy; more emphasis would be placed on consumer goods. By the same token, the Soviet military, an important pressure group, worried that it would mean a shift away from war-related production.

What it boiled down to was this: the Liberman proposals meant change, and the cautious bureaucrats who run the Soviet Union hate change. Khrushchev was ousted in 1964. A watered-down version of the Liberman proposals was implemented in a few factories in 1965 but dropped almost immediately. Liberman's ideas were simply too threatening to the Soviet establishment and so were quietly put to sleep. The Liberman episode illustrates again, however, that political quarrels do take place in the Soviet Union, some of them in public.

outlay for consumption. These were the early Five-Year Plans, designed to make the Soviet Union a military and industrial power quickly. While capital accumulation soared, individual consumption declined—that is, the standard of living actually fell.

The 1941 Nazi invasion convinced many Soviets that Stalin had done the right thing, for without his forced industrialization the Soviet Union would have succumbed. But the intense "storming" of capital-goods construction couldn't go on forever without giving people some incentive. As the slogans wore thin and coercion lost its punch, Soviet workers started demanding more food and consumer goods. By the time Khrushchev took over, he realized that Soviet workers needed more material incentives to get them to produce. Over the next two decades, the Soviet standard of living increased greatly. Soviet consumers did not become content, however; on the contrary, they became more demanding and frustrated that the system was not keeping up with their expectations. Further, the investment in consumer goods cut into investment in capital goods. The managers of heavy industry (especially steel producers) formed a de facto lobby to oppose the shift; Khrushchev derisively called them "metal eaters."

To shift from capital to consumer goods would be a major change in the Soviet system. It would mean putting the consumer in first place, American style, rather than building the future, Soviet style. There is a certain amount of fear that "consumerism" (a pejorative term in Soviet parlance) could get out of hand. Once people started getting enough to eat and wear they became more picky and demanding. And if Soviet planners fulfilled all consumer wishes, there would be nothing left for capital growth and military spending. Consumers are far from kings in the Soviet Union, but now that their appetites have been whetted their demands are increasingly a factor in Soviet economic planning. Failure to obtain adequate food and consumer goods robs Soviet workers of the incentive to produce, and this in turn means fewer foodstuffs and consumer goods.

Who Does Socialism Right?

Wharton Econometrics estimated per capita GNP for East European countries in 1983 as follows:

East Germany	$7,513
Czechoslovakia	6,627
Romania	4,550
Hungary	4,239
Bulgaria	3,987
Poland	3,698
Soviet Union	3,399

Within its own bloc, the USSR is the *poorest* nation, a point that irritates the Soviets. They feel they are providing free security for better-off socialist comrades who don't even say thanks. Instead, from time to time East European satellites try to depart from the Soviet embrace: East Germany in 1953, Hungary in 1956, Czechoslovakia in 1968, and Poland in 1980. What do these comrades want? How could we be nicer to them?

The differences are also a reproach, for they indicate that other countries can do a better job managing a socialist economy. The East Germans are particularly proud of their achievements when they tour the Soviet Union. One East German lathe operator, unimpressed by Kiev, told me, "If you want to see real socialism, come to our German Democratic Republic."

GUNS OR BUTTER?

Not only has Soviet industry been skewed toward metals, it has also been big on defense. Soviet generals favor heavy industry because that is what produces military equipment (guns, tanks, shells). Accordingly, the Soviet military has always been reluctant to see the economy shift too much in the consumer-goods direction. Under Stalin, heavy industry was synonymous with war production.

A good portion of Soviet production is siphoned off by the military. Just how much the Soviets spend on defense is secret; as a portion of their gross national product, estimates range up to 18 percent, some two to three times what the United States spends in proportion to its GNP. It is said that the Soviet military actually stations people at the end of production lines to skim off the best products; the inferior stuff is left to civilian consumers.

In economic terms, armaments are literally worthless; they are neither capital goods nor consumer goods; that is, they can neither produce more things nor satisfy consumer needs. They are a net drain on an economy. One reason for Japan's and West Germany's economic miracles is that they spend relatively little on defense, relying on the United States to protect them. The Soviets will never score an economic breakthrough with so heavy a defense burden, but voices in the Politburo calling for real (as opposed to propagandistic) cuts in military spending have been largely silent since Khrushchev's ouster.

AGRICULTURE: THE ACHILLES HEEL

Soviet agriculture is in poor shape. Long lines outside food shops are common. Two forces conspire: geography and Communist farm policy. Soil conditions, rainfall, and warm weather are simply not as reliable in the Soviet Union as they are in the great American grain belt. Rather than steady and predictable agricultural output, Soviet farm production resembles an uneven fever chart of ups and downs.

And collectivized agriculture makes nature's shortcomings worse. The peasants entered into collective farms only reluctantly—sometimes at gunpoint. No longer owners of private lands and livestock, on the collective there was little incentive to work hard. The government took much of the crop at low prices. Until recently, the income of Soviet farmers lagged far below that of factory workers. Under Stalin, life for many Soviet farmers was a form of forced labor.

Although much better now, things are still far from good. Farm workers still tend to put in unenthusiastic days in collective work and save their energy for their own private plots. Most farm families are allowed to use an acre or two to grow produce for their own table. Not only do they do that, they actually produce one third of the country's meat, milk, and vegetables, just under two-thirds of the potatoes, and about 40 percent of the fruits and eggs (and all this on about 4 percent of the total sown land). Much of what they produce they sell privately. Rather than work for scanty reward on the collective enterprise, they prefer to work for themselves on their private plots. Some believe the Soviet Union could end its food shortages merely by allowing peasants to double the size of their private plots.

Kolkhoz versus Sovkhoz

The first form of Soviet farm collectivization was the *kolkhoz* (short for collective farm), which simply forced peasants to merge their holdings and work them in common. The *kolkhoz,* however, operates as a business, trying to make a profit and paying its members according to the number of "labor days" they accumulate during the year.

More recently, the *sovkhoz* (for state farm) has become the preferred unit, and their number has been growing. The *sovkhoz* is run like a state industry. Labor is paid wages, like in a factory. *Sovkhoz* workers often live in apartments rather than individual houses. The Soviet leaders believe the *sovkhoz* is a more advanced form than the *kolkhoz* and seem to be gradually phasing out the latter.

But this idea is controversial. In the Soviet Union, "bigger" is better, "private" is bad, and "collective" is good. To openly admit the importance of private plots would constitute an admission of the failure of collectivized agriculture. More private farming would also mean that thousands of agricultural bureaucrats would become superfluous. Typically, Moscow restricts private plots when harvests are good, then permits their expansion when harvests are bad. Ideally, Soviet chiefs would like to get rid of private farming, but they know they can't.

Inefficient for an industrialized country, Soviet agriculture employs some 20 percent of the Soviet work force (compared to 2 percent in the United States). This could be remedied, at least in part, by making a greater investment in farm mechanization and wage incentives for farmers. Money that goes to agriculture, however, would have to come from someplace else, such as consumer goods or military spending. Until the Kremlin is prepared to make major reforms in agriculture, it will be stuck with a defective agricultural system.

WHAT DO THE DISSIDENTS WANT?

Much is said in the media about Soviet dissidents, but bear in mind that out of a Soviet population of over a quarter billion people, only a few thousand could be called open and active dissidents. As we discussed, most Soviet citizens are "hardhat" patriots who dislike protesters. Valery Chalidze, a Soviet dissident now living in the United States, claims a great many Soviets, especially educated people, have an "oppositionist" attitude toward the regime, but they keep quiet about their dissatisfactions. It takes enormous courage to go public with criticism of the system or regime. Punishment can range from loss of job to psychiatric confinement to Siberian labor camps.

Not only are Soviet dissidents numerically weak, they are also fragmented into several different groups and do not form a single united front. In addition to the non-Russian nationalities about whom we'll speak later, there are at least three different dissident factions:

Religious Traditionalists: Exemplified by Solzhenitsyn, discussed earlier, a minority of dissidents morally reject the entire Soviet system and would like to recover Russia's spiritual roots and Orthodox Christianity from previous centuries. Although they lack a practical program, these Russian Christians serve as examples of personal strength for other dissidents.

Anti-Stalinist Leninists: Arguing that the present Soviet regime is a Stalinist perversion of Lenin's intentions, dissidents like Roy Medvedev (whose father was killed in Stalin's purges) hold that the original impulses toward both socialism and democracy can be revived. Expelled from the party but never seriously punished for his views, Medvedev criticizes the regime from the Marxist viewpoint that the present system can be made to work right if the party is democratized internally. He would not embrace Western-style liberal democracy, however. His viewpoint too represents a small minority of dissidents.

Westernizing Liberals: Probably the largest dissident faction, liberals would like to democratize the Soviet Union along Western lines, with a free press, political opposition, and guaranteed human and civil rights. Exemplified by Andrei Sakharov (see box), these liberals want as a first step the formal legal rights set forth in the Soviet constitution and pledged in the 1975 Helsinki agreement. Just as Solzhenitsyn is a descendant of the old Slavophiles, the liberals are the descendants of the old Westernizers. People like Sakharov harken not to Russia's past or to an idealistic Leninism but to the traditions and institutions of Western democracy. As such, the Sakharov liberals attract some sympathy among the *intelligentsia,* but they strike no responsive chords among the Soviet masses.

Cooperation among three such disparate groups with such incompatible goals is difficult. In a free democracy, the three strands would represent, respectively, the right, left, and center of the political spectrum. Under present circum-

Andrei Sakharov: The Conscience of Russia

A super-brilliant physicist, Andrei Sakharov zoomed to the top of the scientific establishment for his work on the first Soviet hydrogen bomb. Elected a member of the prestigious Academy of Sciences at the unheard of age of 32, Sakharov seemed to have everything a Soviet citizen could want: apartments, a limousine, honors, and a direct line to the country's leaders.

During the 1950s, though, he began to develop moral qualms about the atmospheric testing of nuclear weapons. Aware of the health hazards of such tests, in 1958 he urged that they be called off. By 1961 he was on the phone to Khrushchev to beg him to cancel a gigantic 50-megaton explosion. Nobody listened, and Sakharov grew more and more critical of the Soviet system as a whole.

By the mid-1960s Sakharov was criticizing many aspects of Soviet life, especially the restrictions on science laid down by the regime. In 1968 he went public with a manifesto for intellectual freedom that was published in the West. For this he was fired from his research jobs (but stayed a member of the Academy).

Gradually Sakharov became the Soviet equivalent of British writer John Stuart Mill, who in the nineteenth century argued that liberty is not only moral but the basis for all social, political, and scientific progress. Cut off the free exchange of ideas, Mill believed, and human progress grinds to a halt. This was precisely what Sakharov began to fear for the Soviet Union.

By the 1970s Sakharov was a bitter critic of the Soviet system, which he described as "the most refined form of totalitarian-socialist society"—closed, corrupt, cynical, and inhuman. Of special concern to Sakharov is the plight of the Soviet Union's non-Russian nationalities, many of whom have been cruelly treated by the regime; like Solzhenitsyn, he feels they should be allowed their independence. Sakharov also worries about Soviet militarism and fears a thermonuclear war; his work on these issues won him the 1975 Nobel Peace Prize (which he was not allowed to go to Stockholm to receive).

The Communist regime tolerated Sakharov because of his high status in the Soviet and world scientific community. His small Moscow apartment became a meeting place and information clearinghouse for the Soviet dissident movement. Sakharov personally went to dissident trials and prison camps to gather information. For Western news correspondents, Sakharov and his network of friends were a pipeline to dissident activity.

Finally, in 1980, the Kremlin lost its patience. Sakharov condemned the Soviet invasion of Afghanistan (just as he had the 1968 invasion of Czechoslovakia) and urged other countries not to participate in the 1980 Moscow Olympics. Sakharov was arrested by the KBG (for the first time) and banished to Gorky, a city about 250 miles (400 kilometers) east of Moscow that is off limits to foreigners.

The Kremlin hoped that isolation would silence Sakharov. But even from exile another Sakharov message was smuggled out:

I am for a pluralistic, open society...for convergence, disarmament and peace; for the defense of human rights in the whole world...for a worldwide amnesty for prisoners of conscience; for doing away with the death penalty. I am for giving priority to problems of peace, the problem of averting thermonuclear war.

stances they are united on only two points: all want freedom of expression for everyone, and all hold each other in considerable personal esteem, whatever their differences.

One crucial point, for example, on which dissidents disagree is U.S. trade restrictions against the Soviet Union. Some, such as Medvedev, argue that American demands merely strengthen the hand of Politburo hardliners, that when faced with Western hostility, Soviet leaders dig in their heels and crack down even harder on dissidents. By pursuing a consistently conciliatory line, this view argues, the West will give reformist and liberal tendencies inside the party a chance to assert themselves. Henry Kissinger's détente policy held the promise of inducing major change in the Kremlin, according to this view.

Most Soviet dissidents, however, are not nearly so optimistic about alleged latent CPSU liberalism, especially in the Politburo. All the CPSU seems to understand is toughness. When they do something unusually beastly, this view argues, only Western embargoes and boycotts get the message through. By showing the Kremlin that the West is strong and resolute, this branch of dissident opinion holds, you may in the long run induce some change and force them to ease up on dissidents. Accordingly, the tough line of President Reagan toward the Soviet Union meets with approval in this group.

Neither case can be demonstrated as valid. Proponents of a soft Western line can argue that détente was not pursued long enough to take effect. Those in favor of a tough Western line are unable to offfer examples of its effectiveness. It may be that the Kremlin is not particularly responsive to any Western line, hard or soft, but makes policy largely on the basis of domestic considerations.

THE NATIONALITIES PROBLEM

Curiously, just as West Germany has a problem with Turks, so the Soviet Union has a problem with its large and rapidly growing Moslem-Turkic peoples of Central Asia. Russians, like Germans, have few babies; Moslems in both countries have lots. Unlike Russians, Soviet Moslems shun alcohol and abortion. From 1959 to 1979, the Russian population in the Soviet Union fell from 54.6 to 52.4 percent, while the Moslem-Turkic population rose from 12.6 to 17.4 percent. Because they are younger, the Moslems provide about one Soviet draftee in four, although they are used mostly for labor battalions rather than combat units, a suggestion the Kremlin doesn't quite trust them.

Is there cause to worry? During the 1920s, anti-Soviet Moslem guerrillas called *basmachi* fought the Communists for years. Although the Soviet Union is opposed to all religions, it treads lightly in dealing with Islam, which is practiced freely. The eruption of Islamic fundamentalism to the south must give Kremlin chiefs sleepless nights. This is believed to be one reason the Soviets invaded Afghanistan in late 1979; if the anti-Communist Afghan insurgents won, the *basmachi* could start all over again. At first the Soviets used Moslem troops—some of whom speak the same languages as Afghans—but withdrew them when they started swapping their Kalashnikovs for Korans.

Soviet theory since Lenin has been that with economic, cultural, and social growth, the nationality problem would gradually disappear; a "new Soviet man" would arise. A great deal of Soviet investment has gone into backward regions to equalize their economic levels with the wealthier ones. In addition to economic growth, the Soviet Union has fostered cultural, linguistic, and social upgrading. Some Soviet nationalities were so backward they were hardly aware of themselves as a nationality and lacked a written language. The Soviets "woke up" these nationalities, taught them that they had a distinctive language and culture, and liberated them from the conservative hand of traditional elites. Bright locals, schooled in the Russian language, could take over as new, revolutionary elites.

Did all this add up to bringing the nationalities of the Soviet Union closer together, as planned? Not precisely. Ironically, just as the British and French inadvertently taught nationalism to their colonial subjects, so did the Soviets to their non-Russian nationalities. By "waking up" the Central Asians, the Soviets created new problems.

One problem takes us back to economics. The Soviets have elevated economic growth to a moral precept: that economy which grows fastest is morally the best. Further, on the practical level, the higher the economic development the greater the rewards for consumers. But investment funds for growth are limited. What one republic gets another doesn't get. If you put a lot of money into Kazakhstan, you're putting less into Lithuania. The result is jealousy and competition among republics for scarce resources.

Further, now that the Soviets have replaced traditional elites with vigorous local Communists, these local party people start demanding a primary role in republic leadership. Before, many of the top jobs in the outlying republics and autonomous areas were staffed by ethnic Russians; they were more highly educated and more reliable. But with ethnic locals now raised on the party spirit and also well educated, the nationalities have started resenting Moscow's continued guidance.

Can the Firing Squad Cure Corruption?

In 1984, the director of Moscow's best food store, Gastronom 1, was executed for corruption. He had accepted some $2 million in bribes from customers eager for scarce foodstuffs. The play the story got in *Izvestia,* the government newspaper, indicated the regime of Konstantin Chernenko wished to carry on the anticorruption drive initiated by Yuri Andropov.

But would it do any good? Soviets say the entire economy works by means of bribes. Food—especially meat—and desirable consumer goods often don't appear on store shelves; they are sold through the back door at inflated prices to friends and benefactors. Soviet elites utilize this arrangement to live well, and it makes average Soviet citizens jealous and angry.

A former Soviet lawyer, Konstantin Simis, who now lives in the United States, says that virtually all factory managers pay bribes to get raw materials, equipment, and transportation. Some of Simis's stories are out of Gogol: one firm put nonexistent workers on the payroll to get their salaries; their names came from a local graveyard. At the Moscow crematorium, corpses were first stripped of clothes and dental gold, which were sold on the black market.

Corruption in the Soviet Union is structural, a combination of scarcity and state control. Bureaucracy and corruption were born twins. The only cure is to cut back the bureaucracy and bring in a market economy, and this the Kremlin is not about to do. Firing squads are to corruption as lawn mowers are to weeds.

The central authorities have repeatedly had to slap down signs of "nationalism" or "nationalist deviation" among party leaders in the outlying republics. As one party report put it: "In Abkhazia a half-baked 'theory' according to which responsible posts should be filled only by representatives of the indigenous nationality has gained a certain currency...."Every few years, leaders at the republic level are removed with hints they were fostering local nationalism. In sum, development has meant more local nationalism and has made it harder for the many Soviet nationalities to draw together to form a cohesive whole. There are, under the Soviet surface, seething resentments against rule from Moscow, the immigration of ethnic Russians, and in some cases the remembrance of past injustices, such as Stalin's deportations of whole nationalities.

ETHNIC NATIONALISM AND DISSENT: AN EXPLOSIVE COMBINATION

The greatest potential for trouble in the Soviet Union is where nationality problems became linked to dissidence, where ethnic resentment ties in with dissidents' rejection of the Soviet system. In fact, members of unhappy nationalities probably contribute the bulk of Soviet dissidents. An ethnic Russian who dislikes the system may keep his or her thoughts confined to a small group of friends; after all, the Russians are the top dogs of the Soviet system, and most Russians approve of it. A Lithuanian, Ukrainian, or Jew feels less restraint in speaking out if he or she feels the system is unjust. Accordingly, the non-Russian nationalities of the Soviet Union are the natural breeding grounds for dissidence.

Some non-Russian nationalities feel like conquered and occupied countries. The Baltic republics—Lithuania, Latvia, and Estonia—gained their freedom from tsarist Russia in World War I only to be swallowed up by Stalinist Russia in 1940. Speaking non-Slavic languages (Lithuanian and Latvian are Baltic tongues, Estonian is close to Finnish) and following non-Orthodox religions (Roman Catholic in Lithuania, Protestant in Latvia and Estonia), the Baltic states have kept alive a strong sense of the cultural differences that separate them from Russians. They fear that ethnic Russian immigration may destroy their native cultures. Lithuanian Catholic dissidents—fired by both nationalism and religion—are reputed to be the bravest among Soviet dissidents.

The second-largest nationality of the Soviet Union also harbors resentment: the Ukrainians. Long treated as the breadbasket of Russia, the Ukraine was the scene of some of the bitterest resistance to farm collectivization. When the Germans invaded in 1941, they found that many Ukrainians welcomed them as liberators; an entire Ukrainian army division even changed to the German side. The Soviets are quietly nervous about continued Ukrainian nationalism. It has been said that one reason for the 1968 Soviet invasion of Czechoslovakia was to stop the bacillus of change from crossing the border into the Ukraine. There have been reports of anti-Soviet riots in the Ukraine.

Jews are the best known of Soviet dissidents. Government policy toward them can be described as semiofficial anti-Semitism. Many Jews welcomed the revolution—the tsarist government was rabidly anti-Semitic—and Jews served the Bolshevik regime in high places. Stalin, however, didn't trust them; he thought Jews were too "cosmopolitan," meaning they had foreign contacts. Jews are under peculiar pressure in the Soviet Union. On the one hand they are forced to be Jews—the internal passports required of all citizens give their nationality as *Yevrei* (Hebrew)—but on the other hand they aren't allowed to be Jews—the practice of their religion is sharply restricted and Hebrew instruction is not allowed. This bind persuades many Soviet Jews to seek emigration to Israel or the United States. During the 1970s, more than a quarter of a million Jews left, including some of the Soviet Union's most talented artists, writers, musicians, and scientists. Those who stay face increasing anti-Semitism—the regime calls it "anti-Zionism"—that keeps their children out of universities, high positions in the military or important government jobs. At times, Soviet anti-Semitism, in the form of officially sanctioned books and pictures, reaches Nazi-like proportions.

Referring to the many different nationalities kept locked within tsarist rule, Lenin called Russia the "prison of nations." In many ways the present Soviet Union is still a prison of nations. Under the right circumstances, some dissidents suggest, the prisoners could rebel.

PETRIFIED

The Soviet system is petrified, in two senses of the term: (1) it resists change, and (2) its rulers are frozen in fear. Most Western observers agree that something has to give before long. But at the same time, most also agree that the tens of thousands of party bureaucrats—the "little Stalins"—fear and hate any change. Loosen one thread, they argue, and the whole system will unravel, as in Poland.

Could it? Predictions of the imminent collapse of the Soviet system are unwarranted. Russians are used to tightening their belts and accepting harsh authority. Too many Soviets have too much at stake in maintaining the system. Still, under the right circumstances radical change could occur. The late Andrei Amalrik suggested that a war with China could trigger an uprising among the non-Russian nationalities. A free labor movement, perhaps inspired by Poland's Solidarity, could galvanize the mass of discontented Soviet workers. It was for this reason that Moscow had to crush Solidarity. Productivity could slump so low and the economy fall so far behind that bright, younger communists could seize power and institute reforms. Moslem unrest could prompt Russian nationalists in the army to take over; the Red Army is known as a hotbed of Russian—not Soviet—chauvinism.

But the Kremlin chiefs are not fools; they are capable of backing down in the face of danger. As Lenin said, a true Bolshevik must be prepared to "take one step backward for the sake of taking two steps forward." Chances are the Soviet system will survive by the judicious choice of a younger leader who will make some reforms but won't threaten the entrenched hierarchy. Mikhail Gorbachev—who was only 54 in 1985, a mere kid in Politburo terms—took over in 1985 as if he had been groomed for the job.

Gorbachev: The New Generation

Since Brezhnev, the Soviet Union had been ruled by a gerontocracy that was more concerned with safeguarding the positions of the Communist elite than in propelling the Soviet Union forward. Suddenly, a new generation of Soviet leaders began to take over. Brezhnev died at age 75 in 1982, Andropov at 69 in 1984, and Chernenko at 73 in 1985. Symbolizing an impatient, younger generation, Mikhail Sergeyevich Gorbachev, age 54, was named the Soviet Union's seventh chief a scant four hours after the announcement of his predecessor's death.

Gorbachev (sounds like "garbage OFF") had long been tipped as the likely choice. He had been given important and visible posts for some years and was even rumored to be in line to follow Andropov, his longtime mentor. On a 1984 trip to Britain—accompanied by his trim and attractive wife—Gorbachev exuded charm and self-confidence, tacitly letting the world know he was the heir to Kremlin power. "I like Mr. Gorbachev," said Prime Minister Thatcher, "I can do businss with him."

Born into a peasant family in the North Caucasus in 1931, Gorbachev graduated from Moscow University's law school in 1955 but immediately returned to his home area for party work. As party chief of Stavropol province in 1970, he made a good impression on Brezhnev, who summoned him to Moscow in 1978 to become a party secretary with responsibility for overseeing agriculture. (Gorbachev had taken another degree, in agronomy, by correspondence.) Something curious happened: the Soviet Union suf-

fered a string of bad harvests, but Gorbachev didn't catch any blame. This suggests that the top Soviet leadership recognizes that they have a defective agricultural system in need of change. It further suggests that Gorbachev may institute a shakeup in Soviet agriculture.

Gorbachev at this time was under the wing of Andropov, head of the KGB, and Mikhail Suslov, a Politburo kingmaker who was also from Stavropol. Gorbachev was elected to the party's Central Committee in 1971, to candidate member of the Politburo in 1979, and to full member in 1980. When Andropov took over in 1982, Gorbachev assisted him closely, and implemented his tough anti-corruption policies.

Gorbachev is believed to share Andropov's concern over Soviet economic stagnation and is willing to reform the economy by means of decentralization and incentives. Gorbachev told party workers in 1984: "We will have to carry out profound transformations in the economy and in the entire system of social relations." Could Gorbachev be the shaker-upper many Soviets have been waiting for? In a 1984 speech to the Central Committee, he said: "Inertia of thinking, as a rule, generates inertia in practical deeds. Questioning and creativity, sensitivity to new phenomena and processes, the decisive eradication of formalism, red tape, and idle talk—such are the demands of life on all workers on the ideological front." It looked like the new generation was getting set to make some changes.

The new generation of Soviet leadership faces some knotty problems, for the Soviet system is fraught with "contradictions," a Marxist term to describe structural problems in capitalist countries. Ironically, "contradictions" describes the Soviet Union, a country that has tried to impose an advanced, complex system on a backward, undisciplined population. Coercion, inefficiency, and uneven development must accompany such an attempt. To see how an even more backward country has tried to utilize Marxism-Leninism to leap over entire historical epochs to a radiant future, let us now turn to China.

VOCABULARY BUILDING

Baltic republics	consumption	innovation	private plots
blat	decentralization	*kolkhoz*	russification
capital	détente	nationality	*sovkhoz*
centralization	econometrics	prison of nations	

FURTHER REFERENCE

Alexeyeva, Ludmilla. *Soviet Dissent: Contemporary Movements for National, Religious, and Human Rights.* Middletown, Conn.: Wesleyan University Press, 1985.

Amalrik, Andrei. *Will the Soviet Union Survive until 1984?* rev. ed. New York: Harper & Row, 1981.

Anti-Defamation League of B'nai B'rith. *Anti-Semitism in the Soviet Union.* New York: Anti-Defamation League, 1984.

Babyonyshev, Alexander, ed. *On Sakharov.* New York: Knopf, 1983.

Carrere D'Encausse, Helene. *Decline of an Empire: The Soviet Socialist Republics in Revolt.* New York: Harper & Row, 1981.

Dunlop, John B. *The Faces of Contemporary Russian Nationalism.* Princeton, N.J.: Princeton University Press, 1984.

Goldman, Marshall I. *U.S.S.R. in Crisis: The Failure of an Economic System.* New York: W. W. Norton, 1983.

Hoffmann, Erik P., ed. *The Soviet Union in the 1980s.* New York: Academy of Political Science, 1984.

Krasin, Victor. "How I Was Broken by the K.G.B.," *New York Times Magazine,* 18 March 1984.

Kushnirsky, Fydor I. *Soviet Economic Planning, 1965–1980.* Boulder, Colo.: Westview Press, 1982.

Nove, Alec. *The Soviet Economic System,* 2d ed. Winchester, Mass.: Allen & Unwin, 1980.

Rubinstein, Joshua. *Soviet Dissidents: Their Struggle for Human Rights.* Boston: Beacon Press, 1981.

Shevchenko, Arkady N. *Breaking With Moscow.* New York: Alfred A. Knopf, 1985.

Simis, Konstantin. *U.S.S.R.: The Corrupt Society.* New York: Simon & Schuster, 1982.

part five

The Third World

22

CHINA

THE IMPACT OF THE PAST

A CROWDED LAND

China's population is slightly over one billion and growing, even though the regime strongly promotes one-child families. Less than one-third of China's territory is arable (suitable for cultivation)—rice in the well-watered South and wheat in the drier North. China's "man-land ratio"—now only a quarter acre of farmland for each Chinese—has long imposed limits on politics, economics, and social thought.

With little new territory to expand into, Chinese society evolved "steady-state" structures that concentrated on preserving stability and making peasants content with what they had rather than encouraging them to pioneer and innovate. Labor-saving devices would render peasants jobless and were therefore not encouraged. China's remarkable achievements in science and technology—which put China far ahead of medieval Europe—remained curiosities instead of contributions to an industrial revolution.

Commercial expansion was also discouraged. Instead of a Western mentality of reinvestment, growth, and risk taking, Chinese merchants sought only a steady-state relationship with peasants and government officials; they depended heavily on government permits and monopolies.

Neither was there much interest in overseas expansion. Once they had their Middle Kingdom perfected, the Chinese saw no use for anything foreign. All outlying countries were inhabited by barbarians who were permitted to *kowtow* (ritual prostration) and pay tribute to the emperor. China had all the technology for overseas expansion but simply didn't bother. Expeditions brought back the news that there wasn't anything worthwhile beyond the seas. Thus for centuries China remained a stay-at-home country.

A TRADITIONAL POLITICAL SYSTEM

Politically too, China was steady-state. Very early China unified. Feudalism was replaced by a centralized empire, complete with impartial civil-service exams to select the best talent. The resulting Mandarin class—schooled in the Confucian classics, which stressed obedience, authority, and hierarchy—was interested in perpetuating the system, not changing it. A gentry class of better-off people served as the literate intermediaries between the Mandarins and the 90 percent of the population that were peasants.

Dynasties came and went every few hundred years in what has become known as the "dynastic cycle." As the old dynasty became increasingly incompetent, water systems went unrepaired, famine broke out, wars and banditry appeared, and corruption grew. In the eyes of the people, it looked as if the emperor had lost the "Mandate of Heaven," that is, his legitimate right to rule. A conqueror, either Chinese or foreign (Mongol or Manchu), found it easy to take over a demoralized empire. By the very fact of his victory, the new ruler seemed to have gained the Mandate of Heaven. Under vigorous new emperors, things go well; the breakdowns are fixed. After some generations, though, the new dynasty falls prey to the same ills as the old, and people, especially the literate, begin to think the emperor has lost his heavenly mandate. The cycle is ready to start over.

Confucianism:
Government by Right Thinking

The scholar Confucius (551 to 479 B.C.) advised rulers that the key to good, stable government lay in instilling correct, moral behavior in ruled and rulers alike. Each person must understand his or her role and perform it obediently. Sons were subservient to fathers, wives to husbands, and subjects to rulers. The ruler sets a moral example by purifying his spirit and perfecting his manners. In this way, goodness leads to power.

The Confucian system emphasized that good government starts with thinking good thoughts in utter sincerity. If things go wrong, it indicates rulers have been insincere. Mao Zedong hated everything old China stood for, but he couldn't help picking up the Confucian stress on right thinking. Adding a Marxist twist, Mao taught that one was a proletarian not because of blue-collar origin but because one had revolutionary, pure thoughts. Confucius would have been pleased.

Two millenia of Chinese empire made an indelible mark on the China of today. Not a feudal system—even though the Communists now denounce it as feudal—it was, rather, a "bureaucratic empire," with an emperor at the top setting the direction and tone, Mandarins carrying out Peking's writ, gentry running local affairs, and peasants, the overwhelming majority of the population, toiling in the fields. New dynasties soon found themselves lulled into accepting the system and becoming part of it. Even the Communists have not been able to totally eradicate the classic pattern of Chinese civilization.

THE LONG COLLAPSE

For some 2,000 years the Middle Kingdom proved capable of absorbing the changes thrown at it in the form of invasions, famines, and new dynasties. The old pattern always succeeded in reasserting itself. But as the modern epoch impinged on China, at least two new factors arose that the system could not absorb: population growth and Western penetration.

In 1741, China's population was 143 million; just a century later, in 1851, it had become an amazing 432 million, the result of new crops (corn and sweet potatoes from the Americas), internal peace under the Manchu dynasty, some new farmland, and just plain harder work on the part of the peasants. Taxation and administration lagged behind the rapid population growth, which hit as the Manchus were going into the typical decline phase of their dynastic cycle in the nineteenth century.

At about the same time the West was penetrating and disorienting China. It was a clash of two cultures—Western dynamism and greed versus Chinese stability—and the Chinese side was no match at all. In roughly a century of collapse, old China went into convulsions and breakdowns, which ended with the triumph of the Communists.

Cyclical versus Secular Change

China offers good illustrations of the two kinds of change that social scientists often deal with. *Cyclical change* is repetitive; certain familiar historical phases follow one another like a pendulum swing. China's dynastic cycles are examples of cyclical change; there is change, to be sure, but the overall pattern is preserved.

Secular change means a long-term shift that does not revert back to the old pattern. China's population growth, for example, was a secular change that helped break the stability of traditional China. One of the problems faced by historians, economists, and political scientists is whether a change they are examining is secular—a long-term, basic shift—or cyclical—something that comes and goes repeatedly.

The first Westerners to reach China were daring Portuguese seamen in 1514. Gradually, they and other Europeans gained permission to set up trading stations on the coast. For three centuries the Imperial government disdained the foreigners and their products and tried to keep them at a minimum. In 1793, for example, in response to a British mission to Peking, the emperor commended King George III for his "respectful spirit of submission" but pointed out that there could be little trade because "our celestial empire possesses all things in prolific abundance."

Still the West, especially the British, pushed on, smelling enormous profits in the China trade. Matters came to a head with the Opium Wars of 1839 to 1842. The British found a product that Chinese would buy, opium from the poppy fields of British-held India. Opium smoking was illegal in China, and there were few addicts. The British, however, flouted the law and popularized opium smoking. When at last a zealous Imperial official tried to stop the opium trade, Britain went to war to keep the lucrative commerce open. Britain easily won, but the Chinese still refused to admit the foreigners were superior. Moaned one Cantonese: "Except for your ships being solid, your gunfire fierce, and your rockets powerful, what good qualities do you have?" For the Chinese, war technology was not as important as moral quality, a view later adopted by Mao Zedong.

The 1842 Treaty of Nanjing (Nanking) wrested five "treaty ports" from the Chinese. (Britain got Hong Kong outright.) In the treaty ports the foreigners held sway, dominating the commerce and governance of the area. The Westerners enjoyed "extraterritorality," meaning they were not subject to Chinese law but had their own courts. In the 1860s, nine more such ports were added.

Around the treaty ports grew "spheres of influence," understandings among the foreign powers as to who really ran things there. The British, French, Germans, Russians, and Japanese in effect carved up the China coast with their spheres of influence, in which they dominated trade. The Americans, claiming to be above this sort of dirty business, tagged along after the British. China was reduced to semicolonial status.

FROM EMPIRE TO REPUBLIC

Internally, too, the Empire weakened. Rebellions broke out. From 1851 to 1864, the Taipings—espousing a mixture of Christianity (picked up from missionaries), Confucianism, and primitive communism—baptized millions in South China and nearly overthrew the Qing (Manchu) dynasty. In 1900, with the backing of some reactionary officials and the empress dowager, the antiforeign Boxer movement killed missionaries and besieged Peking's Legation Quarter for fifty-five days. An international expedition of British, French, German, Russian, American, and Japanese troops broke the Boxer Rebellion and lifted the siege. The foreigners then demanded indemnities and additional concessions from the tottering Imperial government.

Could the Qing dynasty have adapted itself to the new Western pressures? The Japanese had; with the 1868 Meiji Restoration they preserved the form of empire but shifted to modernization and industrialization with spectacular success. Many young Chinese demanded reform to strengthen China, especially after their humiliating defeat by Japan in 1895. In 1898 the young Emperor Guangxu (Kuang-hsu) gathered around him reformers and in the famous Hundred Days issued more than forty edicts, modernizing everything from education to the military. Conservative officials and the old empress dowager would have none of it; they carried out a coup, rescinded the changes, and put the emperor under house arrest for the rest of his short life.

Chinese Words in Roman Letters

Chinese—because it is both ideographic (based on symbolic word-pictures) and tonal (the sing-song pattern)—is terribly difficult to transliterate into English. One system, the Wade-Giles, devised in the 1860s by two Cambridge dons, was used for more than a century. Unfortunately, Wade-Giles didn't sound much like the Chinese pronunciation.

In 1958, Peking—sorry, Beijing—introduced a new system, Pinyin, that is much closer to the correct pronunciation. In 1979 China made Pinyin the official form of transliteration. Most English-language publications went along with it, but stuck with Peking as the nation's capital. Some of the Pinyin spellings used here may look funny if you are familiar with their Wade-Giles renderings, for example:

Wade-Giles	Pinyin
Mao Tse-tung	Mao Zedong
Chou En-lai	Zhou Enlai
Teng Hsiao-ping	Deng Xiaoping
Hua Kuo-feng	Hua Guofeng
Peking	Beijing
Nanking	Nanjing
Chungking	Chongqing
Shanghai	Shanghai (the same!)
Szechwan	Sichuan
Sinkiang	Xinjiang
Yangtze	Changjiang

A system that cannot reform is increasingly ripe for revolution. Younger people, especially army officers, grew fed up with China's weakness and became militant nationalists. Many Chinese studied in the West and were eager to Westernize China. Under an idealistic, Western-trained doctor, San Yatsen (Sun Yatsen), disgruntled provincial officials and military commanders overthrew the Manchus in 1911. It was the end of the last dynasty but not the beginning of stability. In the absence of central authority, so-called "warlords," local strongmen, in effect brought China into feudalism from 1916 to 1927.

Gradually overcoming the chaos was the Nationalist party or *Guomindang* (in Wade-Giles, *Kuomintang*, KMT). Formed shortly after the Manchu's overthrow, the Nationalists were guided by intellectuals (many of them educated in the United States), army officers, and the modern business element. Their greatest strength was in the South, in Guangzhou (Canton), especially in the coastal cities where there was the most contact with the West. It was no accident that they made Nanjing their capital; the word in fact means "southern capital."

Power gravitated into the hands of General (later Generalissimo) Jiang Jieshi (Chiang Kai-shek), who by 1927 had succeeded in unifying most of China under the Nationalists. While Chiang was hailed as the founder and savior of the new China—Henry Luce, the son of a China missionary, put Chiang ten times on the cover of *Time*—in reality, the Nationalist rule was weak. The Western-oriented city people who staffed the Nationalists did not reform or develop the rural areas where most Chinese still lived, usually under the thumb of rapacious landlords. Administration became terribly corrupt. And the Nationalists offered no plausible ideology to rally the Chinese people.

Still, like Kerensky's provisional government in Russia, the Nationalists might have succeeded were it not for war. In 1931 the Japanese seized Manchuria and in 1937 began the conquest of the rest of China. By 1941 they had taken the entire coast, forcing the Nationalists to move their capital far up the Changjiang River from Nanjing to Chongqing. The United States, in accordance with its long support of China, embargoed trade with Japan, a move that eventually led to Pearl Harbor. For the Americans in World War II, however, China was a sideshow. Chiang's forces preferred fighting Communists to Japanese while waiting for a U.S. victory to return them to power.

THE COMMUNIST TRIUMPH

One branch of Chinese nationalism, influenced by Marx and by the Bolshevik Revolution, decided that communism was the only effective basis for implementing a nationalist revolution. The Chinese Communists have always been first and foremost nationalists, and from its founding in 1921 the Chinese Communist party (CCP) worked with the Nationalists until Chiang in 1927 decided to exterminate them as a threat. The fight between the KMT and CCP was a struggle between two versions of Chinese nationalism.

While Stalin advised the Chinese Communists to base themselves on the small proletariat of the coastal cities, Mao Zedong rose to leadership of the party by developing a rural strategy called the "mass line." Mao concluded that the real revolutionary potential in China, which had little industry and hence few proletarians, was among the long-suffering peasants. It was a major revision of Marx, one in fact that Marx probably would not recognize as Marxism.

In 1934, with KMT forces surrounding them, some 120,000 Chinese Communists began their incredible Long March of more than 6,000 miles

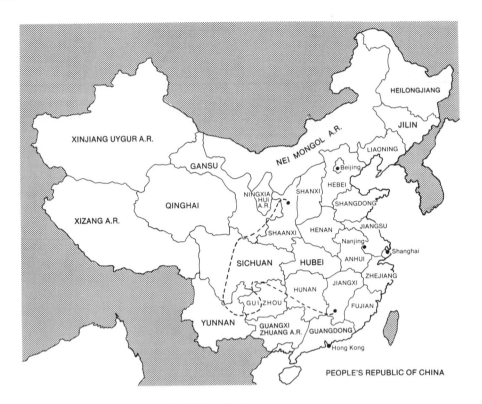

Line shows approximate route of 1934–35 Long March.

(10,000 km) to the relative safety of Yan'an in the north. It lasted over a year and led across mountain ranges and rivers amidst hostile forces. Fewer than 20,000 made it. The Long March became the epic of Chinese Communist history. Self-reliant and isolated from the Soviets, the Chinese Communists had to develop their own strategy for survival, including working with peasants and practicing guerrilla warfare.

While the war against Japan drained and demoralized the Nationalists, it strengthened and encouraged the Communists. Besides some captured Japanese weapons from the Russian take-over of Manchuria in 1945, the Chinese Communists got very little help from the Soviets and felt they never owed them much in return. Mao and his Communists came to power on their own, by perfecting their peasant and guerrilla strategies. This fact set the groundwork for the later Sino-Soviet split.

After World War II, the Nationalist forces were much larger than the Communists', and they had many U.S. arms. Nationalist strength, however, melted away as hyperinflation destroyed the economy, corrupt officers sold their troops' weapons (sometimes to the Communists), and war weariness paralyzed the population. The Nationalists had always neglected the "rice roots" of political strength: the common peasant. The Communists, by cultivating the peas-

Mao and Guerrilla War

In what has become a model for would-be revolutionaries the world over, the Chinese Communists swept to power in 1949 after a decade and a half of successful guerrilla warfare. During these years, Mao Zedong, often in his Yan'an cave, developed and taught what he called the "mass line." Here are some of his lessons:

1. Take the countryside and surround the cities. While the enemy is stuck in the cities, able to venture out only in strength, you are mobilizing the masses.
2. Work very closely with the peasants, listen to their complaints, help them solve problems (for example, getting rid of a landlord or bringing in the harvest), propagandize them, and recruit them into the army and party.
3. Don't engage the enemy's main forces but rather probe for his weak spots, harassing him and wearing him out.
4. Don't expect much help from the outside; be self-reliant. For weapons, take the enemy's.
5. Don't worry about the apparent superior numbers and firepower of the enemy and his imperialist allies; their strength is illusory because it is not based on the masses. Willpower and unity with the masses is more important than weaponry.
6. At certain stages guerrilla units come together to form larger units until at last, as the enemy stumbles, your forces become a regular army that can take the entire country.

antry (Mao himself was of peasant origin), won a new Mandate of Heaven. In 1949, the disintegrating Nationalists retreated to the island of Taiwan while the Communists restored Peking ("northern capital") as the country's capital and proceeded to implement what is probably the world's most sweeping revolution. On that occasion, Mao, reflecting his deeply nationalistic sentiments, said: "Our nation will never again be an insulted nation. We have stood up."

Chairman Mao Zedong proclaims the founding of the People's Republic of China on October 1, 1949. (*Xinhau*)

THE KEY INSTITUTIONS

THE SOVIET PARALLEL

The institutions of China's government are quite similar to those of the Soviet Union—interlocking state and party hierarchies—but China adds a Third World twist: the army is also quite important, at times intervening directly into politics, as happens in other developing countries. China, no less than Brazil (see the next chapter), experiences upheaval and chaos, which leads to army participation. In this regard, the People's Republic of China (PRC) is still a Third World country.

As in the Soviet Union, each state and party level ostensibly elects the one above it. In China, production and residential units elect local People's Con-

Tandem Power:
Mao and Zhou

For over a quarter of a century, until both died in 1976, power in Peking was not concentrated in the hands of a single Stalin-like figure but divided between Party Chairman Mao Zedong and Premier Zhou Enlai. This Chinese pattern of tandem power may now be sufficiently deep to continue into the future.

Both men were of rural backgrounds, but Mao was born in 1893 into a better-off peasant family while Zhou was born in 1898 into a gentry family. As young men, both were drawn to Chinese nationalism and then to its Marxist variation. Neither of them went much further than high school in formal education, although both studied, debated, and wrote in Chinese leftist circles. Zhou was in France from 1920 to 1924, ostensibly to study but actually to do political work among Chinese students in Europe. Mao had no experience outside of China.

As instructed by the Soviets, the young Chinese Communist party worked closely with the Nationalists. Zhou, for example, was in charge of political education at the Nationalist military academy. In 1927, when Chiang Kai-shek turned on the Communists, both Mao and Zhou barely escaped with their lives. Zhou, interestingly enough, was the model militant revolutionist for French writer André Malraux's novel *Man's Fate,* set in 1927 Shanghai.

The next decade set their relationship. Mao concluded, from his work with peasants, that in them lay the path to China's revolution. Zhou, who briefly remained loyal to Moscow's proletarian line, by 1931 had changed his mind and joined Mao in his Jiangxi redoubt. From there, the two made the arduous Long March to the north. By the time they arrived in Yan'an, Mao was clearly the leader of the CCP, and his "mass line" of basing the revolution on the peasantry prevailed.

Mao dominated mainly by force of intellect. Other CCP leaders respected his ability to theorize in clear, blunt language. Mao became the party chief and theoretician but did not concern himself with the day-to-day tasks of survival, warfare, and diplomacy. These became in large part Zhou's jobs. Zhou Enlai became the administrator of the revolution. Never bothering to theorize, Zhou was a master at shaping and controlling bureaucracies, smooth diplomacy, and political survival amidst changing lines.

Was there tension between the two? Probably, but Zhou never showed it. Publicly Zhou dedicated himself completely to fulfilling Mao's desires; although at times, in the shambles of the Great Leap Forward (1958–60) and the Cultural Revolution (1966–69), he seemed to be trying to hold things together and limit the damage.

Mao was the abstract thinker while Zhou was the pragmatic doer. Implicitly, this made Mao more radical and Zhou more conservative. Mao could spin out his utopian dreams, but Zhou had to make the bureaucracy, military, and economy function. Different roles require different personalities.

gresses which then elect county People's Congresses, which in turn choose provincial People's Congresses. China, organized on a unitary rather than federal pattern, has twenty-one provinces. The provincial People's Congresses then elect the National People's Congress (NPC) of some thirty-five hundred deputies for a five-year term.

As in the Soviet Union, this parliament is much too big to do anything but applaud at its brief annual sessions. A Standing Committee of about 175 is theoretically supreme, but it too does not have much power in overseeing the executive branch. The chairman of the Standing Committee is considered China's head of state, a largely honorific post currently held by elderly Li Xiannian.

The top of the executive branch is the State Council, a cabinet of approximately forty ministers (specialized in economic branches) and a dozen vice-premiers led by a premier, China's head of government, now Zhao Ziyang.

The formal structure of the executive does not always correspond to the real distribution of its power. In 1976, after the death of both Party Chairman Mao Zedong and Premier Zhou Enlai, a relative unknown, Hua Guofeng, was installed in both their offices. On paper, Hua appeared to be the most powerful figure in the land.

But an elderly, rehabilitated party veteran, Deng Xiaoping, named to the modest post of senior vice-premier in 1977, was in fact more powerful than his nominal boss, Hua. When Deng toured the United States in 1979, he acted like a head of state. Deng's power grew out of his senior standing in the party and the army. In 1980, he demoted Hua and assumed power himself, still without taking over the job titles, which he left to others. By 1982, Hua was out of the Politburo and out of sight.

THE PARTY

Like the Soviet Communist party, the Chinese Communist party (CCP) is constitutionally and in practice the leading political element of the country. With over forty million members, the CCP is gigantic in absolute terms. Relative to China's population, though, it is proportionately smaller than the CPSU.

In organization, the CCP parallels the CPSU. Hierarchies of party congresses at the local, county, provincial, and national levels feed into corresponding party committees. At the top is the National Party Congress; composed of some 1,500 delegates and supposed to meet at least once in five years, this congress nominally chooses a Central Committee of 210 full members. Since both bodies are too big to run things, however, power ends up in the hands of a Politburo of two dozen party chiefs. But this too is not the last level. Within the Politburo is a Standing Committee which varies from five to nine members and has the decisive voice.

The CCP's structure used to be a bit different from the Soviet model. Instead of a general secretary at its head, the CCP had a party chairman, Mao's title, which he passed on to Hua Guofeng. By then, however, the office was robbed of meaning, and Hua was eclipsed by Senior Vice-Premier Deng Xiaoping, who, to be sure, also held important party and army positions. In

The Mouse Catcher: Deng Xiaoping

Deng Xiaoping's return to power in China in the 1970s seemed to outsiders about as likely as Richard Nixon's becoming president again. The diminutive Chinese leader had actually been purged twice before becoming "senior vice-premier" in 1977, a deceptive title. Actually the former protégé of Zhou Enlai—who, like Zhou, was a pragmatic administrator rather than a theorizer—was China's boss.

Deng was born in 1904 into a rural landlord family. Sent to study in France, Deng was recruited by Zhou Enlai and soon joined the Chinese Communists. As a political commissar and organizer of the People's Liberation Army, Deng forged strong military connections. Rising through major posts after 1949, Deng was named to the top of the party—the Politburo's Standing Committee—in 1956.

Deng was not as adroit as Zhou and kept getting into political trouble. An outspoken pragmatist, Deng said after the Great Leap: "Private farming is all right as long as it raises production, just as it doesn't matter whether a cat is black or white as long as it catches mice." During the Cultural Revolution this utterance was used against Deng to show that he was a "Capitalist Roader." Although not expelled from the party, Deng dropped out of sight and lost his official position. His son was disabled during the Cultural Revolution.

But the little man—Deng is under 5 feet (150 cm) tall—bounced back in 1973 when moderates had regained control. In 1975, he seemed to be ready to take over; he spoke with visiting U.S. President Ford as one head of state to another. But just a month later Deng was again in disgrace, denounced by the radicals of the "Gang of Four" as anti-Mao. Again he was stripped of his posts, but an old army buddy offered him sanctuary in an elite military resort.

Seemingly retired for good now, the amazingly adaptable Deng bounced back yet again. With the arrest of the Gang of Four in 1976, moderates came back out of the woodwork, among them Deng. In July 1977, he was reappointed to all of his old posts. Many Chinese state, party, and army leaders, badly shaken by the Cultural Revolution, felt that old comrade Deng was a man they could trust. Deng's roller-coaster ride in and out of power illustrates two facts of Chinese life: (1) politics is alive and well in China; and (2) it pays to have high-ranking friends who see you as a guarantor of pragmatism and stability.

The pragmatic Deng warmed up ties with the United States. Here Deng chats with President Regan who visited in 1984. (Bill Fitz-Patrick, the White House)

1982, under Deng's guidance, the party abolished the chairmanship—part of a repudiation of Mao's legacy—and upgraded the position of general secretary, so that now the CCP structure more closely matches that of the CPSU. Deng arranged to have his protégé Hu Yaobang named secretary general.

China's nervous system is its party *cadres,* a French word for "framework" now used by Asian Communists to denote local party leadership. There are an estimated eighteen million CCP cadres, and whoever controls them controls China. In 1979, Deng Xiaoping began the ticklish job of easing out both the incompetent old guard—whose only qualification, in many cases, was having been on the Long March—and the extreme leftists who wormed their way into the cadre structure during the tumultuous Cultural Revolution. Quietly, Deng and Hu brought in younger, better-educated cadres dedicated to their moderate, pragmatic line. If successful, Deng, Hu, and their successors will have hand-picked China's first postrevolutionary cadre system and consolidated their own power base.

THE ARMY

Typically the top figures in the Chinese elite hold both high state and high party offices, as in the Soviet Union. In China, though, they often also hold high positions atop the military structure, through the important Military Affairs Commission, which interlocks with the CCP's Politburo. Indeed, from the beginning, the People's Liberation Army (PLA), earlier known as the Chinese Red Army, has been so intertwined with the CCP that it's hard to separate them. Fighting the Nationalists and the Japanese for at least a decade and a half, the CCP became a combination of party and army. The pattern continues to this day. Political scientist Robert Tucker has called the Chinese system "military communism."

Mao wrote that "the party commands the gun, and the gun must never be allowed to command the party." Where the two are nearly merged, however, it's sometimes hard to tell who's on top. As the Communists took over China in the 1940s, it was the PLA that first set up their power structures. Virtually all of China's executive decision makers have had extensive military experience, often as political commissars in PLA units. Said Zhou Enlai: "We are all connected with the army." When the Cultural Revolution broke out in 1966, as we shall discuss below, the army first facilitated, then dampened, and finally crushed the Red Guards' rampages. By the time the Cultural Revolution sputtered out, the PLA was in de facto control of most provincial governments and most of the Politburo. By 1980, a third of the Politburo was still occupied by active military men.

At various times, during mobilization campaigns, the army is cited as a model for the rest of the country to follow, and heroic individual soldiers are celebrated in the media. In only one other Communist country does the army play such a prominent role: Poland.

What does this mean for Chinese governance? In the long run, it probably impacts a conservative twist to Peking's direction. Although the PLA under Defense Minister Lin Biao in the early stages of the Cultural Revolution supported Mao's program of shaking up the party and state bureaucracy, as the chaos spread, military commanders worried that it was sapping China's strength and defense preparedness. Lin, following Mao's lead, emphasized mass enthusiasm in war as opposed to military technology.

Other commanders, aware of the new engines of destruction produced by the Soviets and Americans, decided China needed modern weapons in addition to high morale. Lin, although he was thought to have been Mao's right-hand man, became increasingly isolated among the important military and party people. In 1971 Peking released the amazing story that Lin had attempted a coup and fled to the Soviet Union in a plane that crashed. Outside observers suggest that Lin's death occurred by other means. Lin's supporters were purged from the military.

One of Deng Xiaoping's projects was to make sure the party commanded the gun. Needing all of China's finances for economic modernization, Deng ordered aged officers to retire, and cut the 4.2-million-person PLA by a million in 1985–86. The PLA is poorly equipped, lacking modern weapons, mobility, tanks, and aircraft. In border skirmishes with Vietnam, the Chinese have been clobbered. PLA generals want better equipment, but Deng tried to persuade them to wait for China's industrial recovery rather than expend precious funds for foreign military gear. Many generals were unhappy. In general, the PLA has been a conservative force in Chinese politics, for almost axiomatically, an army stands for order and sees disorder as a security problem. In China, as will also be seen in Brazil, when chaos threatens, the army moves.

Tandem Power Again?

As Deng Xiaoping neared the end of his long life, he gradually surrendered more and more of his government, army, and party positions. Power seemed to shift to his two protégés, General Secretary Hu Yaobang and Premier Zhao Ziyang. In 1985, they were respectively 70 and 66 years old, the *youngest* of the Politburo's six-member Standing Committee. Actuarially, the future seemed to belong to them; everyone else was in his eighties.

Like Deng, Hu was one of the few remaining survivors of the Long March. Also like Deng, Hu was twice purged and twice rehabilitated. During the Cultural Revolution, Hu was sent to the countryside to work and live in the stables.

Zhao missed the Long March but fought the Japanese and Nationalists, like Deng and Hu. He earned a good reputation and caught Deng's eye as party secretary and governor of Sichuan Province, Deng's home. During the Cultural Revolution, he was paraded with a dunce cap through the streets and sent to work on a farm.

Both men are believed to be pragmatic and moderate, more interested in economic growth than in ideological purity. Both, it may be assumed, thoroughly detest what Mao put them through during the Cultural Revolution and don't want another upheaval like that. With Hu in charge of party affairs and Zhao of the government, the two seem likely to rule in tandem.

CHINESE POLITICAL ATTITUDES

TRADITIONAL ATTITUDES

Mao used to say that his countrymen were "firstly poor, secondly blank," meaning that the Communists could start with a clean slate and create the Chinese citizens they wished for. Mao was wrong. Plenty of traditional Chinese attitudes have carried over into the People's Republic. Indeed, even Mao's vision of perfecting human nature by thinking right thoughts is a deeply Confucian notion.

When the Communists restored Peking as the capital in 1949 they were restoring an old symbol; Peking had been the capital for centuries until Chiang's Nationalists moved it to Nanjing. Some government offices and elite living quarters now directly adjoin the old Forbidden City of the emperors, just as the Soviets made the Kremlin their home. Tiananmen (Gate of Heavenly Peace) Square is still Peking's parade and demonstration area, much like Red Square is in Moscow.

In some ways, the Communists' bureaucrats and cadres perform the same function as the old Mandarins and gentry. Reciting Mao instead of Confucius, the new elites strive to place a gigantic population under central control and guidance. Their aim now, to be sure, is growth and modernization rather than conservative stability. But Mao himself recognized the similarity of old and new when he denounced the bureaucrats as the "new Mandarins" during the Cultural Revolution. Like the dynasties of old, the Communists may have been sucked into the old patterns.

Reverence for Age

Just as in Old China, age seems to confer special qualities of wisdom and leadership in the People's Republic. Mao died at 82 and Zhou at 78, both in office. When he returned to power in 1977, Deng Xiaoping was 73. China's Politburo and top officials are much older than their Soviet counterparts.

To become one of the new Mandarins, Chinese youths must undergo twelve and a half hours of grueling university entrance exams. Out of some three million who take them, only about 300,000 pass each year, meaning that only about ten percent of China's college-age youths enter institutions of higher education (as opposed to close to 40 percent in the United States). The three days of exams resemble nothing so much as the Imperial examination system of old China. The new exams, identical and kept secret, are given simultaneously throughout China. They include sections on Chinese literature, math, science, a foreign language, and politics.

Mao argued against the examinations and had them dropped during the Cultural Revolution; they were restored only in 1977. Mao thought the exams were elitist and unrevolutionary, that they created a class of new Mandarin bureaucrats. Mao was quite right, but without the brutally competitive exams, educational standards slid, and incompetent youths got into universities based on their political attitudes. Inferior graduates retarded China's progress in industry and administration, so the post-Mao moderates restored the examinations. It was another example of a long-functional process reasserting itself.

NATIONALISM

Overlaying traditional Chinese attitudes is the more recent one of the nationalism that has dominated China's intellectual life since the turn of the century. Chinese nationalism, like Third World nationalism generally, is the result of a proud and independent culture suffering penetration, disorientation, and humiliation at the hands of the West. This can induce explosive fury and the feeling that the native culture, although temporarily beaten by foreigners, is still better and more enduring. Russian Slavophiles, for example, reacted this way in the last century.

In Asia, Chinese and Japanese nationalists vowed to beat the West at its own game, building industry and weaponry but placing them at the service of the traditional culture. The Japanese were able to carry out their designs in the last century; the Chinese are still in the midst of the process. All of the founding generation of Chinese Communist leaders, including Mao and Zhou, began as young patriots urging their countrymen to revitalize China and stand up to the West and to Japan.

As in the Soviet Union, one prevailing Chinese attitude is the nationalist drive to catch up with and overtake the West. During their best economic-growth years in the mid-1950s, Chinese leaders were intensely proud of their rapid progress. The Great Leap Forward and the Cultural Revolution ruined that momentum. A pragmatic moderate such as Zhou or Deng always has a powerful argument against such disruptions: they harm growth and weaken the country. Basically, this is a nationalist argument.

MAOISM

Maoism, or Mao Zedong Thought, as Peking calls it, is the latest layer of Chinese political attitudes. It draws from both traditional and nationalistic values despite its claim to be totally new and revolutionary. From traditional China, it takes the Confucian emphasis on thinking right thoughts, on the idea that consciousness determines existence rather than the reverse: Willpower has primacy over weaponry in wars; willpower has primacy over technology in building China. The unleashed forces of the masses, guided by Mao Zedong Thought, can conquer anything. This extreme form of voluntarism—the belief that human will can change the world—is consonant with China's past.

From nationalism, Mao took the emphasis on strengthening and rebuilding China so that it could stand up to its old enemies and become a world power. The trouble is that these two strands are partly at odds with each other. Traditional values call for China to ignore the West and its technology, but nationalistic values call for China to learn and copy from the West. The continuing, unresolved conflict of these two streams of thought spell permanent trouble for China.

Maoism is an outgrowth of Mao Zedong's thoughts on guerrilla warfare. According to Maoist doctrine, what the PLA did to beat the Nationalists, China as a whole must do to advance and become a world leader: work with the masses, be self-reliant, and put willpower on a higher plane than technology to overcome obstacles. Mao can be seen as a theorist of guerrilla warfare who continued to apply his principles to governance.

In the Great Leap Forward from 1958 to 1960, Mao tried guerrilla warfare tactics on the economy, using raw manual labor plus enthusiasm to build earthen dams and backyard blast furnaces. Engineers, experts, and administrators were bypassed. The Soviets warned Mao it wouldn't work and urged him to follow the Soviet model of building the economy by more conventional means. As a matter of fact, the Soviets were right, but Mao refused to follow their lead. In 1960, the Soviets withdrew their substantial numbers of foreign-aid technicians, and the Sino-Soviet split came into the open.

For the Soviets, the revolution is over; the proletariat triumphed in 1917 and moved Russia into the most advanced stage of history. For Mao, the revolution never ends. Mao held that at any stage there are conservative tendencies that block the path to socialism: bureaucratism, elitism, and opportunism. Mao understood perfectly well what Djilas warned against in *The New Class* and resolved to combat these tendencies by means of "permanent revolution," periodic upheavals to let the force of the masses surge past the conservative bureaucrats.

Who's right, the Soviets or the Maoists? In terms of traditional Marxism, Maoism is heresy, a complete break with the master. Further, in terms of results, the Soviets are right in prescribing the buildup of industry under the guidance of engineers and experts. For this you need an organized, stable society that trains and rewards the best talent. But this means inequality, rank, and hierarchy, in short a fairly conservative society. What then was the revolution for, ask the Maoists, if you merely go from one conservative society to another? Here Mao was quite right: in bureaucratizing their revolution, the Soviets have become one of the most conservative societies on earth, incapable of producing communism.

Slogans from the Cultural Revolution

"Put destruction first, and in the process you have construction."

"Destroy the four olds—old thought, old culture, old customs, old habits."

"Once all struggle is grasped, miracles are possible."

"Bombard the command post." (Attack established leaders if they are unrevolutionary.)

"So long as it is revolutionary, no action is a crime."

"Sweep the great renegade of the working class onto the garbage heap!" (Dump the moderate chief of state, Liu Shaoqi.)

"Cadres step to the side." (Bypass established authorities.)

"To rebel is justified."

Socialism and bureaucratism are closely connected, but Mao thought he could break the connection. He saw China settling into the bureaucratic patterns he hated and was determined to break them by instituting a permanent revolution before he died. The result was the Great Proletarian Cultural Revolution from 1966 to 1976, during which young people were encouraged to criticize, harass, and oust almost all figures of authority except army leaders. Administrators, teachers, scientists, musicians, even party leaders were humiliated and sent to "reeducation" farms for manual labor; thousands committed suicide. Chaos spread through China, and the economy slumped. As we discussed earlier, the army took over. Shortly after Mao's death, power returned to the bureaucrats; they won and Mao failed.

Mao refused to recognize the unhappy truth that if you want socialism you must accept the bureaucratism that comes with it. By trying to leap directly into some kind of guerrilla socialism without bureaucrats, Mao nearly wrecked China. On balance, Mao Zedong Thought is inherently inapplicable, and in the post-Mao China of the 1980s, Mao is quoted selectively, if at all.

PERSONAL POLITICAL BELIEFS: A GUARDED SUBJECT

It's hard to tell what Chinese really think. The outsiders who visit China—on elaborately staged tours—rarely speak Chinese. Chinese are discouraged from talking with Western reporters. There are few public-opinion polls. Our picture of Chinese attitudes must be pieced together from journalistic glimpses and the tales of refugees who sneak into Hong Kong.

Chinese are required to mouth slogans, one year anti-Confucius, the next anti-Capitalist Roaders, then anti-Gang of Four, later the Four Moderniza-tions, depending on which "campaign" is current. Many get awfully fed up with this and mentally tune out; the slogans become meaningless. During the Cul-tural Revolution, for example, everything had to be related to the Thoughts of Chairman Mao. Pig farmers, scientists, soldiers, and factory workers dutifully intoned that they must "faithfully apply the teachings of Mao Zedong."

In 1976, when Deng Xiapoing was once again temporarily out of politi-cal favor, people all over China solemnly assured visiting foreigners: "We must deepen the criticism of the right-deviationist attempt of Deng Xiaoping to re-verse the correct verdicts of the Cultural Revolution." The slogan had been dis-tributed nationwide with instructions to memorize it.

Later, when Deng was back in and his antagonists, the so-called Gang of Four ultra-radicals, were under arrest, the anti-Deng slogan vanished, replaced by "Smash the Gang of Four." Few Chinese appear to really believe in the slo-gans; they utter them to survive or win advancement. As in the Soviet Union, there is a great deal of opportunism and cynicism.

Further, Chinese are aware of the hypocrisy rife in their system. Chinese workers get poor clothing, housing, and food, while top party officials get neatly cut Mao suits, comfortable apartments, and sometimes access to special stores. Mao was able to tap into class resentment in his Cultural Revolution; many of the Red Guards were ambitious youths who saw their path to advancement blocked by privileged older cadres. Their solution was to overthrow them in the name of Mao and take their place. Mao was right: the revolution never ends.

The average Chinese, after all the upheaval, seem saturated with poli-tics. Many want simply to get on with the job of living and supporting a family. Put another way, could you endure ever-changing campaigns, mobilizations, slo-gans, heros, and villains for years on end without turning away from politics? It is to a longing for some peace and stability that the regime of Deng, Hu, and Zhao successfully appealed in the 1980s.

In sum, it is unlikely that the average Chinese citizen is the politically active animal the regime depicts. Indeed, the constant shifts in political line left many once-active Chinese badly burned. An economist loses his teaching post because he didn't mention Mao's Thoughts in his lectures. A Red Guard youth is sent to work on a communal farm and finds he can return to his city only illegally. An official endorses Peking's line of the moment only to get in trouble the following year for supporting the Gang of Four. Such turbulence taught Chinese to steer clear of politics because they could easily get hurt. Not really in jest, Chinese say: "When two people meet in China they talk frankly. When there are three they tell jokes. When there are four they tell lies."

"Socialism Does Not Mean Pauperism"

With phrases such as this did Chinese ideology move into a post-Mao phase. Strict equality and ideological purity were out; pragmatism and getting rich individually were in. With the "responsibility system" in agriculture and decentralization in industry (discussed below), Peking's ideologues made the necessary flip-flops to explain that the shifts were all good socialism.

They pointed out—quite rightly—that Marx had left no detailed blueprint defining exactly what socialism was to be like. Socialism need not mean poverty, they stressed. In fact, individual achievement throughout China would lift up the whole society. If everyone gets rich then you'll have a rich society—precisely what Marx intended. (It's what Adam Smith intended, too.)

What about Mao and his quotations? Interpret them flexibly, not dogmatically. "There are no quotations for what we are doing now," admitted Su Shaozhi, a top Peking theoretician. "If we used quotations, we would be dogmatic." Mao Zedong Thought now means the collective wisdom and experience of the whole Chinese Communist party, not just Mao's writings. Accordingly, Mao Zedong Thought could be used to criticize Mao. "The thought of Mao Zedong as an individual had many mistakes," explained Professor Su, "especially in his later years. But as far as Mao Zedong Thought is concerned, we regard it as a serious ideology that excludes the ideological mistakes of Mao Zedong himself."

Get it? Neither did many Chinese.

The ironic result of Mao's efforts to politicize the entire population is renewed passivity. Some victims of the Cultural Revolution turned into political zombies, blank to everything around them. Most people just tuned out. Said one Peking woman: "People are fed up with ideology."

PATTERNS OF INTERACTION

CYCLES OF UPHEAVAL

Since the Communists came to power in 1949, there have been three major upheavals plus several smaller ones. Among major upheavals we would count the agrarian reforms (that is, execution of landlords and redistribution of land) of the early 1950s, the Great Leap Forward from 1958 to 1960, and the Cultural Revolution from 1966 to 1976. Smaller upheavals include the brief Hundred Flowers liberalization of 1956, the antirightist campaigns of the early 1970s, and the crushing of the Gang of Four and their supporters in the late 1970s.

The big upheavals and most of the smaller ones can be traced to the same underlying problem: Peking's leaders, having inherited a poor and backward land, intermittently try to make China something it neither is nor can soon be. Mao Zedong Thought teaches that everything is possible: China can leap into the modern age and even beyond it. But the old, stubborn, traditional China is unyielding; it frustrates the bold plans and tugs the system back toward the previous patterns and problems.

As long as China is not what its leaders wish it to be—modern, powerful, and socialist in a way far purer than the Soviets—there is the possibility of another upheaval instituted from the top. It is also possible, however, that with Mao gone, China's leaders will abandon his more grandiose plans and settle for steady industrialization on the Soviet model. Perhaps the Great Leap Forward and Cultural Revolution were uniquely the work of Mao.

But were these upheavals just Mao's doing, or were they something inherent to the "building of socialism"? The latter is probable. Indeed, similar episodes occurred in the Soviet Union as leaders tried to force their country along: Stalin's industrialization and Khrushchev's experiments. The difference with China is that it is far more backward and hence the remedies proferred tend to be more extreme.

For China's periodic upheavals to cease it would require the abandonment of the Communists' central tenet, namely, that they deliver rapid progress. To scale down their goals, even to admit that China may never be a great industrial power and model for the world, would call for a major psychological shift at the top of the CCP, and there's no indication this shift has occurred. Accordingly, although the mid-1980s seemed characterized by moderation and pragmatism among the Chinese leadership, we might keep a lookout for a new round of revolutionary enthusiasm. The potential for extremism is still present, and there are no institutional mechanisms—competing parties, free elections, an independent judiciary—to block a new round of extremism.

The Great Leap Forward: "Twenty Years in a Day"

In 1958 Mao Zedong launched one of the strangest efforts in the Third World's struggle to move ahead: the Great Leap Forward. Vowing to progress "twenty years in a day" and "catch up with Great Britain in fifteen years," all of China was urged to "walk on two legs" (use all possible means) to industrialize rapidly. Most peasants—and China has still a largely peasant population—were herded into gigantic communes, some with as many as 100,000 people. Deprived of their private plots, they were ordered to eat in communal dining halls, leave their young in nurseries, and sometimes even sleep in large dormitories.

The communes were ordered to participate in engineering and industrial projects. Relying on "labor-intensive" methods to compensate for lack of capital, millions were turned out to move earth with baskets and carry poles to build dams and irrigation works. "Backyard blast furnaces" were ordered built so that every commune could produce its own iron.

Within a year the failure was plain for all to see. Even Mao had to admit it; he resigned as president of the PRC but kept his chairmanship of the CCP. The unenthusiastic peasants—as in the Soviet Union—simply failed to produce without private incentives. A serious food deficit developed. The implements produced of locally smelted iron were of miserable quality. The communes were phased out, broken first into "production brigades" and then into "production teams," which were in fact the old villages. Private farming was again permitted. Mao lost; old China won.

The Great Proletarian Cultural Revolution:
"Bombard the Command Post"

If the Great Leap Forward was strange, the Great Proletarian Cultural Revolution was downright bizarre. In it, an elderly Mao Zedong tried to make his revolution permanent by destroying the very structures his new China had created. Of the many slogans from the Cultural Revolution, "bombard the command post" perhaps best summarizes its character. Mao encouraged young people, who hastily grouped themselves into ragtag outfits called the Red Guards, to destroy most authority, even the CCP. They did, and Chinese progress was set back years.

The Cultural Revolution began with a 1965 flap over a Shanghai play some radicals claimed criticized Mao by allegory. Mao turned what could have been a small literary debate into a mass criticism that led to the ouster of several party officials. First university and then high school students aired their grievances against teachers and school administrators. Behind their discontent was a shortage of the kind of jobs the students thought they deserved upon graduation.

By the fall of 1966, most schools were closed as their students demonstrated, humiliated officials, wrote wall posters, and marched to and fro. China was in chaos. Hundreds of thousands of victims of the Red Guards committed suicide. A much larger number were "sent down" to the countryside to work with the peasants and "learn from the people." This sometimes included physical abuse and psychological humiliation. An unknown number of persons were murdered outright. Worried officials set up their own Red Guard groups to protect themselves. Different Red Guard factions fought each other.

Even Mao became concerned and in early 1967 ordered the army to step in. By the end of 1967 the People's Liberation Army pretty much ran the country. To replace the broken governmental structures, the army set up "revolutionary committees" on which sat PLA officers, Red Guard leaders, and "repentant" officials who had been duly cleansed by the Cultural Revolution. By 1969, the worst was over, although Peking's current rulers maintain the Cultural Revolution did not end until 1976 when Mao died and the ultra-radical Gang of Four (headed by Mao's wife, Jiang Qing), was arrested.

The effects of the Cultural Revolution were all bad. Industry suffered. Education, when it resumed, was without standards, and students were chosen on the basis of political attitudes rather than ability. The more moderate and level-headed officials, whom the Red Guards sought to destroy, lay low and pretended to go along with the Cultural Revolution. When it was over, they reasserted themselves and made sure one of their own was in high office: Deng Xiaoping.

And what became of the Red Guards? Claiming that their energy was needed on the farm, the army marched more than sixteen million young city people to rural communes for agricultural labor and forebade them to return to their cities. By hook or crook, many of them managed to get back to their homes to try to continue their studies. Some, utterly disillusioned with the way they had been used, turned to petty crime or fled to the British colony of Hong Kong, the last bastion of the imperialism Mao so bitterly denounced.

RADICALS AND MODERATES

Outside observers have tended to label CCP figures as "radicals" or "moderates" according to their willingness to support the kind of upheavals previously described. This is a bit of a simplification, for there are no distinct groups in China bearing these names. And many party leaders have demonstrated how they can play both sides of the fence, depending on where their career advantage lies.

Still, the radical and moderate labels are useful, for they help us understand the kind of struggles that have been going on within the CCP leadership. The main characteristics are summarized in the box, "Radicals and Moderates in

Radicals and Moderates in Chinese Politics

Radicals	Moderates
celebrate Mao Thought	selectively quote Mao
mass-oriented	elite-oriented
antiauthoritarian	hierarchical
purification	modernization
permanent revolution	stability
breakthrough growth	steady economic growth
politics in command	economics in command
learn from the people	follow the experts
wage equality	wage differentials
expect worker enthusiasm	offer material incentives
common sense	science and education
economically self-reliant	import some technology
ideological	empirical

Chinese Politics." Both radicals and moderates, it should be emphasized, want China to progress. But the radicals are unwilling to dilute the revolutionary purity of Maoist socialism for the sake of mere economic progress. The moderates, on the other hand, are willing to sacrifice ideology for pragmatic achievements.

China's moderates were and still are those high up in the party, government, or army. Almost axiomatically, anyone who's part of the establishment will not be a radical. Mao was right: bureaucrats are by nature conservative. China's radicals were drawn largely from those peripheral to power but ambitious for it: students, junior cadres, some provincial leaders.

One of the prime motivations for radicals, especially during the Cultural Revolution, was (and still is) the scarcity of job openings in party, state, army, industrial, and other offices. For the most part, positions until recently were staffed by aging party comrades who go back to the 1949 liberation or even the Long March. They never retire, and their longevity in office breeds impatience and resentment among younger people with ambitions of their own. A further element fueling youthful discontent is the previously mentioned difficulty of getting into a university. Only about 10 percent of university candidates pass the stiff entrance exams. It is no coincidence that one of the educational "reforms" of the Cultural Revolution was the abolition of these exams.

These kinds of tensions underlay the radical outburst of the Cultural Revolution. Those who aspired to power enthusiastically attempted to carry out Mao's designs. Those who held power pretended to go along with it, often by mouthing the correct slogans and self-denunciations. In Mao's words, they "waved the red flag to oppose the red flag." When the campaign burnt itself out, the bureaucrats and cadres took over again, and it appeared that the moderates had won.

LIBERALIZATION AND ITS LIMITS

Another cyclical pattern in Chinese politics is periodic liberalization campaigns that hint briefly at democratization but then are snuffed out. The most famous arose in 1956 when Mao urged intellectuals to come forward with their criticism. "Let a hundred flowers bloom, let a hundred schools of thought contend," wrote Mao. In response to Mao's call, criticism of the system, the party, even of Marxism came in torrents. Shocked by the candid outpouring, Mao abruptly turned the Hundred Flowers Campaign into the 1957 Antirightist Campaign, and many critics were jailed. On balance, the Hundred Flowers period appears partly to have been a device to get critics to identify themselves so they could be dealt with.

A similar liberal thaw occurred in 1978. "If the masses feel some anger, we must let them express it," said Deng Xiaoping. Demonstrators paraded shouting, "Long live democracy!" In Peking, Democracy Wall became known for its many big-character posters demanding freedom, democracy, and human rights. Chinese of all walks of life earnestly told foreign reporters of the ills of Chinese society and how they hoped for democracy.

Again, the liberalization episode was brief. By early 1979, most of the wall posters had been torn down, some overly outspoken democrats arrested, and private contacts with foreigners banned. Deng, like Mao, saw things going too far; he warned of the dangers of "bourgeois democracy."

Deng Xiaoping, certainly no democrat, had simply used a dash of liberalization to confirm his leading position. Some observers mistakenly thought Peking's moderate leadership would usher in a kind of democracy. Americans especially have always overestimated China's democratic potential. But neither moderates nor radicals have any intention of giving up the party's control.

The Rise and Fall of "Spiritual Pollution"

The four-month campaign against "spiritual pollution" illustrates what can go wrong with Chinese politics: one word from the top and nuttiness can break out again. This time the word was Deng Xiaoping's October 1983 warning that "spiritual pollution essentially means the spreading of various decadent and declining ideologies of the bourgeoisie and other exploiting classes, and the spreading of sentiments of distrust regarding the cause of socialism and communism and the leadership of the Community Party."

Nobody knew what this meant, but that didn't stop them. Some took it as a warning against Western influence, so they stopped speaking to foreigners, clipped too-long hair, and shunned Western clothes and music. Others thought it meant to not go too far with free enterprise, so they interrupted production with study sessions. Hard-liners in the party saw the campaign as a chance to roll back China's liberalization. Deng probably saw this last as a threat to his power and line of succession, so he called off the "spiritual pollution" campaign in January 1984.

The campaign sent shudders through some Chinese, for it reminded them of how the Cultural Revolution began. Compared to the Cultural Revolution, the spiritual-pollution campaign was nothing, but it did show that within the CCP there are plenty of leftists just waiting for the opportunity to go back to the Mao line. What Deng gave, Deng could take away, and Deng was still very much a Communist.

WHAT THE CHINESE QUARREL ABOUT

WAS MAO A WRECKER?

With Mao dead and the Gang of Four jailed, some Chinese, especially within the political elite, have criticized the Great Helmsman, raising the question that Mao may have had at least a partially destructive impact. Symbolically, in 1980 the gigantic portraits of Mao that festooned China came down. Whether Mao was good or bad for China became a major political debate.

Criticism focuses on the last two decades of Mao's life; virtually everyone agrees that during the 1930s and 1940s Mao was a great revolutionary leader and thinker. But in power, Mao couldn't leave well enough alone. He instituted one harmful campaign after another, disorienting the people and CCP cadres, and retarding economic growth. Some Chinese call the period of 1966–76 "the lost decade." Mao, many Chinese believe, simply lived twenty years too long, becoming an underminer rather than a creator.

Economically, China has not been quite the success story touted by its friends abroad (see box, "China's Economy: A Success Story?"). China had good growth in the mid-1950s when Soviet aid flowered generously, administered by Soviet technicians. That ended with the disruption of the Great Leap Forward and withdrawal of Soviet help in 1960. In 1967 and 1968, the Chinese GNP actually declined owing to the Cultural Revolution. China, having turned to the West for capital and technology, is no longer a model for Third World radicals seeking a magic formula for quick economic growth.

Much, if not all, of the blame for China's laggard economic performance points to Mao and his meddling. A Chinese leadership that wishes to modernize and industrialize may therefore directly or indirectly permit criticism of Mao. But the criticism is limited. Mao was indeed a wrecker, but he was also the founder of the People's Republic. If criticism of Mao goes too far, it could un-

---

China's Economy: A Success Story?

For twenty years, from 1957 to 1977, China released no economic statistics, an indication that its performance was poor. With Deng Xiaoping's pragmatic efforts at economic growth, however, China began releasing economic figures and even let in Western experts. The figures are double-edged. During the early 1980s, the Chinese economy improved hugely—GNP grew an astonishing 12 percent in 1984—but only because China at this time abandoned strict socialism for a partially market economy. This kind of success is embarrassing, for it shows that private enterprise works and socialism doesn't.

In the Third World, China is one of the better-off countries. Its life expectancy of sixty-seven years is by far the highest and rivals that of many middle-income countries. Its 69 percent literacy rate is also very high for the Third World. With the "responsibility system" in agriculture, China has enjoyed excellent harvests, and food rationing has disappeared. Rent is very cheap, but apartments are small and scarce. The Chinese press has admitted that 35 percent of urban dwellers have inadequate housing; many families have only about 2.5 square yards (2 square meters) per person. Few have toilets or running water.

dermine the legitimacy of the entire system. Accordingly, whatever the Chinese political elite say about Mao among themselves, they will not permit public criticism to go very far. Just as destalinization had to be stopped in the Soviet Union, demaoization has its limits in China. The great question of post-Mao politics in China is how much to repudiate Mao, a lot or a little? Deng Xiaoping tried to strike a judicious balance: "Mao was 70 percent right and 30 percent wrong."

A MARKET ECONOMY FOR CHINA?

In the 1980s, some amazing changes took place in the Chinese economy. China, like all Communist countries, faced the question of how centralized the economy should be and decided on decentralization. Under Mao, this would never have happened, and people advocating it would have been purged as "capitalist roaders." We still cannot be sure how far it will go.

The most sweeping changes came in the countryside, where 80 percent of China's population still live. Collectivized agriculture was reduced and families were permitted to go on the "responsibility system," a euphemism for private enterprise. Peasants lease land from the state—still no private owners—and must deliver a certain quota to the state at set prices. Beyond that, they can sell their produce on the free market for the best price they can get. They can choose their own crops and how to use fertilizer and farm machinery, which they buy at their own expense. When farmers complained that their one-to-three year leases discouraged them from putting in capital improvements, the leases were lengthened to fifteen years, in many cases with right of inheritance.

Farm production soared, food stands bulged, and farmers' incomes went up; a few even got rich. Since China has perhaps twice as many farmers as it needs, the state encouraged peasants to go into other lines of rural work. Country entrepreneurs started trucking, machine-repair, construction, and other businesses, all private.

The "responsibility system" spread to the cities. Faced with substantial unemployment, the regime let individuals open small shops, restaurants, repair stations, and even manufacturing facilities. It was even permissible to hire workers, something any Marxist would call capitalist exploitation. But it worked. Chinese applied individual hustle to produce and sell more and better products than the indifferent state factories and stores ever could. Hole-in-the-wall "department stores" had customers waiting in line to buy the fashionable clothing and footwear Mao used to scorn. People swarmed to outdoor markets to buy home-produced chairs and sofas. It was enough to bring tears to the eyes of an old-fashioned capitalist like Ronald Reagan or Margaret Thatcher.

State enterprises were told to shape up and make money or get closed down (some were). China decentralized its industrial decision-making, somewhat like Hungary and Yugoslavia, with firms competing in a market and trying to make profits. China's GNP and living standards went up appreciably.

But was this socialism? The bulk of the economy was still state-controlled and much of it not very productive. China's responsibility system resembled the Soviet Union's NEP of the 1920s when state ownership retreated to the "commanding heights" and private enterpreneurs took over farming and small businesses. But NEP didn't last; it was just a breathing spell before Stalin's brutal industrialization drive. Could China's responsibility system go the same way? Could it be just a pleasant interlude between socialist storms?

While the vast majority of Chinese liked their taste of the free market, many cadres did not. The problem parallels that of the Soviet Union. If you really go to a market system, what do you do with the cadres who make a good living by supervising a controlled economy? They dig in their heels and try to block major change. Deng and Hu tried to purge or retire the old guard and Maoist cadres and replace them with young technocrats who would pursue economic growth. But even the newer cadres were not interested in putting themselves out of jobs.

Further, market economies produce problems of their own (see box) and awaken resentments and jealousies. If a Chinese leader some time in the future decided to bring the economy more fully back under state control, he would not lack for helpers. And there would be nothing to stop him, for China is still very much a one-party dictatorship. American journalists and scholars reported glowingly of China's opening up and revival of capitalism, but some of them forgot that economic and political lines in China tend to swing back and forth. No reform in China is the last.

The Trouble with Markets

When a country such as Yugoslavia or China brings elements of a market economy into its socialism, it generally experiences improved economic performance but also starts to suffer some of the problems of capitalism:

- UNEMPLOYMENT appears. In most Communist systems unemployment is disguised by the gross labor inefficiency, but once firms have to compete on a market and make profits, they prune unproductive workers. Chinese workers under Mao had an "iron rice bowl"—jobs for life. Deng broke the iron rice bowl and made millions unemployed. China had to permit small-scale private enterprise to soak up some of these unemployed. Still, unemployment is an embarrassment for a Communist country.

- INCOME INEQUALITIES develop. Under the "responsibility system," some Chinese farmers, factories, and whole provinces get richer than others. The ones who don't do so well—especially the provinces with poorer soil and natural resources—become jealous and complain to Peking to redistribute some of the wealth. The richer provinces object, claiming they work harder and deserve more. Regional tensions seem likely to develop in China. A new leader from a poor area could attempt to push China back to Maoist egalitarianism.

- INFLATION kicks up. In a Communist economy, there is hidden inflation. Prices are set by the state, but many items are not available, so people use the "back door" to get them at higher cost. With much of China's food, clothing, and other consumer goods now sold on a more-or-less free market, and with demand high, a climb in prices is likely. Inflation makes people angry and jealous; they demand higher salaries. If inflation is strong, the regime becomes discredited and longs for the old days when they could control these things.

The problem of an economy that mixes socialism and capitalism is its instability. It tends not to settle in a middle ground but to slide more and more toward full capitalism until blocked by central control. The result is a zig-zag every few years as the government alternately tightens and relaxes supervision of the economy, never finding a stable balance. China is apt to be caught in this situation.

SOVIETS OR AMERICANS?

China was never the faithful Soviet puppet we thought it was. The CCP fought its own way to power by *ignoring* Stalin's advice, a point that underlies the Sino-Soviet dispute. Many scholars believe the split started with Khrushchev's destalinization and liberalization, all done before checking with Mao, who was still using Stalin as a revolutionary symbol. Then strategic issues arose. Mao wanted the Soviets to utilize their atomic and missile capability to stand up to the West and to protect China. Khrushchev, however, hoped for some kind of understanding with the West. Finally, the Chinese, against Soviet advice, plunged into the disastrous Great Leap Forward.

By the 1960s, the Chinese were denouncing the Soviets as unrevolutionary revisionists, cowards, and even imperialists. Old territorial claims were revived; Peking demanded return of certain border areas taken in previous centuries by Russia in "unequal treaties" with old China. In 1969, the two sides even fought briefly on the Ussuri River, which forms the eastern border of Manchuria. Neutral analysts believe the Chinese started the shooting.

By the 1970s, Peking was defining the Soviets as their greatest danger, imperialists of a new type, worse than the Americans. Discreet contacts opened between Peking and Washington, leading to President Nixon's 1972 visit and finally to the establishment of full diplomatic relations in 1979. China had gone a long way, from being a pupil of the Soviets to becoming their bitterest enemy.

It is ironic that it was the ultraradical moves of Mao and the Gang of Four that shoved China away from the Soviet Union and toward the United States, not that it was their intention to turn to America. By deliberately alienating their Soviet benefactors, however, they gave China little recourse. Ultraradical meant anti-Soviet, and this ultimately turned into pro-American and pro-Western policies generally.

Realistically, the quarrel has probably gone too far to patch up totally. Especially bothersome to the Chinese is the Soviet-protégé status of Vietnam on their southern border. The Chinese feel they're encircled. Deng Xiaoping called the Vietnamese "the Cubans of Asia" for their invasion of Cambodia. In 1979, China briefly crossed into Vietnam to teach upstart Hanoi a lesson. If anything, the lesson was that China was not prepared for a war.

It is doubtful if Peking will ever be pro-Soviet, but there are degrees of anti-Sovietism. At various times, Peking has put out conciliatory gestures to Moscow—some by "moderate" Deng Xiaoping—aimed at getting their stalled border talks going. Thus to say a Chinese leader is "moderate" or "pragmatic" does not define a pro- or anti-Soviet position. If the Western connection does not pay off, pragmatic moderates in Peking may conclude that the Soviets aren't so bad after all.

Ties with the United States have had only a modest payoff. The Sino-U.S. rapprochement of the early 1970s produced euphoria on both sides. Americans were relieved to learn that the Chinese were not the world-conquering fiends depicted by John Foster Dulles and Dean Rusk. In fact, the Chinese, worried about a possible Soviet strike, were downright friendly to the Americans, who they thought would deliver development assistance, military aid, and—most important—Taiwan. Washington was able to be of only small assistance in the first two categories and failed totally in the third. Although the Carter administration broke formal ties with Taiwan in order to establish them with Peking, informal ties linked Washington and Taiwan as closely as ever. Taiwan says no to any deal with the mainland.

Peking was especially unhappy with the pro-Taiwan and anti-Peking rhetoric Ronald Reagan used in the 1980 election. In office, Reagan did relatively little—his vice president, George Bush, had served as U.S. ambassador in China and was fully aware of its value—but was certainly not about to hand friendly, capitalist Taiwan over to the People's Republic. Reagan's cordial visit to Peking in 1984 partially patched up United States-China differences. Both sides now have a realistic appraisal of their relationship and do not expect too much.

China could go either way—or neither. Bad relations with one great power could push it to the other. If Reagan had delivered on his campaign rhetoric, it could have led to Peking's returning to Moscow's embrace. Trade is one problem between the United States and China (see box). Currently, Peking defines itself as a member—the leading member—of the Third World and votes that way in the U.N. China doesn't belong to anyone; it goes its own way, looking out for what's best for China.

Trade Wars?

All right, Americans. You told us to introduce a market system, and we did. You told us to make more consumer products, and we did. You told us to open up to international commerce, and we did. You sold us machinery. Now, who's going to buy all this stuff we're producing? You buy practically nothing from us. Big talk, Americans, but little action.

That, in a nutshell, is China's complaint about trade with the United States. United States-China trade expanded to $5 billion a year in the early 1980s, but still only 0.65 percent of United States imports were from China. Particularly galling to the Chinese were U.S. quotas on Chinese textiles. China is the world's biggest textile producer and is desperate for markets—but so are a lot of other East Asian nations;

they all want to get into the U.S. market. To protect the local textile industry, already hard hit by imports, the United States assigns quotas to textile exporters.

Potentially, China can make anything Taiwan, Hong Kong, South Korea, or even Japan can. But how many low-cost competitors can the world stand? The West is already vexed at Japan's ability to dominate the automobile, photo, and consumer-electronics markets. How would the West react if China utilized its low labor costs to produce such items? We coaxed China out of its shell; now we have to let her compete on the world market. If we don't, we're going to have a justifiably angry China to deal with.

DISSENT AND DEMOCRACY

Because we have better contact and communication with the Soviet Union, Americans have tended to focus on Soviet dissent and repression and to ignore the fact that human rights in China are no better than in the Soviet Union and possibly worse. In some ways, repression in China is more insidious than in the Soviet Union, for it is social as well as legal. In the Soviet Union, police may cart off a dissident for a harsh prison term, but in China the entire society is mobilized against dissidents. Instead of jail, a Chinese dissident—and there is no way to discern their number—is under "mass surveillance," meaning he or she is ostracized, observed, and reported on by all others in the community.

For thirty years after liberation and the brutal land reforms, former "rich peasants" were systematically discriminated against for their "bad class background." They were verbally abused, couldn't participate in politics, were barred from medical services, and got lower wages. Sometimes even their children were stigmatized.

Jail seems superfluous in China. One official explained to U.S. journalists why prisoners don't escape from Chinese jails that have no bars or locks. "All throughout China, we have mass surveillance," he replied. "Where would they go?"

Some, however, do go to jail. In 1979, former Red Guard member Wei Jingsheng, then 29 and editor of an underground newspaper, was sentenced to fifteen years in prison for advocating democracy, which the prosecutors called "agitating for the overthrow of the dictatorship of the proletariat." What really got Wei into trouble was a wall poster he put up, revealing that Chinese political prisoners are tortured, deprived of food, and not allowed to see relatives. The Chinese Gulag seems about as bad as the Soviet one, with near-starvation, little medical care, and overwork called "reform through labor."

Deng Xiaoping touted his "Four Modernizations" of agriculture, industry, science, and defense. Wei Jingsheng advocated a "fifth modernization" in a wall poster—democracy—which, in the Chinese context, is more like constitutionalism than the clash of parties in elections. Hardly anyone expects that. Prodemocratic Chinese seek the rule of law, curbs on arbitrary power, and basic civil rights. As Sakharov observed about democracy and free speech in Russia, the freedom to discuss questions openly is the foundation for progress in all fields. In the long run, Deng's Four Modernizations may fail without Wei's fifth one.

Babies as Politics

One Mao program continues in the Deng-Hu era: birth control. China is desperately trying to curb population growth—and with an annual increase of only about one percent, must be counted as highly successful. Much of the Third World increases at 3 percent; only Europe has a growth rate lower than China. But the costs in human terms are high. Urban Chinese couples are instructed to have one baby. If they have more, they can lose benefits and even their apartment. And Chinese love children. In some cities, women pregnant for the second or third time must undergo involuntary abortions. Some hide until it's too late for abortion.

Birth control is difficult to enforce in the countryside because children add to a family's labor force and provide social security for elderly parents. Under the new "responsibility system," children are once again a blessing on Chinese farms. Pressure from zealous Communist officials forces some Chinese parents to resort to the hideous but ancient practice of female infanticide. Peking denies encouraging the murder of newborn girls, but neither does it make an all-out effort to stop it.

Peking feels it has no choice. Even with low birthrates, China adds more than ten million new mouths to feed every year. There simply will not be enough food, jobs, or housing if China's population grows.

VOCABULARY BUILDING

arable	Great Leap Forward	mass surveillance	sphere of
Boxers	*Guomindang*	National Party	influence
cadre	Hundred Flowers	Congress	Standing
CCP	incentives	National People's	Committee
Confucian	*kowtow*	Congress	State Council
Cultural Revolution	Long March	Opium Wars	steady-state
cyclical change	Manchus	*pinyin*	Taipings
decentralization	Mandarin	PLA	Tiananmen
dynasty	Mandate of Heaven	PRC	Square
Four Modernizations	man-land radio	Red Guards	treaty ports
Gang of Four	Maoism	responsibility system	Wade-Giles
gentry	mass line	secular change	warlords

FURTHER REFERENCE

Bonavia, David. *The Chinese.* New York: Penguin Books, 1982.

Bulletin of Concerned Asian Scholars. *China from Mao to Deng: The Politics and Economics of Socialist Development.* Armonk, N.Y.: M. E. Sharpe, 1983.

Butterfield, Fox. *China: Alive in the Bitter Sea.* New York: Times Books, 1982.

Chen Jo-Hsi. *The Execution of Mayor Yin and Other Stories from the Great Proletarian Cultural Revolution.* Bloomington: Indiana University Press, 1978.

Dittmer, Lowell. "Chou En-Lai and Chinese Politics," in Edward Feit et al., eds. *Governments and Leaders: An Approach to Comparative Politics.* Boston: Houghton Mifflin, 1978.

Fairbank, John King. *The United States and China,* 4th ed. Cambridge, Mass.: Harvard University Press, 1979.

Fraser, John. *The Chinese: Portrait of a People.* New York: Summit Books, 1980.

Frolic, B. Michael. *Mao's People.* Cambridge, Mass.: Harvard University Press, 1980.

Gardner, John. *Chinese Politics and the Succession to Mao.* New York: Holmes & Meier, 1982.

Griffith, Samuel B. *Mao Tse-Tung on Guerrilla Warfare.* New York: Praeger, 1961.

Karnow, Stanley. *Mao and China: Inside China's Cultural Revolution.* New York: Penguin Books, 1984.

Lee, Hong Yung. *The Politics of the Chinese Cultural Revolution.* Berkeley: University of California Press, 1978.

MacFarquhar, Roderick. *The Origins of the Cultural Revolution,* 2 vols. New York: Columbia University Press, 1974, 1983.

Mathews, Jay and Linda. *One Billion: A China Chronicle.* New York: Random House, 1983.

Moody, Peter R. *Chinese Politics after Mao: Development and Liberalization, 1976 to 1983.* New York: Praeger, 1983.

Nathan, Andrew J. "An Analysis of Factionalism of Chinese Communist Party Politics," in Frank P. Belloni and Dennis C. Beller, eds., *Faction Politics: Political Parties and Factionalism in Comparative Perspective.* Santa Barbara, Calif.: ABC-Clio, 1978.

Nee, Victor, and David Mozingo, eds. *State and Society in Contemporary China.* Ithaca, N.Y.: Cornell University Press, 1983.

Pye, Lucian W. *The Dynamics of Chinese Politics.* Cambridge, Mass.: Oelgeschlager, Gunn & Hain, 1981.

Schell, Orville. *To Get Rich is Glorious: China in the Eighties.* New York: Pantheon Books, 1985.

Schram, Stuart R. *Mao Zedong: A Preliminary Reassessment.* New York: St. Martin's Press, 1984.

Spence, Jonathan D. *The Gate of Heavenly Peace: The Chinese and Their Revolution, 1895–1980.* New York: Viking Books, 1981.

Waller, Derek J. *The Government and Politics of the People's Republic of China,* 3d ed. New York: New York University Press, 1982.

Wang, James C. F. *Contemporary Chinese Politics: An Introduction,* 2d ed. Englewood Cliffs, N.J.: Prentice-Hall, 1985.

Wolfgang, Marvin E., ed. "China in Transition," *Annals of the American Academy of Political and Social Science* 476 (November 1984).

Zagoria, Donald S. "China's Quiet Revolution," *Foreign Affairs* 62 (Spring 1984) 4.

23

BRAZIL

THE IMPACT OF THE PAST

THE PORTUGUESE INFLUENCE

Portugal had a claim to Brazil even before its explorers arrived there. In 1494 the Treaty of Tordesillas gave Portugal lands in the yet-unexplored New World. The treaty drew a line 370 leagues (some 1,100 miles) west of the Cape Verde Islands; land to the east of the line went to Portugal; and land to the west, to Spain. This arrangement sliced off the easternmost bulge of present-day Brazil; subsequent Portuguese settlements pushed their control further westward to give Brazil its present borders. The first Portuguese arrived in 1500, when Pedro Alvares Cabral, claiming he was blown off course, took formal possession of the land for the king of Portugal.

Portugal did not administer its new colony in the way Spain did. The Spanish charged quickly into Latin America in search of "gold, God, and glory." The Portuguese did nothing for thirty years, partly because they were busy with the rich trade route to India and partly because Brazil seemed to offer little gold. About the only Portuguese interest in the new land was in the red wood that could be used to make dye. From the brazed color of brazilwood came the name Brazil (*Brasil* in Portuguese).

It was when the French started to settle there in 1530 that the Portuguese crown began to take an interest. Ordering the French expelled, Dom João (King John) III parceled out the coastline into fifteen *capitanias* or royal grants, which he gave, in the feudal manner, to wealthy Portuguese willing to finance settlement. The original *capitanias,* like the thirteen English colonies in North America, gave initial shape to Brazil's present-day states and laid the foundation for its federalism. Growth in the *capitanias,* however, was slow and spotty. Portugal's population at that time was only around one million, and there were not many people eager to become colonists. Compared to the Spanish colonies, there were no quick and easy mineral riches to be found in Brazil.

Economic life centered on sugar, for which Europe had recently acquired a taste. Sugar raising requires lots of labor, however. The Indians of Brazil were relatively few in number and made poor slaves; some preferred to die rather than work. With many trading posts down the African coast, though, the Portuguese found their answer in black slaves. From the 1530s to the 1850s, at least three million Africans were brought to Brazil and sold, chiefly to work in the sugar-cane fields. Interbreeding among the three population groups—Indians, blacks, and Portuguese—was rife, producing Brazil's complex racial mixture. The Portuguese always prided themselves on being nonracist, and this attitude, in public anyway, carries over into present-day Brazil.

Other Portuguese attitudes distinguish Brazil from the former Spanish colonies of Latin America. Portuguese have been less inclined to violence and bloodshed than Spaniards. As many Portuguese point out: "In a Portuguese bullfight, we don't kill the bull." Flexibility and compromise are more valued in Brazilian politics than in the politics of its Hispanic neighbors.

Black, white, and Indian blood flowed together freely in Brazil, producing a complex racial mixture. (Michael Roskin)

A PAINLESS INDEPENDENCE

Brazil's independence from Portugal is also in marked contrast to the long struggles waged by the Spanish colonies. Slowly Brazil grew in population and importance. When the Netherlands made Pernambuco (now Recife) a Dutch colony in the mid-seventeenth century, Portuguese, blacks, and Indians together struggled to expel them, and in the process began to think of themselves as Brazilians. In the 1690s, gold was discovered in what became the state of Minas Gerais (General Mines). A gold rush and later a diamond rush boosted Brazil's population. Economic activity shifted from the sugar-growing region of the Northeast to the South and stayed there. To this day, the boom area has been in the more temperate climes of the South, while the Northeast, impoverished and drought-stricken, has become a problem area.

By the late eighteenth century, Brazil had become more important economically than Portugal, and thoughts of independence began to flicker in the growing Brazilian consciousness, inspired, as throughout Latin America, by the U.S. example. Brazilian independence, curiously, came about partly because of Napoleon.

In trying to seal off the European continent from Britain, Napoleon sent an army to take Portugal in 1807. The royal court in Lisbon—some fifteen thousand people in all—at British prodding, boarded ships and sailed for Brazil. Dom João VI was at first wildly welcomed in Brazil, but the royal court was horrified at conditions in Rio and irritated leading residents by requisitioning their houses. Dom João ordered Rio cleaned, beautified, and turned into a true capital. In 1815, Brazil was raised in rank from colony to kingdom within the Portuguese empire.

In 1821, the British advised Dom João to return to Lisbon to make sure Portuguese liberals didn't get out of hand. He left his son, Dom Pedro, then age

BRAZIL

23, as regent in Brazil and gave him some parting advice: if Brazilian independence became inevitable, he should be sure he headed the new government. It was a pragmatic, level-headed idea, an example of Portuguese flexibility in contrast to Spanish obduracy. In this way the Portuguese royal house served as a bridge between colonial and independent status. In 1822 Dom Pedro proclaimed Brazil independent, and Portugal did not resist.

FROM EMPIRE TO REPUBLIC

Monarchy is rare in the Western Hemisphere; it appeared only briefly in Haiti and Mexico (Maximilian). Brazil, however, was a true monarchy from 1822 to 1889, another point of contrast with the rest of Latin America. Dom Pedro I proved an inept ruler, and when the army turned against him he abdicated in 1831 while his Brazilian-born son was still a child. Under a regency—a council that runs affairs until a king comes of age—power was dispersed among the various states; an 1834 act set up states' rights and introduced de facto federalism. Politics became a series of quarrels among the states and the rich landowning families that ran them. The instability was so serious that it led finally to widespread agreement in 1840 to declare Dom Pedro II—only 14 years old—of age.

Dom Pedro II was beloved for his calm, tolerant manner and obvious concern for his nation. He did not, however, do much of anything. Basing his rule on big plantation owners *(fazendeiros)*, Pedro was content to let things drift while he exercised the "moderating power" of the liberal 1824 constitution in appointing and dismissing ministers. But the Brazilian economy changed. The large landowners mattered less while vigorous businessmen and bankers gained in importance. The growing modern element came to resent the conservative monarchy and to want a republic. One big question Dom Pedro II couldn't handle was slavery. Under British pressure, the importation of new slaves ended during the 1850s, but slavery continued, deemed humane and necessary by Pedro's landowning supporters. Various formulas for phasing out slavery were considered, but Pedro let the question drift until his daughter, Princess Isabel, acting as regent while he was in Europe, signed an abolition bill in 1888. Brazil was the last Western country to emancipate its slaves.

"Order and Progress"

French philosopher Auguste Comte (1798—1857) developed a doctrine known as Positivism. With its slogan of "Order and Progress," this optimistic philosophy held that mankind can and will progress by turning away from theology and abstract speculation and toward the scientific study of nature and of society. By applying the natural-science methods of empirical observation and data gathering, society can be analyzed, predicted, and then perfected, not in a revolutionary way, but gradually and under the supervision of humanitarian specialists.

Comte's Positivism launched modern social science and took root in Brazil. By the 1880s many Brazilian army officers had been instructed in Positivism by the mathematics professor Benjamin Constant Magalhães, who taught in the national military academy. With the 1889 republic, Positivists put their motto into the Brazilian flag, where it remains to this day: *Ordem e Progresso.*

By now, wide sectors of the Brazilian population were disgusted with monarchy. Intellectuals and army officers, imbued with Positivist philosophy (see box), wanted modernization. Deprived of their slaves, even the plantation owners turned against Dom Pedro. In 1889, a military coup ended the monarchy and introduced a republic without firing a shot.

THE OLD REPUBLIC

The relative stability conferred by Brazil's Portuguese heritage, bloodless independence, and nineteenth-century monarchy wore off during the Old Republic (1889—1930), and Brazil came to resemble its Hispanic neighbors. Revolts, rigged elections, and military intervention marked this period.

The 1891 constitution was modeled after the United States', but in practice, power gravitated into the hands of political bosses (*coronéis*, "colonels") and the military. For most of the Old Republic, the presidency simply alternated between the political bosses of two of the most important states, São Paulo and Minas Gerais.

Grumbling increased during the life of the Old Republic. New sectors of the population became aware that their interests were unheeded by the conservative political bosses. Idealistic army officers revolted in 1922 and 1924, believing they could save the republic. The Brazilian army at this time was by no means conservative. Some officers still had a touch of Positivism and hated conservative politicians, who seemed to block progress. To this day, the Brazilian military sees itself as a progressive rather than as a conservative force.

What probably finally destroyed the Old Republic was the worldwide depression and the collapse of the price of coffee, a crop that Brazil depended upon heavily for export earnings. Further, in 1930 a split developed in the old Paulista-Mineiro combination, and a crafty politician from Rio Grande do Sul—the home of many maverick politicans—took advantage of it to run for the presidency. Getúlio Vargas claimed the election results had been rigged against him (an entirely plausible charge) and, with help from the military and amidst great popular acclaim, took over the presidency in Rio in October 1930.

VARGAS'S "NEW STATE"

Latin American revolutionary strongmen (*caudillos* in Spanish, *caudilhos* in Portuguese) are hard to label, for they appear to be both leftist and rightist simultaneously. They claim to be for the people and are proud of the many welfare measures they institute. Often they create a labor movement and give it a privileged status that is long remembered among the working class. On the other hand, they are no more democratic than the old political bosses they overthrew and often support the interests of existing elites, such as keeping coffee prices high. And they are very much for "order."

Some call such figures as Vargas of Brazil and Perón of Argentina fascists, but they probably are not. Rather than building a party along ideological lines, these populist dictators mobilized the masses with their personal appeal. During the 1930s and 1940s, however, when fascism in Europe was having its day, they did sometimes throw in some fascistic rhetoric.

Vargas, like Perón, looked after the working class. Under Vargas, Brazil instituted an eight-hour day, minimum wages, paid vacations, and collective bargaining. Labor did not fight and win its rights; Vargas handed them over long before there was an organized labor movement to make demands. The result, as in much of Latin America, is a weak labor movement that constantly seeks the protection of a paternalistic state.

Vargas's 1934 constitution brought in a "corporatist" element—one-fifth of the legislature directly represented professional and trade groups—on the pattern of Italy and Portugal. The constitution also limited the president to a single four-year term. By 1937, however, Vargas decided he wanted to stay president and carried out a coup against his own regime. He proclaimed himself president, but this time there was no legislature to limit his powers. Vargas called his regime the *Estado Nôvo*, the New State. His critics called it "fascism with sugar." There was material progress—industry, highways, public health, social welfare—but there was also a loss of freedom. The United States got along well with Vargas, for he did not curb U.S. investments. In 1942, Brazil even declared war on the Axis.

Vargas discovered the power of the urban working class and mobilized them to his cause by setting up labor unions and the *Partido Trabalhista Brasileiro* (Brazilian Labor party, PTB for short). The military, however, became alarmed at his populistic dictatorship and forced him to resign in 1945. By then Vargas had become a hero to many Brazilians, who continued to support his PTB. In both Brazil and Argentina, the working masses longed for the return of their respective dictators and reelected them to office, Vargas in 1950 and Perón in 1946 and 1973. Once mobilized by a populistic dictator, the masses may prefer such rulers to democracy.

THE RISE AND FALL
OF JANGO GOULART

The reelected Vargas was a poor president; corruption and inflation soared. Many Brazilians, including top military officers, demanded he resign in 1954. Instead, he committed suicide, blaming reactionary international (that is, U.S.) and domestic forces for blocking his good works. One of Vargas's appointments had particularly angered the military. Vargas named a neighbor from Rio Grande do Sul, the radical João (Jango) Goulart, as labor minister, but the military forced him to resign in 1954.

Goulart, however, continued to head the PTB and in 1955 helped moderate Juscelino Kubitschek win the presidency with Goulart as vice-president. Kubitschek mobilized into his Social Democratic party (PSD) the old political class of state and local elites who had dominated Brazil before Vargas. Kubitschek tried to focus Brazilians' energies on developing the interior; he pushed construction of Brasilia, which became the capital in 1960. Heedless of economic problems, Kubitschek promoted industrialization and allowed inflation to skyrocket.

Brazil's working masses were still responsive to populist appeals. In 1960 a Paulista populist, Jânio Quadros, won the presidency in a landslide with reformist promises; Goulart was vice-president. An unstable character, Quadros resigned after just seven months, leaving a quixotic note reminiscent of Vargas's. Now Goulart, the very man the military forced out in 1954, was in line for the presidency.

The Brazilian army started talking about a coup, but a compromise was worked out: Goulart could be president but with the powers of that office greatly curtailed. Goulart accepted but played a waiting game. As the economy got worse—inflation climbed to 100 percent a year by 1964—he knew that the Brazilian masses, by now mobilized and seething with demands for radical change, would support him in a leftward course. Goulart's strategy worked: in a January

1963 plebiscite Brazilians voted five to one to restore full powers to the president so he could deal with the economic chaos.

Goulart now veered further left and called for "Basic Reforms": land redistribution, nationalizing the oil industry, enfranchising illiterates, legalizing the Communist party, and turning the legislature, which had blocked his schemes, into a "congress composed of peasants, workers, sergeants, and nationalist officers."

Brazilian society—like France and Germany in earlier decades—split into leftist and conservative wings with very little middle ground. Conservatives, including most middle-class Brazilians, were horrified at Goulart and his appointment of Marxists to high positions. The United States saw Goulart as another Castro, cut off financial aid, and stepped up covert activity to destabilize the Goulart government. Brazil seemed to be on the edge of a revolution.

What finally brought Goulart down was his challenge to the armed forces. Goulart publicly supported some mutinous sailors, which Brazil's generals saw as undermining their military discipline and command structure. On March 31, 1964, with scarcely a shot, the armed forces put an end to Brazil's tumultuous democracy.

THE KEY INSTITUTIONS

THE MILITARY AS POLITICAL INSTITUTION

As in much of the Third World, Brazil's political institutions were—and still are—weak. Unlike Europe with its well-established parliaments, parties, and bureaucracies, Brazil's political institutions were incapable of handling the demands of mass politics in an orderly way. In such circumstances, the army is often the only institution capable of governing.

The Brazilian military had intervened in politics many times before 1964; at the birth and through the life of the Old Republic, at first in support of Vargas and then against him, and at the establishment of reasonably democratic regimes at the end of the two Vargas periods. Prior to 1964, however, the Brazilian military never tried to stay in power. They saw themselves in much the same way as Dom Pedro II had seen his role, that of a "moderating power" to restrain politicians from excesses. Step in when need be, set things right, then step out, was the Brazilian military pattern.

By 1964, both the Brazilian military attitude and the nation's situation had changed. Brazilian officers, partly thanks to U.S. guidance, had redefined their mission from defending Brazil against external enemies to guarding it against internal threats, especially communism. In the Superior War College, the ESG (see box), top officers studied politics, economics, psychology, and counterinsurgency.

Thus the Brazilian military, technically highly trained and newly motivated toward a more active role in their country's politics, was ready to upset a long-held view (especially by Americans) that truly professional military officers do not engage in coups. Looking around, the Brazilian officers found—almost like a case study—that Brazil was sliding rapidly to the left. The Brazilian army chose to intervene, and it did so precisely because it was professionally trained to prevent revolution. This time the officers were determined to stay in power, block the return of divisive politics, and modernize their potentially rich country in an organized, rational manner.

For two decades, Brazil was governed by a succession of generals. The Brazilian military did not rule the country directly, as if it were an army camp. Rather, they structured the political system so that only a military officer or a civilian who had worked closely and cooperatively with the military could attain executive office. Once named president, a Brazilian general usually retired from active service and seldom wore his uniform.

Can an army be a political institution? Historically, the evidence is against the military holding power permanently. Armies are clumsy tools to govern with. After some years, military regimes tend to return power to civilians, or turn into civilian regimes themselves, or get overthrown in a new military coup. The first is what happened in Brazil in the early 1980s.

Brazil's military regime was not just military, and that may be why it lasted so long. The Brazilian military had close ties to civilian bankers, educators, industrialists, and governmental administrators, many of whom trained together in the Superior War College in Rio. The weakness of most military regimes is their isolation and lack of contact with civilian elites. Unable to run the complexities of economy, society, and diplomacy without skilled civilians, military regimes frequently blunder so badly they decide to give up power and responsibility.

Brazil's Powerful Military School

A school facing a luxurious Rio beach would not normally seem a likely spot for a powerful political institution, but in Brazil virtually an entire ruling class emerged from the Superior War College (*Escola Superior de Guerra*, ESG). Founded in 1949 on the model of the U.S. National War College (which trains midcareer officers for higher command), by the 1960s the ESG had shifted its emphasis from external to internal security. Still influenced by the old Positivism—which, in fact, had been spread in the last century through Brazil's military academy—ESG students came to the conclusion that only Brazil's rapid economic development would save it from chaos and communism.

The ESG, it is interesting to note, trains not only the best colonels and generals, but top civilians as well. Government administrators, private industrialists, and leading professional people have tended to outnumber ESG's military students. The ESG draws its ninety students a year from key areas of the political and economic power structure: banking, mass communications, education, and industry. ESG's graduates return to their branches, imbued with the authoritarian developmentalist doctrines they learned at the school.

The ESG actually resembles a French *grande école* such as the Polytechnique or ENA, except that ESG students are generally older and already established in careers. In both cases, however, the schools put their stamp on bright, carefully selected people, training them to think and act the same way and to maintain close ties with each other. This is what gives French and Brazilian policy making its cohesion and continuity. "We don't actually make government policy," said a senior Brazilian officer on the ESG staff. "The great contribution of the school has been to establish an elite of people who can think in the same language and who have learned the team approach to planning here." The French couldn't have said it better.

Brazil's generals mostly avoided this kind of isolation by partially integrating themselves with conservative civilian elites who held views and values close to the military's. Brazil's "military" regime was actually a civilian-military network of authoritarian developmentalists who controlled most of Brazil's economic, political, and military structures. In public, the government looked civilian. Most executive positions were occupied by civilian technocrats. But behind them, making the basic decisions and insuring order, was the military.

THE PRESIDENCY

The military presidents of Brazil were extremely powerful, their civilian successors less so. When generals ran Brazil–and every president from 1964 to 1984 was a general–the only check that kept them from becoming dictators was the fact that they were part of the military and needed the support of their military colleagues. Brazilian generals, trained in teamwork, disliked the flamboyant, personalistic style of civilian politicians. Consequently, no military president tried to turn himself into a one-man dictator or even to stay in office more than one term.

All but one of Brazil's military presidents were chosen from among its sixteen four-star generals. This meant they were older, around 60, experienced, and well educated, having gone through several highly competitive military schools. All attended the ESG. Additionally, most previously headed the important National Intelligence Service, which served as a sort of brain center and watchdog for what the generals called their "revolution."

The Waltz of the Generals:
Brazil's Presidents, 1964–85

1964–67 Gen. Humberto de Alencar Castello Branco	1974–79 Gen. Ernesto Geisel
1967–69 Gen. Arthur da Costa e Silva	1979–85 Gen. João Baptista de Oliveira Figueiredo
1969–74 Gen. Emilio Garrastazú Médici	

The incumbent president had a large say in selecting his successor but usually did it in consultation with a small circle of fellow generals known as "the system." The choice was simply announced to a government-controlled party which adopted him as its candidate. Then an electoral college composed of legislators of both houses and some from the states—and packed with a progovernment majority—rubber-stamped its approval. They called it an election.

In 1985, Brazil's first civilian president since 1964 was chosen indirectly, by an electoral college of 686 federal and state legislators. Although there was a popular outcry for direct elections, the military was afraid that a radical populist of the Goulart stripe might win. The military thought they had the electoral college stacked in favor of the government party, but it split, and the moderate opposition leader, Tancredo Neves, was elected over the generals' objections.

Brazil's "Information" Service

A curious institution gave Brazil's military control over political life and still plays an unclear but probably major role. The National Intelligence Service (*Serviço Nacional de Informaçoes, SNI*) is a combined FBI-CIA-national-planning agency, which not only supervised internal security (for example, the suppression of dissent) but also social and economic policy. Under the generals, every government ministry had an SNI overseer, and several of Brazil's military presidents had earlier been heads of the SNI. The SNI still exists even though Brazil's president is a civilian, implicitly warning him that if things get out of hand the military could step back in.

The President Who Never Was

Tancredo Neves was chosen Brazil's first civilian president in twenty-one years, but on the eve of his swearing-in on March 15, 1985, he was hospitalized and died a month later at age 75, never having taken the oath of office. Although not elected by a popular vote, Neves was a popular personality, a grandfatherly figure of moderation and balance.

In his place stepped José Sarney, who had been elected as vice president. This brought political problems for, unlike Neves, Sarney was not an opposition figure but a former president of the pro-military Democratic Socialist party, who had switched sides only the year before. Accordingly, Sarney, age 54, wasn't trusted by either side. Many Brazilians were convinced that things would have gone better with the beloved Tancredo.

Elected as vice president in 1985, José Sarney took over as president upon the death of President-elect Tancredo Neves. Sarney became Brazil's first civilian president in 21 years. (Reuter)

But they had set up the electoral system and could not very well denounce the results. This gave the civilian presidency at least temporary protection from a new military coup. The military indicated they would let the next presidential elections be direct, that is, based on popular vote.

Brazil's civilian president is not precisely a free agent. He must constantly look over his shoulder at the military and do nothing to upset them. Any major policy that goes too far too fast faces an implicit military veto or possibly even another coup. Brazilian presidents will never be able to rest easy that they are firmly in charge.

BRAZIL'S RESURGENT CONGRESS

Under the military, Brazil's Congress on paper looked like the United States Congress, but its powers were curbed to the point where it was little more than a façade the military found useful to make the system look more legitimate. Only two tame parties were permitted, the progovernment ARENA (*Alicança Renovadora Nacional,* the National Renovating Alliance) and the lightly critical opposition MDB (*Movimento Democrático Brasileiro,* the Brazilian Democratic Movement). Brazilian wags referred to the latter as the party of "Yes" and to the former as the party of "Yes, Sir!" Through a combination of indirect voting, a veto over candidates, and the power to annul political rights, the military had a comfortable majority of the party of "Yes, Sir!" in both houses.

Starting in 1979, the regime permitted a slow democratization called *abertura* (opening) and free elections in 1982 for governors of the twenty-three states, a sixty-nine member Senate (three Senators per state), and a 479-member Chamber of Deputies. Equipped with a fresh, new legitimacy, the Chamber of Deputies began challenging the military regime of President Figueiredo at precisely the time it was weakening and losing legitimacy. Brazil's Congress even managed to reject a few of the government's key bills, something that hadn't happened since 1964.

The transition Brazil made in the early 1980s illustrates the impossibility of holding a political system halfway between dictatorship and democracy . A

Comparing:
Spain Turns Democratic

In 1975, when Franco died, Spain was an authoritarian system with a hand-picked parliament, curbs on the press, and no legal political parties. Just two years later, Spain was a full-fledged democracy with a freely elected parliament, a lively and critical press, and a complete party system. The Franco system had become history. In 1982, the democratically minded Spanish Socialists were elected to power with an absolute majority of seats.

Dictators like to kid themselves that they have built lastingly. Their immediate successors like to think they can give a few tokens of democracy but preserve the authoritarian system. They can't. A little bit of democracy just whets people's appetites for more, and the system tends to slide all the way into full democracy. There are several points of comparison between Spain's rapid shift to democracy and Brazil's. Inside every dictatorship is a democracy longing to get out.

partially democratic system demands to go all the way and is impatient with restrictions laid down by the still-authoritarian executive branch. By 1985, Brazil
was a reasonably complete democracy intent on eradicating the last vestiges of a
generation of military rule. The chief engine of change in this process was the
democratically elected Congress and its parties.

NEW PARTIES

The new Congress was dominated by two large parties, both to some degree outgrowths of the old, tame parties. Most of the old ARENA retitled itself the Democratic Social party (*Partido Demócrata Social*, PDS), which despite its leftish-
sounding name was still conservative and cautious about democratization. A
creature of the military government, PDS lacked legitimacy and split when the
overbearing Paulo Salim Maluf captured its presidential nomination in 1984 by
means of generous favors. The overrepresentation of rural states and the
coronelismo (political bossism) still present there in the form of patronage gave
the PDS 41.5 percent of the popular vote in 1982 and 49 percent of the federal
deputies. The PDS was a weak party, an attempt to continue the policies and
personalities of the military era but with a democratic gloss.

Much of the old MDB turned itself into the *Partido do MDB* (PMDB), a
moderate opposition party pledged to reform but not drastically. Heavily urban
and drawing from the middle and better-off sectors of the working class, the
PMDB rallied behind the grandfatherly governor of Minas Gerais, Tancredo
Neves, who won in the electoral college but died without taking office. The
PMDB, basically a centrist party, was also structurally weak, an agglomeration of
all who opposed the military government but didn't agree on much else. Although the PMDB edged the PDS in the 1982 vote with 44 percent of the ballots,
it received only 42 percent of the seats owing to the overrepresentation of rural
states, where PDS held sway. Still, with help from other, smaller, opposition parties plus breakaway electors from the PDS (including José Sarney) who detested
Maluf, the PMDB gained a majority in the electoral college in 1985.

Three small parties to the left of the PMDB emerged, all with *trabalhista*
(labor) in their names. The PDT (Democratic Labor Party) was the personal vehicle of Leonel Brizola, a supporter and brother-in-law of the radical Jango
Goulart, whom the military had ousted in 1964. Brizola went into exile but was
allowed back in 1979. He built up the PDT and with it won the governorship of
Rio de Janeiro state in 1982. Brizola was one of the reasons the military refused
to allow direct elections to the presidency; they were afraid Brizola might win.
With support concentrated in Rio and Rio Grande do Sul (Brizola's home state),
the PDT won only 6 percent of the votes and 5 percent of the federal deputies in
1982. Bear in mind, however, that the PDT was just getting started and lacked
the resources and networks the two big parties had carried over with them from
the authoritarian era.

The smaller PTB, bearing the magical name of Vargas's old party, won
less than 5 percent of the vote in 1982 and less than 3 percent of the seats. The
most radical party, the PT, won less than 4 percent of the vote in 1982 and under
2 percent of the deputies. The PT was led by the charismatic union organizer

Luis Inácio da Silva, nicknamed by his fans "Lula." Espousing a combination of Marxism and Catholic liberation theology, the PT drew militant workers and radical intellectuals. Most likely, the Brazilian political spectrum has room for only one left party, and that will probably be Brizola's PDT.

"Diretas Ja!"

In 1984, the cry of "direct elections now" rocked Brazil's cities. Millions of demonstrators wanted Brazil's new president elected by popular vote rather than by the electoral college. The military would not budge; they feared that direct elections could lead to another radical populist's taking power. The new president promised that the next elections would be direct, and the military seemed to indicate it would go along with that.

A LACK OF INSTITUTIONS

Part of the reason Brazil got into its political fix was the lack of sturdy institutions that could handle the influx of newly mobilized sectors of the population and their demands. In the absence of firm, well-established parties and parliaments, demagogic leftists aroused both the masses and the military. The military won, and, as we shall see, the masses lost. The trouble was that the Brazilian military did not really found durable institutions either.

The two largest parties, the PDS and PMDB, were weak and prone to factionalism and breakup. The small leftist parties were attempting to play the populist card—arousing the masses, as Vargas and Goulart did—but if they succeeded, the military would step back in. The democratically elected Congress was weak and untried, and its largest party was a carryover from the authoritarian period.

The military and its creations proved that they could not become durable institutions either. For a while, they pleased the generals and their technocratic helpers, but they had nothing to say to the vast majority of Brazilians. One of the principal functions of political institutions is winning and channeling mass loyalty to the system. Without such loyalty, mere technical arrangements, even if they work well in promoting economic growth, become more and more isolated from the population they rule. Franco's Spain supervised an economic boom, but there was little positive feeling among Spaniards for the Franco institutions. After his death in 1975, those institutions were dismantled with scarcely a protest.

To their credit, Brazil's ruling generals saw the same situation developing. Wide sectors of the population voiced their displeasure with continued military rule. Workers wouldn't stay cowed; strikes flared. Students again grew rebellious. Even groups of better-off Brazilians—bankers, industrialists, and big farmers—who were earlier supporters of the military regime expressed annoyance over economic intrusion and mistakes on the part of the regime. During the 1970s Brazil's ruling generals came to appreciate how difficult it is to run a country.

But the democratization of the 1980s has not guaranteed a happy ending either. The demands on the new civilian government have been incredible: growing poverty, joblessness, inflation, crime, and international debt. And all this falling on weak, immature institutions. Can Brazil's infant democracy handle the strain? If it can't, the military may step back in, and that is not a viable solution either. Indeed, by stunting the growth of solid institutions, the Brazilian military did great harm to the country. We hold our breath to see if Brazil can escape from its cycle of weak civilian institutions overthrown by clumsy military institutions, which in turn give way to weak civilian institutions again.

BRAZILIAN POLITICAL ATTITUDES

THE EASYGOING IMAGE

Both Brazilians and resident foreigners tend to describe Brazilians as easygoing people, seldom angry or violent, largely indifferent to politics, and unlikely to rise in revolt. There's a lot of truth to this image. In most of Brazil for most of the year it's too hot to make a revolution. People would rather go to the beach.

Brazilians have better things to do with their energies than take them out in politics. Brazilians are emotional; they laugh, joke, and embrace in public. They love children—possibly, some suggest, because the infant mortality rate is so high—and tend to spoil their offspring, especially the boys. This creates a male-centered society in which the men are expected to indulge themselves but not the women.

Many of the Portuguese who settled Brazil either were minor noblemen or pretended they were. They brought with them antiwork attitudes and looked down on tawdry moneymaking. Until fairly recently this attitude was still present in the Brazilian middle and upper classes, limiting their entrepreneurial energy. Many of the more vigorous business and government people have been of non-Portuguese origin (German, Italian, Japanese, and Eastern European). Avoidance of work is common throughout the middle and upper classes in the Third World; people would rather attach themselves to the state bureaucracy than develop private industry. The elements of hustle and vigor are missing from much

Personalismo and Machismo

Latin American politicians, including Brazilians, frequently rely on personal magnetism—*personalismo*—in politics rather than on clear thinking, party programs, or patient organizing. Most Latin Americans like to be perceived as having a strong personality, the men especially as *macho. Macho* simply means male, but *machismo* has taken on the meaning of a strutting, exaggerated masculinity. The typical Latin American politician, civilian or military, combines *personalismo* and *machismo* in varying degrees.

The Brazilian generals, given the way in which they are selected for power, tend to downplay these qualities. With the return of civilian politics in the 1980s, however, we can expect to see a reappearance of *personalismo* and *machismo* in Brazilian politics.

of Latin American capitalism, a point sometimes offered as an explanation of both backwardness and penetration by U.S. capital.

The image of Brazilians as lazy and laid-back amidst tropical languor, however, may have been overdone. An economy doesn't expand at rates around 10 percent a year without people working hard. The "tropical languor" theory may have been deliberately cultivated in Brazil, for it serves as a rationalization for keeping the broad mass of Brazilians apolitical while leaving elites free to run the country as they wish. Brazilian elites tell themselves that the poor are content in their ignorance and are apathetic by nature. They, the elites, must shoulder the arduous tasks of running government and the business sector, both of which they keep for themselves.

Furthermore, there wasn't anything easygoing about Brazilian attitudes as the country approached the brink of social collapse in the 1980s. Desperate people, some of them reduced from middle-class jobs to street peddling, turned angry. More than a quarter of Brazilian workers were unemployed, and Brazil has no such things as unemployment compensation, welfare benefits, or food stamps. When Brazilians have no more money for food, they starve, or steal.

BRAZILIAN RACISM

One area where the easygoing Brazilian attitude has helped to keep society calm and stable is their proclaimed indifference to race. Some one third of Brazilians are black, giving Brazil the largest African-descended population outside of Africa. Precise classification is impossible, however, because of both racial mixing and the Latin American tendency to let culture decide race. Throughout the continent, a person with the right education, manners, and money is considered "European," with little regard to skin color. Brazilians have dozens of words to distinguish among the combinations that make up the country's racial spectrum: *branco, alvo,* and *claro* for the lighter skinned, *moreno* and *mulato* for the middle shades, and *negro, preto, cabo verde,* and *escuro* for the darker. In theory and in most public places, there is no discrimination in Brazil. Walking down the street, one Brazilian feels as good as another.

Brazil's dirty little secret, however, is that in fact it is a racist society, one that adheres to the old American song: "If you're white you're all right, and if you're brown stick around, but if you're black get back." Career chances are strongly related to skin color in Brazil. If you're white, your chances of going to a university, entering a profession, making lots of money, and living in a nice house are much, much higher. If you're black, you run a high risk of infant death, malnutrition, rural poverty, and the lowest jobs or unemployment.

The Brazilian economic and political elite is white. This holds true whether the government is civilian or military. A small number of blacks have moved upward, but their way is often blocked by job requirements specifying "good appearance" (that is, white or near-white). Individual blacks can succeed in entertainment and sports, but they are a handful. The world's greatest (and highest-paid) soccer star, Pelé, is black. Even he encountered discrimination early in his career. Intermarriage is perfectly legal but seldom takes place.

South Africa, in contrast, classifies population groups and then uses elaborate laws to discriminate against black and brown. From the Brazilian perspective this is not only unjust but expensive and stupid as well. The Brazilian system, pretending that all are equal, assigns people to social roles on the basis of race as the South African system does, but without the obvious unfairness, the many laws, or the social tension that the *apartheid* system brings. By pretending to be color-blind, Brazilian society dampens the black resentment that could lead to rage and revolt.

BRAZIL'S POOR: PASSIVE OR EXPLOSIVE?

Do poor people turn naturally to social revolution, or are they too busy trying to stay alive to bother with political questions? In Brazil, we have a laboratory to test some of the longstanding debates about why people revolt. The answers depend

Marginals in Brazil's Favelas

Brazil's poor are sometimes called "marginals," that is, people on the edge—of society, of the economy, of starvation. They huddle in *favelas,* shantytowns on the edge of cities.

Some *favelados* hold regular jobs, others sell pop on the beach, and some steal. Brazil's crime rates are extremely high. There is no place for the marginals to go, and no one cares about them.

Politically they are on the margin too. Unorganized and too busy just trying to stay alive, they riot only when faced with starvation. Brazilian sociologists point out that however wretched life seems in the *favelas,* it's worse in the countryside. Moving to a *favela* for many is a step up, for there they have access to some education and health services and may even find a job.

Favelas—shantytowns of makeshift housing—on the outskirts of Brazil's cities, are home to much of the urban population. (Louis E. Leopold, Jr.)

not just on people being poor—most Brazilians through history have been terribly poor—but on the *context* in which poor people find themselves.

In the dry, overpopulated Northeast, some people starve. In the crime-ridden *favelas* (shantytowns) surrounding the cities, life is a nasty scramble for existence. Rich Brazilians, on the other hand, live sumptuously. For most of the military era, there was little open class resentment. First and most important, the Brazilian underclass was deprived of its leadership and organizational alternatives. The radical parties and leaders of the Goulart period were, respectively, outlawed and exiled or had their political rights annulled, *cassado* in Portuguese. Anyone caught trying to form a radical opposition got into bad trouble—"disappeared" to torture or death.

Further, during the economic boom years of the late 1960s and early 1970s, many Brazilian poor, or "marginals," as they are called, hoped to improve their condition. They flooded to the cities, and some did find work while others eked out a precarious living from peddling or crime.

With the drastic economic downturn of the early 1980s, however, hope vanished. "I tell you frankly I'm desperate," said one sidewalk peddler whose pregnant wife stood nearby. "They keep telling us that things will get better, but who can afford to wait? Hunger doesn't wait. Yesterday I sold nothing. Our food is ending. When it ends, what do I do?" The answer for some Brazilians was to raid food stores. Everything from corner grocery shop to supermarket was smashed open by hungry crowds and quickly looted. Brazil's 1983 food riots sent chilling warning signs throughout the Third World.

Especially ominous was that this arousal of Brazil's poor from passive to active came at precisely the time Brazil was democratizing and permitting the formation of parties, some of them with radical leadership. Even more explosive was the fact that many middle-class Brazilians found themselves getting pushed down into the lower classes, and middle-class people are far more likely to rise in revolt than those who have always been downtrodden. Sectors of the middle class, desperate to hold on to their tenuous positions, could serve as the sparkplug for major unrest.

In sum, the poor are not automatically passive or active but can become either, depending on the situation. If Brazilian radicals attempt once again to mobilize mass discontent, we can expect the military to intervene.

UNEVEN DEMOCRATIC ATTITUDES

While there was a general will in the early 1980s to return to democracy, not all sectors of the Brazilian population shared it equally. Some Brazilians, especially among elites, were convinced democrats. Others, especially poorer and working-class people, were interested in little besides jobs and willing to support whatever would put some food on the table, democratic or not. This is typical of the Third World—and even much of the First. Commitment to democratic values is stronger among those higher up on the socioeconomic ladder.

Political scientists Peter McDonough of Michigan and Antonio Lopez

Pina of Valladolid, Spain, found that poorer and less-educated Brazilians were more interested in law-and-order and bread-and-butter issues than in civil rights and democracy. According to them, in Brazil "there is an authoritarian, populist streak to the lower strata." Of the illiterates in their survey, 63 percent named the dictatorial Vargas as the best president. Those with high school or college education favored Médici, the toughest of Brazil's military presidents. Their reasons? Poor people liked the way Vargas raised wages and looked after the poor; middle-class people pointed to industrialization under Médici.

One interesting finding of the same study: at the very top of the Brazilian heap—those with the most education and best jobs—there was a falling off of support for the hard-lining Médici and a marked increase in support for old Kubitschek, the democratic modernizer. In other words, each strata of Brazilians picked the personality that suited them: the poor chose a populist dictator, the middle a military technocrat, and only some of the upper a democrat.

It is among better-educated and better-off Brazilians that we find an interest in democracy, and even here it is not overwhelming. And these Brazilian findings are not unique. In many countries—including the United States—commitment to democratic values falls off as one moves down the socioeconomic ladder. The irony here is that democracy—a system that's supposed to favor the broad masses of people—receives its strongest support from elites.

"Authoritarian Depoliticization"

In Brazil—and in many similar authoritarian countries—citizens do not have clearly focused ideas about politics because the regime has deliberately "depoliticized" them; the most common attitudes are apathy and indifference. In such an environment, the regime can do what it wants, but it doesn't build lastingly. While there's not much active opposition, neither is there much positive support. In a crunch, authoritarian regimes may suddenly discover how little legitimacy they have built up among the population.

In their study of Brazil and Spain, Peter McDonough and Antonio Lopez Pina didn't find hatred against regressive regimes but rather they found "a substantial amount of unchanneled dissatisfaction" that was "free floating" and not political. Because of "the absence of organizational alternatives"—and the regime makes sure there are few organizational alternatives—"mass anxieties remain unorganized" and not aimed at the government.

Their study suggests, though, that under the surface there is a "large reservoir of illegitimacy that may, given organizational alternatives, be drawn upon for collective political action." Authoritarian depoliticization, in other words, is not necessarily permanent, and depoliticized people can turn quickly political in the right circumstances.

The above doesn't mean that democracy is impossible in Brazil, but it indicates that it's apt to be shaky. Part of the impulse for Brazil's democratization in the 1980s came from the educated upper-middle class, a group that's relatively small but strategically positioned to make its voice heard. Brazil makes us aware that democracy—or indeed any kind of political system—is usually the work of the few mobilizing the many. If the generals let them, middle-class intellectuals might mobilize Brazil's masses and then say, "The people demand democracy." That is only partly true.

PATTERNS OF INTERACTION

AN ELITE GAME

Politics in Brazil has been—and continues to be—largely a game for elites: big landowners, bankers and industrialists, and top bureaucrats and military people. The stakes of the game are political power and the patronage jobs that come with it. The rules of the game are that none of the players gets seriously hurt or threatened and that nobody mobilizes the Brazilian masses, for that would destroy the game's fragile balance and hurt them all. Accordingly, Vargas, himself a wealthy rancher, was an acceptable player when he supported coffee prices for the growers, but when he started to mobilize poor Brazilians he had to be ousted. Kubitschek was a good player who looked after his elite friends and deflected potential discontent with his grandiose plans to open Brazil's interior. Goulart, also a wealthy rancher, was a very bad player: he threatened all the elites and mobilized the masses at a furious rate.

Brazil's entire political history has been the same elite game: Dom Pedro with his *fazendeiro* friends, the Old Republic with its Paulista-Mineiro alternation, and the military technocracy with its industrial and bureaucratic clientele. Since Vargas, however, the political mobilization of the masses has been a recurring threat to the game. Periodically, a politician who doesn't like the elite's fixed rules is tempted to reach out to Brazil's masses, both to secure his own power and to help the downtrodden. Seeing the threat, Brazil's elites, through the military, remove it and try to demobilize the masses. Mobilization and demobilization can be seen as a cycle.

THE MOBILIZATION-DEMOBILIZATION CYCLE

Scholars of the Third World in general and Brazil in particular often focus on "political mobilization." Mobilization means the masses waking up, becoming aware, and in some cases becoming angry. Prior to the beginning of mass politi-

Political Mobilization, Brazilian Style

The turnouts in Brazilian elections provide a graphic indicator of political mobilization:

1930 and earlier	never more than .25 million
1933	1.25 million
1945	6.2 million
1950	7.9 million
1955	8.6 million
1960	11.6 million
1962	14.7 million

Even in 1962, the figure was rather small compared to the total Brazilian population, then about 76 million. But a literacy requirement held down the size of the electorate and eliminated the poorest from voting. Conservative, better-off Brazilians and the military were horrified at the prospect of Goulart's dropping the literacy test and letting lower-class Brazilians into the election booth, with their potentially radical demands.

cal mobilization in a country, few participate in politics, and decisions are made by traditional elites, such as Brazil's big landowners and political bosses. Some social stimulus, such as economic growth, however, brings new sectors of the population (in Brazil, the urban working class) to political awareness; they are "mobilized" and start participating in politics with new demands.

The problem with Brazil—and many other Third World countries—is that the existing institutions haven't been able to handle this influx of new participants and their demands. Well-organized, strong political parties can channel, moderate, and calm mass demands in a constructive way. But Brazilian parties are weak, often little more than personalistic vehicles designed to get their chief into power. The chiefs, such as Vargas and Goulart, then use the parties in a demagogic way, whipping up support among the newly mobilized and politically unsophisticated masses by promising them instant reforms and economic improvements.

"Praetorianism"

As the Roman Empire ossified and crumbled, the emperor's bodyguard, known as the Praetorian Guard, came to play a powerful role, making and unmaking emperors. Political scientists now use *praetorianism* to indicate a situation where the military feels driven to take over the government.

Praetorianism is not just a problem of a power-hungry army but reflects conflict in the whole society. In praetorian societies, it's not only the army that wants to take power, but many other groups as well: students, labor unions, revolutionaries, and politicians would like to seize the state machinery; institutional constraints and balances have broken down; nobody plays by the rules. In such situations of chaos and breakdown, it is the army among the many power contenders that is best equipped to seize power, so praetorianism usually means military take-over.

The more conservative elements in society—the wealthy who often have close ties to the military—view this process with horror. The military sees it as "leftist chaos" and may end it by a military coup, the story of many Latin American countries. Thus mobilization, which could be the start of democratization, often leads to authoritarian take-overs.

The 1964 military take-over in Brazil ended one phase of what might be termed a mobilization-demobilization cycle. The ruling generals had grown to hate civilian politics, especially political parties and their demagogic leaders. We can to a degree understand their hatred. As guardians of Brazil's unity and security, they witnessed their beloved republic falling into the hands of irresponsible crowd-pleasers.

Typically, the military tries the only solution they know: demobilization. Believing that the solution lies in an end to disruptive political activity, they ban most parties, hand pick political leaders, and permit only rigged elections. Initially, things do calm down. Some people are thankful the army has stepped in to put an end to extremist politics and empty promises. Mass rallies, loud demands, and radical leaders disappear—the latter, sometimes physically.

But the problem isn't solved. The demands—although no longer whipped up by politicians—are still there and growing. Indeed, as the economy grows—and Brazil's has soared—and more people come to live in cities, the pent-up demands for change increase. To repress such demands, the regime turns to the police-state brutality of arbitrary arrests and torture. Once people are awakened or mobilized they can never be fully demobilized, even by massive doses of coercion.

THE INFLATION CONNECTION

Inflation is a political problem the world over, especially in Latin America, where regimes may fall over the rate of inflation. Inflation may also be seen as part of the mobilization-demobilization cycle. In Brazil, inflation in currency corresponds to the inflation in promises made by politicians seeking mass support.

Controlling inflation is an austere, unhappy task. By restricting credit and cutting the amount of money being printed, a regime can lower the inflation rate, but at a cost of unemployment, slow economic growth, and disappointed hopes. Almost by definition, Latin American inflation cutters are conservative authoritarians, usually military men, who can pursue disinflationary measures without regard to mass desires. As in much of Latin America, the Brazilian military in effect say to its citizenry: "We don't care how much it hurts, the sooner inflation ends the better we'll all be. Take the bitter medicine now before inflation wrecks the entire economy."

Encouraging inflation, on the other hand, is easy; regimes can almost do it in a fit of absent-mindedness. Politicians of populist bent, wanting to make everybody happy, just let the national mint's printing presses run to finance government projects. This is the way Kubitschek built Brasilia. Inflation tends to feed on itself and get out of hand, and soon many people are complaining they can't make ends meet. Conservative industrialists and bankers become convinced the politicians have gone insane. The military, whose fixed salaries are eroded by the galloping inflation, seethes in jealous rage and starts planning a coup to save both the republic and their incomes.

When the military does take power, their disinflationary measures correspond to the political demobilization they also try to enforce. In the Brazilian case, this has consisted of controls on wages but not on prices, with the result that lower-class Brazilians have to work like dogs to keep up with food prices while some speculators enjoy an economic boom.

Although the Brazilian generals had excellent economic planners, by 1984 the inflation rate reached 223 percent, double what it was in 1964, when the military seized power. This extremely embarrassing fact undermined regime support among the businessmen and bankers who had welcomed the 1964 takeover. One reason Brazil turned democratic was that the military proved as inept as civilians in controlling inflation.

THE DIVIDED MILITARY:
LIBERALS VERSUS HARD-LINERS

The more we study supposedly monolithic political systems, the more we realize that they are never totally unified. Among Brazil's generals, the split was between relative liberals who favored an easing of military control and hard-liners (*duros*) who believed liberalization only invited chaos once again.

Some Brazilian observers believe that the liberals were concentrated in the intelligence apparatus while the hard-liners controlled the security apparatus—the "brains" of intelligence versus the "muscles" of security. This may be a bit of an oversimplification, since most of Brazil's general-presidents came from the National Intelligence Service.

The liberal generals, however, came to suspect that continuing military rule was bad for the Brazilian armed forces. They first took power with idealistic motives, to save Brazil from irresponsible civilian politicians and move the country toward economic greatness. But after some years in power, they noticed that what happened under civilians was happening with the military: inflation, corruption, petty political infighting, the struggling for political advantage, and loss of a sense of mission. The military government, in other words, began to "civilianize" itself.

Factions within the military developed links with outside groups, and these links sometimes became more important than the sense of loyalty that bound the military together. Having established civilian ties by running parts of the economy, some of the best army officers then left for lush civilian jobs.

The Deindexation Dilemma

One solution to persistent inflation, some economists have suggested, is to "index" wages to the cost of living: as the cost of living goes up, pay automatically increases by the same percentage. That way no one really gets hurt by inflation. Several countries have tried indexation, including Brazil.

Too late, economists realized that indexation was *fueling* inflation and seriously distorting the economy. Prices and wages chased each other upward faster and faster. Many people urged deindexation, to end the merry-go-round. But how? Brazilians had gotten used to the automatic increases. The Figueiredo government tried partial deindexation, but the cries of pain made it back down. Most politicians agreed that indexing had to be ended, but not suddenly. Said one, "It would be like suddenly stepping on the brakes of a car speeding at 200 km. an hour."

Furthermore, the liberal generals noticed the military, which earlier took credit for the economic boom, was now held responsible for things going wrong. Running Brazil was not quite the pleasure it used to be. Before the military became tarnished, the liberals concluded, they should phase out their rule and return to more soldierly duties. This attitude was behind the *abertura* of the 1980s.

The hard-line generals responded, in effect, by pointing out that the forces of communism and chaos that threatened in 1964 were still present, ready to come out of the woodwork the moment the regime showed weakness. The *duros* were willing and even happy to use army troops against strikers and protesters. Continued military rule was better than recivilianization, they argued.

Given this situation, it is possible for the military to split and for one side to carry out a coup. The military *duros* did what they could to slow or stop the democratization of the 1980s. In 1981 a large bomb killed an army intelligence agent as he was on his way to plant it at a May Day concert in Rio. Rumors flew that sections of the army wanted a provocation to reverse the *abertura* or even to prepare for a coup against the Figueiredo administration. Many generals expressed extreme unhappiness at the election in 1985 of Neves. The Brazilian army may be back in the barracks, but there is no telling how long they'll stay there.

THE DECOMPRESSION DILEMMA

Latin America's military regimes often decide, after some years in power, to liberalize. Their original justification for seizing power—to put an end to chaos and communism—is no longer valid, and both domestic and foreign criticism of their dictatorial methods is mounting. Now comes the hard part: how to ease up? As soon as the regime starts to liberalize, the very same forces it overthrew (mobilized masses, militant unions, and demands for reform) reappear. At this point, the regime may change its mind and decide that continued repression is the safest course.

In Brazil, most new general-presidents indicated that the Brazilian people were now mature enough to regain some political rights. But after a year or two in office, the president usually toned down his liberalizaton plans. The cautious measures—say, permitting the opposition to speak out freely—raised anew the specter of disorder and revolution, and "the system" of advisors around the president urged him to pull back.

In 1974, for example, General Ernesto Geisel came to power speaking of *decompressão* (decompression). Press (but not radio or TV) censorship was reduced. The amount of torture decreased, and politicians were even allowed to criticize the government over the grisly issue. Wages were permitted to rise a bit. Partly free elections were permitted, and the MDB gained. By 1977, though, Geisel could see that his cautious decompression was fueling the movement for basic change, and he cracked down. MDB politicians were removed from office and stripped of political rights for ten years—*cassado* (annulled). The trouble with freedom, Brazilian presidents discovered, is that people use it.

In 1979, under President Figueiredo, a major *abertura* was permitted. The dictatorial Institutional Acts were rescinded. Media censorship was re-

The Brazilian Political Cycle

With some oversimplification, Brazilian politics can be seen as a cycle or progression of phases that repeat themselves. It we were to sketch out our discussion of the last few pages, it would look like this:

Mobilization → Demagoguery → Military → Demobilization → Liberalization → Democratization?
(inflation)   Take-over   (disinflation)

We put a question mark by democratization because we do not yet know if it will be permitted to evolve freely without military intervention. If it does, then the cycle could start all over with the mobilized masses falling under the sway of demagogic politicians. That's the way Brazilian politics worked earlier—for example, during the two "Vargas cycles." Beginning in 1985, however, Brazil's civilian rulers were extremely cautious about reforms and proceeded slowly.

duced, and more critical news items and comments appeared. Political parties were again permitted, and political exiles were allowed to return, among them some pre-1964 politicians.

Figueiredo's *abertura* was broader and deeper than Geisel's *decompressão*. Brazil is scheduled to have a freely elected democracy by the late 1980s. But a lot of things could go wrong—inflation, strikes, the rise of populist politicians—that could persuade the *linha dura* among the generals to cancel democracy. In much of Latin America, alas, liberalization and democratization tend to be episodes between periods of authoritarianism.

RESURGENT INTEREST GROUPS

For most of the life of the military regime, the Brazilian government continued the corporatist model that Vargas had borrowed from Italy and Portugal. Under corporatism, interest groups are controlled or coordinated by the government. With the *abertura* of the 1980s, Brazil's interest groups emerged with a life of their own once again.

After the 1964 take-over, the military abolished the big union, the General Workers Command (*Comando Geral dos Trabalhadores*) that had been fostered by Goulart, and placed all labor unions under direct government control. Particularly drastic was the control of rural unions, whose impoverished and militant farm workers threatened the property of the conservative landowning allies of the military government. Union leaders were henceforth hand picked to make sure they would cooperate with the new order and not lead workers in excessive wage demands or strikes.

While this arrangement held down wages, prices rose, until workers could stand it no more. New unions and leaders outside government control emerged. Especially active were the São Paulo metalworkers, who in 1980 shut down Brazil's automobile industry for over a month. Their leader, the aforementioned Luís Inácio da Silva (Lula), had a political goal as well: he organized a workers' party, the PT. The government jailed Lula and set troops on the strikers, but the regime knew the movement was too powerful to break.

Many businessmen had welcomed the 1964 coup only to find that the military technocrats would sometimes ride roughshod over their interests in the name of economic rationality. The "theory of constructive bankruptcy" let weak Brazilian firms go under rather than subsidize them with tariff protection against foregin competition. In 1980, the regime did the unthinkable: it decreed a wide variety of taxes aimed at curbing the sybaritic consumption of the very rich as well as raising revenues. Many wealthy businessmen moved from support of the regime to opposition.

Other groups, such as students and farmers, also began to voice their discontent. Opposition to the rule of the generals developed across a broad front of conservative and radical Brazilians. The most interesting opposition group, however, was the Catholic church, a force to be reckoned with in the world's largest Catholic country.

THE CHURCH AS OPPOSITION

Curiously, the Roman Catholic church was the only large Brazilian group that maintained its autonomy and was in a position to criticize the regime. We say curiously because typically in Catholic countries the church has been conservative and has favored conservative regimes. We saw in France how the long fight between clericalism and anticlericalism split society into two camps. The same thing happened in Spain and Italy.

Brazil never had this kind of split. With the 1891 republican constitution, modeled after the United States', the Brazilian church consented to disestablishment, that is, to losing its special privileges as church and state were separated. Brazil settled this important and divisive issue quickly and early, leaving the church as an independent force.

Still, in social and economic outlook the Brazilian Catholic church was pretty conservative, urging the faithful to save their souls rather than to reform and improve society. With the Second Vatican Council of 1962—65, this conservative attitude changed, and many churchmen, especially younger ones, adopted the "theology of liberation" that put the church on the side of the poor and oppressed. In some Latin American countries, young priests actually became guerrilla fighters trying to overthrow what they regarded as wicked and reactionary regimes.

The church position in Brazil—as throughout Latin America—is far from uniform. Some national hierarchies are still conservative, others radical, and many moderate reformist. A lot depends on individual bishops and the situation in which they find themselves. In impoverished northeastern Brazil, for example, to be in touch with the broad mass of people, the church organizes unions and teaches rural workers. Priests here often talk like leftists. In other parts of Brazil, the church is more moderate or even conservative, especially after Pope John Paul's rejection of the "theology of liberation."

In the late 1960s, Brazilian church leaders denounced the regime for "Fascist doctrines" and for arresting and torturing priests and nuns accused of harboring politicial fugitives. During the 1970s, the Brazilian church developed a strong stand for human rights and against the terrible poverty still found throughout the country. When strikes flared in the 1980s, strikers often held meetings and sought refuge from police clubs in churches. As a whole, the Brazilian Catholic church was the most activist in Latin America, usually to the chagrin of the Vatican.

In 1980, John Paul II visited Brazil. He was visibly shaken by what he saw in the *favelas*. In one, he removed the ring given him by Pope Paul VI when he became a cardinal and gave it to a local priest as a donation. John Paul seemed to be turning into an activist himself. In a Rio slum he called to Brazil's rich: "Look around a bit. Does it not wound your heart? Do you not feel remorse of conscience because of your riches and abundance?" But he stopped short of endorsing active church involvement in politics. Church people should guide spiritually but not politically. In Brazil, this middle road is hard to tread because concern for the poor tends to radicalize people.

The "Red Archbishop": Dom Helder Camara

Many Brazilian churchmen have suffered the wrath of the military regime, but none more than Dom Helder Camara, retired archbishop of Olinda and Recife in the dry, poor notheast of Brazil. Born in 1909 in a family where five children died of dysentery, Dom Helder was called to both the church and to social action.

Like many Latin American churchmen, Dom Helder does not separate the church's spiritual mission from a need to restructure an unjust system to aid the poor. For preaching this type of gospel among the Brazilian poor, priests have been murdered and tortured; even Dom Helder's little house has been machine-gunned and bombed. He has been called—erroneously—the Red Archbishop.

But believing Christians like himself are not easily cowed, Dom Helder continued to expound his philosophy of "peaceful violence" shared by Gandhi and Martin Luther King, "the violence of Christ":

I call it violence because it's not content with small reforms, revisions, but insists on a complete revolution of present structures—a society remade from top to bottom. On a socialist basis and without shedding blood. It's not enough to struggle for the poor, to die for the poor—we must give the poor an awareness of their rights and of their poverty. . . . I say it's possible to "consciencize" the masses, and, perhaps, it's possible to open a dialogue with the oppressors.

WHAT BRAZILIANS QUARREL ABOUT

THE BRAZILIAN MIRACLE

After the 1964 military take-over, the Brazilian economy improved. From 1968 to 1974 the annual growth rate averaged 10 percent. A series of very bright economic technocrats oversaw what soon became known as the Brazilian miracle, the spectacle of a sleeping giant rousing itself to become a major industrial power. Only Japan has enjoyed economic growth like Brazil's.

There were some problems with the miracle, however. For one thing, it was based on foreign capital. There is nothing wrong with this; most developed economies (including the United States) received boosts from overseas investment in their early years. At a certain point, however, a growing economy should be able to generate its own capital for further investment. Brazil hasn't. Brazilian capitalists, instead of reinvesting their money in industrial growth, tend to spend it, speculate with it, or find ways to stash it abroad. For new capital investment they get government or foreign loans. This was one of the reasons Brazil accumulated the world's largest foreign debt—it topped $100 billion in 1985. Foreign bankers feared default; they tightened credit, and the Brazilian economy staggered.

Another reason for the debt was the price of oil, which shot up during the 1970s. Brazil, with little rail transportation, is dependent on trucks and cars and has few oil wells. So Brazil paid for foreign oil and went deeper into debt. Trying to offset its oil dependency, Brazil turned to alcohol distilled from its own crops. Now Brazilian gasoline, which goes for about $3 a gallon, is 20 percent alcohol. Many vehicles run on pure alcohol. The slowdown in the Brazilian economy in the 1970s was heavily related to the fact that the price of oil increased more than tenfold during this period. As the economy slowed, inflation grew, to over 200 percent a year by 1985.

The point here is that the "Brazilian miracle" had feet of clay. The boom of the early 1970s, when it seemed Brazil could soon be one of the world's great powers, gave way to a declining GNP a decade later. Brazil, dependent upon foreign capital and oil, did beautifully when both were abundant and cheap. When the prices of both soared, Brazil stood revealed as highly dependent on its foreign connections.

Brazilian leftists, in fact, have made "dependency" into a theory of why Brazil is underdeveloped (see box). Some radical intellectuals believe the United States, through its multinational corporations, keeps Brazil in a neocolonial economic status. Although this line was spoken only softly under the military, with a return of democracy we hear Brazilian politicans voicing it again.

The Dependencia Syndrome

Many observers of Latin America (and of the Third World in general) argue that what keeps it underdeveloped is its chronic dependency on foreign—U.S. or West European—capital. The view is an article of faith on the Brazilian left. The classic *dependencia* syndrome usually includes these elements:

1. The poor, dependent country provides cheap raw materials (for example, coffee, sugar, minerals) to the rich, capitalist country, which in turn sells finished goods to the poor country at high prices.

2. A class of local middlemen—called *compradores* (from the Portuguese for "buyers," used originally in the old China trade)—handles this trade, in effect siphoning off the hard-earned profits of the dependent country to the rich country.

3. The local government is dominated by *compradores,* who have no interest in changing this situation that keeps them wealthy but their country poor.

4. The poor country fails to develop much because the capitalist country keeps industry at home and uses the dependent country as a market and provider of raw materials. The rich country gets richer while the poor stagnates.

5. If revolutionaries ever threaten to overturn the dependent relationship, the rich capitalist country uses either local forces or its own troops to prevent it.

Radicals and Marxists often describe Latin America as caught in this relationship with the United States. They cite Guatemala in 1954, Cuba in 1961, Brazil in 1964, Chile in 1973, and Nicaragua in the 1980s, as examples of countries where the United States tried to use force to oust local revolutionary regimes and preserve *dependencia.*

By now, even Marxists admit that classic dependency is rare and that things are more complicated. In the first place, some Latin American countries do develop their own industry and show good growth rates. Some have managed to lessen their dependent economic relationship—especially oil-rich Mexico and Venezuela. Some Latin American countries, such as Brazil and Argentina, have grown politically distant from the United States.

Brown University sociologist Peter Evans, in an updating of the dependency theory, coined the term "dependent development" to take account of the fact of Brazil's impressive growth, which obviously doesn't fit the *dependencia* syndrome. Evans argues that the key choices in Brazil's industrialization are made by an alliance of multinational (that is, U.S.) corporations, the Brazilian government, and local capitalists. They enrich themselves, but growth bypasses the majority of Brazilians who stay poor. Accordingly, Evans believes that a type of *dependencia* still exists between the United States and Brazil.

BRAZIL'S STATE CAPITALISM

While leftists point to foreign dependency as the root of Brazil's problems, conservative businessmen point to Brazil's very large state sector and red-tape controls on the economy. Brazil, they emphasize, is not really a free-market country relying on private initiative. About half of total economic investment is from the government. The government owns over 500 firms, accounting for about one-third of Brazil's GNP—including mines, petroleum production, and electric companies—and pays managers fabulous salaries. In addition, the majority of loans come from government banks, giving the state the power to determine what gets built and where.

The technocrats who run this state-capitalist empire say that the projects they undertake are so big and risky no private business people would handle them. Brazilian investors tend to speculate in sure-fire enterprises such as real estate rather than in industrial growth. Consequently, the technocrats say, if Brazil is to expand boldly, much investment must be under state guidance.

State capitalism—where the government is the number-one capitalist—can both accomplish big projects and make big mistakes. Some projects Brazil has poured money into are prestigious but money losers. For example, the government invested heavily in nuclear power in a country where hydroelectricity has scarcely been tapped. The nuclear program was a foolish waste—although it made Brazil look like an advanced country—and by 1980 it was greatly curtailed.

Government loans were sometimes extended foolishly, too. The interest on these loans was so low, and Brazil's inflation so high, that the credits amounted to free money, which the borrower could immediately loan out at high interest. Why work for a living when you can just shift some paper around? The subsidized loans from the government, however, ultimately come from working Brazilians in the form of inflation. Brazil's cheap government loans are another reason the rich get richer and the poor poorer.

State control produces other distortions in the economy. There are so many laws and regulations that businesses have to employ red-tape specialists called *despachantes* (expediters) to jog the bureaucracy into giving a license or allowing a price change. Many *despachantes* are related to the bureaucrats they deal with; some are former bureaucrats themselves. The Brazilian word for getting around a regulation is *jeito*, literally "knack," meaning having someone who can fix it for you. We call it corruption, but in a system choked with controls, *jeito* is a necessity.

Brazilian Wisecrack

"Brazil is the country of the future and always will be."

Another problem area of state control is minimum wages, a holdover from Vargas's populist paternalism. As in other countries, minimum wages dissuade employers from hiring unskilled workers. Many poor people then cannot find entry-level jobs. Minimum wages, aimed at helping the working poor, simply mean more unemployed marginals in the *favelas*.

Even worse, many of Brazil's grandiose projects have been capital-intensive (using lots of machinery) rather than labor-intensive (using lots of workers). Brazil is short of capital but has lots of labor. More labor-intensive projects would kill two birds with one stone, alleviating both the capital shortage and tremendous unemployment. But such projects are not to the taste of Brazil's technocrats, probably because they are less prestigious than mammoth capital investments.

Who's right, the leftists, who point to dependency, or the business people, who point to state strangulation? Actually, the two views complement each other. State control does stunt domestic capital formation, and this makes Brazil chronically dependent on foreign capital. Instead of a vigorous private sector of local businesses, the Brazilian economy is divided between the foreign multinationals and the state. Brazilian entrepreneurs tend to attach themsleves to one of the two. The Brazilian miracle, alas, turned out to be flawed.

Knuckle Under to the IMF?

The International Monetary Fund demands drastic austerity before it will come to the financial rescue of an ailing country. IMF officials argue that there is no point in shoveling more money into a rapidly inflating economy like Brazil's; the loans will simply disappear and do no good. If you want a loan, says the IMF, you've got to bring down your rate of inflation by drastic cuts in government spending and wages.

This prescription is painful and perhaps impossible for countries such as Brazil and Argentina where people are already in dire economic circumstances. IMF demands raised nationalist anger in Brazil and Argentina. They felt they were being pushed around by big capitalist countries. Some politicians vowed not to knuckle under, to repudiate their gigantic debts rather than accept the harsh austerity. It was a bit like saying, "If I go, the world goes too," for a major debt repudiation could wreck international banking and plunge the world into a depression.

Still, Brazilians toyed with the idea, recalling that Getúlio Vargas had declared a unilateral moratorium on Brazil's foreign debt in 1934, forcing foreign creditors to settle for thirty-three cents on the dollar.

GROWTH FOR WHOM?

Another weakness of the Brazilian economy is that its fruits are distributed highly unequally. The richest fifth of Brazilians rake in two-thirds of all income. At the bottom of the heap, an estimated two-fifths of Brazilians are marginals, some with no income at all. Per capita income in the Northeast is lower than in Bangladesh. The "Brazilian miracle" overlooked these people.

Critics on the left argue that the miracle, because it was controlled by U.S. multinationals and Brazilian technocrats, produced semiluxury goods and grandiose projects that benefited the better off. It made cars and swanky apartments rather than public transportation and basic housing. The leftists would redistribute income to the poor.

Those defending the system point out that Brazil contains two economies, a First World economy that is modern and productive and a Third World one that is traditional and unproductive. Actually, most Third World countries have First World sectors within them. In Brazil the contrast is stark. But, argue the defenders, the gap cannot be bridged overnight. Brazil must first build up its modern sector until it gradually takes over the whole country. To simply redistribute income to marginals, who produce little or nothing, would be economic folly. The trick is to keep the economy growing so as to absorb the marginals and turn them into producers and consumers. This is known as the developmentalist solution to Brazilian poverty.

The critic on the left rejoins that Brazilian development, because it is capital-intensive, can't begin to create the 1.5 million new jobs needed every year. What is needed, the leftist argues, is a whole new approach to development, one that stresses human beings instead of percentage growth for its own sake. As even the hard-lining President Médici (1969–74) had to admit: "The economy is going well, the people not so well."

THE POPULATION PROBLEM

Whatever viewpoint you adopt, one nasty fact will foul up the best laid plans: Brazil's hefty population increase. The Catholic church, of course, frowns on any artificial method of birth control, and the military regime until recently thought a high birthrate contributed to economic growth. Accordingly, in Brazil, until the 1970s, there was no emphasis on curbing population growth, and Brazil's population is now over 130 million, half of it under age 18.

As usual, it is poor people, especially peasants, who have the most children. The poverty-stricken Northeast, where people have especially large families, is an inexhaustible reservoir of marginal Brazilians. However many millions of them pour into the cities of the South, there are millions more still coming. The result is "hyperurbanization," common throughout the Third World, where cities are usually surrounded by huge slum belts created by peasants who can no longer live off the land. Two-thirds of Brazilians live in cities, an absurd situation for a big, empty country. In 1980, São Paulo with 13.5 million inhabitants was

Crime and Punishment, Brazilian Style

As Brazil's urban poor turn to crime, making city life unpleasant, Brazil's police turn to extralegal remedies. In the late 1960s and 1970s, unofficial "death squads" of off-duty policemen executed some three thousand suspected criminals without resort to courts of law. In the 1980s similar outfits were at work. Rio's *Mão Branca* (White Hand) and São Paulo's *Mão Negra* (Black Hand) tortured and decapitated suspects, mostly people with petty criminal records.

In effect, the police were trying to frighten the *favelado* underclass into behaving themselves. As a long-term solution, it is no answer at all, for rural poor continue to pour into the *favelas*, where for many, crime is the only way to survive. Most Brazilians, including the press, denounce the vigilantes, but many then add that something has to be done about crime. In principle, traditionally nonviolent Brazilians deplore the acts of savagery, but since the victims are marginal *favelados*, no one cares very much.

the fourth-largest city in the world; Rio, with 10.7 million, was the eighth. And they're growing fast.

The rural immigrants to the cities settle in *favelas*. With no education or job skills, many do not find regular work. Those that do usually must travel hours to and from their jobs. With wages held down but prices rising, most discover themselves getting poorer. If they cannot feed their numerous children, they are forced to abandon them. Some ten to twenty million so-called "nobody's children" sleep on beaches and in doorways. The crime rate soars; people would rather steal than starve.

BRAZIL TRIES DEMOCRACY AGAIN

On March 15, 1985, with the inauguration of José Sarney, Brazil got its first civilian president in twenty-one years. The Congress elected in 1986 is to write a new constitution, and by 1988 direct elections for Brazil's presidency are to be held. Brazil was not alone in its return to democracy. Since 1979, Ecuador, Peru, Bolivia, Argentina, and Uruguay returned to democratic, civilian rule. Democracy may be contagious. Only Chile and Paraguay remained as dictatorships in South America.

But would Brazil's democracy—or any of the others—last? The problems of all of Latin America's nations are incredible: severe economic difficulties, giant foreign debts, growing populations, military establishments accustomed to intervening in politics, and a lack of seasoned political institutions such as parties and parliaments. Some of the above-mentioned nations probably aren't going to make it.

Brazil and some of the other South American lands, especially Argentina, did start their most recent attempt at democracy with a psychological plus: most of them had had enough of dictatorship and wanted to avoid it. The new civilian leaders—especially Brazil's Sarney—generally avoided whipping up demands that couldn't possibly be satisfied. They refrained from promising too much. And the people—some with recent memories of disappearances and torture—generally refrained from asking for too much. In 1985, Brazil's people and politicians were politically more mature than they had been in 1964. In the 1980s few Brazilians—including the military—wanted the generals to have any reason to take over power again.

The net effect of Brazil's military interlude, then, was not all bad. It had served as a period of economic growth and political calming-down. And it ended gracefully. One almost had the feeling that Brazil's generals knew when their time was up. Once again, Brazil's traits of moderation and compromise, inherited from the Portuguese, seemed to be asserting themselves. For a country headed toward revolution and lacking these traits, let us now turn to South Africa.

VOCABULARY BUILDING

abertura	depoliticization	*fazendeiros*	*personalismo*
amnesty	*dependencia*	indexation	PMDB
capital-intensive	*despachante*	*jeito*	populism
corporatism	*disinflation*	labor-intensive	Positivism
death squads	ESG	*machismo*	praetorianism
decompressão	*Estado Novo*	marginals	Second Vatican Council
demagoguery	*favela*	mobilization	state capitalism
demobilization	*favelados*	Old Republic	theology of liberation

FURTHER REFERENCE

Bruneau, Thomas C. *The Church in Brazil.* Austin: University of Texas Press, 1982.

Burns, E. Bradford. *A History of Brazil,* 2d ed. New York: Columbia University Press, 1980.

Daland, Robert T. *Exploring Brazilian Bureaucracy: Performance and Pathology.* Lanham, Md.: University Press of America, 1981.

Evans, Peter. *Dependent Development: The Alliance of Multinational, State, and Local Capital in Brazil.* Princeton, N.J.: Princeton University Press, 1979.

Fallaci, Oriana. "Helder Camara," in *Interview with History.* Boston: Houghton Mifflin, 1977.

Freyre, Gilberto. *Order and Progress: Brazil from Monarchy to Republic.* New York: Knopf, 1970.

Huntington, Samuel P. *Political Order in Changing Societies.* New Haven, Conn.: Yale University Press, 1968.

Jaguaribe, Helio. *Economic and Political Development: A Theoretical Approach and a Brazilian Case Study.* Cambridge, Mass.: Harvard University Press, 1968.

Langguth, A. J. *Hidden Terrors.* New York: Pantheon, 1978.

Lipset, Seymour Martin, and **Aldo Solari,** eds. *Elites in Latin America.* New York: Oxford University Press, 1967.

McDonough, Peter. *Power and Ideology in Brazil.* Princeton, N.J.: Princeton University Press, 1981.

Nordlinger, Eric A. *Soldiers in Politics: Military Coups and Governments.* Englewood Cliffs, N.J.: Prentice-Hall, 1977.

Nyrop, Richard F., ed. *Brazil: A Country Study.* Washington, D.C.: U.S. Government Printing Office, 1983.

Roett, Riordan. *Brazil: Politics in a Patrimonial Society,* rev. ed. New York: Praeger, 1978.

Schneider, Ronald M. *The Political System of Brazil: Emergence of a "Modernizing" Authoritarian Regime, 1964-1970.* New York: Columbia University Press, 1971.

Selcher, Wayne A., ed. *Political Liberalization in Brazil: Dynamics, Dilemmas, and Future.* Boulder, Colo.: Westview Press, 1985.

Stepan, Alfred. *The Military in Politics: Changing Patterns in Brazil.* Princeton, N.J.: Princeton University Press, 1971.

_____. ed. *Authoritarian Brazil: Origins, Policies, and Future.* New Haven, Conn.: Yale University Press, 1973.

_____. "Political Leadership and Regime Breakdown: Brazil," in *The Breakdown of Democratic Regimes,* ed. by Juan J. Linz and Alfred Stepan. Baltimore: Johns Hopkins University Press, 1978.

Van Den Berghe, Pierre L. *Race and Racism: A Comparative Perspective.* New York: Wiley, 1967.

Wesson, Robert, and **David V. Fleischer.** *Brazil in Transition.* New York: Praeger, 1983.

24

SOUTH AFRICA

THE IMPACT OF THE PAST

WHOSE LAND?

Afrikaners—the white South Africans of mostly Dutch descent—like to emphasize that when their ancestors arrived three centuries ago, South Africa was largely empty, and they settled it first. This is not completely true. When the Dutch East India Company sent Jan van Riebeeck with two hundred men to start up a "refreshment station" at the Cape of Good Hope in 1652, they encountered Hottentots, a primitive people whom they enslaved, impregnated, and eventually killed off with smallpox. Needing more slaves, they imported them from the Indies and Madagascar. The resulting mixture—Hottentot, Dutch, Malay, and other—produced the so-called Cape Coloreds, a group that resembles American blacks in that they are a combination of many strands.

South Africa's Population (in millions)

This sign on a bus for blacks in Soweto shows what's on whitey's mind: a rapidly growing black population. (*Michael Roskin*)

	1960	1985	2000 (PROJECTED)
Africans	12.0	23.0	37.0
Whites	3.1	4.7	6.0
Coloreds	1.5	2.8	4.0
Asians	.5	.8	1.2

South Africa's white population increases at a modest 1.7 percent a year (high compared to Europe.) The nonwhite population, however, increases at Third World rates, 2.5 percent for Africans, 2.2 percent for Coloreds (mixed descent), and 2.4 percent for Asians (chiefly Indians). Every year, whites become a smaller minority.

So far, this process is reminiscent of the early settlement of Brazil, which also produced a mixed race. The difference in South Africa was that, fairly soon, the whites developed exclusivist attitudes on race and classified the Coloreds as a different and inferior group.

As the Cape colony expanded, Dutch farmers *(boers)* pushed outward, taking whatever land they wanted. When the soil was exhausted, they moved on. Their constant movement earned them the name *trekboers,* or farmers on the move. Further inland, they encountered the even more primitive Bushmen, whom they shot as thieving pests. Very early, Afrikaners developed the attitude that the land was exclusively theirs and that the natives were to be either enslaved or exterminated.

Although the Dutch didn't pay much attention to it, the Cape colony grew, aided in part by the arrival in 1688 of French Huguenots, who brought the many French names found today among Afrikaners and also brought their skills in wine-making. As the *trekboers* pushed along the Indian Ocean coast, they encountered, in the late eighteenth century, their first African Negroes, bigger, stronger, much better organized, and more warlike than Hottentots or Bushmen. These Africans were themselves slowly moving south, away from population pressure, tribal wars, and slave raids. In a series of battles over a century, the so-called Kaffir Wars, the Boers subdued the Africans and again took all the land they wanted.

Just as stimulus from Napoleonic France triggered the rise of modern Brazil, France also set in motion the rise of present-day South Africa. When a French revolutionary army occupied the Netherlands, the Dutch in 1795 let the British take over the Cape to keep Table Bay—around which Cape Town is built—out of French hands. The British stayed as welcome guests until 1803 but returned in 1806, this time for good. In 1814, the Netherlands officially turned over the Cape to Britain, and the English moved to remake it into a British colony.

THE GREAT TREK

Many Boers bristled at British rule. Not only did the British want everybody to speak English, they wanted everybody to be equal before the law. Even Hottentot servants could bear witness against their masters. In 1834, to the outrage of many Boers, slavery was abolished. The Boers became convinced that the English were destroying their language, institutions, way of life, and freedom.

Between 1836 and 1838, an estimated twelve thousand Boer men, women, and children—about a quarter of the Cape's Dutch population—loaded up oxcarts and, like American pioneers, moved into the interior seeking land and freedom. The epic is known as the Great Trek and is celebrated by Afrikaners today as a symbol of their toughness, courage, and go-it-alone attitude. At times the *voortrekkers* (pioneers) had to disassemble their wagons to get them over roadless escarpments. Some columns fought battles with Africans, drawing their wagons into a circle called a *laager.* One column disappeared without a trace. Members of another were treacherously slaughtered by Zulus (see box).

The *voortrekkers'* dealings with Africans paralleled the Americans' with Indians. Sometimes by force and sometimes by persuasion, the *voortrekkers* made treaties with chiefs to obtain land. The Africans, who had no concept of *owning* land, thought they were letting the Dutch *use* the land for a while. Disputes were settled by the pioneers crushing the natives.

Dingaan's Kraal: Still Remembered

In 1838 the Zulu king Dingaan invited the *voortrekker* leader Piet Retief and some seventy Boers to a feast at Dingaan's *kraal* (group of huts forming a courtyard). They had been on friendly terms; Retief had recovered some stolen cattle for Dingaan from another tribe, and Dingaan had given the Boers land around present-day Durban. But Dingaan was suspicious of the ultimate intentions of the white man and with the cry, "Kill the wizards!" had them dragged to a hill and beaten to death. Then he killled five hundred settlers—including women and children—in Retief's column.

Later that year, the Boers got their revenge. Setting up a strong *laager* on a river and letting the Zulus attack, the Boers gunned down three thousand of Dingaan's warriors with no loss of their own. Before the battle, the *voortrekkers* vowed that if God granted them victory they would commemorate the day for evermore. December 16, the anniversary of the Battle of Blood River, is still celebrated as the Day of the Covenant.

On a monument at Dingaan's *kraal,* Afrikaners can read the names of the massacred. It must come as a shock, for the names are the same as in a present-day Pretoria phone book. There is even the name of Botha. The all-too-obvious link with the past is one that Afrikaners deliberately emphasize.

The rich soil and good rainfall of Natal, fronting the Indian Ocean, was the goal of most *voortrekkers*. But the British also took an interest in this lush province and annexed it in 1843. The British claimed it was to prevent further bloodshed between *voortrekkers* and Africans; the Boers retorted that it was to rob them of their land once again. In disgust, many *voortrekkers* repacked their ox wagons and moved back inland where, they thought, they would be forever free of the hated British.

The *voortrekkers* consolidated their inland settlements into two small republics, the Transvaal (meaning on the far side of the Vaal River) and the Orange Free State. Here the Boers were at home. The language, religion (Dutch Reformed), governmental institutions, and way of life were all theirs. The Boer republics lived in uneasy peace with the British in the Cape and Natal, until diamonds and then gold were discovered.

THE BOER WAR

With the discovery of diamonds in 1870 and gold in 1886, English-speaking people poured into the Boer republics, chiefly the Transvaal. There, on the Witwatersrand (literally, "white-water ridge"), gold was mined in such quantities that a new city, Johannesburg, was built atop the waste rock. It soon became South Africa's largest city—and English-speaking.

For the Boers, it looked as if the English were once again pursuing them and destroying their way of life. By 1895, the English-speaking *uitlanders* (outlanders) out-numbered the Boers more than two to one. The Transvaal government under Paul ("Oom Paul" or Uncle Paul) Kruger, worried it would be swamped by *uitlanders,* made life difficult for them, denying them the vote and ignoring their petitions. Disenfranchising other groups has become a permanent Afrikaner tactic in preserving their dominance.

Meanwhile to the south in the Cape, the British were plotting to add the Transvaal and Orange Free State to the British Empire. Sir Cecil Rhodes, the Cape millionaire who set up the Rhodes scholarships to Oxford, hankered after the mineral wealth of the Boer republics. He had already sent a column around the Boers to the north to found Rhodesia. Said Rhodes: "Expansion is everything." Agreeing with him was the British high commissioner in the Cape, Alfred (later Lord) Milner, who dreamed of a white empire ruled by London. Using the issue of *uitlander* rights in the Transvaal, Rhodes and Milner provoked Kruger into declaring war in 1899.

British propaganda portrayed the conflict as a crusade to liberate Africans from Boer misrule, but that was window dressing. The English treated blacks no better than the Boers did. The English simply wanted to consolidate their rule over the southern part of Africa, and they found the Boers a nuisance. It was the high point of British imperialism and, some say, the beginning of its decline, for the surprisingly long and cruel war drained Britain militarily and morally.

The Boers fought tenaciously. Good riders and marksmen—and equipped with modern arms from a sympathetic Germany—the Boers at first sent the British reeling back and laid siege to British-held cities. Wrote Kipling: "We have had a jolly good lesson, and it serves us jolly well right." Ultimately, Britain's superiority in arms and numbers reduced the Boers to bands of guerrilla fighters. To isolate the Boer commandos from food and supplies, the British resorted to rounding up their women and children and placing them in "concentration camps." Typhoid broke out and some twenty-six thousand died in the camps. Even today, every Afrikaner family has the memory of losing at least one relative in a camp; they have never forgiven the English and depict themselves as the century's first concentration-camp victims.

Finally, in 1902, the Boers caved in and signed the Treaty of Vereeniging. But the British, guilty over the misery they had inflicted, failed to follow up on their victory. Instead of suppressing the defeated foe, they gave them full political rights, and, over time, the Afrikaners used their legal powers to ultimately take over all South Africa. In the end, the Boers won.

FROM DEFEAT TO VICTORY

The defeated Boer republics were made British crown colonies but were soon given internal self-government. In 1908, a National Convention met in Durban to draw up plans for making the four colonies one country, and in 1910, the Union of South Africa was proclaimed. Politically, the English and the Afrikaners, as they increasingly called themselves, managed to cooperate and even formed parties that included members of both language groups. Some of South Africa's leading statesmen, such as the famed General Jan Christian

Smuts, had earlier fought the British. A spirit of good feeling and forgiveness seemed to reign.

A considerable strand of Afrikaner opinion, though, was unhappy with the alliance for two reasons. First, it tied them to British foreign policy, because South Africa was now a British dominion. Fighting for Britain was something most Afrikaners did grudgingly, if at all: when South Africa entered World War I, many Afrikaners rebelled rather than let themselves be used to take over the neighboring German colony of South-West Africa. Again in 1939, when a bare majority of parliament voted to enter World War II, an Afrikaner fascist movement known as the *Ossewa-Brandwag* (flaming oxcart) sprang up to oppose South African help for a traditional enemy against a traditional friend.

"Workers of the World Unite for a White South Africa"

When the price of gold dropped in 1922, white miners, most of them Afrikaners, staged a major and violent strike because the mine owners wanted to employ more blacks to save on wages. To give a white man's job to an African is an outrage for white South African workers. At this same time the Bolsheviks were consolidating their power in Russia and spreading Marx's old slogan, "Workers of the world unite!" This struck the miners as a good slogan for them too, but they added a South African twist: "workers" meant white only.

The so-called Rand Revolt of 1922 illustrates how Afrikaners viewed themselves as a downtrodden class, crushed first by the British and then by capitalists (all of whom were English-speaking too): We may laugh at the juxtaposition of a Marxist slogan with a white-supremacist phrase, but the Afrikaner miners, worried about jobs, saw nothing funny in it.

Second, and of equal importance, the Afrikaners were economic underdogs to the English, who nearly monopolized industry and commerce. The Afrikaners were largely farmers, and when farm prices collapsed worldwide between the two wars, economically many Afrikaners were scarcely any better off than Africans. Much like characters from the Depression novel *Grapes of Wrath*, Afrikaners streamed to the cities looking for work. Jobs for poor whites became their rallying cry.

Their path to salvation was "ethnic mobilization," organizing themselves to promote Afrikaners in business and politics. They built cultural associations, insurance companies, schools and universities, and above all the National party. The National party was founded in 1914 as the vehicle for Afrikaner political sentiment, but its moderate leaders believed in cooperation with the English. When the party split in 1934, the militant Daniel F. Malan remade the Nationalists into the party of Afrikaner power. Malan stood not only for white supremacy but for making sure every Afrikaner had a job, a pseudosocialist component that survives to this day.

Slowly the Nationalists built their strength. A well-organized party, the Nationalists indoctrinated Afrikaners with the idea that anyone not supporting the party had broken the *laager* and betrayed his brothers. By 1948, they had sufficiently mobilized Afrikaners—who were and still are a majority of the country's whites—to win the general election. Now at last the country was restored to them. No longer would the British push them around. They proceeded to build precisely the system they wished.

THE KEY INSTITUTIONS

THE "NEW DISPENSATION"

In 1984, South Africa implemented a new constitution that had been approved by two-thirds of the whites-only electorate in a referendum the previous year. By including Colored and Indian—but not black—representatives in a new three-chambered parliament, the white government held it was offering a major liberalization. Critics of all colors argued that the "new dispensation," designed by whites and for whites, merely entrenches *apartheid,* the system of white supremacy. The new constitution did open the possibility of major reform, although it was unclear how it would be used in practice.

First, South Africa switched from a parliamentary to a presidential system. Potentially, South Africa's president—elected indirectly for a five-year term and not responsible to parliament—could have a lot of power. Under South Africa's new constitution, if the tricameral parliament deadlocks, the president can rule without it with his hand-picked President's Council.

From 1910 to 1984, the South African government had been structured along British lines—the "Westminster model"—with a prime minister chosen by the all-white House of Assembly. After breaking away from the British Commonwealth in 1961 to become the fully independent Republic of South Africa (RSA), the country had a figurehead president, a largely honorific head of state.

Prime Minister P. W. Botha saw the need to change this. In pushing through a program of cautious reforms, he encountered resistance in the right wing of his National party, some of whom split off to form new parties. A presidential system—where the chief executive could not be ousted by parliament—was better suited to Botha's designs. In a presidential system, he would be able to

What Might Have Been: The Black and Colored Vote

South Africa used to have some black and Colored voters. The Cape colony, under more liberal English rule, permitted them to vote with modest literacy and property qualifications that still discouraged most. Nonetheless, it was a beginning, and one that might have paved the way for the gradual expansion of the franchise. The Cape brought its limited black and Colored franchise with it into the Union in 1910, but parliament dropped the black vote in 1936 and the Colored vote in 1956. Blacks and Colored were to be given separate advisory councils, but these had no power.

One of the keys to democratic stability has historically been the gradual enfranchisement of the population, one slice at a time, to give both the people and the institutions time to adjust. South Africa, in instituting Colored and Indian chambers of parliament in 1984, was paying belated and half-hearted respect to the principle that broadening the electoral suffrage is the main avenue of peaceful change.

South Africa's President P. W. Botha. (South Africa Consulate General)

do what he had to do without worrying about parliamentary sniping or by-elections expressing right-wing anger. As de Gaulle had concluded in France, Botha saw that a presidential system was more effective in enacting changes. As expected, Botha was chosen as the new president in 1984 by an electoral college formed by all three houses of South Africa's new legislature.

South Africa's capital moves twice a year. The parliament buildings are in Cape Town rather than in Pretoria, the administrative capital. When the president comes to Cape Town to officially open a parliamentary session, the capital comes with him. This means that every year hundreds of ministers, bureaucrats, journalists, and diplomats must decamp to Cape Town and then trek back to Pretoria when parliament is over.

Territorially, South Africa, like Britain, is a unitary rather than a federal state. The old colonies—the Cape, Natal, the Transvaal, and the Orange Free State—are now the country's four provinces. Each province has a legislature concerned with local affairs such as education, health services, highways, and fish and game. Provincial administrators, named by the prime minister, oversee the workings of each province for Pretoria and limit the amount of local autonomy.

A TRICAMERAL PARLIAMENT

The curious feature of South Africa's 1984 reform is its parliament, consisting of three houses: one each for whites, Coloreds, and Indians. The trick is that the three meet separately and the latter two cannot override the white chamber. White supremacy is thus effectively preserved. Blacks, over 70 percent of the population, get no representation, on the theory that they are represented in their tribal homelands.

As before, the whites' chamber is the House of Assembly, now consisting of 178 seats, mostly from single-member districts. Coloreds have an 85-member House of Representatives, and Indians have a 45-member House of Delegates. The 1984 elections to these two chambers, however, were heavily protested and boycotted. Fewer than one eligible Colored and Indian citizen in five voted; the turnout was so weak it ridiculed the legitimacy of the new chambers. The most elemental purpose of legislatures is to make people *feel* they are represented. Most Coloreds and Indians felt the new setup was a sham.

There are other problems with the tricameral parliament, especially the likelihood of deadlock. The white chamber, dominated by Botha's National party, is not about to undertake any far-reaching rollback of the laws of apartheid (see box), which is what the two other chambers want. Deadlock between the three chambers therefore seems likely.

A PRESIDENTIAL DICTATORSHIP?

The prospect of deadlock doesn't bother the new president much, for he is very powerful and can govern without parliament at all—a strong point of presidential systems. The president, under the new constitution, can dissolve parliament for any of a number of reasons.

In case of parliamentary deadlock, the president can turn to the President's Council, a 60-member appointive body with nonbinding powers to advise. The white chamber of parliament elects twenty members, the Colored ten, and the Indian five, and the president hand picks twenty-five. If he wants to, the president can even pick blacks for the council to represent "urban blacks."

In sum, the president doesn't really need parliament and may even be able to get more done, in terms of reforms, without one. In a serious emergency, the president can proclaim martial law.

Could this make South Africa's president almost a dictator along the lines of the French presidency? It could, and that power may be necessary for South Africa at this delicate stage. As we will consider later, most white South Africans fear any major change in the system. Change can come about only over the heads of the majority of the white electorate. A strong presidency, insulated from immediate political pressures, has the power and probably the time to accomplish reforms of the system. The parliamentary system, on the other hand, with its frequent by-elections serving as weather vanes, would keep its prime minister on too short a leash. In moving to a presidential system, Botha seemed to suggest that he was getting ready for important reforms that many whites wouldn't like.

The Laws of Apartheid

Every step the Pretoria government has taken in implementing *apartheid* is "legal"; that is, it has been passed as a law. Some of the apartheid laws go back well before the coming of the Nationalists to power in 1948. The Nationalists, however, introduced far more specific, detailed legislation to perfect and make permanent the separation of the races. They passed more than 350 *apartheid* laws. Here are the most important:

Land Act, 1913, prohibits Africans from acquiring land outside of their native reserves.

Natives (Urban Areas) Act, 1923, sets up residential segregation in cities.

Mines and Works Amendment Act, 1926, or "Color Bar" Act, prohibits Africans from skilled work in the mines.

Immorality Acts, 1927 and 1950, prohibited sexual relations between whites and nonwhites. Repealed in 1985.

Mixed Marriages Act, 1949, made marriage between whites and non-whites illegal. Repealed.

Population Registration Act, 1950, requires everyone to carry an identity card specifying race. Borderline cases are decided arbitrarily by bureaucrats.

Group Areas Act, 1950, outlaws racially mixed neighborhoods by specifying which races live where.

Suppression of Communism Act, 1950, allows justice minister to "ban" suspicious persons from normal contacts. Anyone working for major reforms may be defined as a Communist.

Separate Representation of Voters Act, 1951, removed the Cape Colored from the electoral rolls. Finally passed in 1956 after the Nationalist government packed the Senate and high courts.

Native Building Workers' Act, 1951, extends the earlier mining color bar to skilled construction trades.

Prevention of Illegal Squatting Act, 1951, permits destruction of the many African squatter settlements that sprang up near cities.

Natives (Abolition of Passes and Coordination of Documents) Act, 1952, requires all Africans over 16 to carry at all times a passbook specifying where they may live and work.

Native Laws Amendment Act, 1952, prohibits most Africans from remaining in an urban area more than 72 hours. This "influx control" tries to keep Africans from flocking to the cities.

Bantu Education Act, 1953, transferred African education from the province level to the Department of Native Affairs, implicitly to make sure Africans don't get too much education.

Separate Amenities Act, 1953, segregated trains, toilets, restaurants, taxis, beaches, just about anything, according to race. Led to numerous "whites only" signs, which have since disappeared.

Group Areas Development Act, 1955, provided for the forcible removal of nonwhites to make new whites-only areas.

Industrial Conciliation Act, 1956, permits the labor minister to "reserve" job categories for whites only.

Riotous Assemblies Act, 1956, outlaws protest gatherings.

Native Laws Amendment Act, 1957, tightens influx control by granting Africans permanent residence status in cities only if they have been born there, lived there fifteen years, or worked there for ten years. Act also segregates most churches.

Criminal Procedure Amendment Act, 1958, provides for hanging in cases of robbery, aimed at stemming rising black crime rate. (It hasn't.)

Separate Universities Education Act, 1959, prohibited nonwhites from most universities except by special permission.

Promotion of Bantu Self-Government Act, 1959, sets up self-government in the tribal homelands on the theory that here, and only here, can Africans enjoy political participation.

General Law Amendment Act, 1963, lets police hold anyone considered suspicious for renewable ninety-day periods (later reduced to renewable fourteen-day periods) without trial and without recourse to a court of law.

Bantu Homelands Citizenship Act, 1970, the culmination of *apartheid,* makes all Africans citizens of their tribal homelands and deprives them of South African citizenship.

THE PARTIES

The National party has dominated South Africa since 1948. Originally a purely Afrikaner party, it now attracts the votes of many English-speakers as well. Most of the institutions of *apartheid*—now called "separate development"—were drafted by Nationalist cabinets and made law by Nationalist-dominated parliaments. In economics, the "Nats" favor state intervention rather than a free market; they introduced government-sponsored industries and numerous controls designed to secure jobs for Afrikaners and more power for the party. Under the Nationalists, Afrikaners have almost totally taken over the civil service and army. The Nationalists in 1981 won 53 percent of the whites-only vote (down from 65 percent in 1977) and 131 out of 165 seats (down from 134).

The opposition Progressive Federal party, Progs for short, won 18 percent of the vote in 1981 and 26 seats. Founded in 1977 from remnants of the old United, Liberal and Progressive parties, its voting strength is in English-speaking cities such as Johannesburg, Cape Town, and Durban. The Progs would dismantle *apartheid* and devise a power-sharing formula with blacks and browns, although even they shy away from one-man, one-vote enfranchisement. In economics, the Progs are classic liberals (that is, American-style conservatives) and favor private industry in a free market. They combine, in other words, racial liberalism with economic liberalism. In a normal political spectrum the Progressives would actually be considered rather conservative. Although Progressive voters and leaders are mostly English-speakers, in 1979 a dynamic young Afrikaner took over as party chief. He was Dr. Frederick van Zyl Slabbert, a sociologist.

Protesting that Botha was getting ready to roll back the apartheid system, in 1982 the right wing of the National party, led by former Public Works Minister Andries Treurnicht, walked out to form a new Conservative party. This new group won enough support in the *platteland,* the conservative farming districts where the Nats used to hold absolute sway, that Botha and his party saw the possibility of losing their traditional supporters. This was one reason they moved to a presidential system. Even further to the right, the *Herstigte Nasionale* party (Reconstituted National party, HNP) won few votes. However, it contributes to the racist fear that engulfs many Afrikaners.

In Natal, some former members of the old United party calling themselves the New Republic party won eight seats in 1981. They billed themselves as centrists—between the Nats and Progs—but, like the United party before them, offered no alternative to *apartheid*.

The South African party system does not constitute a "normal" political spectrum. The Nationalists are usually called conservative or right wing. They are conservative in the area of race relations but not in economics, for they favor welfare for whites and state control in many sectors of the economy. The Progressives, on the other hand, are "conservative" (that is, classic liberals) in economics, favoring free enterprise, but they are against the *apartheid* race system. What's missing from the South African party spectrum, quite obviously, are black parties.

NONWHITE PARTIES

Legally, there are no black (or even multiracial) political parties in South Africa. Nonetheless, they exist and play an increasing role in both mobilizing blacks and frightening whites. Either labeled as cultural associations or underground and in exile, black parties are a reality that white South Africa cannot ignore.

The oldest and still most important black party is the African National Congress, founded in 1912 by blacks educated in missionary schools. For half a century the ANC practiced nonviolent protest; its leader during the 1950s, the great and gentle Chief Albert Luthuli, won the 1961 Nobel Peace Prize. He was, nonetheless, banished to a remote village, where he died. The ANC was banned in 1960 and, as the Nationalist regime relentlessly implemented its *apartheid* structure, came to the conclusion that violence was the only way to communicate its message. In 1964, its leaders were convicted of plotting revolution and sentenced to life imprisonment.

But the ANC did not die. Operating in exile, it gives young blacks weapons training (with Soviet-bloc help) and has them infiltrate the Republic for sabotage and attacks on police stations. Its spiritual leader, Nelson Mandela, grows more legendary with every year he spends in prison; blacks, especially young blacks, worship him. If South Africa let blacks vote, the ANC and Nelson Mandela would win a national election.

The regime in effect admitted Mandela's importance by offering to release him in 1985 on the condition that he renounce violence, a move probably calculated to split and confuse the ANC. Mandela didn't buy. In a statement read to a cheering crowd by his daughter Zinzi, Mandela said, referring to Botha, "Let *him* renounce violence." In a rare prison interview with a British visitor, Mandela explained: "The armed struggle was forced upon us by the government, and if they want us to give it up, the ball is in their court. They must legalize us [the ANC], treat us like a political party and negotiate with us. Until they do, we will have to live with the armed struggle." In turning down Botha's offer, Mandela acted more like a president than a prisoner, a psychological point that was not lost on his followers.

The ANC's eighteen-member National Executive Committee is based in Lusaka, Zambia, but doesn't advertise its location for fear of South African attack. The ANC's military branch, *Umkhonto We Sizwe* (Zulu for "Spear of the Nation"), has been stepping up guerrilla attacks to include civilian bystanders. ANC president Oliver Tambo (Mandela's former law partner) travels worldwide to seek help for his cause.

The ANC defines itself as a multiracial party, and some of its leaders are white, for example, Joe Slovo, a Communist. During the 1950s, some younger ANC members turned more militant and more dedicated to exclusive black power. In 1958, they split away to form the smaller Pan Africanist Congress (PAC), just in time to be outlawed the following year with the ANC. In exile, PAC withered, so that now ANC is the only game in town for those willing to work underground and in exile for a new "Azania"—the black militants' name for South Africa—with majority rule.

While the ANC and PAC were banned and forced to turn to guerrilla warfare, an above-ground black party is trying to give peaceful change one last chance. *Inkatha*, ostensibly a cultural movement, grew among Zulus during the 1970s, and the Pretoria regime has not outlawed it. Big (a claimed 900,000 members), well-organized (party workers wear tan uniforms), and with a government-approved territorial base (the homeland of KwaZulu), its leader, Chief Gatsha Buthelezi, declares his readiness to negotiate with Pretoria but maintains *Inkatha's* ultimate aim is to liberate blacks nationwide. The movement attracts few non-Zulus, though, and more radical blacks despise Buthelezi as a sellout and Zulu fascist. If it were a serious black-liberation movement, they reason, Pretoria would ban it.

The Colored Labor party and some small Indian parties run candidates for their respective chambers of parliament, but they have little power to change the system.

In 1983 an interesting multiracial alliance sprang up to oppose the new constitution, the United Democratic Front. UDF leaders were arrested and tried for treason, and the organization was banned by the government in 1985. In sum, most of the South African party system is repressed, a condition that cannot last forever.

South Africa's Homelands

THE HOMELANDS

The ultimate aim of *apartheid,* or separate development, is to make Africans citizens only of their homelands and not of South Africa. This policy permits South Africa to treat blacks as temporary workers in the Republic without voting or residency rights. Originally the homelands were native reserves left after the Kaffir Wars of the last century. Americans would call them Indian reservations. The Nationalist policy has been to gradually turn the territorially fragmented reserves into homelands and then into "independent republics," one for each tribe.

These ten homelands, supposedly home to all of South Africa's black population, account for only 13 percent of RSA territory. Most Africans do not live in the homelands but in the cities and on white farms. Many have never seen their homeland and don't want to. The law lets authorities forcibly send Africans to their homeland if they are not needed in an urban area or form a "black spot" in a farming area designated for whites. Some 3.5 million have thus been "resettled" on hopeless, overcrowded, marginal lands.

Home for Three Million People?

(Michael Roskin)

The state of KwaZulu (meaning the "place of the Zulus") is envisioned as eventual home to three million Africans. Broken into twenty-nine fragments and already overpopulated, there is no way it could survive unless (1) many of its people worked outside the homeland and (2) white industry set up facilities to take advantage of the plentiful, cheap labor.

So far, five homelands, under pliant, hand-picked 'leadership, have opted for independence: Transkei in 1976, BophuthaTswana in 1977, Venda in 1979, and Ciskei and KwaNdebele in 1981. Aside from South Africa, no country has granted them diplomatic recognition. Other homeland leaders, following the lead of KwaZulu chief minister Gatsha Buthelezi (also the head of *Inkatha*), have rejected independence as a sham designed to deprive Africans of their national birthrights.

Economically, the homelands are totally dependent on South Africa. In some areas there is said to be starvation. Only money sent from their workers in the Republic and the relocation of South African factories in their territories keep them afloat. The homelands are simply storage bins for humans.

SOUTH AFRICAN POLITICAL ATTITUDES

THE AFRIKANERS

In the last century, the Boers began to think of themselves as Afrikaners rather than Dutch. Their language, *Afrikaans*, had evolved to become quite different from the original Dutch (see box). No longer citizens of the Netherlands, they felt that Holland had turned its back on them. They had become, to all intents and purposes, Africa's white tribe, *die volk* (the people), as they called themselves.

And Afrikaner attitudes are indeed tribal. They even frown on marriage to English-speakers. Like the black tribes in other African countries, they do not willingly share power with other tribes. Afrikaners emphasize that politics in Africa is tribal. They are correct; in fact, they are a prime example of it.

A dour, humorless people, Afrikaners take pride in their steadfastness, religiosity, strength, and determination. They are absolutely convinced they are right and are rarely willing to compromise or admit they might be wrong. They are not, however, arrogant or elitist; among themselves they are quite democratic. Toward foreigners they are friendly if somewhat reserved.

Afrikaners treat blacks firmly but (they think) fairly; on a personal level they may esteem individual blacks but are convinced blacks need perpetual white supervision. They see blacks as centuries behind whites in civilization, work habits, and level of organization. Because blacks are still largely primitive, they must never be accorded political equality with whites. Blacks are still essentially tribal, the Afrikaner believes, and happiest with their own people; that's why the homelands are the best solution.

Toward the British, the Afrikaners feel deep hatred; they stubbornly nurse their historical grudge. They recite tales of their subjugation in the Cape colony, the British take-over of Natal, the British-provoked Boer War, the forced involvement in two world wars, and now having to hear Britain preach human rights to them. To their own English-speaking whites they transfer some of their anti-British sentiment in the form of contempt. They consider English liberals hypocrites and cowards who see blacks exactly the way Afrikaners do but

Afrikaans: A New Language

Cut off from the Netherlands, Boers developed their own language, based on Dutch but with African, Malay, French, and English words added. By the late eighteenth century it was a written language, and by the Boer War it had supplanted Dutch. In defeat, Afrikaners turned to their language as a statement of identity and a focal point around which to rally their people. Many Afrikaner political organizations began as cultural associations to promote Afrikaans language and literature.

Afrikaans has been called the youngest and simplest of the Germanic languages. It now resembles the Flemish of Belgium more than modern Dutch. Grammar complications—such as German's *der, die, das*—disappear in Afrikaans. Everything is *die,* as in *die volk* (German: *das Volk*).

Afrikaans is easy to learn, but English speakers seldom bother, and this infuriates Afrikaners. One Afrikaner fumed: "If there are five Afrikaners and one English speaker, the group will speak English." It's as if the English are still snubbing them as culturally inferior. Most Afrikaners are forced to learn English and speak it well. Both languages are official in the RSA.

To really communicate with an Afrikaner, though, you've got to use his or her language. Arguments and criticism in English are ignored; in Afrikaans they're taken seriously. This has led to the irony that Coloreds, whose native tongue is Afrikaans, can often score points where the English can't.

lack the guts to say so. They regard the English who have joined them in the National party as junior partners at last come to their senses.

One important factor often eludes outside critics of South Africa: the Afrikaners do not see themselves as oppressors but rather as the aggrieved party, the hurt victims of historical injustice. Outside criticism that portrays Afrikaners as villains just bounces off; obviously the critics don't know what they're talking about, thinks the Afrikaner. The whole world is against us? What does that matter? The rest of the world is full of evil Communists or wishy-washy liberals. The Afrikaner is convinced that if only foreigners would come with an open mind to see for themselves, they'd temper their criticism and agree at least partially with the Afrikaners.

Afrikaners expect ethnic solidarity from their fellow Afrikaners. An Afrikaner who joins the English-speakers in criticism has broken the *laager,* the *voortrekkers'* ring of oxcarts, and thus has betrayed *die volk* in their hour of danger. Actually, Boers and later Afrikaners were never monolithic in their views. A minority believed in cooperating with the English and now want a fairer deal for blacks. Today Afrikaners such as novelist André Brink, Reverend Beyers Naude, and opposition leader Frederick van Zyl Slabbert are among the regime's severest critics. Nonetheless, the myth of *volk* unity conditions most to conform in unequivocal support for the Nationalists.

In sum, the Afrikaner is a tough personality who does not bend easily. Under the tough exterior, though, one detects a certain amount of fear and worry; rarely expressed openly, this vulnerability more often surfaces in voices that grow shrill, arguments that depart from the real world, and sardonic, scathing contempt for foreign critics, especially Americans. Many of the points an Afrikaner apologist makes are accurate, but he or she uses them to evade the larger issue: How much longer will South Africa's blacks accept what the Afrikaners are handing them?

THE ENGLISH-SPEAKERS

English-speaking people constitute about 40 percent of South Africa's whites. In terms of ethnic origin, English-speakers can be Greek, Irish, Italian, Jewish, Portuguese, German, or even Dutch. As in Canada, most new immigrants elect to learn English. Sometimes referred to as "the English" for short, they are actually a diverse group who have clustered around the original British colonials of the last century.

As mentioned earlier, the English, after winning the Boer War, walked away from politics, preferring business instead. As a result, they lost most political power but almost completely dominated commerce and industry. The rural Afrikaners discovered capitalism only recently; the urban English were capitalists from the start. This has given them a more liberal outlook: let economics and market forces take care of social problems, rather than imposing numerous controls and regulations as the Nationalists have done.

The English never formed an "English party" but were happy to join with Afrikaners in fusion parties, such as the old South Africa and United parties, which were usually Afrikaner-led. Even today, the almost exclusively English Progressive Federal party is headed by an Afrikaner.

The Afrikaners' scorn for English liberals is at least partly justified. Few protested as the Nationalists built the *apartheid* system, and many English-speaking business persons benefited from the cheap, controlled labor supply it produced. In the now-defunct United party the English liberals questioned the form but not the substance of *apartheid*. Many English frankly don't know where they should stand on the issue. Their principles lead them to criticize the Nationalists, but their fear of black power makes some silently thank the majority party. In recent elections, many English have been voting Nationalist, and there are even English-speaking Nationalist members of parliament.

The English are more likely than the Afrikaners to voice their fears openly. Some wonder if South Africa will be a good place for their children;

What Might Have Been: If the English Had Retained Power

Would it have made a difference in South Africa if the English had retained political power in this century? Afrikaners argue no, that the English spout liberal rhetoric but are just as concerned about securing their place as the Afrikaners are. Some Africans agree. One told me: "The English say they want to help, but they're pious fakes. The Afrikaners are at least honest. When they call you a bloody kaffir to your face at least you know where they stand."

The British record in other colonial situations where there have been substantial numbers of white settlers is hardly liberal. In Kenya and Rhodesia, English settlers fought for years to prevent the rise of black power. Rhodesia even copied South African *apartheid* legislation. And Afrikaners gleefully point out that some of the country's earliest segregation laws were enacted by the British in Natal in the last century.

Others—especially English-speaking liberals—think continued English power would have made a difference. While many agree that, basically, English racial attitudes are not much different from Afrikaner attitudes, the English are restrained by a sense of fair play, by rule of law, by a more modern business mentality, and by extensive overseas contacts. They might have been less thorough in attempting to separate the races and more willing to listen to blacks and to compromise.

some ask visitors casually about job opportunities and housing prices in the United States. Every year, several thousand quietly emigrate, many to the States. Some secretly retain British passports—illegal under South African law—for a possible speedy escape. (Recall how quickly runner Zola Budd obtained British nationality for the 1984 Olympics.) This causes Afrikaners to scorn them even more.

THE AFRICANS

There is some truth to the white view that the Africans are still tribal in outlook, but this has been exaggerated. For those born and raised in rural areas who speak the native language, it is doubtless the case. But for the many millions—about one-third of all Africans—who reside in urban areas to work in mines, factories, homes, or offices, it is no longer accurate. There, under modern economic conditions, Africans from many tribes are integrated with Africans from other tribes. They come to see themselves more and more as Africans suffering a common fate and less and less as Zulus (the largest group of Africans), Xhosas, Tswanas, or others.

Paradoxically, it is the whites whose policies have broken down tribalism and integrated Africans into a whole. In the mines, for example, they found that work teams composed of only one tribe were prone to fight teams of other tribes. They integrated the work crews and fighting stopped. The mine companies even invented a synthetic work language so men from different tribes could communicate. Typically, though, urban blacks are fluent in several African languages and get along fairly well with people from other tribes. Businesses generally require English, and many Africans speak it well, although they are reluctant to learn Afrikaans, "the language of the oppressor."

Are all Africans revolutionaries, thirsting for black power? Far from it. Many are what might be called pre-mobilized, or not yet politically aware. Most think in terms of specific problems: avoiding arrest for not having one's passbook, the long commute from the black township, decent housing, making ends meet, and so on. For them, worry over voting rights is a distant abstraction.

A growing number of young black South Africans, especially in urban areas, are, however, educated and radicalized. They want sweeping change—some even mention universal suffrage—and consider many of their elders "Uncle Toms" for knuckling under to "whitey." (Terms from the U.S. civil-rights struggle are common.) It was, in fact, high school students who led the massive 1976 Soweto riots—triggered by a government edict that made learning Afrikaans in school mandatory—that left some 700 dead. Thousands of young blacks then sneaked out of the country to join the ANC.

What do South Africa's urban blacks want? First and foremost, they insist on a common citizenship. The progressive revocation of South African citizenship—as the homelands become independent—is robbing blacks of their country. Second, they want the homelands policy scrapped; that is, the homelands must not be turned into independent republics where blacks can be dumped. Third, they want the right to move to the cities and have secure tenure over their homes. As it stands now, under the heading of "influx control" the regime can expell most blacks from urban areas and even take away their homes. Fourth, and far from least, they want the hated pass laws scrapped. If one thing most enrages South Africa's blacks it's the policeman's gruff demand: "Where's your pass, boy?" Some half million blacks a year are arrested for passbook irregularities.

Black attitudes are not yet explosive. Or, more accurately, the intermittent explosions among Africans—Sharpeville 1960, Soweto 1976, the Eastern Cape 1985—have failed to ignite the broad masses of black South Africans. Every year, though, Africans get more educated, more industrialized, more angry—in a word, "mobilized." Moderation and acquiescence may disappear among the Africans fairly suddenly, leaving violence as the only path.

"Defensive Avoidance"

How can South Africa's white minority fail to take account of black opposition to the apartheid scheme? Africans are over 70 percent of the population and growing more outspoken. Most whites, though, pay little attention. The white press is mostly about whites; to read it one would think that blacks are a *minority* in the country. The few black faces on South Africa's government-controlled television are those of American entertainers. Blacks have their own channel. It's as if the Africans with their problems and demands weren't there.

Yale psychologist Irving Janis calls this "defensive avoidance," a kind of mental dodge ball in which people defend their mental structures by jumping away from unpleasant facts. Defensive avoidance, says Janis, "involves seeking relief from emotional tension by engaging in wishful thinking" and "relying on reassuring illusions and rationalizations." Dissenters who warn of danger are isolated and ignored. The group is convinced it's right and powerful enough to carry out its plans. Although Janis developed his "groupthink" concept to help explain U.S. foreign policy, it describes white South Africans, especially Afrikaners.

In an ominous sign, when an ANC car bomb killed nineteen—including some blacks—in Pretoria in 1983, South African blacks were generally understanding; some were even jubilant. Said one black, "They long ago gave up any hope for peaceful change. What they are saying is that the African National Congress is finally hitting real targets. That is why you are having crowds of blacks drawn to the street where the bomb went off. They want to see the place where a white man died." For many blacks, white violence is finally being met with black violence.

THE BROWNS

Perhaps the saddest, most worried South Africans are neither the whites nor the blacks but the "browns," as the Indians and Coloreds are known collectively. They are neither in the privileged position of whites nor in the numerical superiority with blacks. The browns are the classic middlemen, squeezed between forces they cannot control. Held to an inferior status by whites, they cannot look forward to being treated any better by blacks.

There is little feeling of solidarity between the Coloreds, most of whom live in the Cape, and the Indians, most of whom live in Natal. The Coloreds, who once had the vote in the Cape, are now more politically restless and resentful. The Indians, many of whom inched their way up from indentured sugar-cane workers to prosperous merchants, are more inclined to leave national politics alone and settle for self-governance within the Indian community. The Indians brought with them a strong sense of identity and culture from their native country. The Coloreds have severe identity and culture problems: they long wanted to be the little brown *baas* (Afrikaans for boss), but, having been rejected, they increasingly call themselves black, although it's not clear the Africans want them either.

The Indians generally stay apolitical, hoping to avoid the crossfire in any upheaval. The Coloreds, once docile, have turned increasingly angry and militant. In 1980, as many as 100,000 Colored schoolchildren struck against their inferior educational conditions—crowded classrooms, untrained teachers, no books—but what they were really striking against was inequality in general. The regime, as usual, handled the matter with tear gas, batons, and mass arrests. In the dusty, crime-infested Colored townships of Cape Town, where unemployment is near 25 percent, young Coloreds responded with rocks, arson, and looting. The police, under an order of "shoot to kill," opened up with buckshot (instead of the usual automatic rifles), leaving some forty dead. The strikes and riots marked a turning of the Coloreds from quiet anger to open rebellion.

In 1984, the leadership of the Colored Labor party went along with Botha's reforms and entered the new Colored House of Representatives to work for change within the system. But there was violent protest in the Colored community against cooperating with the system, and four out of five eligible Colored voters stayed away from the polls. The relatively moderate Labor party may no longer speak for a majority of Coloreds.

PATTERNS OF INTERACTION

THE PARTIES AND THE ELECTORATE

Until the 1980s, the National party had a hammerlock on the Afrikaner vote. The Dutch Reformed church, only half in jest, was called the "National party at prayer." In terms of social class, the Nats also drew working-class whites, even English speakers. As noted earlier, one of the Nationalist mobilizing devices was protection of poorer white workers. The Nats' unwritten motto could have been: "No white man will ever lose a job."

But in the 1980s, the Afrikaner vote began to splinter (see below). The Nationalists saw some of their traditional electoral base picked off by the Conservative party, which was founded by breakaway right-wing Nationalists. They argued that Botha was experimenting with foolish reforms that would only result in the destruction of the *apartheid* system, the loss of white power, and ultimately a take-over by black Communists. Afrikaner organizations—churches, cultural associations, student movements, even the *Broederbond* (see box)—split, the majority staying with the Nats but a significant minority supporting the Conservatives, especially in white farming areas of the Transvaal and Orange Free State. The Conservative electorate was precisely the Nats' old bedrock. A 1984 poll found that 16 percent of Afrikaner voters favored the Conservatives, compared to 69 percent for the Nationalists.

While some Afrikaners left the Nats to go to the right, some English-speakers entered from the left. The 1984 survey found that 35 percent of English-speakers favored the Nats, almost as much as the 39 percent who favored the Progs. Many English-speakers sensed that Botha had the only practical plan for moderate reform; even more felt that whites had to close ranks during the difficult period ahead.

Curiously, it is better-off whites—largely English-speaking business and professional people—who support the Progressives, the party more liberal on race. Their comfortable positions allow them to advocate a new dispensation for Africans. An example of upper-class liberalism is Harry Oppenheimer, head of the Anglo-American Corporation (gold, diamonds). Probably South Africa's richest individual, Oppenheimer freely funds black-development projects and discussion and research groups. He is, of course, a Prog and encourages his corporation's executives to work for the party and sometimes stand for election.

The South Africa situation, in which white workers are conservative and white capitalists are liberal—at least in racial matters—stands on its head Marx's formulation that the working class is always progressive. One of the ironies of South Africa is that a flexible, compromise-ready government will have difficulty coming to power as long as the white working class has the vote. Or, viewed another way, a Pretoria government that does strike a compromise deal with blacks will have to do so on an elite basis, disregarding the feelings of most white voters.

POLITICS WITHIN THE NATS

Although the Nationalists have always stressed unity, during the 1970s two informal groups grew up in its ranks, *verligtes* and *verkramptes*, meaning respectively "enlightened" and "narrow-minded." The terms were coined by a relatively liberal Afrikaner newspaper editor, Willem de Klerk, to substitute for liberal, which had developed a pejorative connotation in South Africa.

A *verligte* Nationalist is not as liberal as a Prog in that he or she does not favor actual power sharing. What the *verligtes* (the *g* is pronounced like a German *ch*) are prepared to admit is that Africans have grounds for complaint and that some of their demands should be heeded. The *verligtes* would rescind "petty *apartheid,*" the barring of Africans from previously all-white jobs, hotels, and public facilities. Under *verligte* prodding, virtually all of South Africa's famous "whites only" signs disappeared. (Some Africans report, however, that the system largely continues without signs.) *Verligtes* favor black economic improvement and are willing to invest government money in it.

When pushed into a corner, though, *verligtes* are not so different from *verkramptes.* Both favor carrying on with separate development by pushing the African homelands to independence. The *verligtes* acknowledge a role for the urban blacks and would permit them to reside permanently in the urban areas.

Black leaders, however, think the *verligtes* are frauds and what they advocate is "*apartheid* with a human face."

The dividing line between *verligtes* and *verkramptes* is the disagreement over Botha's call to "adapt or die"; the former agree with Botha whereas the latter do not. Life became somewhat simpler for the Botha government when many of the more extreme *verkramptes* walked out in 1982 to form the Conservative party. True, Botha had to worry about losing some *platteland* seats to the Conservative party, but it broke the cabinet paralysis that had come from *verkramptes's* blocking and stalemating *verligtes*. The following year, Botha presented his new constitution to the white electorate in a referendum. Two-thirds supported it; some Progs and all Conservatives opposed it. The following year, the new presidential and tricameral system went into operation. The split in Nationalist ranks had actually been a good thing, for it rid the party of an immobilizing element.

The Powerful Band of Brothers

All agree that the single most powerful interest group in South Africa—some say it's the ony one that counts—is the secretive *Broederbond,* "band of brothers." Founded in 1918 to promote Afrikaner cultural, economic, and political power, the Broederbond came to dominate first the National party and then the government. Members—who are never publicly identified—must be white, male Afrikaans-speakers of the Dutch Reformed religion.

With its 10,000 members inserted in all key spots of Afrikanerdom—churches, universities, government, journalism, and industry—the Broederbond is the South African equivalent of the Soviet Communist party, which also functions as a control and communications network. Most Nationalist cabinet members are in the Broederbond. Especially important is the Broederbond's control of the Dutch Reformed churches—most pastors are Broederbond members—for Afrikaners are faithful churchgoers and heed what their *dominee* tells them.

The direction the Broederbond takes determines much of what Afrikaners and the Nationalists do. Since the late 1970s, the Broederbond is reported to have come under the influence of *verligtes,* and their viewpoints began turning up in Afrikaner churches, newspapers, and the Nationalist cabinet. A *verligte* Broederbond could go a long way in reorienting government policy toward peaceful compromise with the black majority. But, like other Afrikaner organizations, the Broederbond split, and some of its members and leaders formed the fascistic *Afrikaner Volkswag* (Peoples' Guard).

POLITICS AMONG THE BLACKS

The Pretoria regime views the African majority as essentially ignorant and passive, willing to follow the "separate development" plans devised by the Nationalists. This view, if it ever was true, is now dead wrong. Black politics in South Africa is at least as complicated as white politics.

On the revolutionary side, as mentioned earlier, is the ANC which, by its very nature, is underground and in exile. On the conservative side, in some of the homelands, are traditional tribal chiefs who go along with separate development and homeland independence because it secures their power. The Pretoria regime presents these people as the authentic voice of South Africa's blacks, but no fair election or accurate poll can support this contention.

In a middle position—treading a tightrope between revolution and Uncle Tomism—are African leaders such as *Inkatha's* Buthelezi, Soweto's Dr. Nthato Motlana, newspaper editor Percy Qoboza, and Anglican Bishop Desmond Tutu. On the one hand, they are appalled by the prospect of violence, for they know that the police would calmly gun down thousands of Africans. On the other, they also know that only violence and the threat of more violence force the Nationalists to change their attitude. ANC guerrillas are probably the only reason the regime pays any attention to African leaders.

Furthermore, African leaders know that if they work with the regime they lose all credibility with activist militants. Buthelezi may have already suffered this fate: at the 1978 funeral of the PAC's Robert Sobukwe, he was stoned by young radicals and had to flee. The fate of Rhodesia's Abel Muzorewa, who worked with the white regime of Ian Smith, is also on the minds of South Africa's black leaders. In 1980 elections, Muzorewa was trounced by Marxist guerrilla leader Robert Mugabe. The lesson was not lost: don't get too close to whites.

This situation makes black-white dialogue exceedingly difficult. Black leaders willing to talk with the Pretoria regime run the risk of having informed, educated black opinion turn against them. A moderate such as Buthelezi, trying simultaneously to lead a national political movement (*Inkatha*) and a homeland (KwaZulu), found himself hopelessly compromised. As a homeland leader, he had to work with the white regime on all manner of economic, political, and territorial questions. But this meant that he was not a credible nationwide black leader, and *Inkatha* remained a largely Zulu movement.

Black leaders who could plausibly speak for and reassure urban Africans—Dr. Motlana, Qoboza, and Bishop Tutu—were reluctant to meet with the government because they knew they would get little to show for it and would lose credibility among their followers. Their respected status among blacks is due at least in part to the fact that all three have been jailed by the regime at one time or another. They live on the edge of arrest and banning.

PROTEST AND REPRESSION

In the absence of a constructive dialogue between blacks and whites, the regime governs with coercion and repression. With avenues of legal protest systematically closed off, black and brown protests are automatically illegal. Faced with illegality, the South African police enforce the law, often with bloody results.

It sounds like a prescription for revolution: plenty of injustice but no way to protest it legally; unavoidable illegal protests met with police violence, with increased hatred on the part of the blacks leading to a heightened sense of injustice. Soon the cycle of protest and repression could produce a nationwide black uprising. In 1985, black youths in the townships started firebombing the homes of black policemen and other servants of the white regime. Pretoria sent army units to help police. Violence seemed to be approaching a take-off point; the old tools of coercion no longer worked.

Coercion is applied in massive doses in South Africa; it is part and parcel of the system. Riot police, clothed in camouflage fatigues, use dogs, tear gas, clubs, shotguns, and sometimes automatic rifles to disperse crowds of Africans. When a disturbance breaks out, the authorities assume it is the work of "outside agitators" and proceed to round up the usual suspects. In Cape Town a Colored pastor the author spoke with one morning was arrested that afternoon for allegedly inciting Colored schoolchildren to strike. They had no evidence against him, but the regime needs outside agitators and he seemed a likely one. For anyone seriously wanting to change the South African system, protest can mean arrest, trials, bannings, prison terms, and sometimes death.

South Africa's contribution to the art of coercion is the "ban," an order from the justice minister—no court is involved—prohibiting the banned person from normal contacts. A typical banning order might specify that for five years the subject will not be allowed to work where there are many other people (such as a factory); may not have more than one visitor at a time; may not be quoted by anyone else including the press; and must be home by six P.M. Each banning order is different, tailor-made to the individual, to make sure he or she is politically ineffective. Banning can also include exile to remote villages—as happened to Albert Luthuli or Nelson Mandela's wife, Winnie—or round-the-clock surveillance by the Security Police.

South Africa jails more than 1 percent of its population each year, a world record. Most jailings are for simple passbook violations, and the violator is soon released. Political detainees suffer a harsher fate. They can be held for virtually unlimited periods without charge. If convicted they usually go to Robben Island off Cape Town. Conditions are said to be harsh, but no one can say for sure: it's a crime to talk about prison conditions.

Steve Biko: Death in Prison

Steven Biko was a threat to the South African system, for his "black consciousness" movement sought to make blacks aware of their dignity as human beings, a first step toward challenging the system. Black consciousness in South Africa was a more subtle, psychological movement than the proscribed ANC and PAC, but in the long run it was just as dangerous for the regime. If it had succeeded in changing blacks psychologically, it would have led to the overthrow of the present system, which is based on keeping the African majority cowed.

Unable to convict the young Biko, a former medical student, on treason charges, the regime banned him to a small town in the Eastern Cape in 1973. But Biko's name and ideas continued to spread, especially among black students, who worshiped him as a hero. Some white liberals also saw the mild-mannered Biko as the last best hope for a nonviolent transition to power sharing.

In 1977 Biko was jailed indefinitely and without trial for allegedly advocating violence. Twenty-six days later the justice minister announced Biko was dead—of an eight-day hunger strike. People doubted that the healthy, strapping thirty-year-old could have died so fast from starvation or even that he had tried to. An autopsy showed his skull had been crushed in. Later police changed their story: Biko had attacked them during interrogation and was hurt in the scuffle.

A worldwide outcry followed Biko's death, forcing the regime to stage an unusual public inquest to show its fairness. Police admitted they kept Biko stripped and chained. A lawyer for Biko's family asked the police colonel if he would treat a dog that way. He replied: "If a dog is absolutely dangerous, I would probably do it." The lawyer asked for the statute allowing police to keep a man in chains. The reply: "We don't work under statutes." The judge found that the police had done nothing wrong. The justice minister, James Kruger, said Biko's death "leaves me cold."

South African police often beat prisoners to death and say they died from slipping in the shower, from falling down stairs or from a high window, or by hanging themselves. The bodies, if an autopsy is permitted, usually show multiple abrasions. Since 1963, some fifty political suspects have died in police custody. The policemen involved never receive more than a slap on the wrist. Both police and courts are largely in Afrikaner hands, and Afrikaners understand what they must do to maintain the system.

BURNING BRIDGES

The agony of South Africa is that there are so few constructive interactions between black and white. Instead of building bridges between the two groups, the Nationalists have deliberately, over the decades, destroyed them. Few whites know Africans outside of a master-servant or boss-employee relationship. There is no church, club, university, sports association, or political party that serves as a meeting ground for an exchange of views. By crushing black political movements and their leaders, the Nationalists now have only their own stooges to speak with.

Is it too late? Is revolution now inevitable? Africans and Coloreds are not yet totally aroused, and most want to avoid violence. There are responsible black leaders who could calm and guide their people *provided* the regime gives major concessions. There are among the whites—even among the Afrikaners—people who realize things can't go on like this any longer and that sweeping reforms are necessary.

But time is running out. Black thinking and white thinking are developing at different rates, the black fast and the white slow. Whites congratulate themselves for the liberalization of their ideas over the last few years. But this does nothing for blacks; they want concrete improvements across the board. What to whites is a major change and display of their goodwill (for example, dropping petty apartheid) is to blacks just a token. Now, at a time whites discover they need communication with blacks, the whites find that their apartheid program has been all too successful: there is no communication.

WHAT SOUTH AFRICANS QUARREL ABOUT

TARNISHED PROSPERITY

The South African economy which earlier had shown strong growth rates, went into steep recession in the 1980s, deepening the political crisis. The material prosperity had not been confined to whites. Shortages of skilled workers have meant that blacks, previously confined to manual labor, have been allowed to move up as construction workers, waiters, auto workers, and even small-business people. Although on the average, whites earn several times as much as blacks, black wages have been climbing faster, narrowing the gap. Job reservations have fallen by the wayside in many areas due to the skilled-labor shortage.

But this very prosperity raises a number of crucial political questions. White South Africans argue that because "their" blacks are better off than Africans in black-ruled states they have neither the need nor the desire to change the present South African system. Blacks know that white rule gives them a growing standard of living, claim white South Africans, and they are therefore content.

There are a number of holes in this facile argument. First, not all of South Africa's blacks are doing well. Figures on African wages are for people *employed,* and there is massive black unemployment, partly concealed by the homelands system that keeps blacks out of the cities. South Africa needs an estimated 250,000 new jobs a year to absorb Africans looking for work, a problem similar to Brazil's. In the meantime, most blacks stuck in the homelands face a marginal existence in subsistence agriculture and cattle herding.

More serious, though, is the presumption that material progress means political contentment. Historical evidence seems to suggest otherwise. As de Tocqueville observed in connection with the French Revolution, it is the good times, not the bad, that raise revolutionary expectations. Especially difficult is when the economy turns down after a period of growth, leaving people with heightened expectations but fewer means of achieving their hopes. Recession hit South Africa in the early 1980s—the world price of gold slumped from $850 an ounce in 1980 to $300 an ounce in 1985. Many blacks lost their jobs. Far from

The Disinvestment Question

One question current on U.S. campuses is integral to South African politics: disinvestment. Over 350 U.S. firms have holdings in South Africa. Do their investments help perpetuate the apartheid system? If they pulled their investments out—disinvested—would it help end injustice? At stockholders' meetings in recent years corporations have been urged to disinvest in South Africa, and some have cut back or sold off their South African operations.

South African diplomats dismiss the disinvestment campaign. In the first place, they point out, if a college, for example, sells its stocks in a U.S. firm doing business in the RSA, someone else buys them and nothing is accomplished. Second, if the college keeps its stocks but coordinates with other institutions to bring pressure on the American company to improve black wages in their South African factories, it's all to the good. The more African workers are paid, the better for the RSA. (This does not, however, mean political contentment. The most progressive American firm in South Africa, Ford, located in Port Elizabeth, was the scene of political strikes.)

What white South Africans don't like to admit is that U.S. investment, although only a tiny portion of total capital in South Africa, is technologically important to the South African economy. Doing without it would be unpleasant. Further, Pretoria planners worry that the psychological climate created by the disinvestment campaign could *slow down* the rate of new foreign investment in those key technological areas.

Some liberal South African whites oppose disinvestment, arguing that if it worked it would just heighten tensions and make violence more probable. Some South African blacks also oppose disinvestment, pointing out that it is African workers who would suffer the most, for they need all the jobs they can get.

South African black leaders appear to generally favor disinvestment; they see it as one way to budge the regime. "Better a few years of belt tightening than an eternity of apartheid." one told the author. Black leaders are reluctant to speak openly in favor of disinvestment, however, for that is a crime in South Africa.

satisfying Africans, South Africa's economic growth makes its blacks *more* discontented. As they become increasingly urbanized, industrialized, and educated, Africans start thinking new thoughts, about why they are continually at the mercy of the white man and his laws, about their lack of tenure over their small homes, about the hated passbooks.

In Brazil, one can envision a "developmentalist" solution, but not in South Africa, for economic development without some political participation to go along with it is a recipe for unrest and possibly revolution. No matter how prosperous South Africa becomes, it will never be able to buy a quiet, obedient underclass.

THE HOMELANDS AND THE TOWNSHIPS

Ideally, white South Africa would like to detach black labor from black bodies, sending the labor to work in the cities and returning the bodies to the homelands. South African industry needs and wants African workers, but white South African society doesn't want black residents. The upshot is that Africans dribble into the cities, but the regime always tries to control their numbers and keep them at a distance.

The pass system was developed as part of this "influx control." Only Africans who already had employment (often through a labor broker) could come to the urban areas. Men were preferred; they would live in hostels outside of the city to earn money for a few months and then return home. But especially with the industrial development of World War II, Africans came to live permanently near the cities with their families. This created, as in Brazil, shantytowns, something the orderly whites disliked. Shantytowns meant uncontrolled black migration to the cities.

So "townships" were designated for African settlement several miles from the white cities. Cheap housing was built, often without sewers or electricity. The Africans were only "temporary sojourners" in white South Africa, so there was no point in making them too comfortable. Shantytowns were bulldozed and their inhabitants either sent back to their homelands or, for a lucky few, allowed to rent a small house in a township.

Soweto—standing for Southwest Townships—outside of Johannesburg is the biggest and best-known township. Soweto doesn't look horrible; indeed, by Third World standards it's good. Then you learn that each little house is occupied by one to two dozen persons, that most houses have no plumbing or electricity, that the commute to Johannesburg is long and crowded, and that it's the only place a black, no matter how wealthy, can live in the Johannesburg area. Because its residents were only "temporary"—although many are second- and third-generation Sowetans—until 1979 Soweto didn't even have a municipal structure to provide for roads, schools, and street lights. Its population—some 1.4 million, about half of them illegal (that is, without the proper residence permits in their passbooks)—is almost twice that of white Johannesburg's.

For white South Africans, one of the debates is over urban blacks. For a

Soweto began with single-men's hostels like these but soon mushroomed into a major city. *(Michael Roskin)*

growing number of black South Africans, living in or near a city is a virtual necessity. The homelands can't support more than a fraction of their tribal population. The situation is actually parallel to Brazil's—and much of the Third World's—where an impoverished hinterland with an enormous birthrate sends its surplus population to the cities. The difference is that South Africa tries to stem this flow with influx controls that are only partly successful. The results, however, are similar; both Brazil and South Africa have astronomical crime rates.

President Botha seems to be following a two-pronged strategy: (1) send as many blacks as possible to homelands and encourage the homelands to opt for "independence," and (2) improve conditions for the remaining urban blacks and offer them some kind of representation within the "new dispensation." The Botha strategy tried to split Africans so as to allow a tame minority to continue in the townships as an industrial labor force.

Urban blacks aren't buying, though. As the new constitution swung into operation in 1984, rioting broke out in the black townships near Johannesburg and Port Elizabeth that left more than 300 blacks dead. Their immediate grievances were a rent increase and poor school conditions, but everyone agreed that they were basically protesting the system as a whole. In 1985, police encountered violent resistance when they tried to remove the black squatter community of Crossroads outside Cape Town; 18 Africans died from police bullets. It seems unlikely that South Africa will be able to buy the peaceful acquiescence of urban blacks. Offering them small token improvements may simply whet their appetites.

ROLLING BACK *APARTHEID*

All of the approximately 2,000 laws and regulations of *apartheid* contain discretionary or delegated powers, giving officials room to make modifications and exceptions without repealing or making important concessions to nonwhites. Authorities can designate more and more job positions as open to blacks without disturbing laws reserving jobs for whites. They do this when there aren't enough whites to fill the jobs. Without repealing any separate-amenities acts, authorities can grant hotels "international status" so they can serve blacks.

These wide-ranging discretionary powers provoke at least two kinds of controversy. Critics of the system say that merely making exceptions to bad laws is no substitute for repealing them. Few have been repealed. Any reform granted by the government can be taken back the next year; and discretionary modifications are no solid base for serious reform, they argue. The regime argues the opposite, that given the *verkrampt* view of many Nationalists, it is better not to come before parliament to repeal an act; it might provoke a serious reaction. Better to do it slowly and gradually by using ministerial discretionary powers, they say, for those are ideal mechanisms for reform.

This latter argument would be plausible but for one drawback: the bureaucracy. The *apartheid* bureaucracy of close to half a million mostly Afrikaner civil servants has everything to lose if their system is seriously reformed. They are perfectly capable of sabotaging any minister's reform rulings. When a *verligt* minister attempted to liberalize the pass laws, bureaucrats shrewdly enforced existing rules to make the move look like a crackdown. South Africa cannot roll back *apartheid* with its *apartheid* bureaucracy still in place.

The Sex Laws:
Major Shift or Token?

In 1985, the white government repealed the Immorality and Mixed Marriages Acts that had outlawed relations across the color line. It was the first time any *apartheid* laws had been rescinded and the first major legislation passed by the new tricameral parliament. The Colored and Indian chambers insisted on scrapping the insulting anachronisms. Mixed relationships that occur in South Africa are usually between whites and Coloreds or Indians.

Some hailed the repeals as a major change, the undermining of the entire logic or *apartheid*, which is based on racial separateness. New changes must now follow. "Group areas" will have to make way for mixed couples. Racial designation will blur.

Critics laughed at the repeals. The changes may affect a small percentage of whites, Coloreds, and Indians, but will do nothing for the black majority. For an unemployed homeland black or an angry township youth, the repeal of the sex laws was merely the regime's belated effort at forming a front of nonblacks to stand against blacks. What some whites viewed as a major liberalization, many blacks saw as a symbolic token.

WOULD A BLACK VOTE MEAN CHAOS?

Some black South African leaders, such as Bishop Desmond Tutu, predict the country will have a black president within the next decade or so. Most whites recoil in horror at the thought. Blacks don't even have the vote, and most whites

What to do with Namibia?

In 1915, South African forces seized the German colony of South-West Africa; in 1920, the League of Nations named South Africa as the mandate power to oversee the largely desert area. South Africa treated South-West as virtually part of itself and implemented all its apartheid laws there. In the 1960s, local nationalists formed the South-West Africa Peoples Organization (SWAPO) to agitate for independence. The RSA reacted by jailing its leader, Herman Toivo ya Toivo, and outlawing SWAPO. In 1966, the United Nations, as successors to the League, revoked South Africa's mandate, but Pretoria wouldn't budge.

With Angola's independence from Portugal in 1975, however, SWAPO had a base of operations just to the north. SWAPO guerrillas, trained and armed by the Soviet bloc, launched raids into the land they now called Namibia, after its Namib desert. South Africa responded in kind with raids deep into Angola. A low-level war continues across the Namibia-Angola border. South Africa permits practically no first-hand news coverage

The main Western powers, including the United States, urge Pretoria to grant independence, but the Nationalist government stalls, fearing that Namibia would become an example and springboard for a similar uprising in the Republic. An independent Namibia under militant SWAPO control would place black revolution right on the Orange River.

Can South Africa keep stalling forever? Some white South Africans say they should never pull out; others point to the expense and frustration of a long, inconclusive war. In 1984, Pretoria made an interesting move that may indicate its aims: it freed Toivo ya Toivo after only sixteen years of a twenty-year sentence, something unheard of in South Africa. Pretoria's probable intention was that Toivo would reclaim SWAPO leadership from the radical Sam Nujoma and lead SWAPO into moderate paths. There is little chance of this happening, however, for it's hard to turn off a revolution in midcourse. South Africa seems to be stuck with Namibia for some time to come.

would like to keep it that way. They point to black Africa and the turmoil that has afflicted most countries since the British, French, Belgians, and Portuguese left. There are few economic or political success stories in black Africa. Corruption, famine, economic stagnation, military coups, and dictators have been the fate of much of the postcolonial continent.

One of the problems in African politics is the strong tribal attachment most Africans still feel. Elections, political appointments, business investments, and civil wars all run along tribal lines. If blacks had the vote in South Africa, whites argue, they would just vote for their tribal leaders; there would be no democracy at all. The biggest tribe—the Zulus—would win, and there's no guarantee that Zulu domination would be any better than Afrikaner domination. Whites would lose their guiding role, and the entire system would dissolve into chaos. It's a valid fear. P. W. Botha did not equivocate when he said: "One-man, one-vote is out. That is to say, never." Most whites agreed.

Tribalism is a constant in Africa, including South Africa, but, argue both white liberals and moderate blacks, it can be held in check. In the first place, the franchise would not have to be extended immediately to everyone. Virtually no whites want universal suffrage, but some would consider a qualified franchise based on education or income that would gradually extend the vote to Africans. Some black leaders reluctantly agree that universal suffrage is unrealistic for the time being and would accept temporarily a partial franchise.

A qualified franchise would skim off the most-educated and least-tribal Africans, chiefly urban residents. They would produce new political formations in combination with whites and browns, not separate tribal parties. As the new multiracial parties established themselves, the franchise would slowly expand as Africans gained education and/or income. The end result could be parties that cut across racial and tribal lines. David Curry, a leader of the Colored Labor party, notes that there is no party currently in parliament that represents the working class; he looks forward to the time when blacks and whites can vote Labor in free elections.

Admittedly, it's a speculative scenario, but if the vote were extended in the right manner it could avert chaos. Extending the franchise is as urgent in South Africa as it was in the last century in Britain, when one English parliamentarian said: "We count ballots so we won't have to crack skulls."

GUERRILLA WARFARE

For a long time, white South Africans scoffed at the possibility that blacks could wage effective guerrilla warfare inside the Republic. They don't scoff any more. During the 1980s, guerrilla warfare began in the RSA. ANC infiltrators bombed economic targets with increasing frequency.

Things had changed in South Africa's security picture. The South African Defence Force was still good, the best on the continent. But the geography had shifted. In 1975, Portugal withdrew from its colonies of Angola and Mozambique after years of guerrilla fighting. In 1980, Rhodesia turned into black-ruled Zimbabwe. South Africa had lost its territorial security belt of white-ruled states that had insulated it from black Africa. Formerly friendly border states became staging areas and sanctuaries for ANC guerrillas.

Further, the fragmented African homelands within the RSA gave guerrillas bases close to targets. In the homelands guerrillas blend in with the population and benefit from the more lax police administration of homeland governments. The homelands do not openly defy South Africa, but their security arrangements are less efficient than the RSA's. From a security standpoint, the South Africans in setting up the homelands committed a strategic error. Some chunks of BophuthaTswana are within commuting distance of Pretoria, Johannesburg, and the industrial areas of the Rand.

The crux of guerrilla warfare is the insurgent's ability to move among his or her own people "as a fish in water," to use Mao's words. The guerrilla, using a combination of persuasion and intimidation, gets the local population to help with recuitment, food, intelligence, or, at a minimum, silence. As long as no one informs, the guerrilla can operate under the noses of the police and army. South Africa will have a tough time winning the loyalty of its Africans in a guerrilla war, for the white regime preaches separateness of blacks and whites. The political package they have assembled is virtually unsellable to the black majority. A black man can sell black power to another black man, but how can a white man sell white power to a black man?

At last, South Africa has come down to the bottom line of the apartheid system. They had wanted racial separateness, and they have achieved it. All other countries in the world try to perfect their integration and unity. Some fight

Bishop Tutu: "We are Humans, Too"

For Anglican Bishop Desmond Tutu, leader of the South African Council of Churches and winner of the 1984 Nobel Peace Prize, "This is our last peaceful chance" to bring change to South Africa. But he warns, "We could very well have a blood bath." The mild-mannered churchman is an outspoken foe of apartheid and has been in continual trouble with the authorities. Tutu has campaigned worldwide to bring political and economic pressure—through disinvestment—on the Pretoria regime.

Like Dom Helder in Brazil (see p. 339), Bishop Tutu believes "we are all involved in the liberation struggle. Jesus Christ is involved in the liberation struggle. He liberated us from the bondage to sin—and oppression is an expression of sin." His message to the Pretoria government: "For goodness sake, will they hear, will white people hear what we are trying to say? Please, all we are asking you to do is to recognize that we are humans, too."

(General Theological Seminary)

civil wars to hold the country together. South Africa, eager to rid itself of potential black voters, takes away the citizenship of a majority of its population and fragments its national territory.

The simple truth is that the races of South Africa are intertwined and interdependent. To forcibly separate them is political and economic folly. White industry needs black workers and customers. Blacks need the jobs, education, and organization the white structure can provide. Together, they could forge a truly remarkable system. But set against itself, the South African house cannot stand.

VOCABULARY BUILDING

Afrikaans	defensive avoidance	laager	township
Afrikaner	disinvestment	Namibia	Soweto
ANC	homelands	PAC	*uitlanders*
apartheid	influx control	*platteland*	Union of South Africa
Boers	*Inkatha*	separate	*verkramptes*
Broederbond	*kaffir*	development	*verligtes*
Colored	*kraal*	*trekboers*	*voortrekkers*

FURTHER REFERENCE

Adam, Heribert. *Modernizing Racial Domination: South Africa's Political Dynamics.* Berkeley: University of California Press, 1971.

————— , **and Hermann Giliomee.** *Ethnic Power Mobilized: Can South Africa Change?* New Haven, Conn.: Yale University Press, 1979.

Ballinger, Margaret. *From Union to Apartheid: A Trek to Isolation.* New York: Praeger, 1969.

Butler, Jeffrey, Robert I. Rotberg, and John Adams. *The Black Homeland of South Africa: The Political and Economic Development of Bophuthatswana and KwaZulu.* Berkeley: University of California Press, 1977.

Frederickson, George M. *White Supremacy: A Comparative Study in American and South African History.* New York: Oxford University Press, 1981.

Goodwin, June. *Cry Amandla!: South African Women and the Question of Power.* New York: Holmes & Meier, 1984.

Gordimer, Nadine. *Burger's Daughter.* New York: Viking, 1979.

Hill, Christopher R. *Change in South Africa: Blind Alleys or New Directions?* New York: Barnes & Noble, 1983.

Leape, Jonathan, Bo Baskin, and Stefan Underhill, eds. *Business in the Shadow of Apartheid: U.S. Firms in South Africa.* Lexington, Mass.: Lexington Books, 1984.

Leonard, Richard. *South Africa at War: White Power and the Crisis in Southern Africa.* Westport, Conn.: Lawrence Hill, 1983.

Lodge, Tom. *Black Politics in South Africa Since 1945.* New York: Longman, 1983.

Luthuli, Albert, *Let My People Go.* New York: McGraw-Hill, 1962.

Nolutshungu, Sam C. *Changing South Africa: Political Considerations.* New York: Holmes & Meier, 1982.

Parker, Frank, J. *South Africa: Lost Opportunities.* Lexington, Mass.: Lexington Books, 1984.

Rotberg, Robert I., et al., eds. *Conflict and Compromise in South Africa.* Lexington, Mass.: Lexington Books, 1980.

Study Commission on U.S. Policy Toward South Africa. *South Africa: Time Running Out.* Berkeley: University of California Press, 1981.

Thompson, Leonard, and Andrew Prior. *South African Politics.* New Haven, Conn.: Yale, 1982.

Woods, Donald, *Biko.* New York: Paddington Press, 1978.

25

LESSONS OF SEVEN COUNTRIES

1. The past is alive and well and living in current politics. The past forms a country's political institutions, attitudes, and quarrels. The past is especially lively in the resentments of aggrieved people, for example, among regions and social groups that feel they've been shortchanged.

2. Wars are dangerous to political systems and other living things. War, said Marx, is the midwife of revolution, and that seems to be true. Several of our seven countries have undergone total system change as a result of war. Moral: think twice about going to war; it may mean the end of your entire system.

3. Economic growth is destabilizing, especially rapid growth. Economic growth and change bring new people into politics, some of them bitterly discontent. Don't think economic growth solves political problems; it often makes them worse. Political change must accompany economic change in order to head off revolution.

4. A system that cannot change to meet new challenges may be doomed. The wisest rulers are those who make gradual and incremental changes in order to avoid sudden and radical changes. Rulers who wait until revolution is nigh to reform may actually fan its flames by offering concessions. All regimes tend to petrify; the good ones fight the trend.

5. Revolutions usually start at the top—in disagreement among elites. Conflict among elites brings latent mass discontent to the surface. Most of the revolutions in our book were preceded by the breakup of elite consensus and the efforts by some elites to mobilize the masses to serve elite ends. Only rarely is revolution a strictly mass affair.

6. Watch those middle-class intellectuals; they're the revolutionaries. Most revolutionary movements we can think of are headed by middle-class intellectuals rather than by common folk. Brains and education help make a revolutionary leader just as they help make any leader.

7. Really want to bring down a regime? Try inflation. At least three of our countries endured revolutions after periods of galloping inflation that destroyed people's means of making a living and their confidence in government. The next question: When does inflation get dangerous?

8. Solid, time-tested institutions that people believe in are a bulwark of political stability. No political leader, however clever, has pulled a functioning institution out of a hat. Even revolutionaries have years of experience building their revolutionary parties and armies. A country with good institutions is immune to revolution. In a certain sense, a revolutionary is replacing defective institutions with better ones. How do we know they were defective? Because they lost.

9. Constitutions rarely work the way they're supposed to on paper. Many factors modify the working of constitutional machinery: popular attitudes, usages that change over time, powerful parties and interest groups, and behind-the-scenes deals.

10. Everywhere parliaments are in decline. Some have become little more than window dressing; some are under such tight executive and/or party control that they have lost their autonomy, and only a few are fighting to regain it. As governance becomes more complex and technical, power flows to bureaucrats and experts.

11. Everywhere bureaucracies are in the ascendancy. In some systems, the permanent civil service is already the most powerful institution. No country has yet devised a way to control its bureaucracies. Control mechanisms simply add another layer to the bureaucracy. Attempts to crush or bypass the bureaucracy end in chaos. Bureaucracy is simply part and parcel of modern government. Still, some bureaucracies are better than others. Bureaucrats may be indispensable, but that doesn't mean they don't bear watching.

12. Multiparty systems tend to be more unstable than two-party systems. Much depends on other factors, such as the rules for forming a cabinet or choosing the executive. Deft institutional reforms can stabilize multiparty systems so that their behavior is not much different from two-party systems.

13. Electoral system helps determine party system. Single-member districts with a simple plurality required to win tend to produce two-party systems because third parties have difficulty surviving in such systems. Proportional representation tends to produce many parties.

14. There are no longer purely federal or purely unitary systems. Instead, the trend is for federations to grant more and more power to the center, while unitary systems set up regional councils and devolve some powers to them. Eventually, it appears, federal and unitary systems could become about the same.

15. Most cabinets consist of about twenty ministers, more in Communist systems. By American standards, other cabinets are large and their portfolios rather specialized. In the United States, there is a reluctance to add new departments. In Europe, ministers are added, deleted, or combined as the prime minister sees fit; the legislature almost automatically goes along.

16. In many ways, prime ministers in parliamentary systems are more powerful than presidents in presidential systems. A prime minister, with the assured discipline of his or her party in parliament, can get about whatever he or she deems necessary. There is no deadlock between executive and legislative. The only thing restraining the prime minister is the threat of party or electoral revolts.

17. Most people most of the time aren't much interested in politics. As you go down the socioeconomic ladder, you usually find less and less interest in political participation. Radicals deny this when they call for "power to the people," but they are usually middle-class intellectuals, sometimes intent on power for themselves. Mass participation in politics tends to be simple and episodic, such as voting every few years.

18. Democracy arouses little enthusiasm in most countries. Only countries with a history of democratic rule have democratically inclined masses. More typically, masses admire regimes that give them law and order, a feeling of national greatness, and a sense of material progress. More-educated people have stronger commitments to democratic values.

19. Political culture is at least as much a reflection of government performance as it is a determinant of the workings of government. Political culture can be taught—intentionally or inadvertently—by a regime. Countries with a cynical, untrusting political culture have usually earned it with decades of misrule. By the same token, when a democratic regime does a good job over many years, as Bonn has, it firms up democratic attitudes.

20. Social class is only one factor in establishing political orientations. Often other factors, such as religion and region, are more important. Usually these three—class, religion, and region—in varying combinations explain a great deal of party identification and voting behavior.

21. There is more regional resentment the farther you go from the national capital. Political scientists call this center-periphery tension. Typically at the periphery of the national territory you find the strongest regionalist or antiregime political movements.

22. Religion is important in politics. In some countries, political parties are based on religion or religiosity (degree of religious feeling). West Germany's Christian Democrats were originally based on the Catholic church and South Africa's Nationalists on the Dutch Reformed church. In Catholic countries such as France, the more religious vote for the more conservative parties.

23. Political systems are rarely totally ideological, but neither are they totally pragmatic. Parties and regimes usually have at least some ideological underpinning—to justify themselves to the masses, it for no other reason—but at the top, rulers tend to be rather pragmatic in making decisions. Leaders may talk a certain ideology but find that in actual governance it is not wholly relevant. Using ideology as window dressing is a common political device.

24. Every country has its elites. Elites are the top people with a great deal of influence. Depending on the system, party elites, labor elites, business elites, military elites, even education and communication elites may assume great importance. Elites pay attention to politics, usually battling to preserve and enhance the status of the groups they lead. Elites rather than masses are the true political animals.

25. There are differences between the political culture of the masses and of the elites. Elites pay much more attention to politics and with greater consistency than masses. Elites, especially intellectual elites, create and articulate political ideas (ideologies, reform movements, media commentary), something the masses rarely do. Further, elite attitudes tend to be more democratic than mass attitudes.

26. Education is the nearly universal gateway to elite status. Except in revolutionary regimes, most elites now have university educations or the equivalent. Some elites are selected by virtue of the special colleges they attend. Educational opportunity is never totally equal or fair; the middle class usually benefits the most from it.

27. Much of politics consists of competition and bargaining among elites. Occasionally elites, in order to gain leverage on competing elites, refer matters to the masses in elections or referendums and call it democracy. Of all the political interactions discussed in this book, notice that relatively few of them involve mass participation.

28. Mass politics is easier to study than elite politics. With mass politics—elections, voter alignments, popular attitudes—political scientists can usually get accurate, quantified data. But since much of elite politics is out of the public eye, we have to resort to fragmentary anecdotal and journalistic data. This means that some of the most crucial political interactions are hard to discern and even harder to document.

29. Democracy exists when elites open their decisions and deals to public scrutiny and approval. Typically, bargains are struck among elites and then presented to parliament and the public. Much legislative and electoral behavior is in ratifying decisions made earlier among elites. The difference here between Communist and democratic governments is one of degree.

30. Of the several elite groups, bureaucratic elites are becoming the most important. Many decisions are made by top civil servants who negotiate from a position of strength with business, labor, and other elites. Some scholars label this tendency "the rise of technocracy," for the civil servants are often technical experts. The process has gone the furthest in authoritarian regimes, such as the Soviet Union.

31. Parties are balancing acts. Parties are invariably composed of different groups or factions. To hold the party together, politicians dispense favors, jobs, and promises to faction leaders. This holds for both democratic and Communist parties.

32. Every party has a radical wing. Social-democratic and labor parties have Marxist wings; conservative parties have reactionary wings. Even Communist parties have moderates and radicals, conservatives and liberals. Radical wings tend to be the home of young party militants, especially in leftist parties. How to control their radical-youth wings is one of the hardest tasks facing party chiefs.

33. A party that lets its radical wing dominate is headed for trouble. When radicals push the party to take extreme stands, average voters tend to go the other way. Pragmatic politicians therefore always fight domination by the radical wing, knowing it frightens away voters.

34. In the Third World, radical parties provoke reactionary impulses. In most of Latin America, for example, the coming to power of a radical or leftist party triggers an automatic military take-over, welcomed by conservative sectors of the society, which fear for their status and property.

35. Third World reformist politicians tend to move to radicalism. The problems of developing areas are so big and the gap between rich and poor so huge that reformers are often drawn to radical, socialist prescriptions. Sometimes these prescriptions are demogoguery, aimed at arousing the masses without thought of consequences. This then often leads to reactionary military take-over. Perhaps only time and economic growth—leading to a large and moderate middle class—can move Latin American and some other Third World countries out of this pattern.

36. Once the army has taken over a government, chances are it will do so again. Once a country catches praetorianism, it seems never to fully recover from the disease. Democracy and reformism are often short-lived phenomena between periods of military rule. Praetorianism can be seen as an incurable, self-reinfecting illness endemic in the Third World.

37. The Third World is trying to get into the First. One of the big problems of West Europe is the new class of foreign workers—Indians in Britain, Algerians in France, Turks in Germany—that have come seeking jobs. In many cases they have come to stay. Likewise, the United States has become a magnet for Latin Americans. Given the differential rates of economic growth—high in the First World, low in the Third—the trend is likely to increase, especially with the high birthrates of the Third World.

38. Within Third World countries, people are flocking to the cities. High birthrates and few jobs in the countryside push people to the cities, where they often live in squalor. The Third World already has some of the globe's biggest cities, and they're growing fast. Some countries, such as China and South Africa, attempt "influx control," but most countries just let the slums grow.

39. Racism can be found nearly everywhere. South Africa isn't the only country mentioned in this book that practices racial discrimination. Most nations would deny it, but discrimination based on skin color, religion, or ethnic group is widespread. When asking if there is racism, look to see what a country does, not what it says. Underdog racial and ethnic groups are locked out of economic and political power.

40. Cutting welfare benefits is extremely difficult; recipients protest too much. Conservatives often come to power with promises to "clean up the welfare mess," but they seldom touch the problem. Once a benefit has been extended, it's almost impossible to withdraw it. The most conservatives can do is restrain expansion of the welfare system.

41. Much of what people and politicians quarrel about is economic. Some economists go so far as to claim that economics is the content of politics. That's going a little too far, since there are important political conflicts that are not directly economic, such as questions of region, religion, and personality. Still, on any given day, people are most likely to be arguing who should get what. Study economics.

42. At almost the same time, countries are rediscovering the market economy. Leaders as diverse as America's Reagan, Britain's Thatcher, France's Mitterrand, and China's Deng hold that statist economics retards growth. Capitalism is now the intellectual trend.

43. No political system has a sure-fire method of motivating people to work hard. All the countries we've considered in this book are making efforts to stimulate populations to harder work; none is consistently successful. Neither capitalist incentives (as in Britain), Stalinist terror (as in the Soviet Union), Maoist sloganeering (as in China), nor technocratic planning (as in Brazil) has proven effective over the long term.

44. Unemployment is nearly everywhere a problem and one that few governments solve. Worldwide, there is a struggle for jobs, ranging from difficult in Western Europe to desperate in the Third World. The Soviet Union seems to have no problem providing jobs—they have a manpower shortage—but that's only because Soviet industry and agriculture are grossly inefficient.

45. Many political issues are insoluble. They are the surfacing of long-growing economic and social problems that can't be "fixed" by government policy. Often only time and underlying economic and social change gradually dissolve the problem. Politics has been overrated as a way to cure problems. Often the best politics can do is keep things stable until time can do its work.

46. Things are getting more political, not less. As government gets bigger and takes on more tasks, what were previously private social interactions (such as those of the marketplace) become political interactions with all the fighting that entails. Modernization brings increased politicization. As more areas become political footballs, we can look for more political quarrels. Even trying to cut the role of government is an intensely political act that generates new frictions.

47. No country has ever run out of problems or political controversies. As soon as one problem is solved—and they're rarely solved by politics alone—new ones appear, usually relating to the administration of the problem-solving mechanism. No country is so advanced that it has no more problems. Indeed, the more advanced a country, the more political problems it seems to have because everything becomes political.

48. Political movements, parties, ideologies, and regimes are hard to judge by *a priori* criteria. We never know how something is going to work until we see it in practice for a while. We learn to judge what's good and bad politically by consequences. What may strike us as an unjust regime may lead to a long-term improvement. But once that regime *has* led its country into ruin it may be safely judged bad.

49. Whenever you look closely at political phenomena, you find they are more complicated than you first thought. You find exceptions, nuances, and differentiations that you didn't notice at first. You can modify and sometimes refute generalizations—including the ones offered here—by digging into them more deeply.

50. Ultimately, in studying comparative politics we are studying ourselves. One of the lessons that should have emerged from this book is that neither our country nor we as citizens are a great deal different from other countries and peoples. When you compare politics, be sure to include your own system in the comparison.

GLOSSARY

Below are some frequently used words or technical terms from the field of comparative politics. Each is defined here in its *political* sense. The country where the term originated or is most commonly used is given, but often the word is now used worldwide.

abertura   (Brazil) Portuguese for "opening," the liberalization of a military regime.

absolutism   tendency of some European monarchs, starting in the sixteenth century, to amass power until they ruled singlehandedly.

affect   individual citizens' feelings of fondness toward a political system.

Afrikaner   (South Africa) ruling white group of South Africa which speaks the Dutch-derived language *Afrikaans*.

agitprop   (Soviet Union) combination *agitation* and *propaganda* the mass-mobilization arm of the Soviet Communist party.

ancien régime   (France) the old regime that preceded the 1789 Revolution.

anticlericalism   movement aimed at curbing influence of Roman Catholic church in politics.

apartheid   (South Africa) system of strict racial segregation.

apolitical   taking no interest in politics.

apparatchik   (Soviet Union) person of the party apparatus, a full-time Communist party worker.

arable   land that can be cultivated; denotes sufficient water for farming.

authoritarian   political system that concentrates power in hands of a few and is not responsible to the public.

autonomy   degree of self-government granted to a region.

autocracy   one person rule, as in tsarist Russia.

backbencher   (Britain) a less-important member of Parliament, one who does not sit on the front bench.

Basic Law   West Germany's 1949 constitution.

bicamerale   a legislature that has two houses.

blat   (Soviet Union) Russian for "influence" or "pull."

Boers   (South Africa) name by which Afrikaners were formerly known; Dutch for "farmers."

Bolshevik   (Soviet Union) Russian for "majority"; faction of Russian Social Democratic partly that Lenin led to seize power in 1917; became the Soviet Communist party.

bourgeoisie   French for "middle class"; connotes procapitalist conservatism; pejorative in Marxist usage.

Bourbon   (France) ruling royal family prerevolutionary France and currently of Spain.

Boxers   (China) late-nineteenth-century Chinse patriotic society, which rose against foreigners in 1900.

Bundesrat   West German upper house of legislature, which represents *Länder* (states).

Bunkdestag   West German lower house of legislature, more powerful than *Bundesrat*.

bureaucracy   the civil service of a country; connotes rigid, hierarchical administration.

by-election   (Britain) a special election to fill a vacant seat in Parliament.

cabinet   the group of ministers or secretaries who head the executive departments of a government; in Europe, synonymous with *government*.

cadre   (China) originally the French word for "framework," it now denotes th Communist structure for mobilization and leadership.

caesaropapism   the combining of head of state and head of a national church in one office, as was done by the tsar of Russia.

capital   accumulated wealth, either money or goods, that are used to produce more goods.

catchall party   a large, ideologically loose party that aims to enlist as many groups of supporters as possible.

center   politically moderate or middle-of-the-road, neither left nor right.

center-periphery tensions   resentment of outlying regions at rule from nation's capital city.

centralization   the concentration of administrative power in the nation's capital, allowing little or no local autonomy.

chancellor   German equivalent of prime minister.

charismatic leader   one who is capable of moving people through force of words or personality.

chauvinism   extreme and prideful nationalism.

civility   preserving good manners in politics and public life.

class bias   the slanting of jobs, schools, and political power to favor one class at the expense of another.

class struggle   basic tenet of Marxism that social classes, especially the woring class and the rich, are of necessity antagonistic toward each other's inerests.

class voting   tendency of a given class to vote for a party that claims to represent its interests.

coalition   in a parliamentary system, th combining of two or more parties to form a cabinet.

Colored   (South Africa) a person of mixed Hottentot, white, Malay descent, found Chiefly in Cape Province.

common law   (Britain) system of laws based heavily on previous court decisions, "judge-made law."

Common Market   oficially the European Community, a grouping of non-communist European nations that eliminates tariffs and trade and labor restrictions between its member nations.

Commons   (Britain) the lower, popularly elected and more important house of Parliament.

Communist party   a political party combining Marxist economics with Leninist organization aimed at building a socialist utopia.

conservatism   political mood or movement aimed at preserving older or traditional values, economic systems, and laws.

constituency   the district or population that elects a legislator.

constitution   document structuring the political and sometimes social institutions of a nation.

corporatism   legislative representation based on profession rather than district or party, often a component of Fascist systems.

coup d'état   the sudden and extralegal take-over of state power by armed groups, usually the millitary.

decentralization   the diffusion of administrative power from the nation's capital to regions, localities, or economic units.

defensive avoidance   psychological mechanism whereby individuals or groups ignore or rationalize unpleasant facts that threaten their convictions.

deferential   political attitude in which lower classes defer to the rule of their perceived superiors.

deification   the glorification of a leader into an artificial god.

demobilization   the tranquilizing or even anesthetizing of mass interest in politics, often attempted by dictators.

democracy   political system in which the power and authority of leaders is accountable to the broad mass of the population.

demagoguery   the ambiguous or tricky use of political issues to enable the user to attain power.

dependencia   Spanish for "dependency"; theory that developing countries are economically tied and subordinate to rich capitalist nations.

département   one of ninety-six administrative districts into which France is divided.

depoliticization   either a loss of political involvement or the turning of political issues into neutral administrative matters.

destalinization   (Soviet Union) the criticism and downgrading of Stalin that occured under Khrushchev.

détente   a French term meaning relaxation of political tensions, usually referring specifically to improved relations between the United States and Soviet Union; policy associated with Nixon and Kissinger.

devolution   the granting of regional autonomy or home rule by the central authority.

dissident   (Soviet Union) person who openly criticizes his or her political system.

Dolchstoss   German for "stab in the back"; myth fostered by German right that Germany had been betrayed during Wold War I by disloyal domestic elements.

Dreyfus Affair   French trial in late nineteenth century over alleged treason by Jewish artillery officer; badly split France into liberal supporters of Dreyfus and conservative detractors.

Duma   Russian parliament permitted by tsar in early twentieth century.

electoral system   laws structuring the manner in which persons are elected to office, such as from single- or multimember districts, and by proportional representation or simple plurality.

electorate   that part of a population entitled to vote.

elites   the top or most influential persons in a society or institution.

Elysée Palace   French equivalent of the White House.

emergency powers   clause in most constitutions permitting chief executive to take on extraordinary powers under certain circumstances.

environmentalism   political movement of the late twentieth century stressing industrial, chemical, and especially nuclear dangers to the environment.

equalitarian   a policy aiming at making persons more equal in income, political power, or life opportunities; a leftist political viewpoint.

Establishment   (Britain) the alleged unofficial club of British elites who work to support the status quo and keep themselves in power.

Estado Novo   (Portuguese for "New State") Fascist-appearing system of Brazilian President Vargas from 1937 to 1945.

Estates-General   seldom-convened French parliament before the Revolution.

étatisme   (French "statism") government prodding of the economy by means of plans and subsidies.

Eurocommunism   alleged independent movement of West European Communist parties (chiefly the Italian, French, and Spanish) from Moscow's rule and their commitment to democratic norms.

Events of May   euphemism for French student and worker strikes of 1968.

Exchequer   (Britain)medieval revenue officer, now chief treasury official.

factious   tending to break up into quarreling factions.

favela   (Brazil) urban shantytown or slum.

federation   political system in which component territories enjoy a high degree of autonomy or home rule.

feudalism   political pattern of medieval Europe in which power was spread among lords rather than concentrated in a king.

Five-Year Plans   (Soviet Union) series of coercive plans initiated by Stalin in 1928 to industrialize country rapidly.

fragmented   condition of political cultures with marked divergence of views among subgroups and little or no consensus.

franchise right to vote.

Gang of Four (China) group of alleged ultra-radical conspirators who brought on chaos of Cultural Revolution; arrested after Mao's death in 1976 and later tried.

Gastarbeiter (German; "guest worker") foreign worker in Federal Republic of Germany, usually from poor Mediterranean country.

Gaullism (France) policy of President de Gaulle aimed at making France stable, unified, prosperous, militarily strong, and independent in foreign policy.

general will theory of French philosopher Rousseau which holds that underlying the many and conflicting "particular wills" in society is a unanimous consensus.

gentry better-off, educated class in traditional societies.

gerontocracy rule by the elderly.

gerrymander the drawing of electoral-district boundaries so as to favor one party.

Gosplan (Soviet Union) central economic-planning authority.

grand coalition coalition of two or more large parties who previously opposed each other.

grande école one of France's elite schools, considered superior to universities, which train the country's leading administrators, engineers, industrialists, and teachers.

Great Leap Forward (1958-60) Chinese effort at overnight industrialization; failed.

Great Purge (Soviet Union) Stalin's murder of thousands of Communist party members from 1936 to 1938 on faintest suspicion of disloyalty.

Gulag (Soviet Union) central prisons administration.

Guomindang (China) Chinese Nationalist party ousted from mainland in 1949; earlier spelled Kuomintang and abbreviated KMT.

Habsburg royal house and empire that grouped Austria and Spain on Catholic side in sixteenth- and seventeenth-century wars of religion.

head of government the chief executive of a country's government, either a prime minister or a president, who engages in day-to-day political affairs.

head of state the symbolic national leader, either a monarch or a president, who normally stands above the political fray.

Holocaust the destruction of six million European Jews by the Nazis during World War II.

homelands (South Africa) tribal reserves for black natives.

Hundred Flowers (China) 1956 campaign to encourage expression of different views; crushed when views grew too critical.

hyperinflation an extremely high inflaton rate that makes currency utterly worthless.

identity recognition on the part of the people as to their nationality, ethnic group, region, or party.

ideology interrelated set of ideas for the improvement of society.

immobilism inability of a government to decide important issues, often due to quarreling of coalition partners.

infant mortality rate number of infants who die in their first year, usually expressed per thousand.

indicative planning (France) governmental economic research and suggestions for business expansion; not the same as Soviet-style central economic control.

industrialization the shifting of a country's economy from agriculture to industry.

inequality degree of difference in wealth, income, social status, or political power among individuals.

influx control (South Africa) measures to limit number of black persons in urban areas; important component of apartheid.

infrastructure the network of highways, railroads, electricity, and other basic prerequisites of economic growth.

institution a web of political relationships lasting over time, an established structure of power; may or may not be mentioned in a constitution or housed in a building.

intelligentsia Russian (from Italian) for "educated class."

intendants (France) central administrators sent out to the provinces; started by Cardinal Richelieu.

interior ministry in most countries, the important ministry that controls police and internal security.

Jacobins radical clubs in revolutionary France.

jeito (Brazil) Portuguese for "knack," meaning bureaucratic connections that get things done, implicitly by means of bribes.

Junker (Germany) Prussian aristocratic class.

Kaiser (German; "caesar") title of Germany's kings.

kolkhoz (Soviet Union) collective farm.

Komsomol (Soviet Union) Communist youth organization.

kowtow (China) ritual prostration before emperor.

Kremlin (Soviet Union) ancient walled fortress in Moscow that serves as center of government.

kulaks (Soviet Union) class of better-off peasants Stalin ordered liquidated as part of farm collectivization during first Five-Year Plan.

laager Afrikaans for "camp"; specifically, a circle of ox wagons drawn up for defense.

Land West German equivalent of U.S. state (plural, Länder).

laissez faire French for "let it be"; doctrine advocating no government interference in a free-market economy.

left politically more radical; aiming at greater equality.

legitimacy   popular attitude that regime's rule is rightful; not the same as *legal.*

liberalism   in its original late-eighteenth- and nineteenth-century sense, an ideology that proposed free economic, social, and political arrangements rather than government supervision; in the belief that such individual freedom would lead to the greatest happiness. In the twentieth-century United States, the favoring of welfare measures and greater equality.

liberation theology   in Third World Catholic countries, especially Latin America, the view of some clergy that helping poor through revolution is proper Christian duty.

Long March   (China; 1934-35) exodus of Chinese Communist party from southrn to nothern China to escape *Guomindang.*

Lords   (Britain) upper, aristocratic house of Parliament; minor government body compared to *Commons.*

lycée   French academic high school.

machismo   (Latin America) strutting, exaggerated masculinity.

Magna Carta   (Britain) agreement nobles obtained in 1215 from the king to preserve their rights.

Mandarin   (China)   traditional   administrator, schooled in Confucian classics.

Maoism   (China) Communist leader Mao Zedong's Marxist ideological variation that revolution can be based on poor peasantry and must continue indefinitely to prevent bureaucratization.

Marshall Plan   program of U.S. economic aid for Europe after World War II.

Marxism-Leninism   or communism, the ideology combining the economic and historical theories of Marx with the orgnizational techniques of Lenin.

Menshevik   Russian for "minority"; the less radical faction of the Russian Social Democrats whom Lenin repudiated.

mercantilism   economic policy of absolutist monarchs, especially French, favoring state guidance of industry and amassing of gold.

minister   head of an executive department or ministry and usually member of cabinet.

Mitbestimmung   (German;   "codetermination") worker participation in company policy in present day West Germany.

mobilization   the awakening of political awareness in previously apolitical masses.

monocolor   in parliamentary systems, a cabinet composed of a single party, not a coalition cabinet.

multiparty   party   system   of   three   or   more competing parties.

Narodniki   Russian student radicals of the 1870s who tried "going to the people" to mobilize peasants.

nationality   belonging to a nation or, in the case of the Soviet Union, to an ethnic group.

nationalization   governmental take-over of private industry.

New Class   term   coined   by   Yugoslav   writer Milovan Djilas to describe the new Communist elite of party leaders, bureaucrats, and security officials.

no-confidence   parliamentary motion to oust the current cabinet.

nomenklatura   (Soviet Union) list of sensitive positions reserved for carefully screened partly members.

October Revolution   1917 Bolshevik seizure of power in Russia.

Old Republic   1889-1930 Brazilian regime of limited, conservative democracy.

Opium War   1839-42 British war against China that Britain waged for the right to sell opium to Chinese.

opportunist   calculating   person   bent   only   on pursuing his or her own self-interests.

opposition   in parliamentary systems, the parties not in the government or cabinet.

Ostpolitik   policy of West German Chancellor Willy Brandt for improving relations with the Soviet Union and East Europe.

Oxbridge   (Britain) the elite universities of Oxford and Cambridge.

paranoid   unreasonable   suspicion   toward   other persons; not the same as *fearful.*

parliamentary system   political system in which cabinet is responsible to, and can be ousted by, parliament; chief executive is a prime minister who is not elected directly.

parochial   focused on local concerns only; ignorant of national politics.

participation   citizen involvement in politics in such ways as voting, helping a party or candidate, or contacting an official.

party identification   psychological attachment of a voter to a particular political party.

party image   the way the electorate perceives a given party.

party list   in proportional-representation systems, a party's list of candidates for parliament, elected in descending order of priority according to portion of the vote the party obtains.

party system   the number and competitiveness of parties in a given country; five general types; no-party, one-party, two-party, dominant-party, and multiparty systems.

personalismo   (Latin   America)   the   respect-commanding qualities and governing style of a leader, often connected with *machismo.*

personality cult   adulation and deification of political leaders such as Stalin and Mao.

plebiscite   a mass vote on an issue, often concerning national status and boundaries.

pluralism   political system that openly acknowledges interplay of many groups–interest, ethnic, regional and political; also, theory that politics works in this manner.

Politburo in Communist systems, the highest ruling body of the party, above the Central Committee.

political culture the psychology of the nation in regard to politics, the pattern of a country's political attitudes.

Popular Front combination of all leftist parties especially Communist and Socialist, in France and Spain in the 1930s.

praetorianism tendency of military to take power.

pragmatic nonideological politics, adopting whatever policy works.

prefect (France) centrally appointed supervisor of a *département*.

presidential system political system in which powerful president is elected directly and separately from parliament and cannot be ousted by parliament.

prime minister in parliamentary system, the chief executive officer and head of government, confirmed by and answerable to parliament.

proportional representation electoral system that assigns parliamentary seats in proportion to party vote.

public schools (Britain) private boarding schools; so named because they train boys for public life.

Question Time (Britain) period in Commons reserved for questioning governmental ministers.

redistribution taxation and welfare measures that generally take from the wealthier and give to the poorer.

referendum a mass vote on an issue rather than on candidates.

reformism political movement aiming at change and improvement in a moderate and noncoercive way.

regionalism political movement that emphasizes regional autonomy and distinctiveness.

regressive tax tax that is lighter on rich than on poor.

Reform Acts (Britain) nineteenth-century series of reforms broadening the electoral franchise.

regierungsfähig German for "able to form a government."

Reign of Terror (France) period of mass executions led by Robespierre after Revolution.

right politically more conservative, favoring preservation of or return to previous status quo.

revisionism changing or rethinking a political ideology or conventional view of history.

Roman law legal system in most of Europe and Latin America based on relatively fixed codes, as opposed to judge-made common law.

russification (Soviet Union) policy begun under tsars and continued to present day of spreading use of Russian language and culture among non-Russian ethnic groups.

Red Guards (China) radical youths who, at Mao's behest, attacked traditions and authorities during Cultural Revolution.

safe seat (Britain) constituency where voting has long favored a given party.

samizdat (Soviet Union) Russian for "self-published"; manuscripts, often by dissidents, circulated underground.

scapegoating unfairly blaming persons or groups for the ills of a political or economic system.

secular change long-term, irreversible trends.

secularization removing church influence from social and political institutions.

single-member district constituency that elects only one legislator, usually by simple plurality, as in Britain and the United States.

social class a portion or layer of society, usually determined by wealth or income.

social cleavages the splitting of society along class, regional, religious, or ethnic lines or over important issues.

socialism political movement aiming at greater equality by means of welfare measures and/or nationalization of industry.

sovereignty legal concept that national government is supreme in its territory.

soviet Russian for "council"; name of 1917 revolutionary bodies and of present-day legislatures in Soviet Union.

sovkhoz (Soviet Union) a state farm where workers are employees of the state, as opposed to members of a collective farm or *kolkhoz*.

Sozialmarkt German for "social market; the economic policy of West German Christian Democratic governments promoting a generally free market with progressive social goals.

sphere of influence foreign area under the control or influence of a powerful nation.

Stalinism (Soviet Union) policies and style associated with Stalin, namely, coerced industrialization, personality cult, and brutal control over society and party.

state capitalism economic system where government is an important investor, as in France and Brazil.

Supreme Soviet national legislature of Soviet Union.

technocrat official who governs by technical as opposed to political or humane criteria, a pejorative term.

terrorism use of political murder and fear thereof to win or consolidate power.

Third Estate (France) the third house of the Estates-General representing commoners, as opposed to the First and Second Estates, representing clergy and nobles.

threshold clause   a numerical minimum required to win seats in parliament, as the 5 percent national vote required of a West German party.

Tory   (Britain) nickname for Conservative.

totalitarian   a dictatorial regime that attempts to impose total ideological, economic, and political control over society.

Treaty Ports   (China) series of seaports on China coast in which foreign powers established by treaty their spheres of influence during the nineteenth century.

unicameral   parliament with only one chamber.

unification   process of pulling a nation together out of diverse and sometimes recalcitrant regions.

unimodal   a single-peaked distribution of political attitudes or opinions; a bell-shaped curve.

unitary   a political system governed by the center with little or no autonomy allowed to subunits or regions.

urbanization   the shift of population from countryside to city.

value-added tax   a large, hidden sales tax used throughout West Europe.

Vatican II   short name for Second Vatican Council; meetings in 1962-65 that turned Catholic church toward problems of the poor.

Versailles   palace near Paris, originally that of Louis XIV, where treaty–highly punitive to Germany–was drawn up after World War I.

Vichy   French government during World War II that collaborated with German occupation.

Volk   German for "people"; used by Nazis to connote racial superiority of Germans.

warlords   (China) independent regional military rulers who took over in the 1910s and 1920s.

welfare   redistributive measures that provide health care, food, housing, and insurance to poorer classes.

Weimar   democratic republic set up in Gemany after World War I and destroyed by Nazis.

Weltanschauung   German for "world view"; the comprehensive ideologies European parties once tried to inculcate into their members.

Westernizers   nineteenth-century Russian intellectuals who favored borrowing from and imitating the West.

Westminster   (Britain) building housing Parliament.

whip   party official in legislature who makes sure party's members are present and voting correctly.

Whitehall   (Britain) chief government executive offices.

xenophobia   fear and hatred of foreigners.

Yalta   town in Soviet Crimea where the wartime leaders of the United States, Britain, and Soviet Union decided the post-World War II status of Germany and East Europe.